THE ARDEN SHAKESPEARE

THIRD SERIES
General Editors: Richard Proudfoot, Ann Thompson
and David Scott Kastan

JULIUS
CAESAR

THE ARDEN SHAKESPEARE

ALL'S WELL THAT ENDS WELL	edited by G.K. Hunter
ANTONY AND CLEOPATRA	edited by John Wilders*
AS YOU LIKE IT	edited by Agnes Latham
THE COMEDY OF ERRORS	edited by R.A. Foakes
CORIOLANUS	edited by Philip Brockbank
CYMBELINE	edited by J.M. Nosworthy
HAMLET	edited by Harold Jenkins
JULIUS CAESAR	edited by David Daniell*
KING HENRY IV Parts 1 and 2	edited by A.R. Humphreys
KING HENRY V	edited by T.W. Craik*
KING HENRY VI Parts 1, 2 and 3	edited by A.S. Cairncross
KING HENRY VIII	edited by R.A. Foakes
KING JOHN	edited by E.A.J. Honigmann
KING LEAR	edited by R.A. Foakes*
KING RICHARD II	edited by Peter Ure
KING RICHARD III	edited by Anthony Hammond
LOVE'S LABOUR'S LOST	edited by H.R. Woudhuysen*
MACBETH	edited by Kenneth Muir
MEASURE FOR MEASURE	edited by J.W. Lever
THE MERCHANT OF VENICE	edited by John Russell Brown
THE MERRY WIVES OF WINDSOR	edited by H.J. Oliver
A MIDSUMMER NIGHT'S DREAM	edited by Harold F. Brooks
MUCH ADO ABOUT NOTHING	edited by A.R. Humphreys
OTHELLO	edited by E.A.J. Honigmann*
PERICLES	edited by F.D. Hoeniger
THE POEMS	edited by F.T. Prince
ROMEO AND JULIET	edited by Brian Gibbons
SHAKESPEARE'S SONNETS	edited by Katherine Duncan-Jones*
THE TAMING OF THE SHREW	edited by Brian Morris
THE TEMPEST	edited by Frank Kermode
TIMON OF ATHENS	edited by H.J. Oliver
TITUS ANDRONICUS	edited by Jonathan Bate*
TROILUS AND CRESSIDA	edited by David Bevington*
TWELFTH NIGHT	edited by J.M. Lothian and T.W. Craik
THE TWO GENTLEMEN OF VERONA	edited by Clifford Leech
THE TWO NOBLE KINSMEN	edited by Lois Potter*
THE WINTER'S TALE	edited by J.H. Pafford

*Third Series

THE ARDEN SHAKESPEARE

JULIUS CAESAR

Edited by
DAVID DANIELL

The general editors of the Arden Shakespeare have been
W.J. Craig and R.H. Case (first series 1899–1944)
Una Ellis-Fermor, Harold F. Brooks, Harold Jenkins and
Brian Morris (second series 1946–82)

Present general editors (third series)
Richard Proudfoot, Ann Thompson and David Scott Kastan

This edition of *Julius Caesar*, by David Daniell,
first published 1998 by Thomas Nelson and Sons Ltd

Thomas Nelson and Sons Ltd
Nelson House Mayfield Road
Walton-on-Thames Surrey
KT12 5PL UK

I(T)P® Thomas Nelson is an International Thomson Publishing
Company
I(T)P® is used under licence

Editorial matter © 1998 David Daniell

Typeset in Ehrhardt by
Wyvern 21 Ltd, Bristol

Printed in Italy

British Library Cataloguing in Publication Data
A catalogue record for this book is available from the British
Library
Library of Congress Cataloguing in Publication Data
A catalogue record has been applied for

ISBN 0–17–443547–9 (hardback)
ISBN 0–17–443490–1 (paperback)

NPN 9 8 7 6 5 4 3 2 1

The Editor

David Daniell is Emeritus Professor of English at the University of London. For 25 years he taught Shakespeare and much else at University College London. He has been Visiting Professor at King's College London, and Visiting Fellow at Magdalen College Oxford. He has taught at Dartmouth College, New Hampshire, and lectured widely in Europe, the USA and the UK. His publications include books on *Coriolanus* and *The Tempest*, and many articles on Shakespeare and also on the English Bible, particularly its first translator, William Tyndale.

For Dorothy, Chris and Andy Daniell,
with love

CONTENTS

LIST OF
ILLUSTRATIONS

GENERAL EDITORS' PREFACE

The Arden Shakespeare is now nearly one hundred years old. The earliest volume in the series, Edward Dowden's *Hamlet*, was published in 1899. Since then the Arden Shakespeare has become internationally recognized and respected. It is now widely acknowledged as the pre-eminent Shakespeare series, valued by scholars, students, actors, and 'the great variety of readers' alike for its readable and reliable texts, its full annotations and its richly informative introductions.

We have aimed in the third Arden edition to maintain the quality and general character of its predecessors, preserving the commitment to presenting the play as it has been shaped in history. While each individual volume will necessarily have its own emphasis in the light of the unique possibilities and problems posed by the play, the series as a whole, like the earlier Ardens, insists upon the highest standards of scholarship and upon attractive and accessible presentation.

Newly edited from the original quarto and folio editions, the texts are presented in fully modernized form, with a textual apparatus that records all substantial divergences from those early printings. The notes and introductions focus on the conditions and possibilities of meaning that editors, critics and performers (on stage and screen) have discovered in the play. While building upon the rich history of scholarly and theatrical activity that has long shaped our understanding of the texts of Shakespeare's plays, this third series of the Arden Shakespeare is made necessary and possible by a new generation's encounter with Shakespeare, engaging with the plays and their complex relation to the culture in which they were – and continue to be – produced.

THE TEXT

On each page of the work itself, readers will find a passage of text followed by commentary and, finally, textual notes. Act and scene divisions (seldom present in the early editions and often the product of eighteenth-century or later scholarship) have been retained for ease of reference, but have been given less prominence than in the previous series. Editorial indications of location of the action have been removed to the textual notes or commentary.

In the text itself, unfamiliar typographic conventions have been avoided in order to minimize obstacles to the reader. Elided forms in the early texts are spelt out in full in verse lines wherever they indicate a usual late-twentieth-century pronunciation that requires no special indication and wherever they occur in prose (except when they indicate non-standard pronunciation). In verse speeches, marks of elision are retained where they are necessary guides to the scansion and pronunciation of the line. Final -ed in past tense and participial forms of verbs is always printed as -ed without accent, never as -'d, but wherever the required pronunciation diverges from modern usage a note in the commentary draws attention to the fact. Where the final -ed should be given syllabic value contrary to modern usage, e.g.

> Doth Silvia know that I am banished?
> (*TGV* 3.1.221)

the note will take the form

221 **banished** banishèd

Conventional lineation of divided verse lines shared by two or more speakers has been reconsidered and sometimes rearranged. Except for the familiar *Exit* and *Exeunt*, Latin forms in stage directions and speech prefixes have been translated into English and the original Latin forms recorded in the textual notes.

COMMENTARY AND TEXTUAL NOTES

Notes in the commentary, for which a major source will be the *Oxford English Dictionary*, offer glossarial and other explication of verbal difficulties; they may also include discussion of points of theatrical interpretation and, in relevant cases, substantial extracts from Shakespeare's source material. Editors will not usually offer glossarial notes for words adequately defined in the latest edition of *The Concise Oxford Dictionary* or *Merriam-Webster's Collegiate Dictionary*, but in cases of doubt they will include notes. Attention, however, will be drawn to places where more than one likely interpretation can be proposed and to significant verbal and syntactic complexity. Notes preceded by * involve editorial emendations or readings in which the rival textual claims of competing early editions (Quarto and Folio) are in dispute.

Headnotes to acts or scenes discuss, where appropriate, questions of scene location, Shakespeare's handling of his source materials, and major difficulties of staging. The list of roles (so headed to emphasize the play's status for performance) is also considered in commentary notes. These may include comment on plausible patterns of casting with the resources of an Elizabethan or Jacobean acting company, and also on any variation in the description of roles in their speech prefixes in the early editions.

The textual notes are designed to let readers know when the edited text diverges from the early edition(s) on which it is based. Wherever this happens the note will record the rejected reading of the early edition(s), in original spelling, and the source of the reading adopted in this edition. Other forms from the early edition(s) recorded in these notes will include some spellings of particular interest or significance and original forms of translated stage directions. Where two early editions are involved, for instance with *Othello*, the notes will also record all important differences between them. The textual notes take a form that has been in use since the nineteenth century. This comprises, first: line reference, reading adopted in the text and closing square bracket; then: abbreviated reference, in italic, to the earliest edition to adopt the accepted reading(s), beginning with the rejected original reading, each with abbreviated italic reference to its source.

Conventions used in these textual notes include the following: the solidus / is used, in notes quoting verse or discussing verse lining, to indicate line endings. Distinctive spellings of the basic text (Q or F) follow the square bracket without indication of source and are enclosed in italic brackets. Names enclosed in italic brackets indicate originators of conjectural emendations when these did not originate in an edition of the text. Stage directions (SDs) are referred to by the number of the line within or immediately after which they are placed. Line numbers with a decimal point relate to entry SDs and to SDs more than one line long, with the number after the point indicating the line within the SD: e.g. 78.4 refers to the fourth line of the SD following line 78. Lines of SDs at the start of a scene are numbered 0.1, 0.2, etc. Where only a line number and SD precede the square bracket, e.g. 128 SD], the note relates to the whole of a SD within or immediately following the line. Speech prefixes (SPs) follow similar conventions, 203 SP] referring to the speaker's name for line 203. Where a SP reference takes the form e.g. 38 + SP, it relates to all subsequent speeches assigned to that speaker in the scene in question.

Where, as with *King Henry V*, one of the early editions is a so-called 'bad quarto' (that is, a text either heavily adapted, or reconstructed from memory, or both), the divergences from the present edition are too great to be recorded in full in the notes. In these cases the editions will include a reduced photographic facsimile of the 'bad quarto' in an appendix.

INTRODUCTION

Both the introduction and the commentary are designed to present the plays as texts for performance, and make appropriate reference to stage, film and television versions, as well as introducing the reader to the range of critical approaches to the plays. They discuss the history of the reception of the texts within the theatre and scholarship and beyond, investigating the inter-dependency of the literary text and the surrounding 'cultural text' both at the time of the original reproduction of Shakespeare's works and during their long and rich afterlife.

ACKNOWLEDGEMENTS

The ideas of more people than I can possibly mention have gone into my thinking about *Julius Caesar* over the years, and more recently into the making of this edition, from books and articles read, and performances seen and commented upon. I hope that, inadequate as it is, a general acknowledgement here of so much wisdom and understanding may be counted to me for righteousness. I have valued T.S. Dorsch's previous Arden edition of *Julius Caesar* (1955): though I often disagree with it, I am honoured to carry the baton forward from his hand. I have benefited particularly from communications from Robert Henke, Blair Worden and Ronnie Mulryne, and the scholarship of Robert Miola. Robert Ireland and Brian Vickers answered complicated questions promptly, at length and with enthusiasm. Robert Ireland read the final proofs and made many valuable suggestions. Some pages of the Introduction first appeared in public at a seminar directed by Robert Miola at the Shakespeare Association of America Conference in Atlanta in 1993. Another section was a paper to the Renaissance Literature Graduate Seminar in Oxford, led by Emrys Jones and Barbara Everett. I learned much from these experiences. Steve Sohmer put at my disposal his insights into the context of the first performances of *Julius Caesar*: more, he made primary and secondary documents available to me at home, a treasure-chest indeed – the publication of this edition means that I have to return that large box: there will be a void in my study in several senses. The librarians of University College London, Magdalen College Oxford, the British Library, the Bodleian Library, the Shakespeare Institute and the Shakespeare Centre at Stratford-upon-Avon, and the London Library, have been unfailingly helpful. Georgianna

Ziegler successfully guided me in locating pictures in the archives of the Folger Shakespeare Library. Jane Kingsley-Smith checked collations and other references with speed and skill. Special gratitude goes to Jessica Hodge of Thomas Nelson: she has been notably efficient, helpful and patient. Roger Fallon was an assiduous copy-editor. To Meg Bradt I owe a particular debt: she arranged for me a research assistant, Sean McBride, who worked in the British Library for four months of solid application; I greatly valued his quick intelligence and accumulated wisdom about the play. The three General Editors of the Series, David Scott Kastan, Ann Thompson and in particular Richard Proudfoot, have made invaluable comments, without which this edition would have been the poorer. Michael Parsons has been important in my thinking about much related to *Julius Caesar*. Thanks are due to Routledge for permission to reproduce excerpts from Bullough: *Narrative and Dramatic Sources of Shakespeare*, vol. 5 (1964). My wife Dorothy, and my sons Chris and Andy, have been a constant source of inspiration, and not only in the years in which I have been so occupied with Shakespeare's first great tragedy.

David Daniell
Leverstock Green

INTRODUCTION

THE PLAY

Julius Caesar is Shakespeare's first great tragedy. It tells the story of the conspiracy to kill Caesar, his assassination, and the civil war that followed, as Caesar's ghost bloodily pursued the chief murderers across the Roman world. Nothing like it had been seen on the stage before. It was a new kind of political play combining fast action (it is a short play – just over half the length of *Hamlet*) and compelling rhetoric. Julius Caesar and the people of Rome, patricians and plebeians alike, have an immediacy that can be felt: the recent history of Rome, and of Caesar himself, is rapidly (and unobtrusively) sketched. Yet in the first three acts the momentum builds to the few seconds of the killing of Caesar – and then builds again until Antony has so skilfully inflamed the mob that, frenzied, they tear an innocent man to pieces on stage, a man who was a poet and maker of good words. From that point, rhetoric, so cleverly used by the conspirators and by Antony, is overtaken by cruelty, revenge and war; on the final battlefield, the two chief conspirators commit suicide, with 'Caesar' on their lips.

Since that fatal moment in Rome on the morning of 15 March 44 BC – the most famous historical event in the West outside the Bible – people have been divided (and still are) about the brutal action to which Brutus gave his power. Was it a necessary culling to save Rome? – King Henry V would have had no hesitation. Or was it, as Goethe called it, the most senseless deed that ever was done? Shakespeare's achievement in this play is to call up widely differing responses. The only political endorsement he gives is to his observation, which was at the

1

heart of his earlier English history plays, that if a ruler is usurped, civil war will follow.

This tragedy has an emotional range from the tender intimacy between a loving man and wife in a garden at night to the most frightening street blood-lust; from stirring music at near-royal processions to the cold listing of people to be purged. Politically, it gives us, from the inside of each person as is Shakespeare's way, the whole of Rome: the 'colossus' of Caesar himself, and an impertinent cobbler; the malcontent urban intellectual Cassius, and the working soldiers in the field; men of the older republic, and the ruthless young politician, Octavius, who says little but will shortly be the first emperor.

Like *Hamlet*, written immediately after it, the play makes a moral puzzle. As in *Hamlet*, the figures on stage are absorbingly interesting, both revealing about themselves and caught up in a drama that drives them on. Their rhetoric, which at first seems full of certainties, four-square like a marble building, on a second glance shows fissures widening as if the ground were moving. The solidity of the city dissolves, to reveal metaphysical experiences; a presence of omens, superstitions, mysteries, misconstruings, supernatural events, delusions and doubtful reports, the senses turning wholly fallible, all making the finding of any truth impossible. As *Hamlet* at its heart expresses doubt, so *Julius Caesar* expresses ambivalence: Caesar did, and did not, deserve to die.

Brutus has by far the most lines in the play. He is, and is not, the tragic hero. Antony calls him 'noble, wise, valiant and honest' (3.1.126), and all are true. Brutus is admirable, and most profoundly flawed. He is loved by Caesar, by Portia, by Cassius, by his servant Lucius, by his fellow-patricians and by Rome, of which he is named the 'soul' (2.1.320). He loves in return, Caesar above all: yet he is easily, by one man's specious self-pity, persuaded to kill him. He is a Roman of refinement who leads the public butchery of his ruler, and then bathes his arms in the blood on the ground. He leads Rome, and quarrels like a spoiled infant. He loves and admires his wife, and abandons her so that she kills herself in despair. He speaks a logical, lucid, spare verse, apparently quite unaware of the illogic, hypocrisy and violence inside it. In the last lines of the play, his death is moving.

Julius Caesar, probably written to open the new Globe theatre in 1599, is remarkable on stage: the assassination in 3.1 has twelve named people consummating it, and at every move we have no doubt who everybody is and why they are there and what is done. The violent thunderstorm in which the conspiracy is brought to a head in 1.3 and 2.2 is Shakespeare's first extended thunder, and most probably his first in the new Globe.[1] He will next use a long thunderstorm in *King Lear*, to show a king's breakdown mirrored in the heavens. There, it is integrated to the fragmentation of the central figure: here, it is oblique to the conflict in Brutus, whose decision 'It must be by his death' (2.1.10) is made in the quiet of his orchard, apparently dissociated from the heavens' violence in the scenes before and after. Caesar, though superstitious, is affected by the storm only through his wife's alarm (2.2). Cassius fails to unite with it: he has 'bared [his] bosom to the thunder-stone' (1.3.49) and tried to read portents, and that is all.

Cicero tells the over-excited Cassius in that storm that 'men may construe things after their fashion' (1.3.34), and in the play everyone is engaged in trying to understand, from Brutus labouring to assess Caesar as tyrant, to Caesar, Calphurnia and Decius solving contrarily the riddle of a dream; from Portia needing to

---

1 Shakespeare's earliest thunder was probably that in *2 Henry VI* 1.4, where, as the Duchess attends the conjuring, '*It Thunders and Lightens terribly: then the Spirit riseth*'; that storm lasts for twenty-three lines, while the Spirit is present. Shakespeare's next thunder after *Julius Caesar* may be at the start of Act 2 of *Othello*, though the twenty lines describing the storm seem to limit it to high winds. By contrast, the explicit thunder and lightning in *Julius Caesar*, from the stage direction at the start of 1.3 to the end of that scene (kept going by a '*Thunder still*' at line 100), and from the stage direction at the start of 2.2 for an indeterminate time, perhaps twenty lines, will probably cover more than two hundred lines in the Folio. Similar calculation in *King Lear* gives not far off four hundred lines of, at least, rumbling in the heavens.

interpret Brutus' disturbance at home, to Cassius on the battlefield fatally misunderstanding the shouts around his friend and fellow-officer Titinius. A tragedy in which the hero of the title dies before it is half over sounds odd indeed, something we might need help to understand, a need big enough to cause a modern critic to dub it a 'Problem Play' (Schanzer, *Problem*). The difficulty of grasping the meaning of rhetoric and events is compounded by what one might call an extra dimension. *Julius Caesar* has unique high moments of the experience of being inside a theatre and at the same time overhearing a different crowd being worked on – it happens in several ways in the first and second scenes. It is almost overwhelmingly powerful in the Forum scene in 3.2.

From its opening in 1599 the play has held the stage in almost every decade and across the world (*Juliasi Kaizari* of 1963 is Shakespeare's play translated into Swahili by Julius K. Nyerere). Modern attempts to confront it have sometimes taken it away from Rome, as if the only way now to make sense of it were to make Caesar a modern Fascist dictator and Brutus and Cassius the leaders of a popular front. One may perhaps sympathize with the urge to comprehend at a stroke a work of art so large and baffling; but such simplification offers us Shakespeare's play shorn of mysteries and resonances. That 'the story is familiar, the republic interesting, and the language public' (S.McB.) makes *Julius Caesar* as it is stand entire.

Shakespeare's verse in *Julius Caesar* is dense with experiment, especially in changes to the iambic line, a movement between regular and irregular pentameters. Compared with the plays written in the five years before and after, *Julius Caesar* has little prose: but it leads the way in the higher proportion of another variation, short and shared lines, a mark of Shakespeare's mature tragedies, especially *Antony and Cleopatra*. *Julius Caesar* is a long step forward in Shakespeare's development of a quite new flexibility of dramatic verse, where speeches travel from mid-line to mid-line. Such prosody is beyond that of his contemporaries, who are themselves ahead of the block verse paragraphs and couplets of the great body of English blank verse down the centuries. It gives a new suppleness to the long 'two-handers' which dominate 1.2, 1.3 and 4.3.

Like piling coloured transparencies one on top of another, examining the structure of the play shows different shapes all present at once. It is clearly in two parts, before and after the assassination. Hamlet says Caesar 'kept the world in awe' (*Ham* 5.1.209), a phrase which captures the ambivalence of his tyranny and the admiration he drew. Immediately after his death, however, the legend of him begins, and now the scale of reference is far, far greater, to 'states unborn and accents yet unknown' (3.1.113). This play is also in three parts, to the conclusions of three quarrels: between the conspirators and Caesar as he dies in Act 3, between Brutus and Cassius at the end of Act 4, and between Caesar's pursuing ghost and Brutus as he dies at the end of the play. The text as we receive it in the First Folio is (probably authorially) in five acts, a standard classical structure. Across those contrapuntal phrases are linked pairs: Portia pleads with her husband, Calphurnia pleads with hers; Brutus shakes bloody hands with the conspirators as a symbol of his sincerity, Antony does the same to gain desperately-needed political time; Caesar's inflexibility in the first acts becomes Brutus' in the last. Some pairings telescope, so that as the end approaches, first Cassius, and then Brutus, die uttering almost the same line and a half. As often in Renaissance texts, a web of number-symbolisms can be detected – for example, an urge to make groupings in fours (McAlindon, 'Numbering').

Recent commentary on the play has found in it a rich hinterland of Elizabethan communal life. *Julius Caesar* can be seen to show some of the patterns, for example, of the older mystery plays: the strong central narrative with a great sacrificial act at its heart is watched and shared by tradesmen and common people (see, for one example, 3.2.160n.). Linked to that are suggestions of popular ritual: the second line of the play sets off the notion of holiday, of subversive and inverting carnival, developed in the Lupercal. Such studies are beginning to reveal more of the religious thought in the play, often Christian and English. The pagan story is told with reference to Elizabethan bibles and Elizabethan religious experience.[1] Everything in *Julius Caesar* points forward to Shakespeare's six further mature tragedies. Beyond the verbal or symbolic references, those seven great plays, *Julius Caesar*, *Hamlet*, *Othello*, *King Lear*, *Macbeth*, *Antony and Cleopatra* and *Coriolanus*, are in a profound sense biblical. Shakespeare inherited a necessarily pagan and Greek view of tragedy: but inside each of these plays is a sense of the scale of human experience in the vastness of the cosmos only found elsewhere in the pages between Genesis 1 and Revelation 22. One comes away from a Roman tragedy of Shakespeare aware of that scale as one does not from those of Jonson or Massinger.

The first part of this introduction will suggest what might have led Shakespeare and his company to put on a play about Julius Caesar in 1599, with something of the long history of the debate about tyranny which his death almost immediately provoked. There follows examination of two of the structures: the language of the play, related to the principal roles; and the larger movements of structure proper. *Julius Caesar* was Shakespeare's first play almost wholly dependent on Plutarch, and this section ends with some analysis of Shakespeare's use of that writer. Some of the life of the play in the study and on the stage is recounted. The last section considers the probable transmission of the play from Shakespeare's pen to the text we have in the First Folio, our only source.

---

1 North translates Plutarch's *pontifex maximus* as 'chief bishop of Rome'.

JULIUS CAESAR IN LONDON IN 1599

We cannot know why Shakespeare, in 1599, took as his subject the assassination of Julius Caesar: but we have strong clues.

Julius Caesar was Shakespeare's twenty-first play. In ten years, he had brought to dramatic life the long English civil war called the Wars of the Roses: first in the three *Henry VI* plays and *Richard III*, and then in *Richard II*, the two *Henry IV* plays and *Henry V*. These battles led to the long peace under the Tudors: Shakespeare may have had in his mind all along that Rome's most significant civil war led to the long peace under Augustus. Shakespeare had learned, among other things, to create ambivalence. The play he had just completed in the summer of 1599, *Henry V*, celebrates an ideal king in heroic actions blessed by God: yet he is a king caught in casuistical politics, whose famous victories ended in civil war. In *Julius Caesar*, Shakespeare 'transformed a confused welter of historical fact and legend into taut, balanced, and supremely ambivalent drama' (Miola, 'Tyrannicide', 273). The morality of rebellion, the subject of all the Wars of the Roses plays and *King John*, is taken to greater dramatic heights in *Julius Caesar*.[1] The history plays already contain a dozen references to Caesar. In *2 Henry VI*, almost the last words of Suffolk are 'Brutus' bastard hand / Stabb'd Julius Caesar' (4.1.136–7; on 'bastard' see *JC* 3.1.77n.). Queen Margaret, seeing her son Prince Edward stabbed to death by the York sons before her eyes, cries, 'They that stabb'd Caesar shed no blood at all' (*3 Henry VI* 5.5.52).

By the spring of 1599 Shakespeare had also written nine comedies. He had invented and developed a form of romantic comedy that ended with the marriage of young men and women in love. Their pleasure in each other is partly the result of triumph over

---

1 Emrys Jones shows (following J.P. Brockbank) that the structure of *Julius Caesar* is modelled on *2 Henry VI*, with ideas of sequential events from *Richard III*, and other material from *1 Henry IV* (*Form*, 106–13).

darker human experiences: gross restraints, delusion, calumny, banishment, grief. Instead of the clashing blood-lines of the history plays, Shakespeare's comedies are rich with attractions. Caesar was in Shakespeare's mind in comedy. Boyet mocks Don Armado's bombastic use of '*Veni, vidi, vici*' in *Love's Labour's Lost* 4.1.70, and at 5.2.607 likens Holofernes' face to 'the pommel of Caesar's falchion'. Rosalind in *As You Like It* quotes Caesar to illustrate the speed with which Oliver and Celia fell in love: 'There was never anything so sudden but the fight of two rams and Caesar's thrasonical brag of "I came, saw, and overcame"' (5.2.28–9). Soon, wanting a boy's name for his disguised heroine Viola in *Twelfth Night*, Shakespeare will call her Cesario. On a grand scale, Shakespeare's romantic comedies speak of high blood and worlds won or lost, of dangerous plots and sudden outcomes, of intended futures and longed-for happiness, of communities threatened and in the end remade, and of the most powerful human feelings. It is not so long a step to *Julius Caesar*, a play in which the word 'love' and its variants appear fifty-six times.

> There is love expressed or suggested between Brutus and Cassius, Brutus and Caesar, and Antony and Caesar; Brutus and Portia, Brutus and Volumnius, Brutus and Lucius; Caesar and Decius, Cassius and Lucius Pella, Cassius and Titinius; Ligarius and Brutus, Artemidorus and Caesar.
>
> (Knight, 63)

Rome was also present in Shakespeare's mind in tragedy, in *Titus Andronicus* (1594) and *The Rape of Lucrece* of the same year. *Hamlet*, being written in 1599, was first performed soon after *Julius Caesar*: four minutes into that tragedy, Horatio tells of the omens surrounding the death of 'the mightiest Julius' (1.1.113). Polonius later says he acted in a university play about Caesar being killed in the Capitol. *Hamlet* was a new kind of play for the Elizabethan stage, the first English tragedy to fulfil Aristotle's observations. *Julius Caesar* before it goes a long way down that Greek road.

> The two elements which Aristotle thought necessary for the profoundest tragedy, *peripeteia* and *anagnorisis*, an ironic turn of events which makes an action have the very opposite effect of that intended, and the realization of this by the agent, are thus seen to be fundamental [to *Julius Caesar*].
>
> (Schanzer, *Problem*, 56)

Brutus may be seen as Hamlet without the Prince, that is, without a royal court. *Julius Caesar* bounded in a nutshell is 'purposes mistook / Fall'n on th'inventors' heads' (*Ham* 5.2.376–7). *Hamlet* uses names from Rome: Claudius, Cornelius, Marcellus, and Horatio – who claims to be 'more an antique Roman than a Dane'. Those Roman names take with them into *Hamlet* a characteristic of *Julius Caesar* and the following Roman plays, where dilemmas, like actions, are clearly stated and made: it is the Dane Hamlet, not the 'Roman' Claudius, who has bad dreams. Even while Shakespeare was planning *Hamlet*, it seems that he saw in *Julius Caesar* a new tragic potential.

Shakespeare found interest in this year, 1599, in retelling well-known stories. How Prince Hal became Henry V, and the victory at Agincourt, were familiar to audiences, not only from the chronicles of Hall and Holinshed, but from at least one play previous to Shakespeare's, the anonymous *Famous Victories of Henry the Fifth* of (1598). *As You Like It*, also from 1599, is Thomas Lodge's popular prose fiction of 1590 and thereafter, *Rosalynde*, adapted for the stage – transformed by a playwright of genius, but still an adaptation. The story of Prince Hamlet was well known before Shakespeare wrote of him. And, as already noted, the assassination of Caesar was the single best-known story from the pagan ancient world. To make something quite new out of something older would be attractive to an experienced poet and playwright, knowing that people would come to the playhouse not to find out what happened, but to see what William Shakespeare did with the story. That he prepared his play of *Julius Caesar* for the opening of his company's new custom-built theatre on Bankside, the Globe, in 1599 seems likely. Reading the opening scene of this play as spoken to an excited crowd in a new theatre supports the point.

Shakespeare, plunging into Roman history, might have written a play about Pompey, who interested him all his life – the Spevack concordance lists, from all the canon, ninety-one references to Pompey. That general's tragic story was well known: his life is told by Plutarch, and in 1581 at least one, and possibly two, plays about Caesar and Pompey are recorded (Harbage and Schoenbaum, 48). Thomas Kyd had translated Robert Garnier's *Cornélie* (about Pompey's wife) under the title of *Cornelia* in 1594 and as *Pompey the Great His Fair Cornelia's Tragedy* in 1595. This was not for the theatre, but a Senecan tragedy dedicated to the Countess of Sussex, a dramatic poem for reading at Wilton: but Pompey's name is in the dramatic air. There were two anonymous plays (now lost), *1* and *2 Caesar and Pompey*, on the popular stage, acted by the Admiral's company in 1594 and 1595. *The Tragedy of Caesar and Pompey, or Caesar's Revenge*,[1] could have been written in the 1590s. Shakespeare changed the Nine Worthies in *Love's Labour's Lost* 5.2.485–557 to replace Julius Caesar with Pompey the Great (see Barroll, 336); it is Pompey who gets the first treatment, and receives the gracious 'Great thanks, great Pompey' from the Princess. Indeed, *Julius Caesar* begins with a scene about Pompey. It is not totally unthinkable that some of the political dissatisfaction in London in 1599 with the all-powerful Queen Elizabeth's treatment of her rivals (which will be touched on below) could have been reflected in a play by Shakespeare called *Pompey the Great*.

Shakespeare could also have considered opening the Globe with a play about Antony. Well known from the longest and most

---

1   Extracts are printed in Bullough, vol. 5.

dynamic life in Plutarch, Antony had also been the subject of recent closet plays. Mary Herbert, Countess of Pembroke, 'Sidney's sister, Pembroke's mother', translated and adapted Robert Garnier's 1578 *Marc Antoine* as *The Tragedy of Antony* in 1590; it was published in 1592 and 1595. Samuel Daniel, a member of her circle, dedicated his *The Tragedy of Cleopatra* to her in 1595. Samuel Brandon published *The Tragicomedy of the Virtuous Octavia* (about the wife of Antony) in 1598, dedicated to Lucia Audelay, and Samuel Daniel wrote *A letter from Octavia to Marcus Antonius* in 1599, dedicated to the Countess of Cumberland. Shakespeare could have used such topical and political interest in Antony.[1] Fulke Greville, Sidney's friend and biographer, author of a long poetic treatise *Of Monarchy*, wrote a play on Antony and Cleopatra which is of interest for the reason for it not surviving: Greville 'had thrown it in the fire fearing that it was "apt enough to be construed, or strained to a personating of vices in the present Governors, and government"' (Rees, *Greville*, 122). In these years, Greville wrote the first version of his tragedy *Mustapha*, in which oriental tyranny is offensive. The aristocratic circles were using history, especially Roman history, to express easily-decoded criticism of 'the present Governors, and government'.

For such interest as had become fashionable through Roman history, however, a certain kind of play about Julius Caesar and his death would be especially timely. It would extend Shakespeare's skill with ambivalence beyond the just-finished *Henry V*. The single most significant act of rebellion in ancient history, and its outcome, could be set by a dramatist in a play-world of *Julius Caesar* where the common people were healthy and content ('Unlike the Plebeians in *Coriolanus* [the worthy commoners of *Julius Caesar*] have no grievance. They seem to be quite happy, and fairly prosperous', not feeling themselves victims: Hunter, 117–18). Yet the world of *Julius Caesar* is one where all those who rule are weak or ill ('epilepsy, fever, deafness,

---

1 See Wilders, 61–3.

shortsightedness, ague, fainting, illnesses real and pretended':
Miles, 134; see Foakes, 'Approach', 262–3). A nation's state of
health could be portrayed, where the 'Governors' were seen to be
sick. Shakespeare could orchestrate a Roman world in the musical key, so to speak, of a very Roman concept that was complex,
ambiguous and suddenly fashionable – Stoic constancy. 'As the
defining virtue of the Romans, it is central to his reconstruction
of the ethos of ancient Rome' (Miles, 15). Shakespeare's *Julius
Caesar* does not set out historical blame. It belongs to a group of
his historical plays (*King John*, *Richard II*, *1* and *2 Henry IV*)
interested in the illusive, and elusive, identity of governors.

Shakespeare's *Julius Caesar* was topical in other ways. In
London in the middle of 1599 Caesar was in many people's minds,
it seems, with pressing thoughts both about evaluation of his death
as a political act, and, to us surprisingly, about an urgent matter of
the calendar. First the date of writing must be confirmed.

Date

Thomas Platter, a Swiss doctor from Basle, wrote in 1599:

> On the 21st of September, after dinner, at about two
> o'clock, I went with my party across the water; in the
> straw-thatched house we saw the tragedy of the first
> Emperor Julius Caesar, very pleasingly performed, with
> approximately fifteen characters; at the end of the play
> they danced together admirably and exceedingly grace-
> fully, according to their custom, two in each group
> dressed in men's and two women's apparel.[1]

Platter's words have long stood as the marker for the latest possible date for *Julius Caesar*. He was in England from 18
September to 20 October 1599, and he wrote in 1604–5 an
account of his travels in the years 1595–1600. *Julius Caesar* seems

---

1 Given here in the more approachable translation by Ernest Schanzer in 'Platter'. The
   suggestion that what Platter saw was something else, and at the Rose, has no evidence
   to support it. The original German is reprinted in Chambers, *Stage*, 2.364–5.

to have been the first of several plays he saw in different theatres, all making a strong impression.

We can say that *Julius Caesar* is not likely to have been written before the autumn of the previous year, 1598. It does not appear in Francis Meres's list of Shakespeare's plays in his *Palladis Tamia: Wit's Treasury*, registered on 7 September 1598 and published shortly after. Had as notable a play as *Julius Caesar* been performed before September 1598, Meres, we might have thought, would surely have included it, though there are other omissions. The earliest date can also probably be confirmed from allusions by Shakespeare himself. We know that Shakespeare was finishing *Henry V* in the summer of 1599. In the Prologue to the last act, Chorus matches the return of the victorious English king from France to London with the return to Rome of Caesar:

> How London doth pour out her citizens!
> The mayor and all his brethren in best sort –
> Like to the senators of th'antique Rome,
> With the plebeians swarming at their heels –
> Go forth and fetch their conqu'ring Caesar in . . .
> (*H5* 5. Chorus. 24–8)

The next lines note, if the Earl of Essex should return from Ireland having successfully put down rebellion there,

> How many would the peaceful city quit
> To welcome him!

Plutarch in his life of Antony wrote: 'Nowe when Caesar was returned from his last warre in Spayne, all the chiefest nobilitie of the citie road many dayes jorney from Rome to meete him' (*Antonius*, 262); Shakespeare adds the 'plebeians swarming' and, for Essex, 'How many'. While finishing *Henry V* in 1599, Shakespeare could well have been planning, or starting, *Julius Caesar*, with the plebeians celebrating a triumph already in his mind. This would confirm the first half of 1599 for the starting, if not more, of the Roman play.

It is possible that phrases in the play echo books published that year, though such references are less reliable as evidence for dating, as they could have been part of a common pool of ideas. Sir John Davies's long poem *Nosce teipsum* of 1599 (the title means 'Know Thyself') may have suggested Cassius' lines on the eye seeing other things but not itself (see 1.2.52–8n.). Davies's book was entered in the Stationers' Register on 4 April 1599. Other echoes of that poem have been suggested, and also from Samuel Daniel's *Musophilus*, registered 9 January and published that year: both might have suggested Cassius' notion of Caesar's death being acted out 'many ages hence' (see Taylor).

Some help is given with the latest possible date by a crop of allusions to *Julius Caesar* which sprang up after 1599: Jonson has two in his *Every Man out of His Humour*, registered 8 April 1600, where his 'reason is long since fled to animals, you know' (3.4.28–9) parodies 'O judgement, thou art fled to brutish beasts / And men have lost their reason' (*JC* 3.2.105–6); and his '*Et tu, Brute*' (5.6.70) is probably a direct reference to *Julius Caesar* 3.1.77 – though that famous phrase, an adaptation of Suetonius' Greek 'and thou, my child', appeared first in 1595 in the so-called 'Bad Quarto' of *3 Henry VI*, entitled *The True Tragedy of Richard of York*, as 'Et tu Brute, wilt thou stab Caesar too?'[1] The identical line occurs again in 1600 in Samuel Nicholson's *Acolastus His Afterwit* (sig. E3^r). William Percy, in his play *Arabia sitiens* of 1601,[2] has the line 'Et tu Brute of the Faemine gender?' (RP). We are probably right to think that the occurrences in 1600 were triggered by Shakespeare using it at the heart of his play.

Julius Caesar is one of the plays of Shakespeare most referred to in the early seventeenth century. This is important. Because it was not in print until the 1623 Folio, knowledge of it must have come from stage performances. It is extremely unlikely that there could have been access to a manuscript copy. Because income came from

1 In *3 Henry VI* 5.1.81, said by King Edward to his brother Clarence, as he declares for Lancaster.
2 Huntington Library HM4, fol. 44a.

14

performances, Shakespeare's company, the King's Men, would carefully guard their property. The play written out, in individual parts or in the theatre's definitive 'prompt' copy, would not be seen or copied again without very special reason indeed, and we have no evidence of that here. So the thick crop of allusions grew most probably from the play being seen on the stage. One more example may suffice. John Weever in his *The Mirror of Martyrs, or The Life and Death of Sir John Oldcastle*, printed in 1601, has, in stanza 4:

> The many-headed multitude were drawn
> By Brutus' speech, that Caesar was ambitious.
> When eloquent Mark Antony had shown
> His virtues, who but Brutus then was vicious?

The dedication says it had been 'some two years ago . . . made fit for the print', though an allusion to Edward Fairfax's *Godfrey of Bulloigne*, published in 1600, suggests it is later than 1599.

We may accept that *Julius Caesar* was begun in the first half of 1599 (when *Henry V* was being finished), and finished by the late summer of 1599 (when *Hamlet* was already on the stocks), for a performance of it seen by Platter at the new Globe on 21 September 1599.

September or June 1599?

Whether what Thomas Platter saw was a first performance, or even one soon after the opening of the new building, is not so certain. Recent research has suggested the possibility that *Julius Caesar* opened the Globe earlier in that year, on 12 June 1599 (Sohmer).[1] From signing the ground lease for the site on Bankside on 21 February, the new theatre (reconstructed from the materials of the old Theatre in Shoreditch) could have been ready in just over a hundred days. The company could have had the new Globe opened from early June 1599. The inquisition (legal investigation) on this Bankside property left by the lessor's father,

1 Sohmer notes that new building, whether the Roman Capitol or the walls of the City of London, was traditionally associated with sacrifice. Thus a play about letting Caesar's blood was appropriate for a new theatre (Sohmer, chap. 4).

Thomas Brend, dated 16 May 1599, described the Globe as '*de novo edificata . . . in occupacione Willielmi Shakespeare et aliorum*' (Chambers, *Stage*, 2.415). It may not then have been quite finished. A sharp, and permanent, drop in Henslowe's takings at the nearby Rose Theatre after June 1599 suggests the presence of a rival on Bankside.

The twelfth of June 1599 was astronomically useful and astrologically significant. Astronomy showed on that day a new moon, and a high tide at Southwark at 1 p.m., more than convenient for the arrival of an audience of three thousand. (The alternative, arriving at a low tide, would have meant a long slog through smelly mud.) To the learned, astronomy also showed the phenomenon on 12 June of the twice-monthly conjunction (alignment) of sun, moon and earth coinciding with the summer solstice, the shortest night, a fact that brought even higher tides. Astrology suggested that a new moon on the summer solstice made 12 June unusually propitious for a new venture, and readings of the stars supported this. To open a theatre on the summer solstice, coinciding with the sun–moon–earth conjunction and exceptional high tides, on a date which was as well astrologically promising, would show wisdom.[1]

Time and the calendar conflicts

Shakespeare carefully crafted our sense of the movement of time in *Julius Caesar* before the assassination. The dramatic pressure up to the end of the third act seems to allow us to compute a sequence of events over two days. Cassius says at the end of 1.2 that he will throw writings in at Brutus' windows 'this night', and it seems reasonable to assume that this is the night of the day with which the play began. Cassius and Caska meet at night and set

1 There is little in *Julius Caesar* that might immediately confirm this suggestion, though Sohmer's assembly of many secondary factors, like the astronomical data, is impressive. In the Scripture readings prescribed in the Book of Common Prayer for the days around 12 June, Sohmer has noted some interesting parallels. In the Book of Common Prayer in use in 1599 the second lesson at Matins on 12 June is Mark, 12, with its reiteration of the name 'Caesar', rare in the Gospels (Sohmer, chap. 4).

out for Brutus' house, where Lucius discovers a letter in the window. They are joined there by the conspirators, looking forward to 'tomorrow' when Caesar goes to the Capitol. In 2.2, the next day, they are welcomed by Caesar, and there can be no break from that point to the fury of the mob after Antony's funeral speech. So a scheme can be made of day–night–day, an apparent effect of 'double time', because an audience would know that from the Lupercalia on 15 February to the Ides (the 15th) of March was not two days. Nineteenth-century critics, thinking of the narrative 'realism' of novels, made much of this. 'The important thing about the sequence of days and nights, is, precisely, their sequence and not (as is so often thought), their duration' (Jones, *Form*, 47). Shakespeare has, by stitching what is invisible in the theatre, joined together the night of the Lupercalia and the eve of the assassination: 'the transformation is one of history into poetry' (Jones, *Form*, 50).

In 1968 Sigurd Burckhardt alerted students of this play to the importance of the bitter struggle at the very end of the sixteenth century which affected everyone in Europe: the warring systems of calendars. As everyone knew and Plutarch emphasized, in 44 BC Julius Caesar had himself sorted out discrepancies in the calendar that had by his day developed, with his institution of the Julian calendar (see Appendix, p. 323). It was, says Plutarch, one of the reasons why he was hated. 'The Roman conservatives felt it to be an arbitrary and tyrannical interference with the course of nature' (Burckhardt, 6). By the 1580s, however, the Julian calendar (for long the Christian calendar) had drifted out of phase again by almost ten days. Pope Gregory in 1582 decreed reform, restoring the 'lost' days, and making the summer solstice on the 21st, not the 12th, of June. The Catholic countries accepted this 'New Style'. The Protestant countries did not, on the grounds that the Julian calendar was that of Christ's revelation (Sohmer, chap. 3). We should remember that under Elizabeth I all editions of the Book of Common Prayer, and most Bibles, opened with pages of the Julian calendar. After the Bible, the most frequently

2

A brefe explication of the Leape yeere.

Ecause the present Almanacke is made for the yere.1584. called in Lattin Annus Intercalaris, oi Biſſextilis, in Engliſh, a Leape veere. hauing ſo good occaſion and fit opportunitie, I ſuppoſe it not inconuenient to treate ſomewhat here concernyng the oiiginall of the ſame.

Iulius Cæſar, the firſt and moſt renowmed Emperour of Rome, perceiuyng the aunctent Romans a long tyme to haue laboured, and paynefully trauayled in ſearchyng out the direct courſe and true ſpace of the yeere, and withall conteyning how many errours they were wrapped in, how muche they were troubled, how manifoldly intangled, and how greatly deceyued in the obſeruation of the ſame, knowyng their woonted and common yeere to be coireſpondent neither to the Sphæricall Reuolution of the Sunne, noi to the Adæquate motion of the Moone, he vndertooke a piofitable iourney from Rome to Egypt, where he piectſely learned of the Egyptians, whoſe computation Eudoxus and Hypparchus folowed, the true & exact quantitie thereof : and then returnyng from thence againe to Rome, he there, by the helpe of Soſigenes an Aſtrologer of ſpecial account, amongſt other his noble enterpiiſes, & glorious actions woithy eternall fame, did ſufficiently coirect, & fully amende their foimer errours. Foi as Numa Pompilius, ſucceſſour to King Romulus (who publiſhed the ſecond Romane Kalender) did therein ad. 50. naturall dayes more vnto the yeere, then were befoie him aſually obſerued, after the inſtitution of the firſt Romane Kalender of Romulus (accoidyng to whoſe ſupputation the yeere conſiſted only of. 304. dayes, that is, but of. 10. Monethes.) So this moſt puiſſaunt Captayne, and learned Aſtronomicall Emperour, in the. 45. yeere befoie the happy byith of our Sauiour *C H R I S T*, did lykewyſe adde vnto the yeere of Numa Pompilius (who nothing eſteemyng the annuary circuites, oi circular piogreſſe of the Sunne, trai-
A. ii. eating

printed documents in the sixteenth century were calendars and almanacs (Thomas, 248).

At the turn of the century the bitter controversy was felt everywhere:

> a situation existed in Europe exactly analogous to that of Rome in 44 BC. It was a time of confusion and uncertainty, when the most basic category by which men order their experience seemed to have become unstable and untrustworthy, subject to arbitrary political manipulation.
>
> (Burckhardt, 6)

In 1599, Easter was five weeks apart between Protestants and Catholics. England, a Protestant nation, felt out of step, celebrating the Church festivals on the 'wrong' days, failing to match what the heavens declared. There was in print in the middle of that year a good deal of strong feeling on the subject. Here is another reason, to add to those below, why Caesar seems to have been a topical subject in 1599. 'Like the Romans of Julius Caesar's age, Shakespeare and his fellow-Elizabethans found themselves compelled to live . . . in "Caesar's time"' (Sohmer, chap. 9).

If there was a question whether, as Midsummer Day, 12 June was a holiday at all, rather than the 21st, the second line of the play, 'Is this a holiday?', could well have produced a powerful response. London City fathers opposed the public theatres, and objected to working men turning the day into a holiday. The tribunes could be echoing that. A more obvious clarification, however, has long been obscured by textual interference. In the play, the eve of the Ides, 15 March, begins with Caska and Cicero in thunder and lightning at the start of 1.3, and finishes at the end of 2.1 with Ligarius and Brutus in the early hours going off to join the others to fetch Caesar to the Capitol: we do not need telling that that journey is on the date it is, 15 March, the Ides. Brutus, however, does. In the Folio text, at 2.1.40, sending

Ianuarie hath.xxxi.dayes.

The common Ianuarie		The Romane Ianuarie, and Februarie partilis.		The progreſſion of the Moone.			The changes and aſpeɛts of the Moone with the Sun.
Dayes.	Vſuall Feaſtes.	Dayes.	Vſuall Feaſtes.	G.	M	Signes	
i	A	ri	D	21	1	Aquar	
ij	b	rii	e	3	25	Piſces	
iii	c	riii	f	15	35	Piſces	☽．✳．☉．
iiii	d	riiii	g	S.Hillary	27	35	Piſces	
v	e	rv	a	9	43	Aries.	Firſt quarter,
vi	f	Epiphanie	rvi	b	12	12	Aries.	the. vi. day, at
vii	g	rvii	c	4	53	Taur.	viii. of ẏ clocke
viii	A	rviii	D	17	15	Taur.	at nyght.
ir	b	rir	e	29	22	Taur.	☽．△．☉．
r	c	rr	f	Sunne in	11	37	Gemi.	
ri	d	rri	g	Aquarius.	24	7	Gemi.	
rii	e	rrii	a	6	55	Cancer	Full Moone,
riii	f	rriii	b	20	1	Cancer	the. riiii. day,
riiii	g	rriiii	c	3	20	Leo.	at two of the
rv	A	rrv	D	Conuertiõ	16	57	Leo.	clocke after
rvi	b	rrvi	e	of Paul,ẋ	0	49	Uirgo	noone.
rvii	c	rrvii	f	Septuage-	15	8	Uirgo	
rviii	d	rrviii	g	ſima.	29	48	Uirgo	☽．△．☉．
rir	e	rrir	a	14	42	Libra.	Last quarter,
rr	f	rrr	b	29	9	Libra.	the. rri. day, at
rri	g	rrri	c	13	6	Scorp	ir.before none.
rrii	A	i	D	Februarie.	26	53	Scorp	
rriii	b	ii	e	Purificati.	10	52	Sagit	☽．✳．☉．
rriiii	c	iii	f	of Mary.	24	52	Sagit	
rrv	d	iiii	g	8	27	Capri.	
rrvi	e	Conuertiõ	v	a	21	39	Capri.	New Moone,
rrvii	f	of Paul.	vi	b	4	31	Aquar	the.rrviii.day,
rrviii	g	vii	c	17	11	Aquar	paſt. iii. of the
rrir	A	viii	D	Shroue	29	32	Aquar	clocke after
rrr	b	ir	e	ſunday.	12	0	Piſces	noone.
rrri	c	r	f	24	5	Piſces	

2 One of many late sixteenth-century almanacs, this by William Farmer
shows the English and Roman calendars current in 1586 and explains how
to compare them

Lucius back to bed, he has an afterthought. 'Is not tomorrow, boy, the first of March?' (and see Appendix, p. 335). Theobald in 1733 with ingenuity and asperity emended to correct the 'error', and most texts ever since have printed his 'Is not tomorrow, Boy, *the Ides* of March?' Brutus is confused about many things, having lost not only his moral bearings: from the stars he cannot tell the time without knowing the date. He does not know the date without the calendar. He sends Lucius to fetch one. In Folio he is asking – is tomorrow the 1st or the 15th? Lucius comes back to say it is the 15th, and immediately on those words there is a '*Knock within*'; the arrival of the conspirators begins the great dramatic movement which does not end until Caesar is dead. Brutus may not have known what we know, that the Soothsayer, by his 'Beware the Ides of March' early in the second scene, meant death to Caesar. But he is contemplating great events, and his question to Lucius would have been familiar to all Elizabethans: he needs to know what calendar he is working under. Then he can read the heavens, and 'Give guess how near to day' (2.1.3) and not be out by fifteen days.[1]

Moreover, we may observe Shakespeare making the good government of Caesar a structure, a grid, within which the events can happen, for Caesar himself had, just before the events in the play, set the date with his calendrical reforms. As Shakespeare's audience knew, he also set the clocks of Rome: Caesar's *Commentaries* (from which Shakespeare quotes at *2 Henry VI* 4.7.56) make clear his concern for timekeeping. When Brutus is publicly committed to killing Caesar, '*Clock strikes*' (2.1.190.1), and Brutus insists they all listen and count. Caesar's first words

---

1 Hinman (2.169–71) tells us that the page, kk3ᵛ, containing 'the first of March', was the first of *Julius Caesar* to be set, by Compositor A. It is suggested that as it would have been the first time he had met the word, he was puzzled by the original 'Ides', and rationalized it as 'first', taking the 'I' as a number 1: Lucius with his 'March is wasted fifteen days' can be seen as much confirming 'Ides' as correcting 'first' (RP). This does not entirely explain, however, the later correct setting of 'Ides' by Compositor B, at 1.2.18, 19 and 23, on kk1ᵛ, and at 3.1.1 on kk5ᵛ. If A did not recognize the famous phrase in the context of the date for the assassination of Caesar, why should B have done so?

21

to Brutus in the morning are 'What is't o'clock?' (2.2.114). The striking clock amused and irritated eighteenth- and nineteenth-century commentators for its anachronistic ignorance – poor Shakespeare did not know that the Romans did not have striking clocks. The point is the reverse: just as Brutus is taking the lead to kill Caesar, Shakespeare makes the setting itself, a room in a house in Rome, demonstrate the triumph of Caesar's time down the ages (and see Burckhardt, 9). Brutus had to decide whether to go with the newness that Caesar could represent, and his new calendar, or kill him and that newness, and stay with the older way. In 2.1, at the very moment that he silently commits himself to Cassius' plot, their whispering is covered by discussion of the seasons, the calendar and the orientation of the Capitol. Then the clock strikes. Caesar had brought the heavens and the business of daily life into harmony, and Shakespeare seems to want to make Brutus especially aware of it.

Caesar in London in 1599

When *Julius Caesar* was being written, there was in England, and associated with Caesar, a sharp political awareness that it was possible to challenge rigidity of rule: a rigidity probably extending to tyranny; a challenge possibly extending to conspiracy leading to rebellion. These possibilities were discussed in the 1590s more widely by way of the death of Richard II as a victim of tyranny, and Caesar's assassination out of a fear of tyranny. We shall here consider the first, on our way to the second – which itself arises from the centuries-old debate: was Caesar a hero or a tyrant? Was Brutus a patriot or an assassin?

Samuel Daniel's *First Four Books of the Civil Wars* of 1595, on the Wars of the Roses, had, out of all proportion, devoted 160 of its stanzas to the deposition and death of Richard II. Shakespeare knew and used that poem, and the same year wrote his own play *Richard II*, which was the only play of Shakespeare's to have three editions in two years (1597, 1598) – editions, however, which pointedly cut 160 lines, the scene of Richard's deposition.

In the late 1590s the faction supporting the Earl of Essex took a special interest not so much in the deposition of King Richard as in his murder. Essex, even in the summer of 1599, two years before the day of his out-and-out rebellion (and that famous special performance, the previous afternoon, of what is always taken to be Shakespeare's play of *Richard II*), was already attracting rebellious conspiracy. He was then still in the middle of his six months' expedition to subdue rebellious Ireland (where, like Richard II before him, and so many since, he failed). Shakespeare himself expressed in the Chorus to Act 5 of *Henry V* the hopes that London had set on the adventurer's triumphant return. The words are ambivalent, to the point of not being hopeful:

> As, by a lower but as loving likelihood,
> Were now the General of our gracious Empress –
> As in good time he may – from Ireland coming,
> Bringing rebellion broached on his sword . . .
>
> (*H5* 5. Chorus. 29–32)

In those months of 1599 the Government was seriously alarmed about Essex. More significant than the later performance[1] of *Richard II* was the appearance in March 1599 of a book by John Hayward, lawyer and scholar (he was knighted in 1619). Hayward's book begins with a whole-page dedication to Essex (to which Essex himself objected) in the most fulsome Latin, including the words '*Magnus siquidem es, et presenti iudicio et futuri temporis expectatione*' ('Indeed you are great, both in present judgement and in the expectation of time to come'), language more appropriate for a monarch. The title of the book is *The First Part of the Life and Reign of Henry the Fourth*: it takes the story only to the end of the first year of the reign. The title is misleading. It is almost entirely about Richard II. He does not yield himself up until page 84, out of 149 pages. Henry is not crowned until page 97. Richard is murdered on page 133. The rest of the book

---

1 Performances, according to the Queen. See Warnicke, 136.

recounts the tragic events that followed. Pages 100–10 are given to the Bishop of Carlisle's speech pleading for the imprisoned Richard as still the sovereign prince: two of these pages are annotated with printed biblical and classical marginal notes and references. The book is effectively about the deposition of Richard and the usurpation by Henry IV. On publication, Hayward was ordered to cut the dedication to Essex: a year later he was, like his patron, in serious trouble – which did not prevent three different printers bringing his book out again when James came to the throne, all three editions separately, and falsely, dated 1599, as if that had been the key year. Hayward's book was later brought into evidence against Essex, and he himself was committed to the Tower and questioned at trials in 1600 and 1601. 'He protested his innocence of any attempt to draw analogies between Richard, Elizabeth, and Essex . . . but he remained in prison apparently until after Elizabeth's death' (Ure, *R2*, lix). Nevertheless, on 1 June 1599, the Stationers received an order mandating a comprehensive sweep of London booksellers to suppress certain classes of books, of which Hayward's was one of the targets (Hayward, *passim*). By that time it had sold between 1,000 and 1,200 copies.

We shall see presently some links between Shakespeare's *Richard II* and *Julius Caesar*. The interest of the Essex supporters in the murder of Richard II overlaps with that in Roman history. (We should remember that the Essex group were also the Sidney circle – Philip Sidney's 'Stella' was Essex's sister: Sidney's widow married Essex.) A special interest can be seen in the need to overthrow a tyrant. Led by Sidney's sister Mary, the Countess of Pembroke, some attempt was made to introduce into English drama the methods of Seneca, to purify the theatre and rid it of its apparent increasing vulgarity and what today would be called 'gratuitous' violence. We have already noted her *Tragedy of Antony* of 1590, Daniel's *Cleopatra* and Greville's play on Antony and Cleopatra. Such English Senecans, influenced by French plays, disliked the onstage killings and blood which English audiences revelled in (witness the continued popularity of Shakespeare's *Titus Andronicus*, picked out by Ben Jonson, with Kyd's *Spanish Tragedy*, for special note twenty years after it was written: Chambers, *Shakespeare*, 2.206). The more decorous plays on the French model (cf. Charlton, cxx) were made of long passionate speeches, perhaps with the occasional entry of a messenger to announce an offstage suicide – we must be thankful that the English theatre kept the robustness of Shakespeare.

As well as such purification (reflected in Sidney's own *Apology for Poetry*),[1] in those Roman plays of the late 1590s the Sidney circle express a particular concern for the way an individual might cope with tyranny. The interest we noted above in Octavia, the faithful wife of the adulterous Antony, makes an example. Mary Sidney's *Antony* makes Cleopatra chaste, loving – and betrayed. All the contemporary men and women mentioned here were members of the Sidney group (Lamb, ch. 3). Greville, who destroyed his play 'on the heroic general destroyed by his love for a false queen' (Bullough, 5.33), was engaged with Sidney at various times in activities which angered the Queen.

The tyrant in view is not hard to find. Even elementary knowledge of Queen Elizabeth's policies in the years up to her death allows parallels between herself and a tyrannical Caesar. Queen Elizabeth, as age advanced, put herself out as immortal, not only as the eternally enduring Faerie Queene or Gloriana. Her control of her portraits, for example, went beyond the natural desire to regulate response to an enormous demand. 'The official image of the Queen in her final years was to be that of a legendary beauty, ageless and unfading' (Strong, 19). After her death in March 1603 there sprang up the cult of 'Saint Elizabeth' in whose presence Time and Death were rendered impotent – a 'final and staggering apotheosis' (Strong, 42–3). A modern historian wrote of Elizabeth:

> Her solution lay in so elevating the queen above the rest
> of mankind that policies in the national interest would –
> along with her personality – pass out of reach of human

1 See Sidney, Philip, esp. 133–7.

criticism . . . As the reign proceeds we are witnessing, in
the field of politics as in literature, the apotheosis of a
woman, a monarch transmuted into a god.

(Hurstfield, 134)

Part of the Senecan tradition, where it touched Julius Caesar,
stressed that final apotheosis. Ovid concluded his *Metamorphoses*
with the elevation of the soul of Julius Caesar into a star. Some
lines before that, for Caesar *'in urbe sua deus est'*, Golding rendered 'But *Caesar* hathe obteynd / His Godhead in his native
soyle and Citie where he reignd'. Golding's version of Venus ele-
vating Caesar's soul extends and elaborates Ovid's image, ending: 'a goodly shyning starre it up a loft did stye / And drew a
greate way after it bryght beames like burning heare . . .'
(Golding, 834–5, 950–6). That had been used by Shakespeare at
the start of one of his own earliest plays: the Duke of Bedford,
lamenting the death of Henry V, says:

> thy ghost I invocate . . .
> Combat with adverse planets in the heavens.
> A far more glorious star thy soul will make
> Than Julius Caesar . . .
>
> (*1H6* 1.1.52, 54–6)

Like Queen Elizabeth, Caesar had been, in this tradition,
'a monarch transmuted into a god', and thus beyond attack.
Shakespeare's Julius Caesar, a moment before his death,
announces that he is even above god-head; see 3.1.58–9 and note.

It is difficult to think that the Sidney and Essex set were not
also aware of the content of a little Italian book first translated
by 'I.B.B.' under the title *Observations upon the Lives of
Alexander, Caesar, Scipio. Newly Englished* in 1602. This was
first published in Turin in 1600. The section in 'I.B.B.' on
Caesar, signatures G–N, is entitled 'Iulius Caesar the Dictator',
where he appears as a self-seeking and cynical opportunist. The
headings include 'That Caesar aspired to the highest greatness',

'How Caesar won unto him the people of Rome', 'How he suppressed the authority of the Senate'. The city of Rome was distracted into factions: Caesar was 'in need of civil war' (sig. Hv^r). The Catiline conspirators were not killed, but kept in prison – presumably for future use (sig. Hvi^v). And so on. This is one of a number of Italian books, strongly for or against Caesar, in the last decades of the century. 'In an age of great monarchs, Caesar became a pattern' (Bullough, 5.21). The debate throughout Europe about what could be done with a tyrant, to which we shall return, had intensified as the century advanced, and usually related to the death of Caesar. In Italy, Stefano Ambrosio Schiappalaria praised Caesar lavishly in *La vita di C. Iulio Cesare* of 1568, and again in his *Osservationi politiche, et discorsi pertinenti a' governi di stato . . . con la vita di Caio Giulio Cesare* of 1600. This has a dedicatory letter from Orlando Pescetti, whose play *Il Cesare* of 1594, largely sympathetic to Brutus, is one probable source for Shakespeare's tragedy.[1] That later interest by Italian intellectuals grew out of new readings of Lucan, Plutarch, Suetonius, Cicero, Appian and Petrarch. Further back, mid-fifteenth-century struggles between republicans and anti-republicans in northern Italy focused on Caesar, those in Florence decrying him: the complex publication history of the Florentine Poggio Bracciolini's *De fortunae varietate*, in which Caesar is attacked, prevents us dating precisely the effect it undoubtedly had. As we observed of the longer debate, in these and other late-sixteenth-century Italian books, Caesar is either hero or tyrant, Brutus is either patriot or assassin.

It is striking that the one work on Caesar that appeared in England near the time of the writing of Shakespeare's play was the translation by 'I.B.B.' of that Italian book seeing Caesar as a dictator and tyrant. Printers – in this case 'A. Islip for John Jaggard' – are not fools: they want to be sure of a return on their

---

1   Bullough, 5.30–2; and see Boecker. There are striking verbal parallels.

investment, and this was a well-produced book for a general high-quality market. Jaggard must have known of London interest which produced knowledge of the Turin book and buyers for a translation so shortly after (and possibly encouraged by) Shakespeare's *Julius Caesar*, seen as revealing a tyrant. England had in the late 1590s a thriving Italian artistic and intellectual community. The most recent Italian opinions of Caesar as tyrant would certainly have reached London.

The very noun 'Caesar' had a rich sixteenth-century life, as referring to the temporal as opposed to the spiritual power, or to absolute monarchy: successive Bibles in English, from Tyndale first in 1526, had made proverbial the phrases in Matthew, 22, 'Give therefore to Caesar, that which is Caesar's: and give unto God, that which is God's.' The use of the form 'kaiser' for an all-conquering absolute monarch goes back to 1225.[1] The verb 'Caesarize', 'to play the Caesar', is recorded by *OED* from John Davies of Hereford, in his *Microcosmos* of 1603, in the line 'This pow'r . . . Caesarizeth o'er each appetite.' The further noun 'Caesarism', more closely meaning the principle of the semi-mythological colossus whose spirit walks abroad after his death – an immortality sought by him before his death – was not recorded by *OED* before its use, by the American Orestes O. Brownson in 1857, for monarchical absolutism. From that date the word had a vogue, particularly in the United States. It was picked up by John Dover Wilson in 1949 in his New Cambridge edition of *Julius Caesar*: he extended the primary meaning to cover the necessity of such absolutism in a city in danger of being almost ungovernable (Cam[1], xix–xxii). These are late applications of an idea which clearly had an older use.

In England almost thirty years before Shakespeare wrote *Julius Caesar*, the homily of 1570, *Against Disobedience and Wilful Rebellion*, had spoken in the strongest terms of rebellion as 'the whole puddle and sink of all sins against God and man', to gen-

---

1   See *OED* kaiser b; also *OED* Caesar 2b.

eral agreement. Yet in the closing years of Elizabeth's reign the question of the right of rebellion against a ruler was being taken so seriously that intellectual leaders in the land were not only discussing it under the cover of Roman history – they were about to move further towards open political and military rebellion led by one of their circle, the Earl of Essex.

Such deposition and tyrannicide were supported with claims of divine sanction. Among the moderate Protestants, by far the majority in the kingdom, those who proposed a system of presbyterian organization were said to question the Queen's authority: her 1593 Act Against Seditious Sectaries led to executions of Protestant martyrs. Some Puritans looked hopefully to Essex as leader. The Pope had excommunicated Queen Elizabeth not all that long before: there were Catholic malcontents who had wanted to assassinate her and replace her with Mary Queen of Scots (executed in 1587) or, now, Philip of Spain. The Jesuit Robert Parsons concluded in his *A Conference about the Next Succession to the Crown of England* in 1594 that Richard II had been justly deposed, and thus it would be just to remove Elizabeth. It is not clear when John Donne wrote his *Pseudomartyr*, published in 1610 but probably written a decade before, attacking those Jesuits who sought martyrdom through refusal to commit themselves to *not* murdering the monarch of England.

The plotted murder of Julius Caesar had divided the minds of men and women even before he died. This Shakespeare vividly demonstrates. The debate about such assassination has continued to this day, quite often taking its form from Shakespeare's play. The questions are: 'how to tell a tyrant from a just king: how to tell envious murderers from heroic republicans: how and when to justify assassination' (Miola, 'Tyrannicide', 273).

The tyrannicide debate

Set going by that death at the base of Pompey's statue in 44 BC, the literature arguing for and against Caesar or Brutus is massive

3 Near-contemporary bust of Julius Caesar, epoch of Augustus

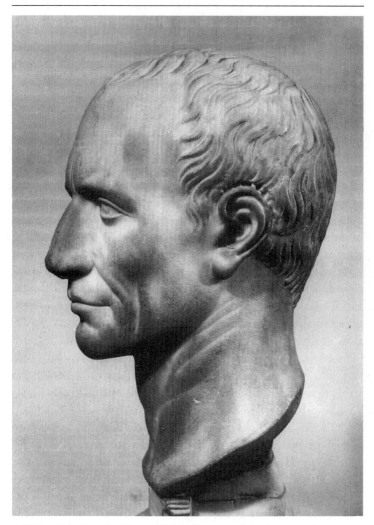

4 This strikingly-refined bust of Julius Caesar was long thought to be
contemporary and was widely reproduced in nineteenth- and twentieth-
century accounts of Caesar. It is now known to be one of many similar
'antiquities' manufactured in Rome in the eighteenth century for the
benefit of visitors

and complex. The intensely-felt legal and moral questions raised by the conspiracy and assassination are tied to the equally intense interest felt by historians and biographers in Caesar himself. 'The range of his activities, his far-flung conquests, his political achievements, the manner of his death and what came after it were so dramatic and well documented . . . [yet] his personality remained an enigma' (Bullough, 5.4).

In the fourteenth and fifteenth centuries, especially in Italy, but not only there, every generation produced its commentary on Caesar, as new political theory emerged, or the classical histories were studied afresh. New analyses of the significance of his death made pinnacles visible above the foothills of medieval absorption in the subject. The argument in Italy that we touched on above goes back through Petrarch's admiration in his biography of Caesar of 1473, widely read in its form as the work of 'Julius Celsus', to Dante, who approved Caesar as founder of Empire, and famously put Brutus and Cassius in the lowest circle of hell: they are the very last figures seen there, with Judas Iscariot. Behind Dante lie the thick forests of medieval Italian and Latin debate: Aquinas had in 1270 offered a Caesar as 'the virtuous, just, and merciful Emperor and as the tyrannical usurper who richly deserved his death' (Schanzer, *Problem*, 16). Those forests of debate became enchanted woods in the medieval European legends of Julius Caesar as the father of Oberon, king of the fairies, or son of the fairy Brunhild and grandson of Judas Maccabeus: Caesar was made a paladin like Hector or Aeneas or King Arthur, the founder of many cities, the builder of the Tower of London (see *R3* 3.1.68–77), the forefather of emperors and popes.

But Caesar was at the same time a tyrant, and hatred of his tyranny can be traced right back down the centuries to the young Lucan and his unfinished epic *Bellum civile* ('Pharsalia'), written not long after that decisive battle where Caesar defeated Pompey. His poem was influential, and shows hatred for tyranny in general and Caesar in particular as a destroyer of the republic.

5 Bust of Cicero, first century BC

Suetonius, like Plutarch, praised Caesar for admirable parts, but declared that his ambition had to be destroyed. Cicero, the commentator who, of course, knew Caesar, greatly admired him for his gifts and his achievements: but he greeted the assassination as a virtuous act, abhorring Caesar's political aims and methods. Cicero's own puzzled ambivalence set the tone for much that followed.

The personal, as opposed to political, fascination that Caesar attracted down all the ages was also usually ambivalent – he was obviously a very great man, with extraordinary abilities, and yet dangerous to friends as well as enemies, and to the state: generous, hospitable, loved and loving, he was arrogant, wilful and unscrupulous. Debate throughout Europe about what would now be called human rights was always at one with the interest in the enigma of his person. On the whole, sixteenth-century political theorists tended to settle for monarchy as the best form of government; but that did not prevent discussion of alternatives with some passion. The rediscovery of Plutarch, through reissues of his work in Latin, and Amyot's French translation (and then North in English), brought to the attention of the educated in Europe Plutarch's surprising sympathy for republican Rome. Mexia in Spain, Luther in Germany, Elyot in England and Erasmus all over northern Europe wrote about Caesar on one side or another, or both. In France, Montaigne admired the republican ideal: Robert Garnier's *Cornélie* of 1573/4, which expresses polarized opinion violently for or against Julius Caesar, was translated in England by Thomas Kyd in 1594, as we saw above, with a second edition in 1595: Caesar appears there as tyrant or as great ruler. The anonymous play *Caesar's Revenge*, probably written in 1595, gives at first a positive picture of Caesar; but he then becomes a tyrant deserving assassination by Brutus.

As the inheritor of over sixteen hundred years of ambiguity, Shakespeare makes the unrolling web of his drama more ambivalent still. He does not endorse anyone.[1] The heavy political negatives from those involved are clear to see. The tribunes fault Caesar for making a triumph when he has defeated not barbarians, but fellow-Romans. The early references to Junius Brutus' revolt against the tyrannical Tarquin (1.2.158–60, 2.1.53–4) are meant to suggest that Julius Caesar came to power unconstitutionally. Cassius declares to Brutus that Rome has degenerated under a ruler who violated the constitution (1.2.150–2, 1.3.108–11). Brutus understands the ancient wisdom of dealing

---

1 Critics have been until recently anxious to have Shakespeare in one camp or another, as if his indeterminacy were too uncomfortable to bear. There is an interesting modern parallel. John Arden's play *Sergeant Musgrave's Dance* has baffled critics and audiences alike as to what it is 'about', yet it was the single most-performed play in England in the 1960s and 1970s, and is still much produced.

with incipient tyrants by killing the serpent's egg in the shell (2.1.32–4). Soon after the assassination, just before Antony speaks to them, the Plebeians agree that 'This Caesar was a tyrant' (3.2.70): by that they mean that he usurped power to himself, and governed viciously.

Yet before long, these same Plebeians are mourning him and seeking vengeance. On the other political side, Shakespeare alters Plutarch to make us suspect Cassius: in his soliloquy about his attempt to win Brutus (1.2.307–21), he speaks as a villain, rejoicing in his own deviousness; he will forge the letters to be thrown in Brutus' way. Shakespeare makes Caska so subjective in his account of Antony's public offering of the crown to Caesar (1.2.234–86) that our judgement is almost completely controlled; all we have of our own is the feeling that it was probably not a trick: Shakespeare significantly makes it happen off stage, denying us a view of it, though it is theatrical in Plutarch. Even Brutus has to 'fashion' justifications, mentioning a record of offences (3.2.37–40) that we never see. Shakespeare ignores incriminating material in Plutarch (Bullough, 5.31, 35ff., 38, 50–1, 57, 60). Again, Shakespeare removes entirely from the sources the long-running antagonism between Caesar and the Senate, which would mark him as a self-willed tyrant, instead making the Senate ready to offer him the crown (1.3.85–8, 2.2.93–4).

Shakespeare was not alone in finding, in the enigma he offered, development within Julius Caesar himself. Political writers in the second half of the sixteenth century from both sides of the religious conflict 'cite Caesar as an example of a tyrant in entrance who eventually became a good and lawful ruler' (Miola, 'Tyrannicide', 279). At first, Shakespeare seems to go out of his way to show Caesar himself as arbitrary, unstable, afraid of plots and conspiracies, a man of arrogant pride whose own will overrides just cause and law, all these being the recognizable marks of a tyrant. His disregard for the processes of 'his' Senate is the opposite of the investigative clemency expected of a good ruler. Shakespeare changes Caesar's dismissal of the tribunes as it is in

Plutarch, for removing diadems from his images, to their punishment for the more trivial 'pulling scarves off' (1.2.284); Caesar putting them 'to silence' (285) has sinister suggestion, an effect which suggests a ruthless and capricious severity. These are the traits called by Brutus 'high-sighted tyranny' (2.1.117) in an image from falconry, related to the stock animal metaphors associated with tyranny.

> For such a ruler, classical, medieval, and Renaissance authorities insisted, there could be only one end: a sudden and violent death. The assassination of Caesar in Act III, then, testifies strongly, if circumstantially, to his tyrannical character.
>
> (Miola, 'Tyrannicide', 282)

And yet, and yet. In Shakespeare's play we also see a Caesar who loves and trusts his fellow-Romans, warmly inviting Brutus and the other conspirators to share wine (2.2.126–7): 'how unlike the typical tyrant who lives sequestered from his people, surrounded by a guard of foreign mercenaries' (Miola, 'Tyrannicide', 282). Wholly unlike a tyrant, Caesar bequeaths to his people on his death his personal possessions (3.2.235–45); and on one crucial occasion, in refusing to read Artemidorus' letter (3.1.8), he puts himself last, where Plutarch has him unable to read it for the pressing crowd. Far from sucking the blood of his people, as a typical tyrant did, and as Shakespeare's Richard III and Macbeth do, Caesar wants 'great Rome' to suck his 'Reviving blood' (2.2.87–8), marking him as a good – indeed, in this imagery, even a Christian – ruler.

Most strikingly, Shakespeare gives Caesar lines that are at the same time soaring images of himself as a great figure in imperial Roman history – 'for always I am Caesar' (1.2.211) – and an ultimate statement of hubristic arrogance. His magnificent lines concluded only moments before his death, beginning, 'But I am constant as the northern star' (3.1.60), are also appalling. Even so,

against that poetic richness the cries of the republican conspirators seem thin, even those immediately on Caesar's death,
'Liberty! Freedom! Tyranny is dead!' (3.1.78). This frighteningly
imperious Caesar in his death caused an Empire stable enough,
under his successor, for what Christians knew as the greatest
moment in cosmic history, when God the Father looked down, as
it were, and said 'Now!', and sent his humble Son, a moment tied
to Roman history as early as the New Testament itself. Luke's
Gospel fixes the Christmas story: 'And it came to pass in those
days that there went out a decree from Caesar Augustus, that all
the world should be taxed ...' (Luke, 2.1., in Geneva 1560).
Christian historians are grateful for Julius Caesar's legacy.

Tyrannicides justify their action by declaring it is the will of
the gods, as well as, or alternative to, the will of the people. Yet
though *Julius Caesar* is full of reference to religious ceremony, it
is just such authority that is missing in the play – and not only
missing.

> The play simply does not support the conspirators'
> assumption of divine approval for the assassination.
> Instead it plunges the viewer into a strange, unfath-
> omable universe, wherein the gods are capricious and
> inscrutable, wherein characters continually misconstrue
> and misunderstand their wishes. ... The sacrifice of
> Caesar itself, the repeated stabbings in the Capitol and
> the gory blood smearing, look more like foul treason than
> divine sacrifice.
>
> (Miola, 'Tyrannicide', 285–6)

Evocation of the will of the people, 'Rome' and 'Romans', so frequent by the conspirators, is equally suspect. Too often, the lofty
claims turn out to be either manipulations for 'the common eyes'
(2.1.178); or performances as 'Roman actors' (2.1.225); or supposedly generous actions like sparing Antony and letting him
speak, which 'shall advantage more than do us wrong' (3.1.242).

After the assassination, the quick slide of the patricians into murder and civil war fulfils Antony's horrific catalogue ending with 'carrion men, groaning for burial' (3.1.262–75). Above all, the volatile citizens of Rome, for whom everything is done, are dangerously unstable, changing their colour and their actions in every scene they have. Their swirling, shifting presence completes a picture showing 'the feckless Senate, the conspiring patricians, and, most important, the ambitious Caesar' (Miola, 'Tyrannicide', 288). In *Julius Caesar*, after all the clear balancing of this against that, and for all the power of the figures on stage to move us, there comes into view no alternative basis of authority at all, either divine or popular. There is only possession of power, the politics of the school playground. While that power was in Caesar himself, his authority and popularity held Rome together: with Caesar gone, there is no larger charter.

THE LANGUAGE OF *JULIUS CAESAR*

The older response to the language of this play was well expressed by E.K. Chambers in 1930: he remarked that:

> Shakespeare is deliberately experimenting in a classical manner, with an extreme simplicity both of vocabulary and phrasing . . . a stiffness, perhaps even a baldness, of diction . . . The element of simple dignity in the style of *Julius Caesar* . . . seems to have made a special appeal to him.
>
> (*Shakespeare*, 1.399)

Bradley in 1904 had found 'a limited perfection . . . We receive an impression of easy mastery and complete harmony, but not so strong an impression of inner power bursting into outer life.' To this he added a note: 'That play is distinguished, I think, by a deliberate endeavour after a dignified and unadorned simplicity, – a Roman simplicity perhaps' (Bradley, 85). Such comments became standard. A.R. Humphreys wrote in 1984: '*Julius Caesar* stands out among Shakespeare's plays as unelaborated in style, and this presumably suggests a "Roman" air' (Oxf[1], 46).

It is surely right to note a certain spareness: even the lively prose of Caska does not come near what Shakespeare was creating only the year before for those three magical speakers of a new prose, Falstaff, Benedick and Rosalind: a prose both controlled and exuberant, both decorous and overflowing with delight in what words can do with feelings. Commentators since Chambers have developed their impression of Roman economy. *Hamlet*, probably being worked on while *Julius Caesar* was being finished, has 4,042 lines (Spevack): *Julius Caesar* has 2,591 lines. For such action, spareness indeed.

Shakespeare's technique is partly one of limitation of vocabulary and phrasing. One never has a sense that a speech in this play is going suddenly to take off into the totally unexpected, like a soliloquy by Macbeth, for example. Both Falstaff and Hamlet can astonish with what they are saying, though Prince Hamlet is in a unique position, released by his 'madness'. The rhetorical figure of hendiadys makes a useful illustration. Hendiadys is the coupling with 'and' of two words related but in some respect not parallel, like Ophelia's 'The expectancy and rose of the fair state' (*Ham* 3.1.152). Shakespeare used it sparingly until *Henry V*: after that it appears richly, sixty-six times in *Hamlet* alone. In *Julius Caesar* it appears eight times. The difference is instructive. A form which Shakespeare used for exploring problematic depths of thought and feeling is far more decorous to Prince Hamlet than to Marcus Brutus. Hendiadys is characterized 'by a kind of syntactical complexity that seems fathomable only by intuitional understanding of the way the words interweave their message, rather than by painstaking lexical analysis' (Wright, *Hendiadys*, 172).

Brutus shows a mind classically restrained. The containment in his phrasing assures us that he is not surrendering to imagination and the sudden, unknown regions of the mind – or, at least, not there. The phrasing, we may put it, is not only decorous to the occasion – it is political: words from a Roman patrician are not going to get completely out of hand. In a tragedy written soon after *Julius Caesar*, passion so drives words that they fail completely:

> It is not words that shakes me thus – pish! – noses, ears, and lips. Is't possible? Confess! Handkerchief! O devil!   [*Falls in a trance.*
>   (*Oth* 4.1.41–3)

They get out of hand, too, with Prince Hamlet when passion and imagination drive them:

> For who that's but a queen, fair, sober, wise,
> Would from a paddock, from a bat, a gib,
> Such dear concernings hide? Who would do so?
> No, in despite of sense and secrecy,
> Unpeg the basket on the house's top,
> Let the birds fly, and, like the famous ape,
> To try conclusions, in the basket creep,
> And break your own neck down.
>   (*Ham* 3.4.189–96)

One has no idea there, from word to word, what is coming next. By contrast, here is Brutus in some state of high feeling:

>   O conspiracy,
> Sham'st thou to show thy dangerous brow by night,
> When evils are most free? O then by day
> Where wilt thou find a cavern dark enough
> To mask thy monstrous visage? Seek none, conspiracy:
> Hide it in smiles and affability . . .
>   (2.1.77–82)

Though Brutus' feelings are powerful, here is intelligence, order and clarity. The cavern and the monstrous visage, though metaphorical, are precisely rational. These qualities create a decorum of phrasing. When logic controls the three elements of vocabulary, word-order and sentence-length, phrasing is going to be neat and orderly, like a civic building where stone and marble stand finished and in place. To compare as phrases 'Unpeg the basket on the house's top' and 'Where wilt thou find a cavern dark enough . . . ?' is to note a similar mixture of five monosyllables and two disyllables, with a pause at the end, and similar everyday vocabulary: Hamlet's is more domestic, and Brutus' 'cavern' is common enough. But Brutus' question is a rational one. Hamlet's imperative is wild: why on earth is he telling his mother the queen, in any case, never mind at this extraordinary moment, to go up on to the palace roof with a basket of birds and an ape?

The first two acts of the play, up to the departure of Caesar for the Senate, have as their core of construction long-paced dialogues. All these Romans have a good deal to say to each other. What they say is – even including Caska's flippancies – weighty matter. Their form of address is thoughtful, measured, directed. They are seeking to persuade. Rome is 'a society of skilled speakers whose rhetorical expertise masks moral and political truth' (Greene, 69). In the third act, this need to persuade is lifted to a high theatricality, but the theatrical is not absent earlier. As in *Troilus and Cressida*, these characters have from the beginning an air of knowing themselves to be important figures on stage, from classical, and remote, history. Unlike those in *TC*, they have no difficulty in recognizing who they are supposed to be – even in the dark, as at 1.3.41 (and as in the opening lines of *Hamlet*). This presented assurance goes with using their own names in the third person. Caesar with nineteen uses of his own name is not alone in his use of this device (see 1.2.17n.) with an added seventy-one pronouns of self. Cassius calls himself 'Cassius' fourteen times (and says 'he' of himself thirty times, out of a total of 201 pronouns referring to himself). Brutus calls himself 'Brutus' thirteen times (with 296 self-referring pronouns). Caska calls himself 'Caska' once (and has forty-six pronouns of self). All the characters use each other's names a great deal: for example, Cassius says 'Brutus' forty-two times (though Caesar says 'Brutus' only four times). 'Caesar' is spoken by all characters more than any other name.

The language throughout the play brings Rome and Roman people to life. Shakespeare had before, from time to time, caught the qualities of contemporary London. In the *Henry IV* plays, he makes England as well as London to be felt under the feet. He seemed not to be interested, as Jonson and Middleton were, in city comedies in the fashion of the time, with their London commercial and sexual intrigue. His only city comedy is set, hardly vibrantly, in Windsor. The action of *Titus Andronicus* happened partly in Rome, but the city in that play acted as a backdrop to dynastic calamity. *Julius Caesar*, in its first three acts, is Shakespeare's first city play. From the first two words, 'Hence! home . . .', to when the action moves out into the field, from 4.2, Rome and its city life is present so strongly that even a reader can feel the marble pavements, hear the bustle of people in the streets, stand by a pillar to watch a procession. Dryden in 1684 first noticed this in Shakespeare, with his 'you more than see it, you feel it too' (Dryden, 415). Much of the immediacy of Rome comes from stage action, without sound. In a street, plebeians in a bunch encounter tribunes and are rebuked; they slink away: that would do on a silent screen. Men meet for a serious talk, pull in a third man as he passes. Two men in turn address a volatile crowd. The shifting visual scenes are urban and vivid. Put in a sound-track, and there are flourishes and music and excited shouts and commanding voices beginning orations – and the sound of two men riding 'like madmen through the gates of Rome' (3.2.259).

A great deal of the painting of Rome is done by small phrases about things not on stage, like 'shop', 'windows', 'chimney-tops'; 'a common slave – you know him well by sight'; and even the surly lion against the Capitol: such an odd sight, in such a recognizable spot. He is like the daytime owl hooting and shrieking upon the market-place. What people are told to do reinforces Rome as a known place: 'run to your houses', 'run to the Senate

House', 'run to the Capitol', 'run hence, proclaim, cry it about the streets'. People, or bits of them, suddenly seen – Cassius standing, thin and unsmiling: 'the angry spot . . . on Caesar's brow', 'Calphurnia's cheek is pale'; people together – 'the rabblement . . . threw up their sweaty nightcaps', 'three or four wenches where I stood' and so on. These examples could be multiplied. Unlike Jonson's careful (usually effective) detail, they have the feel of naturalness, though undoubtedly they are the result of art. (The naturalness fooled the Augustan critics: Dryden in the Prologue to his version of *Julius Caesar* in 1672 has a puzzled Shakespeare looking at what he had written with 'Artless beauty' and wondering 'how the Devil it was such wit' (Ure, *JC*, 28).)

In a patrician's mouth in Rome, words know their place. Patricians speak as Stoics, with 'an attitude of patient endurance, absence of passion, indifference to externals' (Miles, 12). The speakers themselves seem deaf to their own subjective distortions in the use of words. Cicero himself, no less, the authority on Stoic decorum, thought to be the father of the art of classical rhetoric, has to come on stage to warn that 'men may construe things after their fashion / Clean from the purpose of the things themselves' (1.3.34–5). He then exits immediately, having thrown his bomb. Just as characters confidently 'construe' phenomena in opposite directions (like Calphurnia's dream of Caesar's statue spouting blood, 2.2.75–90), so patricians believe, it seems, that words do not get out of hand.

What does obviously get out of hand in Rome is the mob. From the very first lines, the plebeians refuse to play the correct word-game. Flavius and Murellus become unexpectedly inflamed by what seems to be a bit of mild cheeking from a cobbler. But that man makes words jump about and escape logic. He is suggestive with his puns. The proper Roman order of things, like not treating any old day as a holiday, being in the right place ('in thy shop'), or, if on the streets, carrying official identification ('the sign / Of . . . profession'), slips quite away. The tribunes are agitated because agreed meaning is being undermined. It is absolutely not Roman to watch a triumph over Pompey's sons. The mob, of course, gets wholly out of hand in Act 3. They run wild, set fire to Rome and tear a poet to pieces in the street. It is as if the extreme constraints of patrician speech produce extreme licence.

Apart from Antony, a special case in the use of words in Rome, and underneath all the admirable moderation of patrician address, logic and intelligence, there is something kept out of the neat phrasing – violence. Cassius has malice, Brutus sorrow, a few others a grievance. There is in the language of the patricians no towering passion at all. Intelligently and logically, Caesar is stabbed to death. This is what was meant above by saying that the phrasing is political. Prince Hamlet, infinitely rich in unfettered words and phrases, for nearly five acts cannot act to kill Claudius, one to one. Less than half-way through *Julius Caesar*, seven great men of Rome, moderate of word and phrase, coolly and intellectually convinced of their rightness, act together to stab Caesar bloodily to death.

Early studies of imagery in Shakespeare usually expressed puzzlement that there was so little in *Julius Caesar*, if they noticed the play at all. G. Wilson Knight in 1931, however, observed that 'The imagery of idea, simile, description, and incident presents a complex pattern of interthreading, dividing, and blending colours'; he suggested that this play was 'ablaze with a vitality not found in previous plays' (Knight, 33). His sensitive comments, though searching – on blood and fire in particular – are often more enthusiastic for a unique high enamelling than the play may be thought to justify, but his understanding of 'interthreading' is valuable, and should help to keep us away from imagery as purely linguistic. R.A. Foakes in 1954 showed how, for example, 'the various themes are all used to suggest a full circle of events' (Foakes, 'Approach', 260) as superstitions and omens (and their defiance), dreams and darkness, blood and sickness, help to make 'the birth and completion of the rebellion'

(263) the structural principle of the play. Rebellion, he writes, works in the very heart of the language of the play, as emphasis on the efficacy of names, especially in relation to ideals, contrasts always with action, which always destroys. Maurice Charney in 1961 located the chief image themes as 'the storm and its portents, blood and fire', all with 'two opposed meanings, depending on one's point of view' (Charney, 42). The storm and its portents indicate the evil of Caesar's tyranny in the body politic of Rome, or the conspiracy to kill him: blood and fire are purging or civil strife. Further, everything interlocks: 'to Calphurnia the storm and its portents point to the murder of Caesar . . . the same storm in which Caska and Cassius have actually plotted his death' (Charney, 46).

Such studies usually focus on what are felt to be the central linguistic images, rich with immediacy, of blood and fire. We may note that blood is hardly at all lineage and nobility, as it is so much in *Richard II*, for example. It is the body-fluid, something that nourishes Romans, is demanded, is spilled on stage, is bathed in. Fire is vast heavenly disturbance, and light as well: the lack of it marks Brutus' disturbance (2.1.7–8: on the relation of the four central characters to the four humours, cf. McAlindon, *Tragic*, 79). The newness of *Julius Caesar* lies partly in the way that what had been purely verbal images in earlier plays now work, often unobserved, in the very struts and spars of the structure.

Language and character

Julius Caesar Julius Caesar had been a soldier only since his thirty-eighth year. In 44 BC he was 55 years old and in failing health, and had been angered by Marcus Brutus marrying Porcia, daughter of Cato (recently praised by Cicero as a republican ideal), the widow of his great enemy Bibulus. Known for his arrogance, Caesar was 'seeking that short and unambiguous title' of king: his gold statue had been crowned with the traditional symbol of monarchy, a white fillet, which two tribunes had ordered to be torn down and thrown away (Bradford, 205–10).

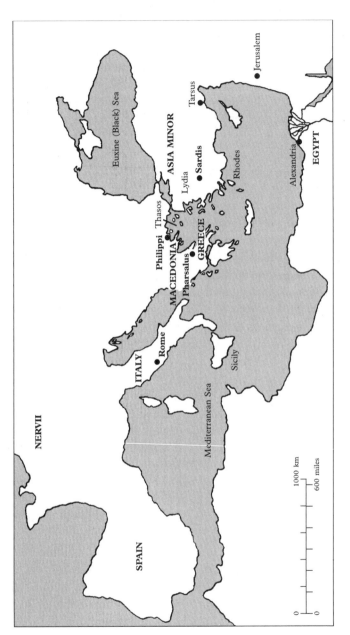

6 The world of *Julius Caesar*. The Parthian empire (see 5.3 37) was about six hundred miles to the east of the area shown here

In a seminal article, T.J.B. Spencer made the general point that sixteenth-century Englishmen saw Rome as imperial, through Suetonius – 'it was the busts of the Twelve Caesars that decorated almost every palace in Europe'. To substitute the Plutarchan, and mostly republican, vision of Rome 'required a considerable intellectual feat' (Spencer, 31).

> The part played by Shakespeare himself in creating our notions of the ancient Romans should not be forgotten . . . we are all in the power of Shakespeare's imagination, a power which has been exercised for several generations and from which it is scarcely possible to extricate ourselves.
>
> (Spencer, 37)

Caesar was freshly interpreted by Shakespeare (Rees, 'Caesar'). 'The most common fault attributed to the Roman leader in the Elizabethan period was pride' (Barroll, 340). In *The Mirror for Magistrates*, Caesar's whole 'pretence' was 'glorye vayne . . . Without remorce of many thousands slain' (Bullough, 5.173). He is a braggart in *Caesar's Revenge*, and his 'strut' was much noticed. 'At all times it is, as it should be, Caesar's play', wrote J.C. Trewin in the *Birmingham Post* (4 May 1972) about Trevor Nunn's 1972 production; he saw a Caesar 'made of coagulated iron filings': Michael Billington in *The Guardian* (13 May 1972) noted his 'testy Fascist omnipotence'. But in Shakespeare's play, even his dismissal of his antagonists just before his killing, 'Hence! Wilt thou lift up Olympus?' (3.1.74), has an elevation as well as arrogance. Shakespeare needed a defining language for this living and vulnerable man.

Within the 130 lines he speaks, Julius Caesar's presence and speech-forms, with the restraints of the patrician decorum we observed, are instantly identifiable and, possibly even when he is talking to his wife, invariably elevated, a tone used by John Gielgud in the National Theatre production in 1977. In a play given almost wholly to oratory and persuasion, the titular hero does not persuade. He is curtly imperious: 'Set him before me. Let me see his face'; 'He is a dreamer. Let us leave him. Pass'; '. . . for always I am Caesar'. He is sharply observant and can sound amused: 'Would he were fatter!' He speaks in lofty aphorisms: 'Cowards die many times before their deaths; / The valiant never taste of death but once.' Before he leaves for the Senate another new register is briefly heard, as he greets each of the conspirators:

> Good friends, go in, and taste some wine with me,
> And we, like friends, will straightway go together.

Rhetorically, Shakespeare's Caesar is right and wrong: the line that Ben Jonson mocked, almost certainly removed from the printed play (see pp. 136–7 below), caught him precisely. Shakespeare's Caesar has been called 'enigmatic and unrevealing' (Schanzer, *Problem*, 32) and 'a public man caught up in posturing and posing . . . [which] confuses our judgement of the assassination and the assassins' (Greene, 70; cf. Pelling). His usual high resonance can go over into bombast, as at 2.2.44–8: 'Danger knows full well / That Caesar is more dangerous than he . . .'. Caesar's will, Caesar says, is immovable: that is, unlike the plebeians, he will not change his mind, is unmoved by emotion, and cannot be shaken by external pressures (see Miles, 129–30). This 'constant' Caesar is wholly Shakespeare's own: but Shakespeare does not let his 'constancy' survive his wife's pleading – nor Decius' counter-plea.

Poetically, his 'northern star' speech (3.1.58–73) reads like Virgil in English. This is a higher verbal authority than has been heard anywhere in the play. It would be recognized by Elizabethans as royal in its imagery of 'constancy', 'firmament', 'fire', 'one in all', and 'one . . . Unshaked of motion'. To the Globe audience, the vocabulary of that speech alone makes the conspirators regicides.

Brutus Brutus' language has a signature, we might say, that fits the body-patterns we are told about. He is surprised to be given a mirror to look in – metaphorical, of course, but bringing with it a certain posture. Later he is troubled that he cannot read the night sky. Later still, he has not slept, but he is determined to 'look fresh and merrily' (2.1.223).

In the second scene of the play, Cassius, beginning his corruption of Brutus' mind, wishes 'That you might see your shadow' (1.2.58). Brutus' knowledge of himself is challenged. He had up to that moment properly assumed that his inner world was private, 'Conceptions only proper to myself' (41). Cassius now begins to give Brutus a new view of himself which will soon be dangerously political: he will have to make a violent challenge to all structures of rule in the person of Caesar. The word 'shadow' here means reflection, by a subsidiary and not infrequent use (see 1.2.58n.). Cassius is not telling Brutus, using 'shadow' in the more regular sense, to project his inner self-esteem out to the public world, where other, powerful, people would be in his shade: he is creating for Brutus a new inner world altogether, in which he will be actively looked at by 'many of the best respect in Rome' (59). Cassius is image-building. When Brutus has met his replacement 'shadow' as Cassius means it, the visitation will destroy him. This new 'shadow' calls on him to kill Caesar, before which action 'all the interim is / Like a phantasma or a hideous dream' (2.1.64–5). Shakespeare's development of this a little later in *Othello* is obvious, as Othello, abused by Iago, knows himself bound to kill his new young wife. It is also clearly at the root of *Hamlet*, where the Prince's own 'hideous dream' comes from the command to kill Claudius: it chimes with Hamlet's own disturbance. The Ghost intrudes into Hamlet a reflection or 'shadow' of himself as the one person able to put right what is wrong in Denmark. The tragedy that follows from Hamlet taking on this new 'shadow' of himself brings about the fall of a royal house.

7 E.L. Davenport as Brutus, Jarrett-Palmer Company, New York, 1875

Shakespeare had always been interested in a clash between inner world and public statecraft. In his first history plays, this was not always too subtle: King Henry VI, sitting aside from the Battle of Towton and letting his wife get on with it, wishes he were a shepherd not a king (*3H6* 2.5). As the histories were written, Shakespeare's interest became more complex, as kings and statesmen in the *Henry IV* plays and *Henry V* demonstrate, though in those plays there is not much revelation of tragic inner conflict. *Julius Caesar* and *Hamlet* show a striking development. In both plays the state is destroyed, not by rebellious challenge arising from a rival blood-line, though there are factions, but from the interior dilemma of the tragic hero. And in these plays that conflict is now profound – indeed, in *Hamlet*, almost fathomless. In *Julius Caesar*, Brutus' inner life is in conflict with itself, as he fights the 'shadow' presented by Cassius.

Though this was indeed new in *Julius Caesar* (and in that way there had been nothing like it on the English stage before), *Richard II* foreshadowed some of it. The climax of the King's deposition in Westminster Hall is Richard breaking the mirror (see Pye, 82–105), and then seizing on the word 'shadow':

> *Bol.*   The shadow of your sorrow hath destroy'd
> The shadow of your face.
> *Rich.*   Say that again.
> The shadow of my sorrow?
>
> (*R2* 4.1.292–4)

Bolingbroke, not given to metaphysics, means simply that the darkness of grieving has made Richard do something compulsively (smash the glass) that now prevents him seeing his reflection at all. But Richard, very much given to metaphysics, seizes on the word. In Cassius' sense, he suddenly understands the projection of his inner world – and, unlike Brutus, suddenly rejects it. What in Brutus was the supposed reflection of his inner self, which Cassius was imposing on him, is in Richard the opposite, the true reflection of his inner self for the first time. Richard's moment of recognition of the 'shadow', precisely as a monarch is deposed, helps us to see clearly, in Brutus, its opposite, the imposition of that inner conflict with, for the first time, truly tragic force. It will depose not just a monarch, but a republican nation. Brutus the Stoic increasingly fails to hold back a breakdown.[1] His earlier individual speech-signature had matched a physical shape – careful, politely attentive, limited. From Act 2, he begins to lose such poise.

It is possible that the vocabulary of alchemy points to a subversive movement in Brutus. The large literature of sixteenth-century alchemy can make a swamp that it is hard to get out of clothed and in one's right mind, and commentary must be cautious. But Cassius in his first soliloquy, on the exit of Brutus, introduces a distorting alchemical metaphor:

> Well, Brutus, thou art noble: yet I see
> Thy honourable mettle may be wrought
> From that it is disposed.
>
> (1.2.307–9)

'Noble' and 'honourable' metals, like gold or silver, cannot properly be 'wrought' (transmuted) into baser substance. 'From that it is disposed' suggests both the natural state of the metal, and the human temperament. The idea is sinister, that Brutus might be so, and improperly, changed. Cassius continues with the idea that Brutus should keep his natural chemical state of mind – 'it is meet / That noble minds keep ever with their likes': in other words, Cassius wants him base but still noble, a confused impossibility.

---

1 Plutarch in *Brutus* says categorically on the first page that Brutus was a Platonist, and thus by implication not a Stoic. There has been much discussion. An illuminating exploration of how Shakespeare draws on Stoic tradition for Brutus is in Miles, 125–7. That there was confusion about Brutus even in his lifetime is interestingly conveyed by Cicero in a letter from Rome shortly after the assassination in 44 BC. He reports 'that Caesar used to say [about Brutus] "It's a great question *what* he wants; but whatever he wants, he wants it with a will"' (Cicero, 197).

Caska, next, at 1.3.157–60, agrees with Cassius to bring in Brutus immediately, saying:

> O he sits high in all the people's hearts:
> And that which would appear offence in us
> His countenance, like richest alchemy,
> Will change to virtue and to worthiness.

There 'virtue', as well as in its modern sense, is (*OED sb.* 9) the great value produced by that alchemy. It seems that Cassius' suggestion of alchemy works, because Brutus himself begins to use alchemical vocabulary, with the underlying idea of transforming Rome into gold by the chemical effect of killing the overreaching Caesar. It is possible that there are alchemical references in Brutus' terrible comment on his own state of mind in 2.1:

> The genius and the mortal instruments
> Are then in council, and the state of man,
> Like to a little kingdom, suffers then
> The nature of an insurrection.
>   (2.1.66–9)

Certainly 'genius' in the seventeenth century survived with an astrological sense (*OED* 1d) for the combination of sidereal influences represented in a person's horoscope. Charles Nicholl's *The Chemical Theatre* (1980) reminded us of the power of alchemy in the thoughts and creations of the last years of the sixteenth century and the first of the seventeenth, to say nothing of Jonson's timely play in 1610. Tentatively one could argue that Brutus' long passionate speech against taking oaths to kill Caesar, 2.1.113–39, ends in its last nine lines with alchemical reference, in 'stain', 'even' (that is, just, level), 'virtue', 'insuppressive mettle', 'spirits', 'performance', 'drop', 'bastardy' and 'particle'. Brutus wants not oaths, but the highest Roman qualities, to act together to make new gold. The fantastic chemistry claimed for Brutus' power and then taken over by him makes him less a moral exemplum, and more distressing – and interesting.

At 2.1.161–82, in the speech containing 'Let's be sacrificers but not butchers, Caius', Brutus thinks he is talking about some activity that can be given nobility, like hunting a deer. His words, however, give way to specific violence. He is trying to claim the high moral ground: he reveals himself to be seriously disturbed in his inner world – as was memorably expressed in the third part of his soliloquy opening this scene:

> Between the acting of a dreadful thing
> And the first motion, all the interim is
> Like a phantasma or a hideous dream . . .
>
> (2.1.63–5)

'Our course will seem too bloody' (that is, if they kill Antony too); and the near-homophone 'cause' expresses the larger ideal. The death is to be clean, a purifying stabbing. His lofty aim is lowered by the technical images of the work of an ordinary high-street butcher – 'cut the head off', 'hack the limbs', 'limb', 'blood', 'dismember', 'must bleed', 'hew him as a carcass', 'hearts', 'eyes', 'arm', 'head'. Whatever Brutus *thinks* he is saying, warning against, when it comes to it, being a town slaughterer, he now reveals his wish. Plutarch's descriptions of the murder of Caesar include a brutality in which Brutus gave Caesar 'one wound about his privities' (see Appendix, p. 329). What Chambers described as the 'element of simple dignity', and Bradley 'unadorned simplicity', will not do.

Brutus is trying to pretend that the Caesar, or 'Caesarism', they are killing is only a spirit and therefore will shed no blood. The idea of sacrifice is extended, so that killing Caesar is dressed up as something strategic ('boldly') and then culinary ('carve'), as at a superior junket ('a dish fit for the gods'). To express the latter elevation, he would need the vocabulary not of the butcher's shop but of the aristocratic hunt – the Scottish word 'gralloch' makes a modern example. Plutarch notes that Caesar 'was hacked and mangled among them, as a wilde beaste taken of hunters' (see Appendix, p. 329). Brutus, not wanting to 'hew'

Caesar 'as a carcass fit for hounds', sets off with a high hunting image, for 'course' means also a hunt (*OED sb.* 7), surviving in 'hare-coursing'; the noun can include the beast hunted. Further, and confusingly, six lines into the speech he says 'We all stand up against the spirit of Caesar', and *OED* (stand *v.*) defines 'stand up' as 'to make a stand against' (definition 103n.), citing this line as first use. But definition 103h gives 'stand up' of a hunted animal, meaning hold out or endure, though first recorded only in 1656. Advising not to kill Antony, whom at this point Brutus despises for 'sports . . . wildness and much company' (2.1.188), Brutus is trying for superior 'sport', and failing.

Brutus is afraid of feeling. His funeral oration, 3.2.12–47, though interrupted at its climax by the unwelcome and distracting arrival of Antony with Caesar's body, is so coldly effective that at the end the confused people want him to have either a statue or a triumph or be crowned Caesar – disturbing echoes of the people's reaction to Caesar at 1.2.222, 229–30, 243–4, 270–2. Logical, balanced, heavily patterned, economical to a fault, coolly self-justifying in 'as he was ambitious, I slew him', in its self-consciousness of gesture, the oration matches the individuality, the physical shape, of Brutus. The triple 'If any, speak, for him have I offended', and 'I pause for a reply', are guaranteed to produce an automatic 'None'. This is the technical art of oration, and Brutus is an intelligent master of it. 'There is tears, for his love; joy, for his fortune; honour, for his valour; and death, for his ambition.' The intense patterning swallows the personal feeling. The speech is in prose, the natural medium of oratory. Brian Vickers noted 'the remarkable rhetorical symmetry in which all the figures aiding clarity and balance (*isocolon, parison, anaphora, epistrophe* . . .) are used over and over again, harnessed to an argument of some simplicity and even speciousness . . . Caesar had to be killed because *otherwise* he would have become a tyrant and the Romans would have lived in slavery (a spurious *enthymeme* . . .)'. This logical flimsiness is matched by the 'ice-cold clarity . . . the totally emotionless attitude . . . terms as if of comparable emotional strength: "tears, joy, honour, death" ' (Vickers, 240–5). Our sense is of a prepared speech detached from both the moment of delivery and the effect on the audience. Brutus is revealed as efficient in word-patterns and indifferent to feeling. His reliance on tight logic frustrates by not leaving room for explanation of the events.[1] In private, Brutus has equal difficulty releasing his feelings to his wife. The brevity and formality of his only warm words to Portia –

> You are my true and honourable wife,
> As dear to me as are the ruddy drops
> That visit my sad heart.
>
> (2.1.287–9)

and

> O ye gods,
> Render me worthy of this noble wife!
> (2.1.301–2)

– speak of a man whose mind is elsewhere. After the last remark, though moved, he sends her from the room; the knock on the door ensures that the momentum of the conspiracy takes over. The seriousness of the interior split is confirmed by his sensitivity to supposed attack, shown by his being at his best only with those who are no threat: Lucius, and his 'poor remains of friends' (5.5.1). His wife, though so symbiotically sensitive herself to her husband's self-wounding 'sick offence' within his mind (2.1.267) that she gives herself a wound, becomes in her challenge someone who has to be driven away (2.1.303), and then left behind grieving (4.3.150).

The Quarrel scene, 4.3, changes our responses to Brutus and Cassius. They show some human warmth, and Cassius has more stature. Here is Brutus in anger; but we must note the intellectual control, and the contrast with Hamlet, or Othello:

---

1 A full account of the rhetorical devices in Brutus' oration, including word-by-word commentary and comprehensive schematic analysis, may be found in Fuzier, 26–32, 59–61.

All this? Ay, more: fret till your proud heart break.
Go show your slaves how choleric you are,
And make your bondmen tremble. Must I budge?
Must I observe you? Must I stand and crouch
Under your testy humour? By the gods,
You shall digest the venom of your spleen
Though it do split you; for, from this day forth,
I'll use you for my mirth, yea for my laughter,
When you are waspish.

(4.3.42–50)

Faced with the anger of Henry V, Hamlet, Othello, Macbeth, King Lear, Cleopatra, Timon or Coriolanus, one wants to run away and hide. At that speech of Brutus, one thinks: 'Goodness, how rude!' – though his earlier 'Away, slight man!' (37) is splendid. It is said that his lament over the dead Cassius is movingly modulated. So it may be, but it is very short. Half of it consists in saying that he cannot stop now:

The last of all the Romans, fare thee well:
It is impossible that ever Rome
Should breed thy fellow. Friends, I owe more tears
To this dead man than you shall see me pay.
I shall find time, Cassius: I shall find time.

(5.3.98–104)

Shakespeare's Brutus in public address has neither rhetorical figures nor arguments to move an audience; his private words with his wife are formal. Yet he reveals intense inner feelings of violence. This split in him has a double cause. Genuinely fearing that Caesar is becoming a tyrant, his upright nature rebels against the political necessity of killing him. Second is a cause among the profoundest there can be: he knows Caesar loves him as a son, and he loves Caesar as a father, but he has to kill that father. Shakespeare keeps out of sight the possibility that Caesar was Brutus' real father. Plutarch notes Caesar's orders for special care of young Brutus when he was first in battle with Pompey against Caesar, possibly for Brutus' mother Servilia's sake:

> For when he was a young man, he [Caesar] had been acquainted with Servilia, who was extreamelie in love with him. And bicause Brutus was borne in that time when their love was hottest, he perswaded himself that he begat him . . .
>
> (*Brutus*, 92)

Suetonius records Caesar's dying words to him, in Greek, as 'and thou, my child', not '*Et tu, Brute?*' Shakespeare keeps the two men apart, exchanging few words, their first close contact being the stabbing. So deep is the fracture caused by the double need to kill Caesar that this upright, intelligent statesman, of such well-known probity and good judgement – Caius Ligarius calls him 'Soul of Rome' (2.1.320) – finds himself seduced by Cassius. The flaw is apparent as early as 2.1.10, where his soliloquy starts with its conclusion, and then proceeds to rationalize that conclusion. (We may note that the Latin *brutus* means 'stupid', the name given to his great ancestor Lucius Junius Brutus, who feigned idiocy to save his life.) Brutus' admired good judgement breaks down too quickly in the play for us not to suspect an older, deeper mischief at work in him against Caesar than Cassius' alarm.

In the Quarrel scene, at 4.3.1–12 he condemns Cassius for condoning, and practising, extortion and then demands the fruits of that extortion: in itself bad enough, but done with such an ideal picture of himself – 'armed so strong in honesty . . . I had rather coin my heart . . .' (67, 72–5) – that the split in him is by then distressingly visible. Brutus is from the beginning, as he observed to Cassius at the start of the play, 'with himself at war' (1.2.46). The reason for his 'passions of some difference' (1.2.40) is at first undeclared. So it will be for Hamlet, who has 'that within which passes show' (*Ham* 1.2.85), until the Ghost's tale of the uncle's villainy makes unconsciously-prepared ground fertile. Cassius' bad story of Caesar, similarly, seeds Brutus' 'Conceptions only

8 Brutus and the Ghost of Caesar, drawing by Fauchéry from a painting by
   Westall, engraved by Lafond, undated

proper to myself' (1.2.41). As King Claudius will say, Brutus
from the beginning is saying to Cassius, 'O, speak of that; that I
do long to hear' (*Ham* 2.2.50). This is the difference between
Brutus and the other conspirators. They 'Did that they did in

envy of great Caesar', as Antony says at the end of the play (5.5.70): Brutus had other reasons. Antony goes on to say that it was the 'common good to all' (72), but Shakespeare has not shown that. Brutus conspicuously had thought of no provision at all for the future of Rome 'When Caesar's head is off' (2.1.182).

Brutus as tragic hero is limited in poetic expression. He does not, like Hamlet, grow throughout all the action to integrate his entire universe in one stroke – '*Stabs the King*' (*Ham* 5.2.314). Yet he pulls always at the interest of everyone within the play, and those attending or reading. He is more than just a Hamlet insufficiently moulded. He is far more than just a flawed hero for later republicans. He is the first tragic hero with any significant interior life to appear in English drama. The greater tragedy of Brutus is that this inner life is so empty of larger meaning. Shakespeare has withdrawn the gods from Rome: since there are no kings in Rome either, nothing can be sacred, and Brutus' personal moral tragedy, unlike that of Hamlet, though huge in its effects, meshes with no fuller interior cause than himself.

Cassius Cassius is Brutus' intimate in a play about the rivalry of intimates (which reaches its peak in Caesar's three words '*Et tu, Brute?*'). Linguistically, the thin, unsmiling, nervously-articulate Caius Cassius, a modern intellectual and anarchist, is also individually marked, particularly in a way that has not been noticed, for he shows a characteristic of using the most modern vocabulary. This is not absolute throughout the play, but it is notable. Again and again Cassius' words turn out to be first recorded in the mid-1590s or later: Brutus' to be ancient, even to simple things like 'taper' (ninth century), or his 'tide in the affairs of men' speech. Refining the point, Cassius' trick of modern speech appears most sharply in his dialogues with Brutus when he is manipulating him. In such speeches, in the first act alone, we find recent, often very recent, words, as first recorded in *OED* (the newness of many, like 'gusty', comes as a surprise): or words very recent in the special sense intended. Such are 'temper', 'scandal',

9 'Against the Capitol I met a lion / Who glazed upon me and went surly by / Without annoying me.' 1.3.19–22. Henry Tresham. London: Rivington, 1823

'banqueting', 'gusty', 'buffet', 'stemming', 'creature', 'lustre', 'get the start', 'majestic', 'applauses', 'bestride', 'famed with', 'jealous', 'aim', 'chew', 'villager', 'chidden', 'humour', 'trash', 'indifferent' – no doubt there are many more. By contrast, Brutus' opening words, 'gamesome', 'lack', 'part', 'quick', 'spirit', 'hinder' and so on, are all solidly old, and even those later in the first act in an unfamiliar sense, like 'soil' for solution, with a touch of absolution, are old. True, Cassius is at work with Brutus, making strokes and effects: his trick of creating tiny cameo pictures of himself as obviously not untrustworthy, like 'profess myself in banqueting / To all the rout' (1.2.77–8), before sketching fuller, and damning, invented incidents with Caesar (100–15), shows his consciousness of what he is doing. But what might it signify that Cassius 'speaks modern' and Brutus, at least at first, does not? (The difference of idiom was brought out by James Mason as Brutus and John Gielgud as Cassius in Joseph Mankiewicz's 1953 film.)

Othello may help. (The story of the Moor of Venice may have been in Shakespeare's mind as he wrote *Julius Caesar* and *Hamlet*, if, as seems likely, we can accept E.A.J. Honigmann's dating for that play of 1601/2 (Honigmann, *Oth* 344–50). It is Shakespeare's next play set in Italy, and it is about villainy and a secret plot to destroy a military leader. Othello himself is given a language that is as old as geology could find. Iago is a would-be modern, trying at the same time to use language above his position. Iago uses 'corrigible' (*OED* 5. 1601), 'sect' (*OED sb.*[2] 1604, citing this), 'sequestration' (OED 2. 1599, *Henry V*, possibly also 1565) and probably 'locusts' (*OED* 1615 for the cassia-pod, or fruit of the carob tree), all impressively modern but wrong. Iago is a villain: indeed, *the* villain. Does the same trick – but getting the words right – show us something about Cassius? Cassius is not Iago; but he is surely in his first fleshing-out in the play dangerous. Perhaps the modern talk is meant to suggest that. As Brutus in the first half becomes little more than Cassius' instrument ('Since Cassius first did whet me against Caesar . . .', 2.1.61) he himself uses more and more modern words, as a sign of the crumbling of his ancient foundations.

The central relationship of Brutus and Cassius (brothers-in-law, though Shakespeare does not tell us that until 4.2, unless Brutus' remark to Antony at 3.1.174–5, 'our hearts / Of brothers' temper', is meant to contain something more specific than the general community) is always on the move: as it develops, they baffle each other in a dramatically compelling way, until the bafflement bursts into new warmth in that Quarrel scene, 4.3. Conflict is surrendered in wine, and then returns. But however close they get in Acts 4 and 5, Brutus and Cassius never exhibit a linguistic trait visible in some of Shakespeare's plays of those years whereby he uses a ghostly shared quatrain and even sonnet form to show a new mutuality of thought between men who have been distant and who are now close in a particular way. George T. Wright noticed in early Shakespeare, as in Marlowe, a tendency to block dialogue in quatrains and couplets (Wright, *Metrical*, 117–18). It is not surprising to find Shakespeare, in 1598 and after, thinking in something like sonnet forms, for probably many of his 154 sonnets were written then. From that time, he can be seen to have a tendency in the *Henry IV* plays, for particular shared emotional moments, to block ideas out in groups of quatrains marked by punctuation, and even blocked in fourteen lines, including a form of the sonnet 'turn' at the eighth line. Though there is not often straight rhyme, many of the other characteristics remain. Take, for example, the moment in *1 Henry IV* 3.2 when the King and Prince are first together and in private, a father and a once-errant son. From the immediate exit of the lords in line 3, the King's opening words to his son make a speech of fourteen lines of two 'quatrains', with a strong 'turn' at the end of the eighth line at 'Tell me else'. The first 'quatrain' is the speaker about himself: the second about 'thou'. The Prince, picking up the tone, replies in two 'quatrains' and three lines, the final three of the 'sonnet' coming from his father. Such observations must not be forced: but most of the speeches in the 160 lines of this scene in *1 Henry IV* are haunted by thoughts in quatrains, particularly the last ringing speech of the Prince, now fully reunited with his father. Hamlet, by contrast, in his excitement shared with Horatio at the end of the play scene (*Ham* 3.2.282), strongly avoids an obvious rhyme, an avoidance noticed by Horatio: he seems to want to keep clear of even a hint of the 'sonnet' intensity and union. When he has returned to Denmark in

Act 5, and is telling Horatio his story in some intimacy, on the *Henry IV* analogy a moment to expect ghost sonnets, there is no trace of any such system, though there is patterning (for example, in the 'many such-like "As'es"' of 5.2.43).

That Brutus and Cassius most pointedly do not come anywhere near quatrains may be because the making-up was not fully of the heart: as Caesar said of Cassius, 'Such men as he be never at heart's ease / Whiles they behold a greater than themselves' (1.2.207–8). Yet at the start of the play the tribunes Flavius and Murellus have this linguistic sharing. From this opening scene, one would think that the whole play is going to be just as mannered in its structure, with much entwining of linguistic forms between emotionally-involved people. It seems that there is no room in this adversarial, confrontational play, after the first scene, for any such sharing. (Flavius and Murellus, after all, are immediately 'put to silence' (1.2.285).)

Instead, Cassius the realist and genuine friend of liberty, who thinks realistically about himself and fears the consequences of political compromise, keeps for the first Acts some distance from the sharp contrary, the idealist Brutus, whom he admires. Shakespeare removes Cassius from the Forum scene, 3.2, and what must have been his horrific realization that the crucial issues of the future of the state were being put to the judgement of the mob. He enters the play again, somewhat changed, in 4.2. The quarrel flares quickly but, unlike the noble Brutus, Cassius reveals tolerance of the comic 'cynic' poet, and genuine warmth of shock and sympathy at the news of Portia. Now we are shown a Cassius who commands the loyalty of soldiers and friends, and has better military judgement than Brutus. His death – like Brutus', with Caesar's name on his lips – is unexpectedly moving, to those on stage as well as to us. What has changed him? The killing of Caesar, now accomplished? Perhaps simply being out of the political hothouse of Rome and into the open field with his own powers. Linguistically, the earlier rhetorical tricks produced because he 'thinks too much' give way to a new kind of realism:

> Now, most noble Brutus,
> The gods today stand friendly, that we may,
> Lovers in peace, lead on our days to age.
> But since the affairs of men rest still incertain,
> Let's reason with the worst that may befall.
>
> (5.1.92–6)

Portia To read a modern Greek text of Plutarch is to get a strong picture of Porcia (also so named in North: Shakespeare uses the Italian form). She was a young woman who roused strong feelings. Her father, Marcus Porcius Cato, a man of stern morality, had killed himself rather than fall into Caesar's hands (an act which Brutus could not stomach 5.1.101–2). Plutarch in his life of Cato the Younger tells a revealing story. While she was young, married to Bibulus and the mother of his sons, a respected Roman named Quintus Hortensius, 'a man of splendid reputation and excellent character', went to her father and suggested, partly to enhance his social position, that Porcia and he should get together, she being 'noble soil for the production of children[1] . . . a woman, said he, in the prime of youth and beauty should . . . [not] quench her productive power and lie idle' (Perrin, *Cato*, 293). Quintus Hortensius thoughtfully added that if her husband Bibulus loved her very much, he could have her back after she had borne him a child. Cato replied that he respected Quintus Hortensius, but found his suggestion absurd. (So instead Hortensius married Cato's own specially-divorced wife, who was still of child-bearing age.) The story illustrates the limitation of women's power in Rome to that of property. When Bibulus died, Porcia was still young, and we are to think of her as a young wife to Brutus. Plutarch goes out of his way to show her φιλόστοργος δ' ἡ Πορκία καὶ φίλανδρος οὖσα (*philostorgos d' he Porkia kai philandros ousa*) (Perrin, *Brutus*, 152), that is, being of an affectionate nature and fond of her husband: φιλόστοργος (*philostorgos*) has a stronger sexual sense than

---

1 North has 'that he might also cast about the seed of goodly children, in that pleasant fertile ground' (819).

10 'Kneel not, gentle Portia', original etching for *Julius Caesar*, 2.1.269–77, by Frank Howard, London, *c.* 1828

the modern 'affectionate' implies. Curiously, for that word North has 'being excellently well seen in philosophy', noting in the margin that she was '*well studied in Philosophy*' (*Brutus*, see Appendix, p. 337). Amyot probably followed a textual variant in Plutarch which gave instead of *philostorgos* the more common word φιλόσοφος (*philosophos*), meaning loving wisdom.

Shakespeare gave Portia's language something strikingly different again, neither *philostorgos* nor *philosophos*. She lives intimately with Brutus, keeping with him at meals and comforting his bed as she puts it, sympathetic to his extreme disturbance to the point of wounding herself.[1] Yet her language to her husband is in the manner of a formal oration. 'Portia in nightdress uses the rhetoric of the Forum to address her husband about their domestic life . . . Oratory is very nearly coterminous with *Romanitas* at this point in the play' (Velz, '*Orator*', 63). This is important.

1   In *Julius Caesar* and in *Hamlet* there are two senior women (Calphurnia, Gertrude) and two more junior women (Portia, Ophelia): both the latter complain of intimate scenes spoiled by the strange, withdrawn and reticent behaviour of their men; both these women take their own lives in a bizarre way.

Portia, we may say, can only reach Brutus in his political dilemma by 'being' a member of the Forum, that is, a man. Hers is the only voice to challenge Brutus, and she does it at a vital moment in the play. She can be heard because she speaks as a man. Aware of that, she says 'I grant I am a woman' – and then defines womanliness by reference to powerful males, her stern father and her male-leading husband: 'Think you I am no stronger than my sex / Being so fathered and so husbanded?' (2.1.291–6).

Clearly recounted in Plutarch, her ultimate statement, beyond rhetoric, is that surreal 'voluntary wound, / Here in the thigh' (299–300). The position of the gash in her body makes it intimate to the two of them – it is to prove herself (Plutarch's phrase, used twice) as able to share 'a secret . . . with thee' (see Appendix, p. 338), like the married, sexual, secret. The wound, with its unmistakable feminine location, also shares the exclusively masculine quality in Rome of suffering wounds (Kahn, 101 and *passim*). Her action is intended to be symbolic, claiming fearlessness and equality. Brutus' response in both Plutarch and Shakespeare is to hope to be worthy of so noble a wife: the language, again, of the Forum. (Brutus can be tender – to his servant Lucius.) In Plutarch 'he then did comfort her the best he could'; not so in Shakespeare, where he dismisses her with a promise to make a statement 'by and by' (303–7). In the night scene with her husband she wants more than to be patronized as a woman ('in the suburbs / Of your good pleasure', 284–5). Yet what woman in the middle of the night wants to be praised by her man for being noble? As a 'man' of Rome as well as Brutus' woman, she is worthy to be promised entry to the conspiracy. Brutus obviously keeps his promise: in 2.4 she is struggling, now alone as a woman, to keep the great secret: 'I have a man's mind, but a woman's might. / How hard it is for women to keep counsel' (8–9). It is as a woman that she dies. Her death was, as Brutus puts first in his explanation, because she was 'Impatient of my absence', and because the new men 'had made themselves so strong', with no need of women (4.3.150–4).

Antony The exception to the Roman patrician linguistic austerity is Mark Antony. Plutarch explained that his life-style from being a young man was consciously 'Asiatik' (*Antonius*, 255), that is, florid, indulgent, extravagant: he could, notes Plutarch, be debauched and distasteful. Yet his hold on the minds of men ever since has rivalled Caesar's: Shakespeare makes Antony's full entry to his play, exactly half-way through, memorably gripping.

Before Antony's entry to Brutus and Cassius at 3.1.146.1, following his servant, he has only had three brief speeches: 'Caesar, my lord' (1.2.5); 'I shall remember. / When Caesar says "Do this", it is performed' (1.2.9–10); and 'So to most noble Caesar' (2.2.118) – a total of nineteen words. He was not present at the assassination. At 3.1.121.1, his servant comes ahead of him. The quality of Antony's linguistic impact on the play is not foreshadowed by the speech of this servant: he – apparently repeating verbatim what Antony has said – plays to Brutus, as if Antony had heard it, the patterned rhetorical manner of Brutus' funeral oration:

> Brutus is noble, wise, valiant and honest
> Caesar was mighty, bold, royal and loving.
> (3.1.126–7)

Immediately on Antony's own entry, he begins by rhetorically echoing Brutus with a list, 'Are all thy conquests, glories, triumphs, spoils . . .' (149): but from that point forward his rhetoric is quite differently orchestrated:

> I do beseech ye, if you bear me hard,
> Now, whilst your purpled hands do reek and smoke,
> Fulfil your pleasure. Live a thousand years,
> I shall not find myself so apt to die.
> No place shall please me so, no mean of death,
> As here by Caesar, and by you cut off,
> The choice and master spirits of this age.
> (3.1.157–63)

In pace, it might almost be Hamlet with Laertes in Ophelia's grave

11 Bust of Antony, first century AD

('Be buried quick with her, and so will I', 5.1.272), and especially in largeness of reference. Contrast Antony's readiness to kill himself with that of Cassius in the Quarrel scene: Cassius there is unusually elaborate in reference ('I that denied thee gold will give my heart') and dynamic in rhythm ('Strike as thou didst at Caesar') (4.3.103–4); but foremost in his thought is not someone else (Ophelia or Caesar), but himself, Cassius. After this first speech, Antony has twenty-five speech prefixes before the Forum scene (3.2) is over and the plebeians exit with Caesar's body. Seven of these speeches are long orations, four of them part of one interrupted speech. What comes into the play with Antony is a different rhetorical skill in a tone of passionate mourning. By contrast with everyone else in the play (even Portia, who should be similar in this), his language over long passages is apparently driven by feeling for someone else. Towering above the Forum scene is his grief for Caesar. This is the counter to Stoic insensibility to suffering, now challenged through the second half of the play. Antony, it is true, is a master of rhetorical, and thus political, craft, ruthlessly working to make that grief stir his hearers to violence in support of him. 'Effecting the shift of power from Brutus to Antony, [his rhetorical *tour de force*] marks the end of the Republic . . . rhetoric in this play is a theme as well as a style' (Greene, 68–9). But in the Forum scene, whatever he is saying, his linguistic eye, if we may so express it, is on his dead friend and leader, in grief for him. At the start of his first main speech in the play, at 3.1.184, he shakes the blood-dripping hands of the seven conspirators, and then – uniquely for any speaker in the play – is at a loss for words: 'alas, what shall I say?' (190). Momentarily he thinks, Cassius-like, of himself, 'Either a coward or a flatterer' (193). Then the following seventeen lines are addressed in love to Caesar and his spirit, a metaphysical conceit (rare so far in the play) of numbers of eyes weeping like the bleeding of many wounds.

Antony's twenty-two-line soliloquy over the body of Caesar (3.1.254–75) is in a register we have not so far heard. It is efflorescent in imagery, again metaphysical, even baroque:

> Over thy wounds now I do prophesy
> (Which like dumb mouths do ope their ruby lips
> To beg the voice and utterance of my tongue) . . .
>
> (259–61)

Grief opens a new diapason. Shakespeare had before made similar expansions of linguistic range in the expression of grief; there are mothers mourning sons in the three *Henry VI* plays, *Richard III* and *King John*. Ophelia's widening of the spectrum of language in grief for her dead father will stretch even as far as wild nonsense. Antony's, however, is Shakespeare's first soliloquy of grief. As such, it has obvious significance for the making of *Hamlet*. The traditional icon of Hamlet has been the young man in mourning black, holding a skull: Shakespeare makes an entire play, as it were, out of grief. The play of *Hamlet* has a powerful drive: the thrust of the action never pauses, and can be overwhelming in performance. In Antony's soliloquy and his funeral oration is that same combination of linguistic release and onward drive.

The destruction that Antony prophesies has the energetic rhythms of Henry V retorting to the Dauphin – 'And some are yet ungotten and unborn / That shall have cause to curse the Dauphin's scorn' (*H5* 1.2.286–7) – or before Harfleur – 'The gates of mercy shall be all shut up . . .' (3.2.10). The difference is that Antony describes the even greater horror of civil war – one recalls the prophecy, perhaps influential here, by the Bishop of Carlisle in *Richard II* (4.1.136–49). The imaginative liberation in the main conceit, of giving voice to the 'dumb mouths' of Caesar's wounds, acts to open floodgates, and produces in the language sudden violent energy. For the first time in the play this violence is owned by the speaker. True, Antony will soon work it up in the mob, to a point of frenzy: but that is deliberate. Antony, unlike Brutus, knows the violence he feels. The result is exhilarating. There is suddenly in the language a range, movement, authority and release:

71

> And Caesar's spirit, ranging for revenge,
> With Ate by his side come hot from hell,
> Shall in these confines, with a monarch's voice,
> Cry havoc and let slip the dogs of war . . .
>
> (3.1.270–3)

The rhythms are a long way from the sound of Brutus soliloquizing:

> It must be by his death: and for my part
> I know no personal cause to spurn at him . . .

and

> It is the bright day that brings forth the adder,
> And that craves wary walking.
>
> (2.1.10–11, 14–15)

The four long sections of Antony's funeral oration compared with Brutus' (close to 1,100 words, against Brutus' about 350) use rhetoric in a 'less systematic and more devious' way (Fuzier, 32). Our sense, however, is that here is a speaker who knows exactly what he is doing with his audience. He obeys to the letter Brutus' injunction not to blame the conspirators: his irony has an energizing effect on the hearers. The second and third sections of Antony's speech, 3.2.119–93 and 203–52, are dominated by irony and *negatio* – the latter is 'a refusal to speak which nevertheless tells everything, or a refusal to do something which is expressed in such a manner that the audience is spurred to do it' (Fuzier, 35). Woven into these are many other figures and devices of prosody:

> This was the most unkindest cut of all:
> For when the noble Caesar saw him stab,
> Ingratitude, more strong than traitor's arms,
> Quite vanquished him: then burst his mighty heart;
> And in his mantle muffling up his face,
> Even at the base of Pompey's statue,
> Which all the while ran blood, great Caesar fell.
>
> (3.2.181–7)

Here are *demonstratio*, 'defined by Cicero as a device which "so explains things with words that we apprehend them as though before our eyes"'; a form of allegory ('Ingratitude . . .'); but especially 'a very elaborate use of *paroemion*', where the harsh consonants 'k', 'r' and 't' 'stand for the murderous assault upon Caesar' and 'the soft sounds (mainly f and l) . . . echo his fall' (Fuzier, 39).

The man who is 'no orator, as Brutus is . . . a plain blunt man' (3.2.211–12) speaks at three times Brutus' length and uses over twice as many rhetorical figures as Brutus (Fuzier, 62), but gives the impression that they are not contrived; that he is not relying on them as Brutus did, that they are 'used to strengthen points, when they in fact make them' (Fuzier, 45). Antony's is a 'made-to-measure' rhetoric, 'as opposed to Brutus' ready-made and rather ill-fitting speech' (Fuzier, 49). Antony's words are always engaged with the feelings of his audience, and chosen for that reason.

Not only words, of course. A striking moment in performance is something beyond verbal rhetoric, when Antony holds up the blood-soaked mantle (3.2.168). It leads to attention to the silent, deeply-gashed body. The effect is galvanic. Second Plebeian cries 'O noble Caesar!' (196). That 'noble' echoes Brutus' verbal response to Portia's blooded nightgown and gashed body. Brutus dismissed Portia from his mind almost at once. Antony stirs his audience to immediate hot reaction – 'Burn! Fire! Kill! Slay!' (199). Antony, holding up the mantle, takes time to tell his hearers an anecdote – 'I remember / The first time . . .' (168–71). The story is made up, of course: Antony was not there: but that, Shakespeare is saying, is how to be effective in a theatre.

Flavius and Murellus The first speeches of Flavius and Murellus are firmly iambic pentameters, to establish the form for the play and for themselves. Agitated by the Commoners' disturbing replies, they next speak in a loose unscannable prose, returning powerfully to iambic pentameters as they claim the initiative again. Some of the effectiveness of Murellus' long demand, and dismissal, of the Commoners, at 1.1.33–56, comes from the steady regularity of the beat, suddenly broken by 'Be gone!' (53).

Inside these firm iambic pentameters, the tribunes share linguistic devices. One is of making heavy emphasis fall on various 'o' sounds: 'home' (repeated), 'know you not', 'ought not walk', 'Rome' (repeated), and especially in Murellus' 'bonds', 'blocks', 'stones', 'oft', 'towers and windows', 'tops', 'shores', 'do you now' (repeated), 'put on', 'Be gone!', and 'gods' (there are more). These sounds come to rhetorical consummation with 'Pompey's blood' (1.1.52). Flavius' response shows how much he has understood the rhetoric of repeated 'o' sounds, and shares it, 'Go, go, good countrymen, and for this fault . . . the poor men of your sort' (57–8). The two tribunes, further, share a ghostly end-of-line rhyme-pattern as in 'home' / 'Rome' / 'Rome' / 'Rome' (33–43) and the final assonances of 'shout' / 'sounds' (45–7) and 'this fault' / 'your sort' / 'exalted . . . all' (57–61). This relationship rises when they are, for the only time in the play, briefly alone after the exit of the Commoners. Their concluding dialogue is built on the frame of a sonnet; they share fourteen lines with, in the middle, an added four beats of Murellus' detached 'May we do so?' Ghostly rhymes on 'o' and 'ess' in an ABAB pattern can be found (62–7), as at line 67, when the firm 'o's of Murellus' 'do so' respond to Flavius' 'not moved' (62), 'Go you down . . . towards . . . Capitol' (64), 'Disrobe' (65) and 'you do' (66). Flavius' response is set up with the strong 'o's of 'no', 'no' and 'trophies' (69–70). Flavius' sound-pattern then changes to dominant 'i's, from 'I'll about, / And drive' (70–1), to 'fly' (74), and the concluding 'i'-assonance of 'thick', 'wing', 'pitch' (72–4). A final 'couplet' (75–6) has 'men' and 'ness' as near-rhymes.

Lucius We should glance at the Shakespearean skill, present from his earliest work, in making minor characters come to life, taking Lucius as example. In his three scenes, this boy,

Shakespeare's invention, while always speaking verse, has a remarkable naturalness, making him one of the characters one feels one knows, remembered long after the play is over. His language is domestic, of the house (or tent); about a book, a lute, answering the door and going errands, and it is matter-of-fact about sensational events like muffled men arriving in the night, like running to Brutus at the bidding of an unusually agitated Portia, and like Brutus' strange alarm in his tent. His name associates him with light, and his first action, later repeated, is to take a taper to Brutus' darkness (2.1.7; 4.3.155.1). Shakespeare used the name frequently: twice in *Titus Andronicus*, twice in *Timon of Athens*, twice in *Antony and Cleopatra*, and once in *Cymbeline*. Two small parts of that mysterious interior world of significances that can be found in all Shakespeare, and made much, or little, are seen here. First, John Foxe on the first page of his *Acts and Monuments* of 1563 says that he is beginning his huge work from 'the first conversion of christian realms to the faith of Christ (namely of this realm of England and Scotland, first beginning with king Lucius . . .)'.[1] Second, Lucius Junius Brutus was the illustrious ancestor of Marcus Brutus.

STRUCTURES

Julius Caesar is obviously in two parts, before and after the death of Caesar. The re-entry of Antony after the assassination, at 3.1.146.1, is the exact centre of the play. This is presumably not an accident, for Antony from that point begins to change the nature of the action, especially against Brutus and Cassius. To that extent two parts are clearly visible. Emrys Jones found evidence of what he called 'structural rhyming', where the endings of the two halves of a two–part play could be found to be similar in action and tone (Jones, *Form*, 77). It is notable that the moments of deepest feeling come later in the second half.

---

1 Foxe, 1.87 and *passim*. And see Bate, *Tit*, 21.

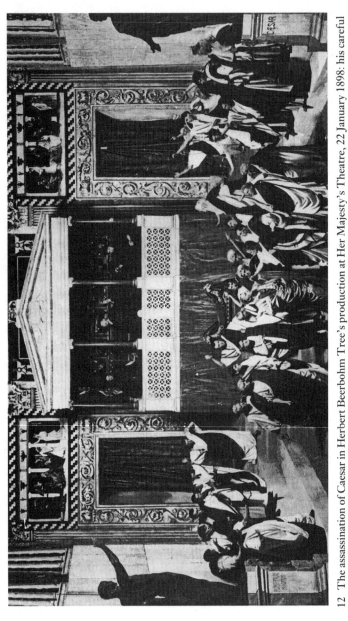

12 The assassination of Caesar in Herbert Beerbohm Tree's production at Her Majesty's Theatre, 22 January 1898: his careful pictorial symmetry for this pivotal – and brutal – moment in the play is striking

Nicholas Grene observed that 'There is a basic theatrical plea-sure in the matching of prophetic image to its fulfilment' (Grene, 26).

Julius Caesar, however, shares with *Henry V* and *Hamlet* a solidly five-act structure. Counterpointing that are other structures, notably three sweeping movements. The five acts of *Henry V* are heavily marked by the Choruses: observable, how-ever, are a first movement up to the excitement and crowding at Harfleur, a second to the surrender of the French after Agincourt, and a last comic duel between Henry and Katherine. In *Hamlet* the five acts are each characterized and independent (though the conventional placing of the beginning of Act 4 in the middle of the Closet scene is unfortunate): across them cuts the first long structural phrase, up to the crowded excitement of the play scene and the exit of Claudius; the second is up to the Prince coming forward at Ophelia's grave as rightful king of Denmark ('This is I, / Hamlet the Dane') – to his mother's astonishment, and the complete alteration of the dynamic of the action; a last to the duel and four rapid deaths in the court (Gertrude, Laertes, Claudius, Hamlet) with the climax in Hamlet's own death.

Similarly in *Julius Caesar*, the five acts have the classical struc-ture (see Baldwin, *Structure*). Cutting across this are three long phrases of action. The first is acceleration to the crowded excite-ment of the assassination and the 'exit' of Caesar; the second is to the re-establishment of Brutus and Cassius together, now with a different emotional tone, in the Quarrel scene; the last is to the battle of Philippi and the four rapid deaths (Cassius, Titinius, Cato, Brutus) with the climax in Brutus' own death. The conflict with Laertes in Act 4 of *Hamlet*, overt in Ophelia's grave and later in Laertes' death in Act 5, parallels Brutus' conflict with Cassius, overt in the Quarrel scene and later in Cassius' death. Just as Hamlet and Laertes fight in the presence of the dead Ophelia, so Brutus and Cassius quarrel in the 'presence', as it were, of the dead Portia.

One mark of greatness in great art is multiplicity: so one can detect other structures. Frank Kermode wrote:

> The play is throughout beautifully built, as in the fast-moving, variously lit passage from II.ii to III.i – the decision of Caesar to go to the Senate, Portia's anxiety, the tense minutes before the assassination, the arrival, large and menacing, of Antony, and finally of Octavius's messenger: five hundred lines tightly written, describing one great dramatic curve; and followed instantly by the next movement: funeral orations, riot, war.
>
> (Riv, 1104)

Adrien Bonjour propounded the structural unusualness of two heroes: Mark Rose found a rhythm of rituals, as did Brents Stirling in a different form, and John Velz a wave-like motion of rises and falls, operating before, through and after the play. *Julius Caesar*, like *Hamlet*, has a compelling drive. Like *Hamlet*, it is open to contradictory interpretations, yet in the theatre the pace of both stories can be so strong that all the contraries are absorbed and accepted in the power of the ending.

It has long been argued that *Julius Caesar* is in that special late-Elizabethan and Jacobean genre known as revenge tragedy, of which Kyd's *Spanish Tragedy* of 1587 is the first popular example, and *Hamlet* is the finest. Some of the marks are certainly there: a noble, wronged victim; the dedicated pursuit of the murderer or murderers over a long period until, at the end, he or they are dead; a supernatural visitation; the sense that by the final deaths some great wrong has been avenged. Not for nothing did the English Senecans use Caesar as a subject. The label will not do for Shakespeare's *Julius Caesar*, however. The avenger is not a flesh-and-blood prince who comes down to the audience to take us so much into his confidence that, as Hazlitt said, 'it is *we* who are Hamlet' (Hazlitt, *Characters*, 64). The avenger in *Julius Caesar* is Roman history. Plutarch notes Caesar's 'daemon':

as an avenger of his murder, driving and tracking down
his slayers over every land and sea until not one of them
was left, but even those who in any way soever either put
hand to the deed or took part in the plot were punished.[1]

One can see the excitement in that for a playwright. But to have
an avenger as a historical principle, even if it does for ten lines
make the lamps burn blue, will not make a revenge tragedy. We
should not force *Julius Caesar* into that mould.

SHAKESPEARE'S SOURCES

Plutarch

Shakespeare's prime source for *Julius Caesar* was Plutarch's *Lives*
in North's English translation. Here he found, principally in the
lives of Caesar, Brutus and Antony, much material about their
characters and the events of their lives (new in its detail: Barroll,
330) and those of their confederates, Cicero, Cassius and Octavius.
Shakespeare used Plutarch freely, sometimes taking the events
over largely as he found them, like the assassination: or phrases,
like Brutus wanting to be 'worthy of so noble a wife'; but most
often he adapted, changed, reversed, compressed, expanded and
invented, so that, famous though details of the story were, the
play's compelling force is Shakespeare's own. As always, he used
material from other places as well: other classical historians, like
Suetonius and Appian; other familiar books, like the Bible or
Ovid; his own experiences in the theatre; and his own work, as
already-written dramatic situations continued to ferment in 'the
quick forge and working-house of thought'. None of these
sources, not even Plutarch, dictated the form of the play. Some
eighteenth-century critics regretted reading North's Plutarch, as
it seemed to them then that Shakespeare's cover was blown: the
supposed child of Nature had simply taken the whole thing from
North: Richard Farmer remarked in 1767, 'It is notorious that

1   Perrin, *Caesar*, 605; cf. Bullough, 5.88. See Appendix, p. 331.

much of his *matter of fact* knowledge is deduced from Plutarch' (Farmer, 9–10). There is still some blindness to the wholly original shaping into dramatic poetry of what he found.

Plutarch was a Greek citizen of the Roman Empire born around AD 45, in the small, historic, town of Chaeronea. He visited Alexandria, and went at least twice to Rome, a city he admired. His house in Chaeronea became a kind of informal philosophical school. He was a disciple of Plato, a student of Pythagoras, a member of the college of priests of Apollo at Delphi, a traveller, a magistrate, a writer on the theory of poetry, a biographer and historian, and principally a moralist. He died around AD 20. He wrote his *Bioi paralleloi – The Parallel Lives of the Most Noble Greeks and Romans* – perhaps in Alexandria (the date is unknown). There are fifty lives: for all but a few, the life of a Greek soldier or statesman, for example Pericles, is paired with a Roman, in that case Fabius Maximus. The pairs of lives are intended silently to comment on each other, like Demosthenes and Cicero. He adds a short essay of comparison to nineteen of the pairs, like Alcibiades and Coriolanus, to bring out important elements revealed. Plutarch was also influential through a collection of brief prose pieces, originally 150: over seventy have survived. They are known as the *Moralia*. The subjects of these are widely various, including conduct, religion, health and philosophy.

In the *Lives*, Plutarch is more interested in moral character than political events, though he is always aware that the course of the world's history is being shaped. He can write set pieces, like the catastrophe of the Syracusian expedition in *Nicias* (North, 590–2), or the murder of Pompey (North, 717): or huge battle-pictures in, for example, the victory of Caius Marius over the Cimbri (North, 465–7). What, however, has appealed to readers, and writers, ever since is his skill in the choice of anecdotes to reveal the nature of the man. He wrote in the life of Alexander, as translated by North:

The noblest deedes doe not alwayes shew mens vertues

and vices, but oftentimes a light occasion, a word, or some
sporte makes mens natural dispositions and maners
appeare more plaine, then the famous battells wonne . . .

(North, 722)

The most dazzling displays of his powers of selection, description and narrative are in the Roman lives – not surprisingly as his
narratives are of critical times in Roman history.

Julius Caesar Plutarch paints a powerful picture of Caesar's
life and achievements, beginning with his marriage to Cornelia
(it is thought that the paragraphs giving his ancestry, birth and
boyhood are lost). He stresses his remarkable authority as a young
man, and his extraordinary energy and skill in war, in spite of a
pale, sick body and epilepsy. What comes across is something of
the breadth of his interests, the distances over which he ranged
as conqueror, and, always, his political awareness and achievements. Plutarch gives a good deal of space and emphasis to
Caesar's almost unbelievable campaigns, especially in Gaul, to
the crossing of the Rubicon, and to that decisive battle of
Pharsalus in which he defeated Pompey. The language of the
brief passage on Caesar with Cleopatra leaps with life.

Caesar does not fatally enter the Senate until eleven-twelfths
of the life have passed, and the pages after that give almost a
leisurely account of what followed – Brutus does not address the
people until the day after the assassination, and then the Senate
takes its time. Indeed, it was thought that everything was all over,
and settled in the best way, until Caesar's will was opened: even
then the account of the riot of burning in Rome is overtaken by
the story of Cinna being torn to pieces. The brief coda tells of the
portents linked with the suicides of Cassius and Brutus.

Brutus Plutarch's life of Brutus tells the story of an upright,
studious, active politician, weighty of character, for whom reason and noble principles operated most strongly. The narrative

81

gets quickly to reasons for Brutus' hostility to Caesar, and to Cassius, and develops the conspiracy in detail. The climax of the conspiracy is approached through Porcia and her wounding herself, and the story catches fire at the killing of Caesar and what immediately followed: it moves quickly to a long-paced account of the battle of Philippi. From Cassius' first speech seducing Brutus, early in Plutarch's story, to Antony finding Brutus dead in the last paragraph, most, but not all, of Plutarch's incidents are familiar from Shakespeare in *Julius Caesar*.

Plutarch's life of the Roman Brutus is paired with that of the Greek Dion, who was a Sicilian, a friend and pupil of Plato: he brought that philosopher to Syracuse. Plato later wrote his *Epistles* to friends in Syracuse about Dion and his struggle against the evil tyranny of Dionysius. Dion was a man of culture and high ideals, who successfully rid Sicily of Dionysius, but was himself tragically assassinated: Plato wrote in lament for him – and Wordsworth a poem in seven longish stanzas about his death (he 'stained the robes of civil power with blood / Unjustly shed, tho' for the public good'; the poem ends, 'Him, only him, the shield of Jove defends / Whose means are fair and spotless as his ends').

Brutus and Dion were famous for their hostility to tyrants. Brutus, as Plutarch writes, without any private grievance risked his life for the common liberty; even his enemies praised his single-minded aim to restore to the Romans their ancient form of government. Yet Brutus in killing Caesar struck down his preserver with his own hand, as Plutarch also notes. Yet again, killing Caesar at such a public moment implied high generalship and the ability to win the total loyalty and silence of many people.

Antony Antony, in Plutarch's vivid account (his longest), has great strengths and great weaknesses. In the political world of people, pressures and pretences, Antony is always contradictory. He is larger than life, greatly loved by his soldiers in spite of his dissipations and irregularities of life. The slower, rather gossipy pace of the earlier part of the story changes with the staged entry of Cleopatra half-way through. Cleopatra brings Plutarch's liveliest writing, which has the gusto, detail and long reach of a novel. The relationship of Antony and Cleopatra dominates three-quarters of the life, even though Plutarch leaves her for a lengthy account of Antony's extraordinary desert war against the Parthians (famous, incidentally, as impossibly skilled enemies: see 5.3.37). In Plutarch's account, it is as if the ever-renewed energy and contrariety of the Parthians are one with Cleopatra (and their story is embedded in hers) in persistent engagement, total unpredictability and changeableness.

> The generally unfavourable portrait that results from the political bias of [Plutarch's] sources and the moral prejudices of the author does not exclude the recognition of Antony's good qualities: his courage, generosity and humanity. It is this of course that makes Plutarch's Antony a potential tragic hero, not an unsympathetic adventurer.
>
> (Russell, 135; and see Wilders, 52–61)

The later life of the Lives

The *Lives* were translated from Greek into Latin, and so circulated throughout the Roman world, and in Europe in the Middle Ages. From the second century, the *Lives* have had a great number of readers (Shackford). Their many-sided appeal kept the interest in the *Lives*, and the *Moralia*, alive. Both were influential in Renaissance Italy and northern Europe – Erasmus translated three essays from the *Moralia*. In England, Humphrey, Duke of Gloucester had copies of both in his new University of Oxford library (eventually the Bodleian). References began to appear widely in English Renaissance writers; Thomas Elyot in *The Book Named the Governor* (1531) and William Painter in *The Palace of Pleasure* (1566) to name but two.

  In 1559 the *Lives* were translated by Jacques Amyot (1513–93) into French directly from the Greek, corrected both from the Latin and from earlier French versions. Amyot turned to Plutarch's *Lives* from translating the Greek novelists. He was a scholar and cleric and skilled translator: 'he made countless original contributions to the interpretation, and sometimes the reading, of the text' (Russell, 150). Amyot combined faithfulness to the original with ease and facility through, first, 'additions and interpretations, the innumerable *c'est-à-dire* of which his critics complained': and, second, the freeing and considerable expansion of phrases: 'the Plutarch that he created . . . was something new and exciting' (Russell, 151; and see 152–8). Shakespeare read Plutarch in Amyot's version, with the further vigour and independence that North brought into the English in his translation, from Amyot, of 1579.

In the 1580s and 1590s, Thomas Nashe sarcastically pointed out William Lyly's habit of plundering classical authors, singling out Ovid and Plutarch. Gabriel Harvey, Edmund Spenser and the circle around Philip Sidney and his sister Mary referred directly to Plutarch. By then, Plutarch was the most widely-read Greek author after Plato. 'An age that promoted individualism and persistently sought personal fame, that admired a strong-willed despot while hating tyranny itself, found Plutarch congenial and suggestive in both his wisdom and his enthralling narrative' (Shackford, 5). The sixteenth and seventeenth centuries 'mark the widest diffusion of the notion of antiquity and its values that the Renaissance had constructed, and for this notion Plutarch was, as he had been in the late empire, a central and inescapable text-book' (Russell, 159).

The great Elizabethan translation of Plutarch was made by Thomas North. Shakespeare could have read Plutarch without North: the French and Latin versions were in print. He could not have avoided him. North's Plutarch, like an English Bible and Holinshed, was becoming a book to be found in households, with five editions between 1576 and 1626. Shakespeare was a reader, and he would know that in Plutarch, as in the other two large books, he would find varieties of human experience, good narratives, conflict and passion, and unforgettable phrases. Plutarch's biographies set their subjects, their motives and reversals, both closely within their times, and under a larger arch of destiny. There could hardly be greater reversals of fortune than Caesar's fall and the defeat of Brutus and Cassius. Shakespeare found in Plutarch this sense of tragic drama, shaping the lives of noble Greeks and Romans as if they were figures in Sophocles or Euripides. Consider the detail in Plutarch, taken up in Shakespeare, of the dramatic events of Caesar's progress to his death: the bad omen in the sacrifice, his wife's dream, the voices from the crowd (as if from a chorus) to beware, or to read the vital document, the final climactic and theatrical location at the base of Pompey's statue. More largely, Plutarch's awareness of heroic falling-short and the accompanying ironies, unseen by the protagonists, could be seen as Sophoclean.

T.J.B. Spencer, as we saw above, p. 47, produced evidence for the Elizabethans' idea of Rome being limited: no Elizabethan writer, he noted, dared to match Livy and Tacitus, and popular views of the Twelve Caesars were formed largely through the gossipy eyes of Suetonius (Spencer, 31; and see Barroll). By contrast, moral Plutarch brought (as we might put it) a Greek humanist's picture of Rome and its people, with republican sympathies. Spencer notes the bulk of that thick volume: 'We have to read 1,010 folio pages in the 1579 edition before we come to the death of Cleopatra' (Spencer, 33). True. But the evidence from the references down the ages is that people did not read Plutarch only for the history of Rome, but for the men and women so alive within his pages.

Thomas North, a son of the first baron North, was born about 1535. He was apparently a Cambridge man, who for an unknown reason was given the freedom of the city of Cambridge in 1568. Soon after his great translation of Plutarch was published in 1579, Leicester wrote to Burghley that 'He is a very honest gentleman and hath many good things in him which are drowned only by poverty.' About 1591 he was knighted. He was Justice of the Peace for Cambridge in 1592 and 1597. He is thought to have died about 1601. In 1557 he translated as *The Dial of Princes* Antonio de Guevara's *Libreo aureo*, an adaptation in Spanish of Marcus Aurelius: equally popular was his translation from Italian of a collection of oriental fables. All his translations went through several editions. The first edition of the *Lives* was printed in London by Thomas Vautrollier, who had just taken as apprentice Richard Field of Stratford-upon-Avon: Field himself (who in 1593 had been Shakespeare's first printer, with the admirable Quarto of *Venus and Adonis*) in 1595 printed the second edition of North's Plutarch. North's translation of the *Lives* has been widely praised for its expressive English: W.W. Skeat in 1875, introducing his *Shakespeare's Plutarch*, found parallels in its 'nervous idiomatic English' with the Authorised Version of the Bible. In 1929 Martha Hale Shackford noted, rightly, that 'its energy, its clarity and its essential sympathy' attracted readers who, through lives of saints, had been prepared to find biography essentially didactic (Shackford, 27). It had always been suggestive to Shakespeare. Probably almost ten years before *Julius Caesar*, he had shown familiarity with it in *1 Henry VI* 4.1. It belongs in the making of *A Midsummer Night's Dream* in 1595: the opening table of fifty lives begins with Theseus, and not far below are Demetrius and Lysander. In the right-hand column, the two walk-on characters who visit the oracle at Delphi in Act 3 of *The Winter's Tale*, Cleomenes and Dion, appear close to one another (and Shakespeare may have remembered that Plutarch himself spent the last thirty years of his life as a priest in the temple of Delphi).

Shakespeare and Plutarch

In writing *Julius Caesar*, Shakespeare used Plutarch freely, just as he used his main sources in the English history plays, where adjacent dramatic events can be seen to be taken from passages in Hall or Holinshed as many as a hundred pages apart. Using Plutarch's *Caesar*, Shakespeare made his drama from the point where Caesar goes to the Senate. The accumulated power and presence of Caesar in Rome come indirectly, by allusion to the war with Pompey and the campaign in Spain early in the first act. Events before the climax, like the Lupercalia, or Calphurnia's dream, are strongly dramatized. Yet the white heat of Shakespeare's drama, even from the Lupercalia, comes from four folio pages, 786–9, of *Caesar* in North's 1595 Plutarch. The play is also steeped in Plutarch's *Brutus*. As well as the great paradox of Brutus' character, detail after detail went straight from Plutarch to the play – Brutus being unable to keep his public control of himself when he was private at home at night, and Porcia perceiving perplexities; or Brutus before his death sitting with a few officers and friends by 'a great rock'. Shakespeare took from Plutarch Brutus' objection not to the loss of republican freedom, but to the act of crowning which would make Caesar, to Elizabethan eyes, irrevocably and irremovably the monarch (Kermode, 1103a). Caesar's preference for fat and long-haired men like Antony and Dolabella, and fearing pale and thin ones, meaning Brutus and Cassius, appears in *Brutus* exactly as it does also in *Caesar*. It appears again in *Antony*, from which Shakespeare noted that Antony's revels in various cities included theatricals. He took from this *Life* the rite of the Lupercal, and the mock-crowning after it; Antony's seizing of the moment with his funeral oration; the 'pricking scene' as the triumvirate, alone together, trade murders; and details of the deaths of Brutus and Cassius.

Plutarch's account of the celebrated storm and portents in 1.3 (which Horatio describes in *Hamlet*) does not include the lion that 'went surly by' (21) – it is the only detail not in Plutarch. Shakespeare alone chose to bring that creature in. Lions, however, feature earlier in *Brutus*, in North some pages before the portents. They are given as one of the injuries that Cassius felt that he had suffered under Caesar, 'for that he had taken away his lions from him' (see Appendix, p. 334). Shakespeare has made Cassius invent the malicious stories of Caesar's feebleness in fever and inability to swim (both the opposite of the truth): but he has ignored both Cassius' grievance over getting only the second praetorship, and Cassius' lions. Instead, by dramatic alchemy, he has transmuted the Megarian lions into one preoccupied animal born of the storm, to stand for dangerous creatures that may turn against their masters and, perhaps more suggestively, for the final tearing-in-pieces of the conspirators.

What reading North left on Shakespeare's creating mind makes him not so much a 'source' as an opportunity. Plutarch gives a passage to Cassius as Epicurean, telling Brutus of his opinion of spirits (see Appendix, p. 351); cf. Palmer, 'Error'). The tenor of these two hundred words is the very fallibility of the senses and of forming judgements, the difficulty of finding truth, which so pervades the play of *Julius Caesar*: Shakespeare does not use the passage as a 'source'; but Plutarch at that point may have given him a dramatic scheme which grew out of the mind of Cassius as Plutarch presented him.

Moreover, there is in these biographies something that we might call a plasticity of dramatic potential. For example, Plutarch on three separate occasions, in all three central *Lives*, called both Brutus and Cassius 'leane and whitely faced fellows'. Why did Shakespeare so pointedly make it apply to Cassius alone? Obvious answers are to defend his more 'noble' Brutus, and that at that point (1.2.193) only Cassius is on stage in Caesar's line of sight. In order to get a useful edge on the force of the changes from Plutarch, we should be considering further what it might have meant if Shakespeare had included Brutus in the description, as everything in Plutarch would encourage him to do. One effect would be staying closer to Plutarch's Caesar, who is much more intimately involved with Brutus; another, making Caesar refer to Brutus early in the play. As it is, in Shakespeare Caesar does not mention Brutus at all until just before he goes to the Senate, with the casual line 'What, Brutus, are you stirred so early too?' (2.2.110). Until moments before he stabs Caesar, Brutus relates directly and on stage only to Cassius, to Lucius, to Portia and to the six conspirators as a group. Examination of a combative change such as this brings sharply into sight the fact that the names 'Caesar' and 'Brutus' are first, strongly and at length, planted together by Cassius (1.2. 58–321), with the dramatic point that the relation between Caesar and Brutus *in the play* is at first wholly in Cassius' brain: it is then, in Brutus' soliloquy, developed in his own mind. Even some considerable time later, Artemidorus' attempt to bring the word 'Brutus' to Caesar fails, for Caesar never reads his paper (2.3.1, 5–11). Caesar does not know of Brutus as antagonist until a second or two before his last words, '*Et tu, Brute?*' (3.1.77). The implications of making Cassius alone 'lean and hungry', without Brutus, reverberate, and no doubt go on reverberating.

Out of the plotting of Caesar's death, so diffusely shown in Plutarch as to be only implied, over many widely-separated pages in all three *Lives* and in *Cicero* (see Appendix, pp. 325, 327, 334–41, 367–8), Shakespeare made one unforgettable scene of conspiracy. Act 2 opens with Brutus domestic, studious and doubtful, with the invented Lucius; he soliloquizes, before six men arrive; alone again, he is rebuked by Portia, and the seventh man, the sick Caius Ligarius, comes; his double exit with Brutus clinches the latter's active commitment. Three strokes in the making of that wholly-invented scene are noteworthy. First, by giving us a good view of all the conspirators quite some time before the action of assassination, Shakespeare ensures that that coming crucial moment will be forceful and clear: and he is able to have them disagreeing about two things that were important in related but opposite directions, the exclusion of Cicero and the exclusion of Antony, which determined the early deaths of all of them. Second, and surprisingly, we are not shown the precise moment when Cassius seduces Brutus to commit himself to his cause. At 2.1.99, Cassius says to Brutus 'Shall I entreat a word?' and, as the Folio has it, '*They whisper.*' For eleven lines they are private, while Caska explains the rising of the sun, 'the youthful season of the year . . . his fire . . . the Capitol . . .', with high symbolism. Brutus returns to shake each hand formally. Shakespeare wanted Cassius and Brutus to be especially close to each other within the group, as they were in 1.2 and will be again in 4.2: and as they are, in drawing aside. But Shakespeare does not tell us what they said. Brutus at the end of his soliloquy has committed himself privately. As he comes forward, he does it publicly. Not hearing what words Brutus used to Cassius when he said 'yes', which could have been a dramatic *tour de force*, allows a disconcerting, but very Shakespearean, indeterminacy. This bond between Brutus and Cassius is never pinned down for us. That makes a special, and uncomfortable, effect. Third, the most telling dramatic stroke is setting the scene in Brutus' house at night. There are nights about in Plutarch: the supernatural omens, the letters through the window, Calphurnia's dream, and Brutus' private agitation not letting him sleep. But Plutarch has Brutus joining the others on the morning of the assassination in Cassius' house, from which they all go to Pompey's Porch (see Appendix, pp. 338–9). Smooth dramatic articulation allows a sense of the passage of a short time: a day, a night, and then the day Caesar was killed (and see above, pp. 19–22). That night was full enough of omens, doubts, letters and wifely distresses: yet the knocking, the stealth of the muffled figures entering, the guilty furtiveness of their presences, the identifying of such night visitors, the dank and unwholesome night airs, all seem so convincingly rooted in history that it can be a jolt to realize that Shakespeare made it all up.

In Plutarch it is Brutus who demands the leading of the right wing at Philippi (see Appendix, p. 355). In Shakespeare it is Antony, in a sharp exchange with Octavius (5.1.16–20). The moment allows Shakespeare a chilling line from Octavius (more chillingly still, echoing the Quarrel scene) which sets in ten words the immediate future of Roman history, 'I do not cross you: but I will do so.' But that disagreement would not do for

Brutus disputing with Cassius: it is too external and practical for their history together. Plutarch says of the appointment, 'the which men thought was farre meeter for Cassius: both because he was the elder man, and also for that he had the better experience' (see Appendix, p. 355). After the force of Brutus' Shakespearean inner world, external conflict with Cassius in such a bustling public moment in the field would jar. The switch to Antony and Octavius, which feels so right, is an imaginative invention.

'O Julius Caesar, thou art mighty yet', says Brutus over the dead Cassius and Titinius (5.3.94). Brutus himself dies on 'Caesar, now be still' (5.5.50). Caesar's ghost is not so powerful in Plutarch as in Shakespeare: indeed, Plutarch does not say that the apparition was Caesar. Yet at the bottom of the last full page of *Caesar*, North has:

> But his great prosperitie and good fortune that favored him all his life time, did continue afterwards in the revenge of his death, pursuing the murderers both by sea and land, till they had not left a man more to be executed, of al them that were actors or counsellers in the conspiracy of his death.

> *(Caesar, 88)*

But the phrase 'his great prosperity and good fortune' does not seem strong enough for Shakespeare to take it as a unifying principle in the play, with Caesar as powerful in death as in life. There is a little evidence that Shakespeare could have known Plutarch in Greek. Plutarch wrote, ὁ μέντοι μέγας αὐτοῦ δαίμων (*ho mentoi megas autou daimon*) (Perrin, *Caesar*, 604), which can be translated 'certainly his great demon', the latter a word now carrying unfamiliar freight, by no means all negative. It is closer to Shakespeare's dramatic drive. The Latin version of Plutarch, with '*Magnus ille suus quo vivens usus erat Genius eius quoque defuncti necis ultor subsecutus est . . .*' (literally, 'That great Spirit of his, which he had enjoyed during his lifetime, attended him as the avenger of his murder after he was dead'), gave us 'Genius' at that point, perhaps illuminating Macbeth's 'My genius is rebuk'd; as, it is said, / Mark Antony's was by Caesar' (*Mac* 3.1.55–6; the Caesar there is Octavius). (See Fowler, 270; Thomson, 195–205.)

Suetonius, Appian, Sallust, Tacitus, Euripides

Julius Caesar and his death were so interesting to the ancient world that references are found widely. Shakespeare probably knew Suetonius' journalistic, anecdotal *De vita Caesarum*, about Julius Caesar and the twelve emperors from Augustus to Domitian, written some two centuries after Caesar's death, and making use of Plutarch. There was no published translation of Suetonius in English until Philemon Holland's *The History of Twelve Caesars* in 1606, though among others there were printed translations in French in 1541 and 1556, Italian in 1539 and Spanish in 1547 and 1596; the text was widely available in Latin and Greek. Bullough suggests that 'it contributed to the balanced view of the dictator' (5.14, 147–56; and see above, p. 47, and Spencer).

About the same time as Suetonius, Appian of Alexander, a lawyer in Rome, compiled narratives in Greek of the Roman wars. Part of what survives was translated into English by 'W.B.' as *The Civil Wars* in 1578. Shakespeare could have known the fine funeral oration which Appian gives to Antony: Appian calls Caesar's wife Calphurnia, as Shakespeare does, though in North's Plutarch she is generally Calpurnia. No other parallels are convincing. The translator's dedication demonstrates God's declaration of obedience to the sovereign, with tacit reference to Augustus' peaceful rule. A unique early title-page of the English translation ends, 'Foure Acts of the prophane Tragedie, whereof flowed our diuine Comoedie' (Appian, *History*, sig. Aii): Caesar's assassination led to the rule of Augustus, in which time Christ came. Shakespeare is not unaware of such Christian thinking in his Roman plays. Bullough (5.12, 144–6) suggests influence from

Tacitus' *Annals*, written AD 115–17, and translated in 1598. Tacitus prefers the peace under Augustus to republican freedom. Sallust, the friend of Caesar who later wrote histories in which he is glorifed, was another school-book, not Englished until Heywood's translation in 1608. Sallust's sketch of Caesar may have been in Shakespeare's mind (Bullough, 5.141). The emotions and shape of the Quarrel scene, it has been suggested, came to Shakespeare from Euripides' *Iphigenia in Aulis*, where Agamemnon and Menelaus quarrel and suddenly and convincingly make up. 'There is no other scene like it in classical drama, Greek or Roman' (Jones, *Origins*, 110). Shakespeare's quarrel scene was much imitated, starting with *The Maid's Tragedy* (see below, p. 101).

Renaissance texts

Pescetti's *Il Cesare* and other sixteenth-century Italian works on either side of the Caesar–Brutus argument have been mentioned above (p. 27). Only *Il Cesare* can be said to be parallel to Shakespeare; though interesting, the similarities cannot suggest a source (Bullough, 5.30–3, 174–94). In France, the short Latin play *Julius César* of 1544, by Montaigne's tutor, M.A. Muret, set a pattern of structure which was imitated later by Grévin and to some extent Garnier (Bullough, 5.26–30). We noted above, p. 10, Garnier's *Cornélie* translated into English by Thomas Kyd in 1594, an English play in tune with the new aristocratic Senecan ideas which Shakespeare is likely to have known (Bullough, 5.30; Rees, 'Caesar'). Of Richard Eedes' *Caesar interfectus*, a Latin drama following the new interest in Caesar, performed at Christ Church, Oxford, in 1581/2, only the Epilogue has survived: it shows some parallels with Brutus' manner of speech in his funeral oration (Bullough, 5.33, 194–5). Possibly significant is the long, anonymous drama *The Tragedy of Caesar and Pompey, or Caesar's Revenge* of 1595: based largely on Appian, the play's date, and influence, have been disputed. It resembles Shakespeare's play in some structural matters, and, for a Senecan drama, the unusual range of time covered (Bullough, 5.33–5, 196–211).

Even less likely as influence, though often mentioned, is the expanding, didactic, rhythmically jog-trot, medieval-flavoured *Mirror for Magistrates*, which first appeared in 1559 as a continuation of Lydgate's *Fall of Princes* of the 1430s, itself a version of Boccaccio's *De casibus virorum illiustrium* of the century before. The final version of the *Mirror* in 1587 included a 400-line poem on Julius Caesar, his place in a seemingly interminable moralizing poem about English history justified because he invaded Britain (Bullough, 5.24–5, 168–73). Shakespeare, like most modern readers, would take nothing from it.

The Bible

It is not far-fetched to consider Scripture, and especially the New Testament, as commonly in the minds of both playwright and audience in a way that is wholly alien to the late twentieth century. The seventy years before *Julius Caesar* was written saw the first printed translations of Scripture into English from the original languages, Greek and Hebrew, translations for which many people died violent deaths, including the first great translator, William Tyndale, in 1536. Tyndale translated the New Testament twice, in 1526 (of which only two copies survive) and in 1534, the basis of all English versions that followed. He had translated half the Old Testament from Hebrew before he was killed. All Tyndale's work went forward, the second half of the Old Testament being taken from the version (not from the Hebrew) by Miles Coverdale. English scholars in Geneva, escaping persecution under Queen Mary, prepared in 1560 a revision of the whole Bible which rapidly, under Elizabeth, became the Bible of the English people: it was revised in 1576 and 1599. Its rival, the conservative Bishops Bible of 1568, was the official base for King James's revisers producing the Authorised Version ('King James Bible') of 1611, though they reverted to a high proportion of the original Tyndale phrasing. In *Julius Caesar* it is possible to hear echoes of these versions up to 1599: and see Sohmer, *passim*.

The English Bible was a most powerful cultural as well as religious influence on the people of Britain in the second half of the century. To take one example only: both playwright and audience could know that the Philippi to which Julius Caesar is directed was the place, in Macedonia, of the first Christian church in Europe – to which Paul was especially called in about AD 52 from Troas, not far from Sardis, the location of the Quarrel scene. Acts, 16.9–12, recounts this, and tells that it is a Roman colony, as it had become after the Battle of Philippi in 42 BC. The church in Philippi received a letter from Paul. Understood biblically, even the geography of the Caesar story points to it being in the Providence of God, preparing for the coming of Christ. Shakespeare's age was not squeamish about seeing the Christian God using 'pagan' events. Verbal echoes from the Bible in *Julius Caesar* will be noted in the commentary.

JULIUS CAESAR AND THE CRITICS

Always popular on the stage, *Julius Caesar* was for a long time given a particularly bumpy ride by critics. One Stuart poet, Leonard Digges, in words not printed until 1640, eulogized, 'Oh how the Audience / Were ravish'd, with what wonder they went thence. . .' (Chambers, *Shakespeare*, 2.232). But the first true critics, neoclassical commentators such as Thomas Rymer and John Dennis at the end of the seventeenth century, expressed forcibly their dissatisfaction with the figure of Caesar in a play of that name, both in its historical inaccuracy and in Caesar's relegation to a supposed minor role. This view was long held. Hazlitt wrote in 1817 that the representation of Caesar does not answer 'to the portrait given of him in his Commentaries' (Hazlitt, *Characters*, 21). Since the titular hero was so inadequate, another hero was sought. Charles Gildon, writing his preface to the play in Nicholas Rowe's edition of Shakespeare of 1710 (7, 137) found it in Brutus, and the notion became standard for two hundred years. Even

Coleridge made Brutus central, in spite of his puzzlement about 'in what point he [Shakespeare] meant Brutus' character to appear' (Coleridge, 178). Swinburne can stand for many, then and since, with his Brutus, who is the 'very noblest figure of a typical and ideal republican in all the literature of the world' (Swinburne, 159).

Just as general disappointment was also widespread among the Augustans about the incorrectness of the language and the neglect of the admired unities of time, place and action, so making Brutus central destroyed any hope of finding any integral unity in the play itself, which became 'a set of loosely-connected episodes featuring inaccurate portraits of Roman historical figures, the chief of which is Brutus' (Ripley, 3), though the Quarrel and Forum scenes were treasured as jewels in the dirt. It was Samuel Johnson in his *Preface* of 1765 who first defended Shakespeare, finding in him a study of human kind, 'the real state of sublunary nature' (Johnson, 125). And Herman Ulrici in 1839 found a wholeness in *Julius Caesar* (355–6) which in turn led to a fresh examination by nineteenth-century critics of the characters, especially their relationship to that wholeness. Caesar himself began to be seen in some sort as a controlling figure. Rather than a bad dramatization of history, the play emerged later in the nineteenth century as ensemble drama, political and personal, an identity it has never since wholly lost.

In the earlier part of the twentieth century, it began to be recognized how revolutionary for the Elizabethans was Plutarch's sympathy for the republic. M.W. MacCallum's study in 1910 (MacCallum) began the new trend of appreciation of the play through re-examination of Plutarch, achieving a summit, and a significantly wider view, in T.J.B. Spencer's 1957 essay (Spencer). At the same time, analyses of language and imagery in the 1930s, by Wilson Knight in particular, opened the way for the critics' long love-affair with Shakespeare's ambiguity, a relationship that has lasted through most of the second half of the twentieth century. The new word for Shakespeare as historian was 'ambivalence', and it seemed to open up afresh even the old caskets of character-study. Through such insights into the language (and see above, pp. 38–45) three chief positions about the figure of Caesar in particular emerged: his near-royal greatness (Hunter); his ruthless tyranny (Wilson, Dover, in the New Cambridge); and his ambiguous unknowableness (Schanzer, *Problem*). Brutus, now almost universally secondary, became a mistaken man full of faults.

Shakespeare's Roman plays received some illumination in the 1980s, from American New Historicist critics, and from Cultural Materialist critics in Britain. The new debate, on both sides of the Atlantic, was about power, and the new key word was 'subversion'. New Historicists widened the aperture and colour-range of the pictures they were taking of the period, declaring, often by way of a bizarre contemporary anecdote, that Shakespeare's plays were embedded in the ideological structures.

For his opening anecdote, Richard Wilson, in his influential study dependent on Michel Foucault, ' "Is This a Holiday?": Shakespeare's Roman Carnival', rather stretched the significance of Thomas Platter's account of seeing *Julius Caesar* at the Globe. Wilson tried to show that the presentation of the repression of holiday-making Commoners in the first scene of *Julius Caesar* coincided with a new growth of official attacks on popular, and subversive, carnival, then mistakenly thought to be located in the new theatres. He argued that 'the first scene acted at the Globe can be interpreted . . . as a manoeuvre to legitimize the Shakespearean stage and dissociate it from the subversiveness of artisanal culture' (33). Legitimized subversion surrounded the new Globe theatre in Southwark, he declared, in the brothels and in the hospitals and prisons containing the sick and criminal, so that the area was 'to function as the unconscious of the capital of trade'(34). Antony touching Calphurnia at the Lupercal races, and Caesar theatrically pretending to give ' "the rabblement" the freedom that they shout for' were parts of Caesar's own appropriation of carnival ceremonies, making 'a model of authoritarian populism' (37). Wilson followed through the play a subtext of a many-sided carnival subversiveness, to the point where 'text and body fuse' at the will ('the favourite Shakespearean phallic pun') repeated 'twenty-seven times in thirty lines',[1] after which 'the incendiary brands of carnival are transformed into instruments of counterrevolution' (39). Brutus encapsulates the political programme:

> And let our hearts, as subtle masters do,
> Stir up their servants to an act of rage
> And after seem to chide 'em. This shall make
> Our purpose necessary and not envious . . .
>
> (2.1.174–7)

This is at first draught refreshing: but like other New Historicist critics, Wilson offered historical evidence that was scattered, to put it no higher,[2] and like them he was cavalier with mere facts.[3] These things do not encourage credibility. Interestingly, like other New Historicists, Wilson tried to have his argument both ways at once, so that Shakespeare as subversive is on the side of unbridled carnival licence with potential for great change, and simultaneously, by making the tribunes and senators centre-stage, is 're-presenting' conservative containment.

To sample the Cultural Materialists: Catherine Belsey observed that in *Julius Caesar* the staging of alternative political structures (something that was difficult in the English history plays), offered the possibility of some negotiation (Belsey, 101–3). John Drakakis found in the play 'the unmasking of the

---

1 A compelling statistic, but wrong. Antony first mentions the will at 3.2.129: from that line to the final use of the noun at 233, 104 lines later, it occurs seventeen times. Twenty-seven is achieved by adding general 'wills', and verbs 'will' and 'we'll' (improper even to Wilson's purpose), all occurring in over a hundred lines.

2 Revolts in 1381, 1450, 1517 and 1549; a French carnival in 1580; vague reference to 'the disorders of the 1590s'; documents in Chambers (*Stage*, 4.307, 340–1) relating to comments in 1592 and 1612; the English civil war in the following century.

3 To take one example of many, it is not true that St Thomas's hospital 'flanked' or was 'next door' (35) to the Globe: it was nearly half a mile away, beyond St Saviour's church (Southwark Cathedral). That tall tower, amid the light industries surrounding the theatres, and dominating the London skyline south of the Thames, close to the Globe, undermines Wilson's argument that, when *Julius Caesar* was written, Southwark was, in the dogma of Foucault, 'criminalized' (21).

politics of re-presentation *per se*' (Drakakis, 72). Alan Sinfield in an imagined production hoped to make the plebeians, and Cinna dreaming, the heart of the play 'to check the tendency to add Shakespearean authority to reactionary discourses' (Sinfield, 21).

Feminist critics over two decades have offered new ways of understanding power in women and men. Though *Julius Caesar* lacks a monarch, Caesar and the senators were found to be obvious symbols of patriarchy. Enriching studies came from Gayle Greene, whose work on rhetoric has already been noticed (p. 70, above), and from Coppélia Kahn, whose civilised *Roman Shakespeare* (1997), the first book-length feminist study of these plays, showed how far the Elizabethans' standard idea of Rome was identical to an ideology of maleness (Kahn). Her subtitle was *Warriors, Wounds, and Women*, and in her chapter on *Julius Caesar* she made strong points about male emulation, and especially about shifts in gender: for example, beginning from Portia's puzzling 'voluntary wound', she showed interestingly how ambiguous in gender even Caesar himself was made to be.

The most recent work on *Julius Caesar* has opened a seam of religious symbolism, recognizing that priesthood in various forms within the play, and a central sacrifice, would be recognised by the first spectators, not to mention parallels with biblical events, particularly the passion of Christ (Sohmer, *passim*). Studies of the Roman world as understood by the Elizabethans, in fact, have been the main stream of valuable criticism at the end of the twentieth century. Platt and Miola, both in 1983, and Miola's 'Tyrannicide' in 1985 (and see references in Kahn, 10–14, 21–2) have given criticism of *Julius Caesar* a new and more solid base.

JULIUS CAESAR IN PERFORMANCE

To reveal itself fully, the play requires an uncut text, fluid stagecraft, and actors of heroic power. And these three factors, sadly enough, have never conjoined.

(Ripley, 257)

John Ripley in 1980 felt his own ideal to have been unmet: yet performances follow fashion, decade by decade, and since its first performance in 1599 this play has had a notable place in the history of the stage. Productions make a mirror of the interests and styles (not only theatrical) of every period of English life since 1600, and of American life since 1770. The play is unusually open to contrasting emphases in performance; born no doubt of the long history of conflicting support for Caesar or Brutus, but extended by Shakespeare into rich ambivalences. *Julius Caesar* has been staged, among many other ways, with the Augustan ideals of *romanitas*; with antiquarian correctness on a lavish scale; with a 'realism' of unruly crowds; as a republican manifesto; as a supernatural experience; with the production values of the cinema or television. Performances have partly to be judged by the characters' own indications of theatrical business, uniquely in this theatre-conscious play – 'pluck Caska by the sleeve' (1.2.178). The actions of Popilius Lena and Trebonius a minute before the assassination are in the dialogue: 'Look how he makes to Caesar'; 'For look, he smiles'; 'Trebonius . . . draws Mark Antony out of the way' (3.1.18–26). Even closer to the moment of stabbing, two of the conspirators are instructed by their dialogue to prostrate themselves, but Brutus is only to kneel ('I kiss thy hand', 3.1.52; and see Pasternak, 27, 83).

Hints of London performances not long after 1599 were noticed above in discussion of the date (pp. 14–15). Court performances are recorded in 1611–12 at Whitehall, on 31 January in 1636 at St James's and on 13 November 1636 at the Cockpit (Chambers, *Shakespeare*, 2.343, 353). Details of contemporary staging are unknown, but evidence of some classical costuming, including breastplates and plumed helmets, can be found (Merchant, 71). Among the four commendatory verses prefixed to the First Folio in 1623 are lines by Leonard Digges. There he singles out for praise *Romeo and Juliet* and *Julius Caesar*, significantly showing that the latter must have lived on in performance, as, unlike *Romeo and Juliet*, it was not yet in print. Digges adopts the mode of not believing Shakespeare is dead till he hears 'a Scene more nobly take, / Than when thy half-Sword parlying *Romans* spake' (Chambers, *Shakespeare*, 2.232). That Brutus and Cassius are meant is spelled out in the longer poem by Digges, mentioned above, which appeared in the 1640 edition of Shakespeare's *Poems*:

> So have I seene, when Cesar would appeare,
> And on the Stage at half-sword parley were,
> *Brutus* and *Cassius*: Oh how the Audience,
> Were ravish'd, with what wonder they went thence . . .
>
> (Chambers, *Shakespeare*, 2.233)

The Quarrel scene (4.3) was the celebrated one: for two centuries, just as performances of *Much Ado About Nothing* meant, as Digges wrote in that poem, 'let but *Beatrice* / And *Benedicke* be seen', so *Julius Caesar* meant Brutus and Cassius quarrelling in a tent, partly the result, of course, of Brutus being the star actor's part. The popularity of this scene may have led others to imitate it, including Beaumont and Fletcher in *The Maid's Tragedy* of about 1610 (Beaumont & Fletcher, 2.51–9, 75–82, 86–91).

In 1675, in the Prologue to his tragedy *Aureng-Zebe*, Dryden wrote of himself as author:

> But spite of all his pride a secret shame,
> Invades his breast at Shakespear's *sacred name:*
> Aw'd when he hears his Godlike Romans *rage,*
> He, in a just despair, would quit the Stage.
>
> (Dryden, 507)

A picture emerges of a play that was popular before the closing of the theatres. After the Restoration, *Julius Caesar* was welcomed on stage for dealing with fashionable Roman matters. Audiences were drawn by the acting of the best actors, invariably as Brutus – though a Brutus not very recognizable, both in Dryden and Davenant's own version of 1719, and in others, having lost sentiments and phrases considered unsuitable for a tragic hero, and gained a more dignified death by his own hand, after a new speech added for the occasion. Dryden would have seen as Brutus the great Thomas Betterton, whom Pepys saw in *Hamlet*: 'Betterton did the Prince's part beyond imagination', and 'the best part, I believe, that ever man acted' (24 August 1661 and 30 August 1668: Pepys, vols 2 and 9). Betterton's Brutus had a grave nobility as a republican fighting a despotic tyrant, setting the norm for a long time to come. Colley Cibber wrote of his Brutus that 'with a settled dignity of contempt, like an unheeding rock he repelled upon himself the foam of Cassius' (Cibber, 1.104) – the Quarrel scene again.

Betterton played Brutus last in 1708. So popular was *Julius Caesar* that in the first half of the eighteenth century it was revived almost every year, with 150 London performances. From 1750 to 1780 there were twenty-three. Brutus continued to be central, played, in the tradition already set, as the noble patriot beyond stain. The text was adjusted to fit. Just as Pope in 1725 had given the lines at 3.1.105–7, 'Stoop, Romans, stoop, / And let us bathe our hands in Caesar's blood . . .', to Caska, as being unworthy of 'the gentle spirit of Brutus', so Bell's acting edition of 1774 omitted them altogether. The Proscription scene (4.1) had long been cut, and continued to be. Betterton's successors, Barton Booth and James Quin, both as Brutus, dominated what had become almost a chamber play, with no complexity of scenic effect, no verbal suggestiveness, and certainly no psychological depth. Instead the heart of the play was Brutus' moral authority against the evils of a (somewhat caricatured) Caesar, all expressed with high declamatory style. Sparseness of scenery, however, did allow some speed to the action, and use of an apron stage gave the actors the opportunity for subtlety as well as weight. A reasonably adequate Brutus, even with a weak supporting cast, continued to draw steady audiences.

That great and innovatory Shakespearean actor David Garrick did not stage *Julius Caesar*. He knew it well enough: his letters give free quotations from the play, and glimpses as well of some problems of staging it. He wrote in August 1758 to William Young that he could not lend him 'Shapes' (costumes) for it, partly because the ones they had were 'so scandalously bad & not fit to be Worn Ev'n by ye waiters', and partly because the new ones were needed in his own *Antony and Cleopatra*. 'I cannot well conceive how You can perform the Play [*Julius Caesar*] with less than *two* back Scenes & *Six* Wings.' His 'back Scenes' are:

> 23 feet wide & 16^{F}6^I high; & our Wing's are in proportion, consequently unfit for Your Place – but indeed We have no Useless Scenes – what we have, are in constant Wear, & take their turns as the different Plays & Entertainments are Exhibited . . .
>
> (Garrick, 284–5)

From 1780 to 1810 there were no performances of *Julius Caesar* in London. Francis Gentleman, a great admirer of the play, saw three reasons for decline of interest: it needed more good speakers than could be found; it lacked tender passions; and governments frowned on such strong republicanism (Bell's, 5, sig. A2^r).

On 29 February 1812, *Julius Caesar* arrived again to the fullest public favour. John Philip Kemble astonished London with his production at the Theatre Royal, Covent Garden, where it was revived each year until his retirement in 1817. He came to it at the end of his career, and brought long experience and revolutionary methods. On the big stage of that massive theatre, the large pictorial effects of the well-painted scenery, the figures grouped according to the classical sculptural principles learned from Sir Joshua Reynolds, and the historically 'accurate' costumes were a grand scheme in which the words, though still grandly spoken, were now only a part. Kemble's promptbooks show that Caesar's entry at the opening of the second scene had '*Three Great Shouts, Drums and Trumpets*' and no fewer than seventy-one people (the Garrick Club promptbook has 106) processing on in classical costume, including '*4 Priests . . . 6 Senators.*

Go up to Priests . . . *6 Virgins* . . . *4 Matrons* . . . *2 Golden Eagles*
. . .' (Kemble, 1812, 7). That was all very spectacular; but everyone had to be got off again after twenty-four lines. Over a quarter of the (already short) play was cut, and minor characters were
either absorbed into Trebonius, Metellus and Caska, or simply
omitted. This made adequate acting possible in every part, and
allowed what was felt to be a proper balance in the supporters of
Brutus and Antony. The play was simplified for the sake of spectacle – which must have been sensational. Most of the thirteen
sets would have drawn applause. The play opened with Caska
and Trebonius briefly addressing the even briefer, but artistically
arranged, artisans. The second scene was *Rome. 'A publick Place'*,
which had white marble buildings, a huge triumphal arch, a fire
burning on the Soothsayer's altar, and, again, sculptural groupings. Presently at 3.2, *'Rome. The Capitol . . . The Senate sitting'*
was *'discovered'*, with over fifty figures disposed about the deep
set. To cover the setting of the equally deep Forum scene, jug-
gling lines and heavy cutting allowed a ten-line street scene down
front: the promptbook has *'Take time here'* (Kemble, 1812, 43).
(In 3.3 Cinna the poet, though brought on, simply rushed off,
without speaking, his life spared at every performance, as it was
to be until 1937 in New York.) The four scenes of the fifth act
showed different plains and forests. Kemble's sister, Sarah
Siddons, played Portia: the principals were impressive. Kemble
himself played Brutus, but not to universal praise. Though as *The
Times* reported on 2 March 1812 he was graceful and elegant in
movement eminently suited to the dignity of a Roman senator,
and *Bell's Weekly Messenger* for 8 March 1812 praised Brutus'
'fine poetical conception of a virtuous patriot', both Leigh Hunt
and William Hazlitt (379) found him wooden and lacking suggestion of inward struggle. Hunt wrote in *The Examiner* (5 April
1812)that 'this artificial actor does so dole out his words, and so
drop his syllables one by one upon the ear, as if he were measur-
ing out laudanum for us'. Sir Walter Scott, also in *Bell's Weekly
Messenger*, 8 March 1812, found in Kemble warm affection for

Portia in the Orchard scene, and hot temper in the Quarrel scene, even though 'his stoic mien, arising out of rules of thought and conduct long since adopted, draws a veil over both feelings'. Kemble, apparently aware of weakness, so organized his own ten entries that only one was without music and noise (Rostron, 32). Yet Kemble's promptbooks, with their pages of handwritten notes in Latin and Greek, and their sense of the historic scale of the natures of the men and women in the story being told, record the new direction he gave to the play, even towards a ravishing beauty of scene, after a generation of neglect. Throughout the nineteenth century, few British stagings were not inspired by this production, and his became the standard acting text.

Young America of the Revolution took the libertarian passions of *Julius Caesar* to its soul (and commonplace books). The play was from the beginning of the United States a serious part of North American life for students, politicians, orators and all theatre people: it has been so ever since. The first American production was on 1 June 1770 in Philadelphia, where the advertisement noted 'The noble struggles for liberty by that renowned patriot, Marcus Brutus'. The play was only produced six more times before 1802, but it was read for 'the growing spirit of liberty it breathes [and its] elegant and sublime language' (Ripley, 100). Throughout the nineteenth century, performances led by actors of commanding presence as Brutus (Lewis Hallam, John Henry, Thomas Cooper, the Booths, William Augustus Conway, Edwin Forrest, Laurence Barrett and others) were noted for their dignity, virility and orotundity: the republican ideal was high – indeed, the success of the new nation depended on it. Kemble's influence helped to keep the story strong, simple, relevant and serious.

In London, W.C. Macready, acting in *Julius Caesar* as Cassius or Brutus from the ages of 23 to 58, in middle age produced it at Covent Garden in 1838–9, and Drury Lane in 1843. Very much the actor-manager as star, Macready kept to Kemble's grand vision and at the same time widened its eyes, as it were, so that the people of Rome appeared as living beings rather than as stat-ues – a development which extended to the principals, now allowed to be richer characters. The Cassius to Macready's Brutus was Samuel Phelps, who gave the part a wider spectrum of feeling, as did James Anderson with Antony. When Phelps produced the play himself at the smaller Sadler's Wells between 1846 and 1862, he continued the process.

A force for European change came from Germany. In the 1870s and 1880s, Georg II, ruler of the small German duchy of Saxe-Meiningen, directed his own company on principles which included absolute historical accuracy in the scenic effects and very detailed ensemble work, excluding dominant roles. The Duke toured Europe with his *Julius Caesar*: London saw it in May 1881 at Drury Lane, the first of sixteen performances, spo-ken in German. Critics and public were quite impressed by the scenery and costumes, though such antiquarianism and control of large forces was nothing new (Booth, 13, 18). There was dis-may at the submersion of star roles in the sea of choreography. The detailed crowd-control in the first scene, with each part indi-vidually formed, was familiar, but in the Forum scene Antony's oration was electric. Ludwig Barnay's complex work as Antony, interacting as he fought word-by-word to get the attention of the excited and hostile mob, and then to direct it, brought, ironically, universal praise to this star. The balance of attention was seen to shift from Brutus, and to the Forum scene. The Meininger Company were, again ironically, bringing to a focus develop-ments that had been for some time strong on the English stage: a quarter of a century before, the Duke had found his ideas in a production of *Richard II* by Macready's successor, Charles Kean (Booth, 18). What did impress the English critics was the con-sistency of standard achievable 'by long and patient preparation, quality ensemble work, and generous financing' (Booth, 19). The Meininger Company's crowd scenes, with their hundreds of well-paid and, it seems, over-drilled supernumeraries (recruited from German expatriates living in London), as well as the core

13 Ludwig Barnay as Antony in the Forum scene, 3.1, in the German-
   language production by the Saxe-Meiningen Company, Drury Lane,
   May 1881

company of eighty, showed what was about to happen. In
London it was to become possible, for the first time since
Shakespeare's lifetime, to treat the play as a whole rather than a
set of loosely-connected favourite moments; and to avoid mak-
ing everything after the Forum scene an anticlimax, as the
Meiningers had done.

14 Herbert Beerbohm Tree as Antony in the Forum scene, 3.1, in his production at Her Majesty's Theatre, 22 January 1898

In New York in 1871, Edwin Booth directed the play as a descendant of Kemble, with lavish production values and strong acting. His Brutus had a new breadth of human sympathies; he was a 'poetic idealist ... look[ing] towards a new century' (Ripley, 145). There was high praise for Laurence Barrett's Cassius with its well-aimed waspish sting. Booth later played Cassius, and then Antony.

The London production that gathered up the English nineteenth-century traditions and defined *Julius Caesar* for two decades was Herbert Beerbohm Tree's 'exercise in spectacular realism' which opened at Her Majesty's Theatre on 22 January 1898. The curtain went up to show at some length the daily life of Rome before even the tribunes entered (see Ripley, 155–7). The production offered a magnificence suitable for heroism of several kinds. Brutus and Cassius were somewhat less dominant; Caesar was strong. The drama newly belonged to Antony (Tree himself): the play was heavily cut (well beyond excluding many minor characters and, as always, 4.1) and rearranged so that each of the three main movements ended with a tableau curtain dominated by Antony. Tree had privately noted, 'For the soldier, Brutus; for the actor, Cassius; for the public, Antony' (Bingham, 86). The immense sets and lavish costumes were designed by Sir Lawrence Alma-Tadema, that member of the Royal Academy famous for classical paintings full of sensual luxury. This *Julius Caesar* had over a hundred performances on its first appearance, and many more up to 1913. The realism of detail in the spectacle was much admired. George Bernard Shaw lamented some poor acting and bad orchestral writing, but chiefly the loss of 'the Shakespearean music' throughout the speaking of the verse, a loss noted by other critics. Though, Shaw wrote in the *Saturday Review*, 29 January 1890, 'the real hero of the revival is Mr Alma Tadema', want of discipline and thought spoils effects: 'in Brutus' house the door is on the left: the knocks on it come from the right ... After a battle ... [the Roman soldiers] come back carrying their javelins still undisturbed in their rug-straps, in perfect trim for a walk-out with the nursery-maids of Philippi' (Shaw, 141). The convention of the grand spectacle persisted: Granville-Barker individualized a crowd of over three hundred in 1911: his promptbook notes read 'X186 groans heavily and moves upstage, where he joins a doleful group consisting of Ys 48–54 and Zs 201–10 . . .' (Hesketh Pearson, quoted in Berry, *Anecdotes*, 123).

Between 1890 and 1930, Frank Benson founded a style at the Shakespeare Memorial Theatre at Stratford-upon-Avon which, with a text differently, but still severely, cut, linked the familiar classical declamation and some neo-Elizabethan traditions, like limited scenery. A new development was presenting a Caesar in some decline but powerful enough to be a serious challenge. Also at Stratford, Benson's successor William Bridges-Adams, a director rather than an actor-manager, between 1919 and 1934 made the single most significant change for two hundred and fifty years: he gave Shakespeare's text with no rewriting and virtually without cuts, even 4.1 being restored. He introduced 'Elizabethan' methods of using the forestage almost exclusively, and simplifying sets to allow pace of action and speech – indeed, speeding up everything to get in the whole text in the usual time. Next revived at Stratford after the war, in 1950, by Anthony Quayle and Michael Langham, *Julius Caesar* had momentum, richness of characterization, and Shakespeare's impartial politics: the Cassius was John Gielgud, who brought to the part a richly complex characterization, including great energy.

Meanwhile, in New York, dominating – even swamping – later productions of *Julius Caesar* in the American theatre were the 157 performances (the longest run on record) of a distant version of the play, subtitled *Death of a Dictator*, at the Mercury Theatre, New York, from 6 November 1937, under Orson Welles. Severely pared down to incidents concentrating on Caesar, Brutus and the mob, the play could hardly be called Shakespeare's, though a central experience was the lynching of Cinna the poet (3.3), restored after a centuries-long absence. With the tone harsh, the action fast

15 The conspirators, in the Royal Shakespeare Company's production at the
    Shakespeare Memorial Theatre, Stratford-upon-Avon, 1936

and shocking, and using cinematic effects, Welles's point was the
catastrophic failure of the liberal, faced with the ruthless force of
Fascism. Caesar was Mussolini and some settings were Nazi ral-
lies. True, the impact in the moment was reported as stunning.
True, Caesar was now central, an emphasis becoming common on
both sides of the Atlantic. But Shakespeare's play, in this and
other similar mangled versions, had gone from sight. Heroic
tragedy it was not. A contemporary noted that the conspirators
looked like 'a committee from a taxi-drivers' union' (*New York
Daily News*, 13 Nov. 1937.).

Happily, in the second half of the twentieth century there have
been far too many productions of *Julius Caesar* all over the world
to be recorded here. Again happily, to the standard set by Quayle
and Langham in 1950, the norm has been a full text. But productions in the last decades of the century have sometimes ranged
away from Rome to try to make modern political points. Exciting

111

16 Fascist salutes greet Joseph Holland as Caesar in Orson Welles's version at
the Mercury Theatre, New York, 6 December 1937

as the resulting theatre might be in some moments, to do that is to misunderstand Shakespeare, who responded to that deep interest in the problematic workings of human nature in men and women who had shaped history that he found in Plutarch. The latter did not, as Shakespeare consummately did not, level out men and women as taking political sides. To mention only a few examples, the play as anti-Fascist was set in Latin America at Minneapolis in 1969, at Stratford, Connecticut, in 1979, at Belfast in 1981 and at Oregon in 1982. Audiences in Miami in 1986 were brought to their feet by the spectacle of the assassins bathing their hands in the blood of Caesar as Fidel Castro. In 1996 at Houston, Caesar's body lay in state and the mob threw books on to a bonfire. As Michael Billington wrote in *The Guardian* (10 April 1987), of Terry Hands's 1987 production at the Royal Shakespeare Company, 'if Caesar is so nakedly Fascist, does it not detract from Brutus' moral qualms about his murder?'

17　Orson Welles as Brutus and Muriel Brassler as Portia in his version at the
　　Mercury Theatre, New York, 6 December 1937

An anonymous reviewer in the *Yorkshire Post* on the same day found 'the sort of Brutus who could have been persuaded by an inter-departmental memo'. Nicholas de Jongh in the (London) *Evening Standard*, 5 August 1993, wrote of David Thacker's modern-dress promenade production at The Other Place, the RSC's studio theatre at Stratford, that it 'brought Rome's civil war as close and shocking as the latest television pictures from Bosnia'. At the Barons Court Theatre, London, in March 1993, Caesar was played by a woman, and the symbolized political assassination was of Margaret Thatcher.

A contrary movement, still with almost a full text, was towards

18 *Et tu, Brute?*: John Gielgud as Caesar receiving the final wound from Brutus (Brian Cox), in John Schlesinger's National Theatre production, London 1977

attempts at an 'original', that is Elizabethan, style, notably with mixed results at Stratford, Ontario, in 1955. Harley Granville-Barker had noted in 1927 that 'A Caesar in doublet and hose may offend and will undoubtedly distract us' (Granville-Barker, 127). Similarly, classical costumes, as John Gielgud wrote, though 'becoming and graceful to players of fine physique, can be ridiculous and hampering to men who are too short, too tall, too thin or too fat. There is always a danger of the effect of a lot of gentlemen sitting on marble benches in a Turkish bath' (Gielgud, *Stage*, 48). An 'Elizabethan' student production by the Marlowe Society in Cambridge in 1952 under the very young John Barton, hoping to reproduce Shakespeare's Globe, went the whole hog and included supposed 1599 pronunciation, to strange effect: that, near the Capitol, Caska met a 'lee-on', and that Caesar was warned to beware the 'Ades of March', were two of the more comprehensible moments.

The most important changes have been in the bringing-forward of principals other than Brutus and Cassius; the recognition, for example, that the play is called *Julius Caesar* and that Caesar himself has to be an important dramatic force, not to be lost in bombast and self-delusion. (As long before as 1916, Frank Benson had played Caesar notably, and at Drury Lane had been knighted on stage by George V.) Glen Byam Shaw's production at Stratford-upon-Avon in 1957 presented Caesar as a great leader, the source of all authority, undiminished by his weaknesses. Under John Schlesinger at the National Theatre in London in 1977, John Gielgud's Caesar had such great natural authority that his spirit was obviously unconquerable from the start: Bernard Levin wrote of his Ghost that 'his "Ay", at Philippi hovered in the air like some infinitely shimmering echo' (Gielgud, *Shakespeare*, 28). John Barton's 1968 RSC production had a Caesar in Brewster Mason who in hauteur and grandeur recalled General de Gaulle (Speaight, 373): trying to kill him, the conspirators, shaking and shocked, slumped to the ground. Trevor Nunn in 1972 at Stratford-upon-Avon, in a production still thought the best in recent decades, made Caesar dominate through a colossal statue, always present. Nunn said that the play has to suggest that 'Caesar is dangerous . . . fast becoming a military dictator . . . he has total control of the army . . . he can't be *voted* out' (rather than, as Ralph Berry put to him, Caesar as usually 'a sort of company chairman who's a little bit over the top, and the Board are getting restive about him': Berry, 65). As Sally Beauman pointed out, giving Caesar's entourage Fascistic accoutrements makes sledge-hammer effects which overwhelm 'the hidden nuances of the text' (Beauman, 317). The 1972 Nunn production was part of the RSC's sequence of Shakespeare's Roman plays, and a natural result was the strengthening not only of Antony, but of Octavius – the latter, with 4.1 now commonly restored, first having had full weight in Alan Badel's portrayal in the Quayle–Langham 1950 production. Nunn's Brutus was John Wood, whose performance won high praise for his quality of interior life and thoughtfulness, 'the ultimate and self-deceiving liberal' (Michael Billington, *The Guardian*, 31 March 1983; and see Cook, 90–1; David, 139–63). Elsewhere, Billington found him 'the best indictment of smug and boneless liberalism' (Beauman, 316), with no power to oppose Mark Dignam's unstoppable Fascist Caesar, who, wrote Benedict Nightingale in the *New Statesman* (12 May 1972), received Brutus' 'spinsterish jab at the throat with the amazement of an eagle set on by a white-bellied seed-snipe . . . he quite possibly dies of incomprehension'. At the other extreme, Joseph O'Connor's Caesar in Ron Daniels's 1983 production was described by Michael Billington as seeming to be 'a harmless old party with a baby-doll wife . . . and a certain fondness for processional entries: hardly grounds for assassination' (*Guardian*, 31 March 1983).

Even the Soothsayer had his longer day under Ron Daniels in 1983, when the white-bearded Griffiths Jones witnessed everything that happened in the play – in contrast to a persistent stage convention, with no foundation, that the Soothsayer is blind. Portia has now been allowed a real relationship with Brutus,

19 The conspirators close in on Caesar (Robert Stephens) in the 1991 Royal
Shakespeare Company production, Stratford-upon-Avon

however troubled, and tends to reveal her wound fully: Brutus'
willingness to listen to Portia has itself become a mark
of her power. Conversely, the crowds, for so long so swirlingly
present, disappeared entirely from John Wood's production
at Stratford, Ontario, in 1978, and from Terry Hands's at
Stratford-upon-Avon in 1987, replaced by offstage noises,
to understandable critical disapproval. Absent from many
eighteenth-century and later productions, the essential sense of
mysteries, of supernatural events and references in the play, was
brought to control the whole approach by Jonathan Miller in
1972, where the Oxford and Cambridge Company presented a
terrifying dream-world, an idea partly taken over by Martin
Cobin at the 1981 Colorado Shakespeare Festival. Ron Daniels
at Stratford-upon-Avon in 1983 used the beliefs in omens and
fate as part of a colourful palette of reference, attempting a picture of humanity's smallness.

In the second half of the twentieth century, more fluid stagecraft, a new demotic acting style and the loss of the actor-as-star

have tended to rob the play of its tragic dimension, and a nine-teenth-century (and Stuart) sense of awe. In his review of the RSC production that had just opened, Robert Gore-Langton in the *Daily Telegraph* (25 May 1996) wrote of 'the sight of violence in sandals, not the jarring tragedy of individuals clashing with their destinies'. '*Julius Caesar*'s stage history in this [the twentieth] century is the tale of an heroic play adrift in an anti-heroic age', wrote John Ripley in 1980 (214). He may be right, though there have been some productions closer to that ideal than he may allow. Perhaps the Folio text, in all its austere splendour, still towers above us. Yet performances, no doubt flawed like all their predecessors, can still, even if only with 'bare boards and a passion', move a Shakespeare audience.

Shakespeare on screen presents different opportunities. The newer resources have been used to illuminating effect. Joseph L. Mankiewicz's 1953 Hollywood film, though in black-and-white, stays in the mind for two things: first, the largeness of his vision – big spaces, big crowds (a Forum scene crowd of twelve hun-dred), big gestures, big principals: and second, John Gielgud's tall, neurotic Cassius, unsmiling throughout, given to intense outbursts, compulsively watchable, even to the point of – not intentionally – stealing the film. James Mason's Brutus has great integrity, slow and thoughtful to the point of naïvety. Marlon Brando's very physical Antony grows magnificently in his sense of his power. Caesar (Lewis Calhern) is large in stature but humanly weak. What film can do is done very well, in the elabor-ation of images to make points – as, for instance, Antony alone at the end of 4.1, looking over Rome and stretching to embrace his new empire.

On the small screen, the BBC / Time Life version in 1978 has not been bettered. Though Roman enough in setting and man-ners, the values are of human drama rather than the engagement of colossi. Richard Pasco's Brutus has the authority to make one believe that all is as he planned it, but at the same time subtly con-veying the inner disturbance that will before long destroy him as well as Caesar. The moments of assassination, and of the ritual smearing of blood, are horrific in sudden realizations in Charles Gray's Caesar from half-second to half-second as the daggers smite him. Here is a fine and faithful interpretation, particularly well spoken.

Casting

Julius Caesar has forty speaking parts. This is roughly the same as *Antony and Cleopatra*. The English history plays tend to have more, most tragedies considerably fewer, and the comedies fewer still. The number of actors needed for the crowd scenes, 1.1 and 3.2, and for soldiers on each side in Act 5, obviously cannot be fixed. Thomas Platter in September 1599 counted about fifteen actors. Since we know that a company of about ten, with two or three boys, and hired men, could comfortably stage most Elizabethan plays, his figure is not disturbing. T.J. King calculated that in *Julius Caesar*:

> Nine actors can play fourteen principal and three minor male roles; three boys play two principal female roles and Lucius, a boy. These twelve actors speak 91% of the lines. Eleven men can play twenty-seven small speaking parts and thirteen mutes.
>
> (King, 87)

Since the citizens, or plebeians, do not return after 3.3, they are available as soldiers in Act 5. Flavius and Murellus are in the entry at 1.2, but otherwise vanish, as do, after 3.1, Caska, Decius, Cinna, the Soothsayer, Trebonius, Metellus Cimber and Popilius Lena. Of the boys' parts, Calphurnia and Portia have gone by the end of Act 2. Practically, there is no reason why 'Caska' cannot reappear as Messala from 4.3 on, nor 'Decius' as Octavius from 4.1, nor 'Murellus' as First Plebeian and Lucilius, nor 'Flavius' as Second Plebeian and Titinius (for such possible doubling, see King, Table 56). Platter's fifteen (and there could have been more) is more than King calculates, and the difference may be revealing. Plays and companies were cut to a minimum for touring, it is true, and to that extent counting the smallest number needed to stage a play efficiently has value. Yet the company performing the *Julius Caesar* that Platter saw, far from touring, was in its new permanent home, very probably to open their richly-appointed new Globe theatre. Penny-pinching would not be in the programme: some lavishness would. We do not know what followed *Julius Caesar* at the Globe for the next afternoon performance: the enlarged *Henry V* as newly fitted up for the Globe, perhaps, or even on successive days the *Henry IV* plays – Falstaff was hugely popular – followed by *Henry V*. There would have been no reason to exhaust the principal players by too-heavy doubling.

We cannot unfortunately put particular actors in Shakespeare's company, the Lord Chamberlain's Men, into particular parts. The great Richard Burbage, second only to William Shakespeare in Folio's opening list of twenty-six actors, and creator of Hamlet, King Lear and Othello, had been with the company for some five years: we may assume he played Brutus, at 720 lines a part about as long as King Lear's at 753 lines (but both half the length of Hamlet's 1,507 lines).

Visiting the new and finely-decorated Globe, with its projecting open stage and three thousand spectators in tiers almost all round, would have been an occasion to relish, even, as it was not roofed-in, under leaden skies and rain. The play was the thing. The atmosphere would have been even more charged than, say, at a modern soccer match. The action, unhindered by changes of scenery, would have been fast; Caesar's entry in procession at 1.2, though impressive from the central upstage doors, would take little time – he would sweep on and launch into his part. Brutus soliloquizing down front at the start of 2.1 would have stood alone almost entirely surrounded by spectators: he would have been able to play on them as intimately as Antony later did with the rabble. In other words, whoever the actors in *Julius Caesar* were, their stage presence must have been remarkable. It was for that theatrical effect of magnificently delivered and memorable verse, in acoustic perfection, that the Globe was designed.

THE TEXT

The origins of the printed text

Julius Caesar comes to us from a single printed text, one of the thirty-six plays assembled by Shakespeare's fellow-actors after his death in 1616, and printed by the Jaggards in 1623 in the large volume that we call the First Folio. The title-page calls it *Mr. William Shakespeares Comedies, Histories, and Tragedies. Published according to the True Original Copies* (the order as well as the content is still the basis for most of our complete Shakespeares). *Julius Caesar* is listed in the 'Catalogue' (table of contents) at the front of the book as the fifth tragedy, but *The Tragedy of Troilus and Cressida* is not in that list, and *Julius Caesar* is in fact the sixth in the volume, starting a run of mature tragedies which goes on with *Macbeth*, *Hamlet*, *King Lear*, *Othello* and *Antony and Cleopatra*.

The complete plays of Shakespeare come to a total of not far short of a million words. Printing a big book was easily within the capabilities of a good Jacobean printing house, as William and Isaac Jaggard's was (Isaac, William's son, took over when his father, already blind, died in 1623). To save bulk, and paper, the plays were printed in two columns per page, as were many large books of the time; for example, contemporary bibles, and huge undertakings like Foxe's *Acts and Monuments*. Unlike them, however, Shakespeare's plays are mostly in verse. This could lead to difficulties when a line was too long for the width available, a restriction made worse when the space was narrower still because a speaker's name (even though generally abbreviated) began the line and was already set in from the left. The compositors had a number of solutions for this: one of them was to set the long line as two short lines, occasionally making a problem for modern editors which will be discussed presently. Tightness of space at the foot of a right-hand column on a page also produced difficulties for the compositors. A play in Folio was not set and printed page-after-page from beginning to end, but in groups of twelve pages, working from the inner pages of each twelve outwards.[1] This meant that the calculation of how much copy would fit each page, known as 'casting off', had to be exact. Finding that he had too little copy left to fit the space was not too serious for a compositor, as he could expand his text either by using more white spaces, or by creating two shorter lines out of one, as at 1.2.58, where Folio has:

> That you might see your shadow:
> I have heard,

Having too much could lead to jamming the lines together by missing out white spaces, printing verse as prose or, desperately, leaving something out. Happily, the Folio text of *Julius Caesar* does not suffer from any of these deformities.

The Second, Third and Fourth Folios of 1632, 1663 and 1685 have no authority, as they follow the First Folio, and each other, with occasional very slight corrections and their own new small errors. Once or twice the Second Folio can be seen to correct a minor point, as in the stage direction at 1.2.24.1, where First Folio's '*Manet*' will not do for two people, Brutus and Cassius, remaining, and Second Folio corrects to the plural, '*Manent*'. There are no contemporary Quartos, and the later seventeenth-century Quartos, all after 1684, derive from the First Folio.

Most of the problems for an editor come from the fact that, apart from some questionable sheets from what he may have contributed to *The Play of Sir Thomas More*, none of Shakespeare's plays or poems has survived in his own handwriting. What we

---

1 That is, by formes. A folio forme consisted of two pages of type locked into a frame (chase) for printing on one side of a large sheet. Another forme was used for the other side of the sheet, its pages arranged so as to print back-to-back as appropriate. The compositor began with the innermost pages, six and seven, progressing through five and eight (on the other forme) until he reached one and twelve. Once printed, the double-sided sheets were folded so that the pages, one inside the other, were in the correct order for sewing together.

know as 'Shakespeare' comes entirely from texts printed by other people, with no surviving manuscripts to check against. Indeed, the compilers of the Folio, Shakespeare's friends and fellow-actors John Heminges and Henry Condell, in their interesting preface '*To the great Variety of Readers*', lament that he did not live 'to have set forth, and overseen his own writings'. In that carefully-made First Folio, however, *Julius Caesar* is a strikingly well-printed play. Even so it is impossible to be certain how what Shakespeare wrote in the middle of 1599 became the printed *Julius Caesar* in 1623. What sheets of paper did the compositor in Jaggard's printing house, setting the play in type, have in front of him? How may we be sure that what was set almost a quarter of a century later was what Shakespeare wrote?

The compositor could have been following two documents: (a) Shakespeare's original manuscript from the summer of 1599, probably untidy with crossings-out, later ideas put in, things written hastily and different spellings of the same word. Such original sheets have been known for some time by the inelegant phrase 'foul papers', picking up the playwright Robert Daborne's words 'foule sheet' in a letter of 1613, contrasted with a page written out fair (Greg, 92–3, n. 3). (b) A copy of such original 'foul papers' (or even possibly the 'foul papers' themselves) tidied up to control performances, typically with notes organizing entrances, properties and effects, and perhaps containing the author's second thoughts (and possibly marks of censorship, as all plays had to be submitted to the Master of the Revels to make sure they were politically harmless). This document is the promptbook. It was precious to the company as its full record of a play, and carefully guarded: it was less likely to be given to a printer.[1] (Other offshoots of the original that we know were made, like the actors' parts written out with cues, or occasionally

---

1   A third possibility is a fair copy of the original specially made for the printer. This we know happened with five plays in Shakespeare's Folio (see Jackson, 170–1) including the first, *The Tempest*, which gives the appearance as it is printed of having been prepared not for the theatre but for readers, appropriately beginning a volume to be bought and read. *Julius Caesar* shows none of the marks of such special preparation.

a schematic 'plot' of the sequence of scenes and some technicalities of the staging, would not be useful in setting the whole play.)

In asking what the printer used, we need to be clear what it is we are looking for. A work of art is not a legal document. In the latter, whether handwritten or printed, every mark on the page has to be once and for all precise. Literature is usually looser. A poem by Coleridge, for example, appears differently in print in different places: so does a novel by Virginia Woolf. A play-script is even further from legal sheets. There was very probably no definitive text of *Julius Caesar* in 1599. A play is to be staged and acted: probably two dozen people were involved in making *Julius Caesar* happen. Some of Shakespeare's original directions, and even lines, would no doubt have been changed in the practical work of putting the play on the stage, through rehearsals and successive performances – it is one of the pleasures of theatre as opposed to cinema that the play is different every time. Shakespeare was an actor deeply engaged in the life of his company, and would be part of the process.

Praising his fluency, Heminges and Condell wrote in their preface that Shakespeare's 'mind and hand went together ... what he thought, he uttered with that easiness, that we have scarce received from him a blot in his papers' – suggesting that his 'foul papers' could be good enough to make a promptbook. That may have happened with some plays in the Folio. Perhaps for others he wrote out fair some overwritten sheets that were especially hard to read. No doubt sometimes he would have so worked on all his original that there would have to have been a complete fair copy, made either by Shakespeare himself, or by a scribe: in that case Shakespeare would have overseen it, as he would have been involved in rehearsals and performances.

The second question above may already be reasonably answered. What Shakespeare wrote was important to the company and, since two of his responsible colleagues were assembling the texts for the printer, what they presented would have had to be as reasonably accurate as any play-script is. After all, their preface is addressed to that large constituency, 'the great variety of readers' of their Shakespeare, bidding them 'read him, therefore, and again and again': they were preparing texts partly for 'the most able', some of whom would have remembered the plays accurately and in detail from performance. We live at a time when what is visual is so dominant that we have to make an effort to understand the intense pleasure that Shakespeare's contemporaries could find in spoken words, remembered even if heard only once.

We can now attend again to the first question. What kind of 'true, original copy' (as the Folio title-page has it) were the compositors most likely to have been following? The unusually orderly text of *Julius Caesar* suggests that it came from a fair copy. Shakespeare, like any other writer, changed his mind as he wrote, and his 'foul papers' would be full of the inconsistencies found in other plays set up from such a manuscript – names changed in the course of the play, characters brought on and never used, other characters speaking without having been brought on, or going on speaking after their exit. A notable mark of a printed text set up from Shakespeare's 'foul papers' is idiosyncratic spelling, particularly of proper names. The almost complete absence of such roughnesses from Folio's *Julius Caesar* suggests that such things were sorted out in a fair copy before the text reached the printer. There is, it is true, a slight tendency sometimes to give Italian endings to names, so that Antony is four times 'Antonio', Octavius is twice 'Octavio', and two marginal soldiers in the second half are 'Claudio' and 'Flavio'. Since three of the 'Antonio' uses are from Caesar (and the fourth, from Caska, is reporting Caesar's words) they could be intentional, Caesar using a jocular, almost pet, name for someone close to him. The other Italian endings, though odd, are too insignificant to be made decisive evidence for anything except that the scribe who made the fair copy was following what he found. Shakespeare had previously written five plays set in Italy (*The Taming of the Shrew*, *Two Gentlemen of Verona*, *Romeo and Juliet*,

The Merchant of Venice, Much Ado About Nothing: six if *Titus Andronicus* is counted) and *Julius Caesar* is itself an Italian play. Italian endings were in his mind: he has Antonios in *The Taming of the Shrew*, *Two Gentlemen of Verona*, *The Merchant of Venice*, *Much Ado About Nothing*, *Twelfth Night*, *All's Well That Ends Well* (the last three written close in time to *Julius Caesar*) and *The Tempest*. There is a prominent Claudio in *Much Ado About Nothing*, written the year before; a marginal one in *Hamlet*, probably started as *Julius Caesar* was being finished; a prominent one again in *Measure for Measure* soon after that. None of those Claudios are in his printed sources. Perhaps Shakespeare, had he lived to oversee the printing of *Julius Caesar* in Folio, would have changed these minor characters' names: perhaps not. There are a few other very minor irregularities. The standard form in stage directions, '*Caesar*', appears at 2.2.0.1 as '*Julius Caesar*', and Brutus' servant, having exited as Lucius, re-enters at 4.3.155.1 as '*Boy*'.

None of these small matters detracts from our starting-point, that *Julius Caesar* was set up from a fair copy.[1] Apart from those few Italianate endings, the names in their hundreds are consistently spelled. Though sometimes differing from Plutarch (Shakespeare has 'Murellus', 'Calphurnia', 'Caska'), the text is consistently different. This is notable in the consistent spelling of 'Antony' – not 'Anthony', which is how the name appears in Folio in *Love's Labour's Lost*, *Romeo and Juliet*, *Much Ado About Nothing*, *Henry V*, *Macbeth* and *Antony and Cleopatra*: it is 'Antony' nowhere else in Folio. Speech prefixes are also reasonably consistent, which is rare: and the attribution of speakers to speeches can be trusted. (Transfers at 1.1.15 and 3.1.101–2 are eighteenth-century interference.) Punctuation is regular and consistent (though different from modern conventions): the lack of eccentricity suggests that the compositors had clear guidance

---

1   We may assume that the fair copy was particularly fair: Elizabethan handwriting in 'secretary hand' could give difficulties even to contemporary professionals (see Jackson, 169–70).

(see below, pp. 129–31). Whether the copy included the act divisions is not clear. Only the opening has '*Actus Primus. Scoena Prima.*' The current scene divisions are eighteenth-century additions. The next Roman play in the Folio, *Antony and Cleopatra*, has no divisions of any kind at all, apart from the opening '*Actus Primus. Scoena Prima.*' Nor do *2* and *3 Henry VI*, *Troilus and Cressida*, *Romeo and Juliet* and *Timon of Athens*. One of the several structures that we can observe in *Julius Caesar* is the classical five-act form, but that does not mean that Shakespeare intended sharp divisions and wrote them in his manuscript. Folio prints most plays with at least act divisions, thus reflecting the practice of private theatres from about 1610.

Though a promptbook could be used as compositors' copy for setting a play in type (*Macbeth* may be an example) it is most likely that what was fairly copied for *Julius Caesar* was 'foul papers', the author's manuscript. The idiosyncratic Italianate endings noted above are one small clue. Another is found in the few places where vagueness in stage directions might have had to be corrected if it were in the promptbook. The very first direction in the play is '*Enter . . . certaine Commoners over the Stage.*' The procession opening the second scene has Murellus and Flavius tagging on, though they are silent and do nothing: this is only a suggestive point; as the commentary notes (1.2.0.3n.), their silent presence could make a telling theatrical affect.

More illuminating are the times when a stage direction does not happen. This is not a serious defect. Stage directions are sometimes built into the dialogue (see above, p. 100). On the other hand, some directions that a modern editor might expect do not appear. Some dozen or so exits are missing, like those for Lucius at 2.1.60 and 76. On the other hand again, it is common in Elizabethan texts for exits to be omitted, as the spoken signal for the actor to go is invariably clear. Perhaps more serious are a few missing entries: the 'press' and 'throng' have no entry at 1.2.15 and 1.2.21, nor the 'People and Senators . . . affrighted' spoken to by Brutus at 3.1.82; and missing sound effects, like whatever it is that Caska commands to be silent at 1.2.1 – perhaps the 'music' which Caesar refers to at 1.2.16, rudely described by Caska as 'every noise' and again told by him to be quiet just before. Caesar enters at 1.2.176.1 to no sound effect, though as he leaves at 213 a '*Sennet*' is indicated. On the other hand, at the end of 2.1, as Brutus and Ligarius are leaving his quiet '*orchard*', Folio has a direction in the margin '*Thunder*', which editors have found redundant when three words later as 2.2 opens the direction is '*Thunder and lightning*'. The transition from scene to scene is immediate, however, and Shakespeare may well have written the direction for a preliminary rumble at that point. (This would probably have been the first ever extensive use of the thunder machinery in the new Globe, and the backstage people would enjoy showing off a little. See also above, p. 3n.) Such duplication happens five more times, in each case when tension is mounting, at 4.2.24.1, at the start of 5.2, 5.3.96, 5.5.23 and 29.1; they are all atmospheric, heightening the mood of anxiety, and each time it is as likely that Shakespeare originally wrote them as that they were added at a later stage – which could have been by Shakespeare, of course, in the theatre. One of the marks of genius in this play is Shakespeare's new confidence in setting a tone instantly, and dramatically developing it. Some slight confusions in the comings and goings of soldiers, other than the omission of exits, are understandable and would be immediately sorted at rehearsal (at 4.2.3 and 4 it is clear that Lucilius has been with Pindarus at Cassius' camp, though at 4.2.0 Folio makes Titinius rather than Lucilius accompany Pindarus to meet Brutus). These point again to the fair copy having been made from Shakespeare's 'foul papers' rather than from the promptbook. Complicated theories about suggested partial input to the printers' fair copy from the promptbook (Bowers, 27) are not necessary. The Folio text could stand as a promptbook. Shakespeare was a theatre man, and wrote for performance.

In 1963, Charlton Hinman, developing earlier work, demonstrated from habits of spelling and punctuation that there were five regular compositors in Jaggard's printing house. He assigned sections of the Folio to each with some confidence. His findings have been challenged, and such analysis is now less considered, but it seems that Compositor B, with possibly a little help from A and even E (the 'bad' one), largely set *Julius Caesar*. Compositor B set most of the Folio. He was experienced and fast, and his good work is another reason why the *Julius Caesar* text is clear. Apart from the rearrangement of verse lines (to which we shall come shortly) Compositor B tripped up rarely: once, perhaps because he was going quickly, he misread his copy. At 5.4.7, though he indented the line, he gave no speech prefix, when it clearly should be '*Luc.*', that is, Lucilius; he then wrongly inserted '*Luc.*' at line 9. Mechanical slips like 'Brntus' at 2.1.254 (TLN 896) and 'Btutus' at 3.2.35 (TLN 1564) and a dozen more are so few that they make another reason for celebrating a clean text.

Punctuation

Julius Caesar in the Folio is well, and lightly, punctuated. Elizabethan and Jacobean punctuation was used on rather different principles from those at the end of the twentieth century. One may reasonably suspect that many punctuation points in *Julius Caesar* came from the compositors rather than the author: to reproduce Folio punctuation slavishly now would be folly. Nevertheless, several things need saying. First, since it seems to have been set from a good fair copy of the author's manuscript, every change of punctuation needs to be considered. While a few are wrong by any convention, obscuring the thought, no doubt coming from a compositor's haste or habits, other slightly unfamiliar uses could be an effect that was Shakespeare's own, and deliberate. Second, modern conventions of punctuation are more familiar from more recent prose, and do not relate to the unfamiliar world of Elizabethan verse, with its even more peculiar world of verse drama. True, Heminges and Condell inaugurated a text to be bought and read at home rather than making a performance: even so, we might pause before applying late-twentieth-century prose conventions to forceful address in sixteenth-century iambic pentameters. To illustrate: printers for several centuries used the colon for places where we should prefer a range of stops – full point, semicolon, comma or dash. It has been maintained that Compositor B liked, and over-used, colons: it may be so. Yet deep within the oratorical structure of *Julius Caesar* are several new techniques of expression which Shakespeare went on to develop, like short lines (see below, pp. 131–5), to which we should attend. One of these not commonly considered in the study of Shakespeare's tragic craft is the use of colons. In *Julius Caesar* these are noticeably richer in the passages of higher rhetoric or feeling from Brutus, Cassius or Antony. A colon does not bring the thought to a full stop: there is a sense of carrying-over, or, better, of forward pressure. Consider the punctuation of the following in the Folio, from the climax of Cassius' speeches of seduction of Brutus in 1.2, at 141–6, that is, between full points:

> *Brutus* and *Caesar*: What should be in that *Caesar*?
> Why should that name be sounded more than yours?
> Write them together: Yours, is as fair a Name:
> Sound them, it doth become the mouth as well:
> Weigh them, it is as heavy: Conjure with 'em,
> *Brutus* will start a Spirit as soon as *Caesar*.

In each case, neither a heavier nor a lighter stop will give quite that weight of meditated persuasion, a rhetoric of self-induced anger now being declared, within the five-beat line, that the colons give.

Two colons, those at 2.1.10 and 4.3.293, are especially significant. Both belong to Brutus. The first is in the first line of his soliloquy, 'It must be by his death: and for my part . . .'. Anything less than a colon runs the thought on too quickly: a full point destroys the appalling forward flow into speciousness. The second is in Brutus' reply to the Ghost of Caesar's 'To tell thee thou shalt see me at Philippi'. Brutus answers 'Well: then I shall see

thee again?' Brutus absorbs his evil spirit's sinister announcement, with its overtones of mortal destiny, with one Stoic word,
'Well:'. Then, after one beat, he tests the significance of such
apparitions for him. The punctuation stands as a chasm between
sets of feelings, which Brutus successfully crosses – that movement being the force of a colon. In a play full of conscious high
rhetoric, the colons can be seen to work in the highest positions.
Cassius' last lines to Caesar (3.1.55–7) begin 'Pardon, Caesar:
Caesar, pardon' (the commas are modern). Antony shaking the
bloody hands of the conspirators at 3.1.190 says, 'Gentlemen all:
alas, what shall I say?', where the pressure to go on after 'all' is
palpable, but again a chasm opens. A similar crossing is implied
in Antony's speech at 3.2.181–2: 'This was the most unkindest
cut of all: / For when the noble Caesar saw him stab . . .'. The
mounting rhythms of Antony's 'O pardon me, thou bleeding
piece of earth' soliloquy, from 'blood' at 3.1.258 to the end in
'burial' at 275, allow no full point for seventeen lines – there are
none in the Folio. The force of the 'curse' is in sections divided
only by two colons: the sense of 'all the parts of Italy:' falls over
into 'Blood and destruction', and 'the hands of war:' runs on to
'All pity choked . . . Caesar's spirit, ranging for revenge'.

Short lines

A further problem for a modern editor of *Julius Caesar* is evalu-
ating the short lines. The Folio compositor always sets half-lines
on a fresh line ranged left, even when they are clearly another part
of a pentameter line. How many short lines are thus of the compositors', rather than Shakespeare's, making? Three examples of
the compositor ordinarily at work may help. At 5.1.66–7, he set:

> *Cassi.* Why now blow winde, swell Billow,
> And swimme Barke:
> The Storme is up, and all is on the hazard.

Two pentameter lines: but because the column could not hold
the first line he has split it, something that he does regularly.

131

Sometimes, an opposite fault, he overloads a line. At 5.1.69–72, he set:

> *Luc.* My Lord.
> *Cassi.* *Messala.*
> *Messa.* What sayes my Generall?
> *Cassi.* *Messala*, this is my Birth-day: as this very day
> Was *Cassius* borne. Give me thy hand *Messala*:

Cassius' last lines fall into regular pentameters if they begin 'This. . .'. So editors set the earlier words as one rough pentameter:

> *Messala.* / What says my general? / *Messala*,

Similarly Folio at 3.2.111–112, has '3 [Plebeian] Ha's hee Masters? I feare there will a worse come in his place.' This is in one line, the last two words taken up to a previous space. 'I feare . . . place' is a perfect iambic pentameter, and as such the line is spoiled by the four beats of 'Ha's hee Masters?' Here one can understand what happened, as it is the foot of the right-hand column on the page (sig. ii), and space had run out.

But, considering short rather than long lines, what of the first news of Portia's death at 4.3.145–52? Both Brutus and Cassius convey their feeling in regular pentameters, broken by two telling short lines, each with two strong stresses, which demand pauses. The compositor set:

> *Bru.* No man beares sorrow better. *Portia* is dead.
> *Cas.* Ha? *Portia?*
> *Bru.* She is dead.
> *Cas.* How scap'd I killing, when I crost you so?
> O insupportable, and touching loss!
> Vpon what sicknesse?
> *Bru.* Impatient of my absence,
> And greefe, that yong *Octauius* with *Mark Antony* . . .

Are 'Upon what sickness?' and 'Impatient of my absence' genuine short lines, also implying pauses caused by strong feeling?

Or should an editor try to count a rough five beats with a mental metronome and metrically glue the short lines together? Editors, as in this edition, almost always make a full line, presumably because there can be felt to be advantage in Brutus completing Cassius' medical question with the contrast of four unclinical words, 'Impatient of my absence'. In performance, the difference may not be noted. But the Folio was set to be read, and a point is made by Brutus starting a fresh line.

As Cassius begins to work on Brutus at 1.2.52–3, 58–9 and 63, the Folio's short lines might simply be the result of the compositor's mistake in casting off, calculating how much text could be set on a page. On the other hand, the short line at 2.2.101, ' "Lo, Caesar is afraid"?', could be Shakespeare's: Decius' daring words demand, perhaps, a sharp intake of breath by Caesar and Calphurnia, even a shared glance of outrage: that would make more plausible Decius hurriedly going on to ask pardon and express his 'dear, dear love'. At the Soothsayer's second entrance, Folio's gnomic short lines suit the speaker well: 'None that I know will be, / Much that I fear may chance' (2.4.32–3) – together they make an alexandrine, not a pentameter; Pope, making them one line, cut the last two words to make them fit. The Soothsayer's first appearance, too, at 1.2.12–24 has suggested relining. Asked by Caesar, 'What sayst thou to me now? Speak once again', he repeats the heavy trimeter, 'Beware the Ides of March.' It seems a pity to deny him this second powerful, and solitary, utterance, by altering the Folio to add Caesar's 'He is a dreamer' to his line: in any case, Caesar's 'He is a Dreamer, let us leave him: Passe' is, like his command two lines before, a regular iambic pentameter. Caesar, we might say, perfects his line before he goes on.

On the other hand, relining Caesar's second entrance at 1.2.174–6, as editors have done for a century and a half, allows the angry Caesar '*and his train*' to interrupt Cassius; the half-line 'Of fire from Brutus' gives space to herald that big re-entry. On the other hand again, as the conspirators draw to a close at 2.1.191–2 it is tempting to set the short lines beginning 'Peace!

Count the clock . . .' as three separate statements, as the Folio does, marking a strong sense of period to the discussion – talk is over; what follows are plans for action. Printing them as parts of perfect iambic pentameters, however, which they are, has the simultaneous effect of keeping the pulse of the words and action steady: and in this scene the classically ordered, regular lines are about butchering the greatest man in the world for petty malice. The opposite procedure must be used for 1.2.79–80, where Folio's lining is a nonsense:

> *Bru.* What meanes this Showting?
> I do feare, the People choose *Caesar*
> For their King.
> > *Cassi.* I, do you feare it?

We may admire, however, the setting of two short lines in Brutus' soliloquy in 2.1, and suspect they are Shakespeare's. At 2.1.50 and 62, Folio's separate lines for 'Where I have tooke them up' and 'I have not slept' single out for emphasis Brutus' only actions in the perfect tense, telling us important facts about his state of mind.

There are over a hundred short lines in *Julius Caesar*, and roughly the same number of lines shared between speakers, a proportion of the whole far beyond Shakespeare's plays before this, and heralding the even higher proportions in *Hamlet* and the great tragedies that followed (Wright, *Metrical*, 294). They all demand an editor's decisions.[1]

An editor has also to decide whether what is printed is verse or prose. See, for example, the contrast between the Plebeians' speeches in 3.2 and 3.3: the many short lines are printed the same way in the Folio. In 3.3 the Plebeians must surely speak prose, particularly as lines 7–9, though rhythmically forcible, do not fall into verse however cleverly an editor may adjust them

---

1 Other examples of editorial changes from Folio's lineation, recorded in the textual notes, are at 1.2.33, 79–80; 1.3.39–42, 57–60, 79, 137, 139–41; 2.1.220, 327; 2.2.1; 2.4.40; 3.1.147; 3.2.54, 111–12, 199; 4.3.55, 161, 183, 222, 247, 297–8; 5.1.41, 110; 5.3.36–7, 47.

('Where do you dwell? / Are you a married man or a bachelor? / Answer every man directly'). The tone is sordid viciousness: the words accompany actions of a mob that are base, and prose is appropriate. In contrast, the same people in 3.2 are united and lifted by the high rhetoric they hear, and their rhythmically strong short lines in the Folio grow out of metrically-patterned regular verse that suggests elevation of mood. 'O piteous spectacle! / O noble Caesar! / O woeful day! / O traitors, villains! / O most bloody sight! / We will be revenged!' (lines 196–8) – those lines, unlike the rhythmically slacker last lines of 3.3, have a forceful pulse climaxing in the gunshot monosyllables of 'Seek! Burn! Fire! Kill! Slay!' (line 199). The verse forms survive in their last words in 3.2, from 244 to their exit, beginning, 'Never, never. Come, away, away . . . ', where regular iambic pentameters, 'We'll burn his body in the holy place, / And with the brands fire all the traitors' houses', lead to the short single lines as set in the Folio.

Emendation and possible revision

Some earlier confident changes to the Folio came from a sense of superiority to Shakespeare, something ultimately patronizing. Eighteenth-century editors, knowing themselves not only later but better educated and thus wiser, automatically assumed that Shakespeare needed 'correcting'. That Shakespeare in his world was not only very different, but knew exactly what he was about, did not occur to them. A ludicrous example of this is at 2.1.73: Alexander Pope was so certain that Romans did not wear hats (Pope was wrong, as we know) that in his edition of 1723–5 he could not bring himself to print the word, and has Lucius say 'No, sir, their – are pluckt about their ears'.

At 2.1.40, the Folio text has 'first', and so it stood until Theobald emended to 'Ides' in 1733, a 'correction' that has held ever since. A great deal of ingenuity has been brought to the attempt to explain how 'Shakespeare's mistake' happened. Lewis Theobald was the third editor of Shakespeare; he was knowledgeable and he took trouble. He offered, as he wrote in the Preface to his edition in 1733, 'Nothing . . . altered but what by the clearest reasoning can be proved a corruption of the true text: and the alteration, a real restoration of the genuine reading'. Yet when our modern knowledge of the sharp and all-pervasive controversies over the calendar, at their peak in 1599 (see above, p. 21, and commentary), is brought to the text, we find that there is no need to emend Folio's 'first'.

Three supposed faults in the Folio have attracted most attention, and produced theories of revision of the text: the unexpected arrival of a 'Publius' among the conspirators who visit Caesar at 2.2.107.2, thought to be an error for 'Cassius'; a change resulting from a remark by Ben Jonson at 3.1.46–7; and Brutus in 4.3.145–190 being told twice of his wife's death. The first is, in fact, no problem, as the commentary shows: in performance, the moment with Publius can be felt to be dramatically well made. Ben Jonson's remark in his *Timber, or Discoveries Made upon Men and Matter* of 1640 has set off much discussion (see Var, 136–40). Jonson, in the course of expressing his love of Shakespeare and admiration of his talents, added:

> Many times hee fell into those things, could not escape laughter: As when hee said in the person of *Caesar*, one speaking to him; *Caesar thou dost me wrong*. Hee replyed: *Caesar did never wrong, but with just cause:* and such like; which were ridiculous.

(Chambers, Shakespeare. 2.210)

In the Induction to Jonson's *The Staple of News* (1626) the Prologue says to Expectation, '*Cry you mercy*, you neuer did wrong, but with just cause' (36–7). Both references have suggested to later editors that lines were originally in the play that allowed Jonson's gibe, and later cut. That may well be so. The line would easily fit if after 3.1.46, Metellus said something like 'Caesar, thou dost me wrong', as a powerful short line, to which

Caesar replied 'Caesar did never wrong but with just cause, / Nor without cause will he be satisfied.' Metellus then appealed, as Folio stands, 'Is there no voice . . .?' As part of mounting arrogance, it fits Caesar very well.

The two statements of Portia's death in 4.3, which have also generated a great deal of comment about inadequate revision of the copy from which the printed text was set, need fuller attention. The textual case for revision rests on the fact that each passage mentioning the death of Portia includes an anomaly. First, from the entry of the Poet at 4.3.122.1 until the entry of Titinius and Messala at 160.1, Cassius' twelve speech prefixes are '*Cas.*' instead of the usual '*Cass.*' or '*Cassi.*' (see Fig. 20). Behind that change, it has been argued, lay a different scribe, suggesting a later addition. On the other hand, John Jowett maintained that the '*Cas.*' prefixes indicated not revision but a sudden shortage of '*ssi*' ligatures in Jaggard's printing house, something that happened at other times as well.

Second, though Brutus frequently refers to him as 'boy', at 4.3.155.1 the usual stage direction '*Lucius*' is replaced, for the only time, by '*Boy*'. It is suggested that the section begun by his entry there, until thirty-eight lines later, is a later addition by a different scribe: and it is certainly true that Brutus' remark at 194, 'Well, to our work alive', fits very well with the last thing said before the '*Boy*' came in, Cassius' 'O ye immortal gods!' Revision there may have been: but it does not have to be branded as the result of inadequacy, as if Shakespeare, preparing his play for all the work with actors, could somehow forget that he had announced Portia's death twice. The '*Boy*' section as we may call it, 4.3.156–93, could well be an intentional addition. It has been suggested that Brutus' Stoic stature is shown by his reaction to a momentary hope caused by the disagreement in the letters, snuffed by Messala's 'For certain she is dead' (Smith, Warren). It will be argued here that the double announcement makes an important contribution to the dramatic shape.

137

The Tragedie of Julius Cæsar.   125

Cass. I durst not.
Bru. No.
Cass. What? durst not tempt him?
Bru. For your life you durst not.
Cass. Do not presume too much vpon my Loue,
I may do that I shall be sorry for.
Bru. You haue done that you should be sorry for.
There is no terror Cassius in your threats:
For I am Arm'd so strong in Honesty,
That they passe by me, as the Idle winde,
Which I respect not. I did send to you
For certaine summes of Gold, which you deny'd me,
For I can raise no money by vile meanes:
By Heauen, I had rather Coine my Heart,
And drop my blood for Drachmaes, then to wring
From the hard hands of Peazants, their vile trash
By any indirection. I did send
To you for Gold to pay my Legions,
Which you deny'd me: was that done like Cassius?
Should I haue answer'd Caius Cassius so?
When Marcus Brutus growes so Couetous,
To locke such Rascall Counters from his Friends,
Be ready Gods with all your Thunder-bolts,
Dash him to peeces.
Cass. I deny'd you not.
Bru. You did.
Cass. I did not. He was but a Foole
That brought my answer back. Brutus hath riu'd my hart:
A Friend should beare his Friends infirmities;
But Brutus makes mine greater then they are.
Bru. I do not, till you practice them on me.
Cass. You loue me not.
Bru. I do not like your faults.
Cass. A friendly eye could neuer see such faults.
Bru. A Flatterers would not, though they do appeare
As huge as high Olympus.
Cass. Come Antony, and yong Octauius come,
Reuenge your selues alone on Cassius,
For Cassius is a-weary of the World:
Hated by one he loues, brau'd by his Brother,
Check'd like a bondman, all his faults obseru'd,
Set in a Note-booke, learn'd, and con'd by roate
To cast into my Teeth. O I could weepe
My Spirit from mine eyes. There is my Dagger,
And heere my naked Breast: Within, a Heart
Deerer then Pluto's Mine, Richer then Gold:
If that thou bee'st a Roman, take it foorth.
I that deny'd thee Gold, will giue my Heart:
Strike as thou did'st at Cæsar: For I know,
When thou did'st hate him worst, ÿ loued'st him better
Then euer thou loued'st Cassius.
Bru. Sheath your Dagger:
Be angry when you will, it shall haue scope:
Do what you will, Dishonor, shall be Humour.
O Cassius, you are yoaked with a Lambe
That carries Anger, as the Flint beares fire,
Who much inforced, shewes a hastie Sparke,
And straite is cold agen.
Cass. Hath Cassius liu'd
To be but Mirth and Laughter to his Brutus,
When greefe and blood ill temper'd, vexeth him?
Bru. When I spoke that, I was ill temper'd too.
Cass. Do you confesse so much? Giue me your hand.
Bru. And my heart too.
Cass. O Brutus!
Bru. What's the matter?

Cass. Haue not you loue enough to beare with me,
When that rash humour which my Mother gaue me
Makes me forgetfull.
Bru. Yes Cassius, and from henceforth
When you are ouer-earnest with your Brutus,
Hee'l thinke your Mother chides, and leaue you so.

Enter a Poet.

Poet. Let me go in to see the Generals,
There is some grudge betweene 'em, 'tis not meete
They be alone.
Lucil. You shall not come to them.
Poet. Nothing but death shall stay me.
Cas. How now? What's the matter?
Poet. For shame you Generals; what do you meane?
Loue, and be Friends, as two such men should bee,
For I haue seene more yeeres I'me sure then you.
Cas. Ha, ha, how vildely doth this Cynicke rime?
Bru. Get you hence sirra: Sawcy fellow, hence.
Cas. Beare with him Brutus, 'tis his fashion.
Brut. Ile know his humor, when he knowes his time:
What should the Warres do with these Iigging Fooles?
Companion, hence.
Cas. Away, away be gone.   Exit Poet
Bru. Lucillius and Titinius bid the Commanders
Prepare to lodge their Companies to night.
Cas. And come your selues, & bring Messala with you
Immediately to vs.
Bru. Lucius, a bowle of Wine.
Cas. I did not thinke you could haue bin so angry.
Bru. O Cassius, I am sicke of many greefes.
Cas. Of your Philosophy you make no vse,
If you giue place to accidentall euils.
Bru. No man beares sorrow better. Portia is dead.
Cas. Ha? Portia?
Bru. She is dead.
Cas. How scap'd I killing, when I crost you so?
O insupportable, and touching losse!
Vpon what sicknesse?
Bru. Impatient of my absence,
And greefe, that yong Octauius with Mark Antony
Haue made themselues so strong: For with her death
That tydings came. With this she fell distract,
And (her Attendants absent) swallow'd fire.
Cas. And dy'd so?
Bru. Euen so.
Cas. O ye immortall Gods!

Enter Boy with Wine, and Tapers.

Bru. Speake no more of her: Giue me a bowl of wine,
In this I bury all vnkindnesse Cassius.   Drinkes
Cas. My heart is thirsty for that Noble pledge.
Fill Lucius, till the Wine ore-swell the Cup:
I cannot drinke too much of Brutus loue.

Enter Titinius and Messala.

Brutus. Come in Titinius:
Welcome good Messala:
Now sit we close about this Taper heere,
And call in question our necessities.
Cass. Portia, art thou gone?
Bru. No more I pray you.
Messala, I haue heere receiued Letters,
That yong Octauius, and Marke Antony
Come downe vpon vs with a mighty power,
Bending their Expedition toward Philippi.

Ii 3   Mess.

20 Folio text of *Julius Caesar* at 4.3.60–170, showing on the right the unusual speech-prefixes 'Cas.', and the unique stage direction *Boy*, which have been taken to suggest some form of revision

The death of Portia

The suicide of Portia is recorded in Plutarch only in the last lines of his *Brutus*, as a postscript to his concluding record of what happened to Brutus' body. Plutarch gives no indication either of when the death happened or of when the news reached Brutus. Shakespeare, with no compelling dramatic need to mention Portia's death at all (unlike the death of Ophelia, Portia's death does not set off action), and with the whole of the two last acts available if he wanted, chose to place Brutus' receiving of the news just before the Quarrel scene, and to have him reveal it to Cassius as they begin to make up. We may ask what it might have meant not to have that news in the play at all, and why it has to be there. There is strictly no need for the news: we are not told, to take random examples, what happened to Calphurnia after the death of Caesar, or to Lucius after the end of Act 4. Neither is on record, Lucius because he is invented: but that does not mean that Shakespeare could not have underlined the sense of closure at the end of the play by reference to their fates. A sick Lucius, dying of a broken heart, and then dead for Brutus to find, would have been interesting and touching (and quite wrong, of course). Shakespeare omits or strengthens exits from the story as he wishes. He felt free to underscore the end of Pindarus: by Cassius 'reserved ever for suche a pinche', as Plutarch has it (see Appendix, p. 358), Pindarus kills Cassius and then runs out of the play – 'was never seene more', says Plutarch. But Shakespeare triply strengthens his absence twenty lines later by having Titinius call out for him, then be sent off to find him, and then say he will seek for him, as cover for his own suicide (5.3.72–90). Brutus could convincingly have quarrelled with Cassius without his own private heartbreak.

What if the report of Portia's death were not in the Quarrel scene? Shakespeare was free to put it somewhere else. It could have come much nearer to where Plutarch placed it, early in the final scene, 5.5, for example, where Brutus is trying to find a fellow-soldier who will kill him. Again, Plutarch tells earlier in

Brutus that during the very assembly of the conspirators to kill Caesar, immediately after Popilius Lena had disturbed them by wishing them well, 'there came one of Brutus men post hast unto him, and tolde him his wife was a dying' (see Appendix, p. 340): it was not so, of course; but Shakespeare could have thought briefly about following up that personal blow to Brutus by placing some report of Portia's death at his exit from the Forum scene (3.2.62).

Shakespeare works in his own way with Plutarch to give the news of the death of Portia dramatic force by using it for a purpose which is at first sight plain; to change the emotional tone of the end of the Quarrel scene. Brutus' unusual state of mind is thus explained: though he has always been in command of himself, now we learn that he is unstable through being 'sick of many griefs' (4.3.142), and one in particular. His explanation of his being discomposed is set against, and greatly outweighs, Cassius' quite different reason for his own disturbance: Cassius shifts responsibility for his 'rash humour' on to his mother (4.3.119). It is thus useful to Shakespeare that the revelation is to Cassius rather than to anyone else. Telling Lucius, in a suitable quiet moment, of the suicide of his mistress would have brought expressions of raw sorrow and horror from that young heart, and uncontaminated pity for Brutus. These emotions would have been too directly human for the political complexities of distortion, deceit and distrust which dominate Act 4: from the perfidy within the triumvirate as the act opens to Brutus' command as it closes that Cassius should set his troops in the vanguard at once – as Cassius knows, and later tells Messala (5.1.70–88), a doomed position. What Shakespeare gains by giving the news of Portia's suicide to Cassius at that moment is not, in fact, an excuse for Brutus being temporarily choleric, but the acceleration of an already-rolling counter-movement diminishing 'the noblest Roman of them all'. It seems that Caesar's 'demon' is not just killing the conspirators one by one: it is twisting them out of the way of truth, like a Mephistophilis.

Consider. The Quarrel scene, 4.3, is the first we have seen or heard of Brutus and Cassius since they rode 'like madmen through the gates of Rome' (3.2.259). Now the angry exchanges reveal Brutus, unpleasantly, as too high-minded to recognize in himself the very crimes of extortion of which he accuses Cassius. This is now the 'shadow' from Cassius which Brutus will not see reflected back at him (see 1.2.58: there are parallels between this and the second scene in the play). There follows a sequence of seven more 'reflections' of Brutus before the scene ends. First is the intrusion of the 'Cynic' poet – a moment of lightening of mood in the theatre, an incursion apparently quite without threat. Yet in spite of Cassius' laughter and the incongruousness, the moment is dark. The Poet is mortally serious: 'Nothing but death shall stay me', he says (126). A true Cynic, a fellow of Diogenes, would come with intent to spoil the moment of ease, new-found between the generals. Plutarch has him as one of 'the Cynick philosophers, (as who would say "doggs")' (see Appendix, p. 349). 'Cynic' meaning 'doggish' had a host of derogatory associations. His rhyme, too, though comically clumsy, refers to a quarrel at the start of the *Iliad* which led to disaster for the Greeks. In Plutarch, the intruder is a philosopher who returns that night to cheer up the supper that Brutus gives for his friends. A scrap of that may have got into Shakespeare making Brutus immediately send Lucius out for wine.

So Lucius is off stage for the next 'reflection' of Brutus, his announcement to Cassius alone of Portia's death, and the means. The moment begins as one of union: Cassius and Brutus make up: 'In this I bury all unkindness, Cassius' (157). As it were, they swallow their fire: Portia's strange, echoic death, swallowing fire, is caused by absence: Brutus' absence from her (150), her sanity's absence ('she fell distract' 153), her attendants' absence (154). The ten lines in which Cassius hears the news are marked by being the most extended intimacy in the play. That is intruded upon by the terrible death of Portia – terrible in the means, and also in the reason; as Brutus says,

'Impatient of my absence, / And grief that young Octavius with Mark Antony / Have made themselves so strong . . .' (150–2). Portia was not Brutus' 'harlot': she was passionately engaged to the 'enterprise' of liberating Rome from the tyranny of Caesar. The fourth scene of Act 2 is given to her anxiety about what is happening in the Capitol, an economical and effective dramatization of the dozen lines in Plutarch describing her extreme agitation and the swooning 'in the middest of her house' which led to the servant running to tell Brutus she was dying (see Appendix, p. 340). Now, near the time of the battle of Philippi, the message comes that she has killed herself because she has been without Brutus for a long time, and their enemies have become powerful. Just as in the early parallel scene, 1.2, as we saw, Brutus with Cassius began a new view of himself in his inner world, a replacement 'shadow' or reflection, which visitation not only contained the death of Caesar, but was destroying him, so here with Cassius he has a second visitation to his inner world (sinisterly prefigured by the Poet's 'Love and be friends') containing separation and a hideous death. By placing the true report of the death of Portia here, Shakespeare has completed the movement of Brutus' inner world in the reflection from Cassius; he is now disintegrated by the destruction of one he loves. It is not just his sense of doom, though that is present: it is, in intense intimacy with Cassius, an expression of an inner, and hideous, death.

This explains the third visitation. His friend Messala comes from the outside world with letters full of death. On the curious aside from Cassius 'Portia, art thou gone?' (4.3.164), they hear that Octavius and Antony are not only on their way, with a 'mighty power', but 'Have put to death an hundred senators' including Cicero. Tactfully Messala enquires of Brutus, and then tells him of his wife, 'For certain she is dead, and by strange manner.' The dramatic logic of this is powerful. Always in the play we are asked to consider how distortions in the inner, private, world of Brutus do not match reality (evidences that Caesar was ambitious had to be 'fashioned'), and then in the real world the truth breaks in to Brutus, always of death. Brutus' inner 'shadow' had to kill Caesar for impersonal, political, reasons: Caesar in the outer world died, and saying '*Et tu, Brute?*' In Brutus' inner world, Portia was as 'dear' to him as 'the ruddy drops' that 'visit' his 'sad heart' (2.1.288–9): in the outer world she was dismissed and abandoned, and in that outer world she died, horribly. A messenger brought, significantly with military dispatches of approaching defeat, the news 'For certain she is dead'. Such dramatic logic can override any theory of textual error in the two mentions of Portia's death.

There follows the fourth visitation by Brutus' own 'reflection', the disagreement between him and Cassius about strategy. Cassius had the better reading of the situation with his plan to exhaust the enemy before the conflict. Brutus overrides him curtly and philosophizes about 'a tide in the affairs of men', making a sermon on a worn adage about opportunity stand for practical and detailed discussion with Cassius. Cassius can only give in, understanding that Brutus sees only his own fantasy.

A tender passage with Lucius, and Varrus and Claudio, about sleeping and not sleeping, reflects, fifth, Brutus' own lack of sleep, echoing 2.1 and now suggesting, as inability to sleep so often does in Shakespeare, that Brutus is set aside from what is human and natural. The sixth visitation is by music, murdered by slumber. Again, always in Shakespeare music is a harmony reflecting cosmic harmony. The seventh, and most startling, visitation is by '*the* Ghost *of Caesar*'. It speaks sixteen words only, the first four announcing that it is 'Thy evil spirit, Brutus'. This is straight from Plutarch (see Appendix, p. 351), and it has to come here, before Brutus and Cassius set off with their armies for Philippi. Plutarch's account is anchored at this moment in the story: nothing else in this scene is. The sequence of effects on Brutus, what we called the seven visitations, is Shakespeare's invention. Into that sequence the two reports of the death of Portia fit admirably.

'Path', Erebus and change

One other example will be taken here to support a Folio reading against much emendation. At the crisis of his commitment to Cassius and the conspirators, Brutus uses a curious verb of which the earliest citation in this sense in *OED* is dated 1598. At the beginning of 2.1, Brutus soliloquizes: at the end, and a few seconds before the already-announced entry of the conspirators, which seals for ever his commitment, he apostrophizes conspiracy itself: he comments on its apparent shame even by night (Lucius has told him that the men arriving are muffled), and asks:

> Where wilt thou find a cavern dark enough
> To mask thy monstrous visage? Seek none, conspiracy:
> Hide it in smiles and affability;
> For if thou path, thy native semblance on,
> Not Erebus itself were dim enough
> To hide thee from prevention.
>
> (2.1.80–5)

In the theatre, the meaning is clear enough – conspiracy has to be disguised in smiles. But in 'For if thou path, thy native semblance on', what is 'path'? The First Folio, without the comma after 'path', makes it transitive, meaning 'if thou put thy native semblance on', and several later editors follow. 'Path,' is the reading of the Second Folio, which as a rough rule in this cleanly-set play makes few corrections to the First. There have been many emendations to 'path' as intransitive, like 'march' (Pope), 'pass', 'parle', 'pall', 'pace' and so on. Making it transitive spoils the metaphor, because 'semblance' ceases to be 'native'. A copyist's or typesetter's error for 'put' is unlikely, for a common word like 'put' is unlikely to become so strange a word as 'path'.[1] But if it is intransitive, what does it mean? *OED* path *v.* 3 gives the word as an intransitive verb with this *Julius Caesar* reference, meaning 'to pursue one's course' – an unusual, new, verb.

---

1 Robert Ireland suggests, privately, 'patch' (*OED v.* 4.a); 'if you put your real appearance on (as a temporary cover) . . .'

The verb has unexpected riches. 'Path' may turn out to contain a shadowy image of the road to Erebus, the dark place under the world through which the shades pass on the way to Hades. That is a progress also present at *2 Henry IV* 2.4.147–8 in Pistol's words damning Doll Tearsheet: 'to Pluto's damn'd lake . . . to the infernal deep, with Erebus '. That image of 'path' also shades into 'cavern' (*JC* 2.1.80, three lines above in Brutus' speech) and the following 'monstrous visage'. According to Hesiod's *Theogony*, Erebus was the child of Chaos. A north-country dialect meaning of the noun 'path', still extant in place-names, meaning a deep cutting or chasm, was used in the tenth-century Lindisfarne Gospels to render the Vulgate Latin *chaos* for the deep gulf of the lower world at Luke, 16.26, in the parable of Dives and Lazarus (*OED* path *sb.* 2.a).

Linguistically, what is happening here? An apparently very newly recorded verb ties in rather oddly with a running image of Erebus through an ancient north-country sense of that verb. Erebus, an 'infernal deep', in Pistol's use, includes traitors. Obviously, conspirators are traitors, exactly the sort of people in a political play who would be damned and on the path to Hades. The link apparent in Shakespeare's mind is on the surface not too difficult.

Yet there is more. At the precise moment that Brutus is saying these words, he is dramatically and rather startlingly changing, into the less constricted, even we may say more devious, version of the philosopher (not, in fact, a Stoic, though often called one) of the first act. The change relates to the entry of the stage-full of conspirators already announced. In *2 Henry IV* it is curious that at the precise moment when Pistol makes his Erebus remark, he is making an extraordinary change. He was announced forty lines before he came in: he entered, and he was simply, as somewhat lengthily prefigured by Doll, Hostess and Falstaff, a Roaring Boy. With these lines about Erebus he turns suddenly, and for ever, quite without apparent cause, and to our everlasting gratitude, into a preposterous figure who can speak nothing but the wildest theatrical gobbets. His entry is presently followed by the theatrically far more significant entry of the Prince and Poins.

The only other mention of Erebus in Shakespeare is in *The Merchant of Venice*. Alone together in a doubtful idyll in Belmont, Lorenzo and Jessica discuss the beauty of the night, and the music. Lorenzo says:

> The man that hath no music in himself . . .
> Is fit for treasons, stratagems, and spoils:
> The motions of his spirit are as dull as night,
> And his affections dark as Erebus.
>
> (*MV* 5.1.83–7)

At that moment the scene, and Lorenzo and Jessica's fortunes, change entirely with the entry, announced forty lines before, of Portia and Nerissa, presently followed by the men.

Here in *Julius Caesar* we have the last occurrence in Shakespeare of a constellation not noticed before, of announced entry, dramatic change, treasons and Erebus. Perhaps a single source may be found, possibly an emblem. That would be interesting, but less to the purpose here, where the peculiarly rich word 'path' comes just in the middle of that constellation. Brutus is not simply musing on conspiracy in the abstract. He is in those words deciding to be devious, announcing that he will hide in smiles and affability. He will 'path', pursue his course. And it is a modern verb at the time.

A NOTE ON THIS EDITION

The text is modernized, according to the principles in the General Editors' Preface (pp. x–xiv). Since the Folio text is so good, some attention has been paid to following it, rather than eighteenth-century and later 'corrections'. Thus, names appear as they do in the Folio text rather than in Plutarch. For ease of reference, conventional scene divisions have been included, though they are again eighteenth-century additions, and not in

Folio. Folio's admirably light stage directions have been followed, with a few necessary small adjustments, all recorded in the textual notes. In a few places, lineation has also been changed; again, the changes are all recorded. The good punctuation has been lightly modernized, though the present text has preserved more colons than has been common.

All Shakespeare references outside *Julius Caesar* are to the Alexander edition.

JULIUS CAESAR

LIST OF ROLES

Julius CAESAR

Marcus BRUTUS
Caius CASSIUS
CASKA
DECIUS Brutus
CINNA   } *conspirators against Julius Caesar*   5
METELLUS Cimber
TREBONIUS
Caius LIGARIUS

OCTAVIUS Caesar   10
Mark ANTONY   } *triumvirs after the death of Caesar*
LEPIDUS

CALPHURNIA   *wife of Caesar*

PORTIA   *wife of Brutus*

LUCIUS   *personal servant to Brutus*   15

CICERO
PUBLIUS   } *senators*
POPILIUS Lena

MURELLUS   } *tribunes of the people*
FLAVIUS   20

CINNA   *a poet*

LUCILIUS
TITINIUS
MESSALA   } *supporters of Brutus and Cassius,*
Young CATO   *and officers in their army*
STRATO   25

VARRUS
CLAUDIO
CLITUS   } *soldiers with Brutus and Cassius*
DARDANIUS
VOLUMNIUS   30

PINDARUS

ARTEMIDORUS

A CARPENTER

A COBBLER   35

A POET

A SOOTHSAYER

150

A SERVANT to Caesar
A SERVANT to Antony
A SERVANT to Octavius   40
A MESSENGER

5 PLEBEIANS
3 SOLDIERS   *in the army of Brutus*
2 SOLDIERS   *in the army of Antony*
The GHOST of Caesar   45

[Commoners, Soldiers and others]

LIST OF ROLES Rowe first supplied an (imperfect) list, expanded by later editors.

1 **Julius CAESAR** Military commander extraordinary, he had been consul in Rome since 59 BC. He defeated Pompey at Pharsalia in 48, and Pompey's sons in Spain in 45, the cause of the triumph as the play begins. Now aged 56, Caesar was in failing health, and he had been angered by Marcus Brutus marrying Portia, daughter of his enemy Cato (who had killed himself rather than fall into Caesar's hands), and widow of his enemy Bibulus. *Life* by Plutarch. Shakespeare makes Caesar the fourth-largest part; with 1,126 words, he has only a little more than Caska.

2 **Marcus BRUTUS** fought with Pompey against Caesar at Pharsalia in 48 BC, was pardoned by Caesar, and became governor of Cisalpine Gaul in 46, and a praetor (roughly, senior magistrate) in 44. Gossip maintained that he was Caesar's natural son. His mother was a half-sister of Cato, whose widowed daughter Portia he married. *Life* by Plutarch. In the play, he has by a long way the largest part, with 5,394 words.

3 **Caius CASSIUS** of uncertain parentage; little is known of him before he fought with Crassus in 53 BC. Instigator of the plot against Caesar, in spite of Caesar's favour and honours. Plutarch gives many accounts of him: 'a hot, chollerick, and cruell man, that would oftentymes be caried away from justice for gayne' (Appendix p. 348). Shakespeare gives him the second-largest part, with 3,709 words.

4 **CASKA** a conspirator, so spelled throughout F. His character is largely Shakespeare's invention, from brief notes in Plutarch (Appendix, pp. 329, 341). A tribune, and the first to stab Caesar, he fled from Rome and was deprived of his tribuneship. He fought at Philippi (which Shakespeare does not mention), though Antony there mentions his stabbing Caesar *like a cur* (5.1.43–4)). He died soon after the battle. Caska has the fifth-largest part in *JC*, with 1,074 words.

5 **DECIUS Brutus** a conspirator, though as Plutarch tells, Caesar had made him 'his next heire' (Appendix p. 327). The name 'Decius' is in the Preliminary Table in Amyot's first Plutarch (1565), and in Holland's Suetonius of 1606. Elsewhere in Amyot, and throughout North, it is 'Decimus'. Properly Decimus Junius Brutus Albinus, he persuades Caesar to go to the Senate, is active in the murder and has his house burned down by the mob (3.3.35–6). See 1.3.148n.

6 **CINNA** a conspirator, properly L. Cornelius Cinna the Younger, who was made a praetor by Caesar, but 'in an oration he made had spoken very evill of Caesar' (Plutarch, Appendix p. 345), and approved of the assassination. He is told by Cassius in 1.3 to distribute papers for Brutus to find; is on the fringe of the conspirators in Brutus' orchard in 2.1; is on Artemidorus' list in 2.3; and after the murder of Caesar is the first to cry 'Liberty! Freedom! Tyranny is dead!' (3.1.78).

7 **METELLUS Cimber** a conspirator, properly L. Tullius Cimber, but called by Plutarch both 'Tullius Cimber' (Appendix p. 341) and 'Metellus Cimber' (Appendix p. 328) – which Shakespeare took. Strongly supported Caesar, and was given Bithynia: but is mentioned in 1.3 as a conspirator, and, though greeted specially by Caesar in 2.2, presently gives the signal for the murder in 3.1, having unctuously begun to present a suit. Says ten words after the murder, and then leaves the play.

8 **TREBONIUS** a conspirator. Favoured by Caesar over many years, and made consul by him in 45 BC. In 2.2 Caesar wants him 'near him'. On Artemidorus' list. His role is to keep Antony away from the Senate (*Brutus*, Appendix p. 341; in *Caesar*, Appendix p. 328, it is Decius) and after the murder he reports that Antony has 'fled to his house amazed' (3.1.96), his last remark in the play.

9 **Caius LIGARIUS** a conspirator. Properly Quintus Ligarius, acquitted

by Caesar, after Cicero's defence, of fighting with Pompey: even so, he hated Caesar for what he saw as his tyrannical power. Like Cicero and others, he was deeply ambivalent about Caesar.

10 OCTAVIUS **Caesar** Great-nephew of Julius Caesar, he was the political powerhouse of the triumvirate even before his first appearance at 4.1. With Antony he defeated Brutus and Cassius two years later in 42 BC (when he was 21 years old). In 27 he became the emperor Augustus. In *JC*, his part is very small, with 328 words; a good deal less than half Portia's.

11 Mark ANTONY Marcus Antonius, friend of Caesar, with a vigorous military and personal history. He was kept away from the murder, but seized power after it, and, allied to Lepidus, after internecine war against Octavius, formed the triumvirate in 43 BC. He was given Asia, and had to appeal for clarification of a matter to the Queen of Egypt, Cleopatra. The rest is history. Life by Plutarch. In *JC*, he has the third-largest part, with 2,540 words.

12 LEPIDUS M. Aemilius Lepidus was praetor in 49 BC, consul with Caesar in 46. After the murder, being near Rome with troops, he was able to help Mark Antony. A role in the heart of *JC*, at 3.1 and 4.1, and in the first half of *AC*. Member of the triumvirate from its formation in 43 BC. Was given Africa: after trying to annex Sicily, was deprived of power and retired. He died in 13 BC.

13 CALPHURNIA so spelled throughout F, though Plutarch gives the Latin 'Calpurnia', the normal form in classical times.

14 PORTIA the Latin form of the family name, used by Shakespeare, here in *JC* and in *MV* 1.1.165–6. North has 'Porcia' for Plutarch's Πορκία (*Porkia*). Though a young wife to Brutus, she was the widow of Bibulus, already with sons. Her father, Marcus Porcius Cato, was renowned for his stern morality and hostility to Caesar. See Introduction, pp. 65–7.

15 LUCIUS Shakespeare's invention, though he used the name on seven other

occasions: see Introduction, pp. 74–5.

16 CICERO Marcus Tullius Cicero, philosopher, orator, statesman, letter-writer, founder of a school of rhetoric greatly influential in Europe; he was known to Elizabethan schoolboys as 'Tully'. He largely admired Caesar, but feared the rise of tyranny. In *JC* a sharp observer from outside: the failure of the conspirators (on Brutus' advice) to recruit him was a great error. Popular in Rome but a personal enemy of the triumvirate, he was murdered a year after Caesar's assassination. Life by Plutarch. His character in *JC* is largely Shakespeare's invention.

17 PUBLIUS a senator, Shakespeare's invention, warmly greeted by Caesar on the morning of the assassination (2.2.109). He later brushes Artemidorus aside (3.1.10) and is clearly, though silently, shocked by the murder (3.1.85–91). He is not a conspirator. His sudden arrival in 2.2 has led to the suggestion that Shakespeare originally intended Cassius at that point. See 2.2.107.2n. Not to be confused with that 'Publius Cimber' also invented by Shakespeare as a brother for Metellus in 3.1; see 3.1.44n.

18 POPILIUS Lena Popilius Laenas, a senator, wished Cassius well just before the murder, which he accidentally triggered by talking to Caesar in the Senate House (3.1.13–19). Plutarch, Appendix, pp. 340–1.

19 MURELLUS one of five tribunes of the people, speaking only in 1.1, and probably put to death soon after (1.2). The spelling in F is not otherwise known: Theobald first emended to 'Marullus' to match Plutarch, though only two men of that name occur in classical literature. Shakespeare may have wanted the brighter, sharper sound of the 'e'. See Introduction, pp. 73–4.

20 FLAVIUS another tribune, sharing Murellus' fate.

21 CINNA Gaius Helvius Cinna, poet and friend of Catullus and Suetonius. See 3.3.0.1n. Plutarch calls him 'one of Caesar's friends' (Appendix pp. 331, 343), not mentioning his poetry.

22 LUCILIUS a friend of Brutus who later became faithful to Antony (Plutarch, (Appendix, pp. 360–1). He is active with Brutus from 4.2; taken prisoner at Philippi, he says he is Brutus until Antony recognizes him.

23 TITINIUS according to Cassius at 1.2.127, attended Caesar in Spain. He reappears as an officer in Brutus' army in 4.3, with Messala seeing Brutus respond to the news of Portia's death. At 5.3, in the second battle of Philippi, sent by Cassius to check on troops, he finds Cassius dead, and kills himself with Cassius' sword. Plutarch spells him 'Titinnius', and calls him 'one of Cassius chiefest frendes' (Appendix p. 357).

24 MESSALA M. Valerius Messala Corvinus, a member of a distinguished Roman family. In 4.3 he brings the news of Portia's death to Brutus. Active in the battles of Philippi in 5.1, 2, 3 and 5, where he commends Strato to Octavius. He was later pardoned by the triumvirs, and became a friend and senior general of Octavius (Augustus).

25 Young CATO son of Marcus Cato and thus brother to Portia, he fights bravely for Brutus and is killed in battle in 5.4.

26 STRATO a Greek rhetorician and friend of Brutus. In 5.3 he is one of the group who find Cassius' body. In 5.5 he holds the sword for Brutus to kill himself. He was afterwards treated with distinction by Octavius, according to Plutarch (Appendix pp. 362–3).

27–8 VARRUS, CLAUDIO soldiers who at the end of 4.3 are bidden by Brutus to sleep in his tent before the battle of Philippi. They and their names are Shakespeare's inventions, though the names 'Claudius' and 'Varro' appear elsewhere in Plutarch. (Varro was one of Pompey's lieutenants.) Shakespeare had major characters called 'Claudio' in *MA* just before and *MM* just after

JC. 'Varro', a common Roman name, is used in *Tim*. 'Varrius' occurs in *MM* 4.5, Claudius in *Ham* (only in SDs).

29 CLITUS a soldier and friend whom Brutus in 5.5 first asks (aside) to kill him: his vigorous refusal ends 'I'll rather kill myself' (7).

30 DARDANIUS as Clitus, but asked second.

31 VOLUMNIUS as Clitus, but asked third. At *school* with Brutus (5.5.26), and particulary close. In Plutarch (Appendix, p. 362) Brutus makes the request in Greek.

32 PINDARUS a historically well-attested freed Parthian slave serving Cassius. He was 'reserved ever for suche a pinche' (Plutarch, Appendix, p. 358), the slaying of Cassius at his request: this Pindarus does at 5.3.46, when Cassius misunderstands the situation in the second battle of Philippi. Pindarus disappears 'Where never Roman shall take note of him' (5.3.50).

33 ARTEMIDORUS tries to warn Caesar. Plutarch tells us that he was 'a Doctor of Rhethoricke in the Greek tongue ... verie familliar with certaine of Brutus confederates ...' (Appendix, p. 328), presumably the reason for his knowledge of the conspiracy. He was 'born in the isle of Gnidos': his name suggests 'gift to Artemis' (the Roman Diana); but the Greek ἀρτεμία (*artemia*) means 'safety', and it could be a rhetorical invention by Plutarch.

34 A CARPENTER a heavy worker in wood; see 1.1.6n.

35 A COBBLER Cobblers and shoemakers were known for independence.

36 A POET a Cynic philosopher, one Marcus Favonius, who breaks into the quarrel between Brutus and Cassius at 4.3.122.1

37 A SOOTHSAYER not blind in Plutarch or Shakespeare, as a theatrical tradition has it (Appendix, p. 326)

THE TRAGEDY OF
JULIUS CAESAR

1.1   *Enter* FLAVIUS, MURELLUS *and certain*
Commoners *over the stage.*

FLAVIUS

Hence! home, you idle creatures, get you home!
Is this a holiday? What, know you not
(Being mechanical) you ought not walk

1.1 location: Rome, the setting to the end
of 4.1. (The rest of Act 4 is near Sardis,
and Act 5 is near Philippi.) Except for
2.1, F does not locate scenes as they
open. As well as the eighteenth-
century editors' scene numbers, their
brief locations are kept in the commentary to mark the imaginative
space. Here in 1.1, Rowe supplied
'Rome', Theobald 'A Street'.

The assassination of Caesar was in
March 44 BC, the death of Brutus in the
autumn of 42 BC. Caesar's triumph over
the sons of Pompey was in October 45 BC.

The short opening scene gives us a
city in a crisis of instability. Caesar's
triumphant return was familiar to
Elizabethans (see *H5* 5. Chorus. 26–8),
but Shakespeare sets this famous event
obliquely, suggesting uncertainty and
even contradiction, because the triumph described is that over Caesar's
enemy, Pompey. Instead of firm civic
authority, the play opens with a 'mob'.
By their equivocations they challenge
order (Siemon, 131–42).

0.1 MURELLUS as in F. For the name, see
List of Roles 19n. The five tribunes of
the people (*Cor* 1.1.13) were supposed
to maintain the republican tradition,
but these two, while detesting tyranny,
show no respect for, nor fellow-feeling

with, the people (Hunter, 118).

0.2 *over the stage* The group of celebrating commoners, crossing the stage, or
even climbing up from the yard
(Nicoll, 53), collides with the tribunes,
whose partisanship for Pompey makes
clear an antagonism to Caesar which at
once establishes one theme for the play.
Such an immediate conflict is a mark of
Shakespeare's new skill with openings.

1   **idle** The possible pun on 'idol' may
be the first of a run of ambiguities suggesting religious senses in this and later
scenes. Sixteenth- and seventeenth-
century polemicists used 'idol' as an
adjective, often from the Geneva (1599)
Bible's 'idol shepherd' at Zechariah, 11.17
(and running head). Here there may be,
as well as inactive people, 'idol creatures':
sham, counterfeit worshippers.
creatures implies contempt (*OED* 3.c)

2   **holiday** indistinguishable from a holy
day in Elizabethan times. For a possible holy-day/holiday occasion on the
day of the opening of the Globe
theatre, see Introduction, p. 19.

3   **mechanical** handicraftsmen. The
'rude mechanicals' of *MND* (3.2.9)
are a carpenter, a joiner, a weaver, a
bellows-mender, a tinker and a tailor.
Flavius' contempt implies their inferi-
ority as base and vulgar.

Title] *F*   **1.1**] *Actus Primus, Scoena Prima*   0.1 MURELLUS] *F (throughout)*; Marullus *Theobald*
(after Plutarch)

155

Upon a labouring day, without the sign
Of your profession? Speak, what trade art thou?   5
CARPENTER   Why, sir, a carpenter.
MURELLUS
Where is thy leather apron, and thy rule?
What dost thou with thy best apparel on?
You, sir, what trade are you?
COBBLER   Truly, sir, in respect of a fine workman, I am   10
but as you would say, a cobbler.
MURELLUS
But what trade art thou? Answer me directly.
COBBLER   A trade, sir, that I hope I may use with a safe
conscience, which is indeed, sir, a mender of bad soles.

4–5 **sign . . . profession** mark of occupation: Cleopatra fears being the captive
in such a triumph, uplifted by
'Mechanic slaves, / With greasy
aprons, rules and hammers' (*AC*
5.2.208–9). There is also in the phrase
as used in the sixteenth and seventeenth centuries an echo of a statement
of religious faith.

5 **thou** the pronoun for addressing family or friends affectionately, servants
good-humouredly, strangers contemptuously, animals, and God or others solemnly (Onions, 284; Abbott,
232). Shakespeare is always alert to the
use (Foakes, *KL* 7–8; Gurr, 10).
Flavius is again contemptuous.

6 **carpenter** a heavy worker in wood,
making the frame for ships or houses:
distinct from the joiner, who did finer
work, sometimes overlapping with the
cabinet-maker. The medieval Guild of
Carpenters led the Corpus Christi processions and plays; this first encounter
may carry a suggestion that what follows is a dramatic sacrificial story with
some association with the Bible passion narratives.

7 **rule** measuring-strip, but also with a

sense of regulation of conduct
9 **You . . . you** Murellus uses the correct
non-familiar pronoun, although its
repetition suggests scorn; *trade* is not
contemptuous, as the word then
embraced the professions.
10–32 The shift between verse and the
usual prose for commoners helps the
sense of instability.
10 **in respect of** compared to
11 **cobbler** bungler as well as shoe-
mender. The Cobbler's is the first
vividly individual role, and a subversive one. Max Beerbohm's affectionate
parody of the scene has, opening Act 3
of 'Savonarola', the stage direction,
'*The Piazza is filled from end to end with
a vast seething crowd that is drawn
entirely from the lower orders . . .
Cobblers predominate*' (Beerbohm,
198).
12 **thou** the more insulting pronoun
directly plainly: Murellus is already
disturbed by the Cobbler's quibbles.
Cf. 3.3.9.
13 **safe** morally sound
14 ***soles** The pun on 'souls' is common,
e.g. *TGV* 2.3.15–16; *MV* 4.1.123.

14 soles] *Q 1691*; soules *F*

FLAVIUS

What trade, thou knave? Thou naughty knave, what
   trade? 15

COBBLER   Nay I beseech you, sir, be not out with me: yet
if you be out, sir, I can mend you.

MURELLUS   What mean'st thou by that? Mend me, thou
saucy fellow?

COBBLER   Why, sir, cobble you. 20

FLAVIUS   Thou art a cobbler, art thou?

COBBLER   Truly, sir, all that I live by, is with the awl: I
meddle with no tradesman's matters, nor women's

---

15 **knave** a base and crafty rogue: Flavius, in doubt throughout the scene about what the Cobbler is saying, calls him devious. There is no need to change F's ascription of this speech and give it to Murellus, as most editors have done following Capell.

naughty having nothing (naught); wicked

16, 20 **you, sir . . . Why, sir** The Cobbler takes on, and mocks, both tribunes.

16, 17 **out . . . out** angry, and with holes in shoes. Something provokes Murellus' agitated retort. The Cobbler's insubordination is provocation enough, but he may be saying that he can handle a sexual offer.

18 **mean'st** It is unnecessary to make the line verse by reading 'meanest' or omitting *thou* (Steevens) on the grounds that elsewhere the tribunes are always metrically correct. *Thou* is important in expressing Murellus' personal disturbance about what he thinks the Cobbler might have said to him: and a slight jolt to regularity of form is surely to be expected.

19 **saucy** insolent; lascivious: stronger than today's usage

20 **cobble you** Some of the heat in these exchanges is explained if *cobble* is also

taken as 'couple', a sense perhaps surviving in 'cobble together' (*OED v.*[1] 2). Though *OED v.*[2] records a dialect meaning of the verb as 'To pelt with stones', the earliest recorded use is 1691, and an undercurrent of sexual meaning is more likely to be giving offence.

22 **all . . . awl** a pun common enough to appear as a proverb (Tilley, A406) but also strongly sexual (Bate), leading to the next phrase: awl = a pointed tool for boring holes.

23 **meddle** has strong older senses of mix or blend (*OED* meddle *v.* 5), allowing an explicit sexual sense as in *Cor* 4.5.45–8)

tradesman's matters The Cobbler confines himself to his work (*awl*) and takes no personal part in trade politics.

23–4 **women's matters** F1 switches from a singular 'Tradesmans' to plural 'womens', F2 to 'womans'. F1 suggests more strongly the shift in *matters* from personal politics to licentious sexuality, as Hamlet to Ophelia, 'country matters' (*Ham* 3.2.110–16). There may be a faint echo of Dekker's *Shoemaker's Holiday* (Ard[2]).

---

15 SP] Marullus *Steevens*   18 mean'st thou by] meanest thou by *(Steevens)*   23 women's] *(*womens*)*; womans *F2*   24 withal I] with all. I *Capell*

matters; but withal I am indeed, sir, a surgeon to old
shoes; when they are in great danger, I recover them.   25
As proper men as ever trod upon neat's leather have
gone upon my handiwork.

FLAVIUS

But wherefore art not in thy shop today?
Why dost thou lead these men about the streets?

COBBLER   Truly, sir, to wear out their shoes, to get myself   30
into more work. But indeed, sir, we make holiday to see
Caesar and to rejoice in his triumph.

MURELLUS

Wherefore rejoice? What conquest brings he home?
What tributaries follow him to Rome
To grace in captive bonds his chariot wheels?   35
You blocks, you stones, you worse than senseless things!

---

24 **withal** Capell emended to 'with all';
that is, like *withal*, only part of the pun,
which includes 'with awl'.

24–5 **old shoes** things discarded as
worthless; there may be a suggestion of
female sexuality even here; *OED* shoe
sb. 2l has 'to tread her shoe awry' as to
fall from virtue; cf. *TGV* 2.3.17–18.

25 **great danger** Laertes warns Ophelia
(*Ham* 1.3.35) to keep 'out of the . . .
danger of desire': the Cobbler as *sur-geon* may be claiming to bring unex-pected satisfaction to *old shoes*.
   recover re-cover; restore to health

26 **proper** handsome; cf. *Oth* 4.3.34–5,
'This Lodovico is a proper man . . . A
very handsome man.'
   neat's leather shoes made from the
hides of cattle – a more refined, and
patriotic, English product, contrasted
with shoes made of Spanish leather,
considered tougher. The whole phrase
is proverbial (Dent, M66).

28 **shop** workshop

32 **triumph** his victory, and his proces-sional entrance into Rome. A Roman
general had to leave his army outside

the city: one point of a triumph was
that he was on that occasion allowed to
bring it in. This, in October 45 BC, was
Caesar's second triumph, won in
March that year at Munda in Spain
against Pompey's sons. Plutarch
records the people's resentment at
such a ceremony because the victory,
seven months before, had not been
against barbarians, but 'the sonnes of
the noblest man in Rome, whom for-tune had overthrowen' (*Caesar*, 77).

33–56 This fine speech affects the crowd.
The same process is striking later in
the play, at what can be thought to be
the opening of the second half of the
play, 3.2.

33 **conquest** specifically the traditional
booty; more generally a pointed ques-tion, the victory being not new terri-tory but 'the calamities of his [own]
country' (Plutarch, *Caesar*, 77)

34–5 Antony contradicts Murellus' par-ticular inference at 3.2.89.

34 **tributaries** payers of tribute

36 **senseless** incapable of sense, both as
feeling and as wisdom

33] *Rowe; F lines* reioyce? / home? /

O you hard hearts, you cruel men of Rome,
Knew you not Pompey? Many a time and oft
Have you climbed up to walls and battlements,
To towers and windows, yea, to chimney-tops,   40
Your infants in your arms, and there have sat
The livelong day, with patient expectation,
To see great Pompey pass the streets of Rome:
And when you saw his chariot but appear,
Have you not made an universal shout,   45
That Tiber trembled underneath her banks
To hear the replication of your sounds
Made in her concave shores?
And do you now put on your best attire?

38 **Pompey** Gnaeus Pompeius, 106–48 BC, 'the Great', the subject of one of Plutarch's *Lives*, where he is parallel with Agesilaus. An outstanding general, a first triumvir with Caesar and Crassus, and husband of Caesar's daughter, he took the rise of the upstart Caesar too lightly. Caesar defeated him in Spain and then, decisively, at Pharsalus in Thessaly in August 48, from whence he fled to Egypt: he was murdered as he arrived by hirelings of Ptolemy (his own former centurions) even as he sought asylum. Shakespeare has over ninety references to the name, some, as in *LLL* and *MM*, comic. One, *2H6* 4.1.137–8, is to that stabbing – by 'savage islanders', from a telescoping of Plutarch, who records that the two who were responsible for his death were Theophanes of Lesbos and Theodotus of Chio (North, 716), both places being islands in the Aegean. Pompey's 'spirit . . . presides over the whole play' (Williams, 36).

38–51 **Many . . . way** The vivid scene, not in Plutarch, has the mark of occasions in London, as in *R2* 5.2.7–21; *1H4* 3.2.46–59; *H5* 5. Chorus. 22–34.

40 **chimney-tops** The familiar compound is first recorded here in *OED*. The picture is more London than Rome.

43 **great Pompey** His title was Pompeius Magnus.

45–8 **universal . . . shores** The huge sudden sound from a crowd, and its echo across the river, make the first of many references to the experience of playgoing on London's Bankside, additionally appropriate if *JC* opened the new Globe there.

46 **her** Like Father Thames, the Tiber was traditionally seen as masculine; the feminine possessive adjective (cf. 1.2.101) may have been called up by the trembling reaction to sudden emotion in praise of a male hero: Cassius presently speaks suggestively of Caesar and himself, as males 'buffeting' Tiber 'With lusty sinews . . . And stemming it . . .' (1.2.107–9).

47 **replication** echo: *OED*'s first citation in this sense

48 **concave** hollow (cf. *AYL* 3.4.24, 'I do think him concave as a covered goblet'); inwardly curving and overhanging

38 Pompey? Many] *Rowe*; *Pompey* many *F*   40 windows, yea] *Rowe;* Windows? Yea *F*

And do you now cull out a holiday?   50
And do you now strew flowers in his way,
That comes in triumph over Pompey's blood?
Be gone!
Run to your houses, fall upon your knees,
Pray to the gods to intermit the plague   55
That needs must light on this ingratitude.

FLAVIUS

Go, go, good countrymen, and for this fault
Assemble all the poor men of your sort;
Draw them to Tiber banks, and weep your tears
Into the channel, till the lowest stream   60
Do kiss the most exalted shores of all.

Exeunt all the Commoners.

See where their basest mettle be not moved.
They vanish tongue-tied in their guiltiness.
Go you down that way towards the Capitol.

---

50 **cull** pick (a holiday out of a working day)
51 **flowers** Murellus in the heart of his speech aims at suggestions of domestic, feminine and natural innocence to move the crowd. But picking and strewing flowers can have in Shakespeare a darker quality of madness or death – or both, to look no further than Ophelia (*Ham* 4.5.172–82). A subtext is that Murellus' manipulation is dangerous.
52 **Pompey's blood** literally, and his kin: F's 'Pompeyes' could be plural, to include the sons.
55–6 **intermit . . . light on** suspend the plague that will inevitably fall to their lot
58 **sort** class, kind
59–61 **weep . . . all** a surreal image of emotional excess, whereby the men's tears will raise the level of Tiber to its highest banks: but Flavius' subtext is of the subservience of his hearers, in *poor men . . . lowest . . . kiss . . . most*

exalted. He is a strange republican.
62 **where** ambiguous. The subjunctive in *be not moved* points to *whe'er* as 'whether': in keeping *where*, Flavius points triumphantly to the success of their rhetoric; cf. *TS* 5.1.47, 'see where he looks out of the window'.
  mettle almost invariably ambiguous: the Commoners have the basest spirit, rapidly affected; they are also of the basest metal in creation, lead, which melts most quickly.
64 **Capitol** a significant indicator of location at this point in the play, and one to which all the action of the next scenes will drive. It was the great national temple of Rome, dedicated to Jupiter; it overlooked the Forum, making *down that way* rather odd. Shakespeare, writing for the Globe, may have had the downstream Tower in his mind. Flavius sends Murellus on a risky enterprise into the most politically sensitive part of Rome.

52 Pompey's] *(Pompeyes)*   62 where] whe're *Theobald*

This way will I. Disrobe the images,   65
If you do find them decked with ceremonies.
MURELLUS
    May we do so?
    You know it is the feast of Lupercal.
FLAVIUS
    It is no matter. Let no images
    Be hung with Caesar's trophies. I'll about,   70
    And drive away the vulgar from the streets.
    So do you too, where you perceive them thick.
    These growing feathers plucked from Caesar's wing
    Will make him fly an ordinary pitch,
    Who else would soar above the view of men,   75
    And keep us all in servile fearfulness.   *Exeunt.*

65–6 **Disrobe ... ceremonies.** Statues
of Caesar had been ornamented by his
supporters with diadems (Plutarch,
Appendix, p. 335), *trophies* (below, 69),
scarves (1.2.284), even the laurel crown
(1.2.220 and Plutarch, Appendix, p.
368), all as symbols of state pomp and
rule. Shakespeare, overlapping the
occasion with the Lupercalia (see next
note), makes the tribunes' action dou-
bly sacrilegious.

68 **Lupercal** 15 February; Caesar's triumph had been in October, five months
before. Shakespeare gets dramatic value
out of combining the two: in telescoping the time to the Ides (15th) of March;
in giving religious colour; and in weak-
ening Calphurnia (and thus Caesar) and

strengthening   Antony   (1.2.3–11).
Lupercus, a rural deity associated with
Pan and the legendary history of the
founding of Rome, brought fertility.
The Lupercal was also a cave where a
wolf suckled Romulus and Remus.

71 **the vulgar** the common people: less
pejorative than today, as the Catholic
Church's Latin Bible, 'the common
version', became the Vulgate

73–6 'Disabling Caesar like a falcon will
prevent his rise to a high *pitch* (the
highest point a falcon reaches before
swooping on prey), so far out of sight
of men as to be a god.' Dante (*Inferno*,
4.123) gave Caesar '*occhi grifagni*',
translated by Cary as 'falcon eyes'.

75 **else** otherwise

[1.2] *Enter* CAESAR, ANTONY *for the course,* CALPHURNIA, PORTIA, DECIUS, CICERO, BRUTUS, CASSIUS, CASKA, *a* Soothsayer; *after them* MURELLUS *and* FLAVIUS.

CAESAR
    Calphurnia.

CASKA   Peace, ho! Caesar speaks.

CAESAR   Calphurnia.

CALPHURNIA   Here, my lord.

CAESAR
    Stand you directly in Antonio's way
    When he doth run his course. Antonio.

1.2 location: 'Rome. A public place' (Capell). Eighteenth-century scene numbers were added when the stage was cleared, though not consistently. Nothing should interrupt the flow of the action, and modern productions without interval (as by Terry Hands at Stratford in 1987) have been valued. Since they are conventional for reference, scene numbers are kept in this edition.

0.1–3 Overlapping the exits of the tribunes, probably to opposite sides downstage, Caesar makes a magisterial arrival from upstage (no doubt using the central door of the Globe's *frons scenae*). He is in processional pomp on his way to the Forum, making an entry which comments on Flavius' last words. He comes to attend one of the chief Roman festivals. Shakespeare makes the matter less simple, however, for those around him are all in complex relation to him. He enriches Plutarch (Appendix, p. 324) with great skill, to create a grand entry, to add Calphurnia and Caesar's desire for an heir, and to make a setting for the cryptic warning (Thomson, 236–7).

0.1 *course* Antony, like the other runners offstage, is naked except for a girdle of goatskin. For the Lupercalia cere-

mony, as the young men ran round the bounds of the Palatine (Palace) Hill, they struck with goatskin strips those whom they met, especially women. The superstition (cf. 2.1.194) held that this ritual ended sterility (Plutarch, Appendix, pp. 324 and 367 and see *OCD* Lupercalia).

0.3 MURELLUS *and* FLAVIUS have no action in the scene and do not speak. They come in awkwardly after their exits. But F clearly brings them on at the end of the procession – they can appear (as at Stratford in 1972) under arrest. Their silence may be an expression of their contempt, for at the same time their presence indicates their importance. Kittredge was the first editor to omit them here.

1 **Peace . . . speaks** 'the megaphone of sycophants' (Brooke, 146)

3–6 **Antonio** F's occasional '*Antonio*', followed throughout this text, is suggestive in the light of Shakespeare's seven other Antonios (in *TGV, TS, MV, MA, TN, AW, Tem*), all in Italian-set plays. We should not be quick to assume error, as the eighteenth-century editors in particular were ready to do. Shakespeare can be seen to use 'Antonio' in this play to signal a special address (see Introduction, p. 125).

1.2] *Pope*   3 Antonio's] *(Antonio's);* Antonius' *Pope*   4, 6 Antonio] *(Antonio);* Antonius *Pope (passim)*

ANTONY   Caesar, my lord.   5

CAESAR

Forget not in your speed, Antonio,

To touch Calphurnia; for our elders say,

The barren touched in this holy chase

Shake off their sterile curse.

ANTONY   I shall remember.

When Caesar says 'Do this', it is performed.   10

CAESAR

Set on, and leave no ceremony out.   [*Music.*]

SOOTHSAYER   Caesar!

CAESAR   Ha! Who calls?

CASKA

Bid every noise be still. Peace yet again!

CAESAR

Who is it in the press that calls on me?   15

I hear a tongue shriller than all the music

Cry 'Caesar!' Speak. Caesar is turned to hear.

---

8   **touched** touchèd
9   **sterile curse** curse of sterility
(Abbott, 3). Shakespeare alters
Plutarch to make Calphurnia's curse of
barrenness (or, at least, Caesar's asser-
tion of it) dominant at Caesar's first
entry. He has no legitimate son. He
needs an heir. He is immediately vulnerable in his dynastic ambition.
*****remember** F's comma suggests cyn-
icism, that Antony needed to remind
himself of Caesar's power: that seems
inappropriate here.
11   **Set on** go forward; begin
15   **press** pressing throng: used five times
in the Gospels in Tyndale, *NT*,
Geneva 1560 and KJB for people
pressing about Jesus (e.g. Mark, 2.4)
17   **Caesar is turned** Caesar's use of his
own name here is part of the dramatic
process of striking the audience with

his essential presence: cf. *Ham*
1.2.42–50, where Laertes, when first
addressed, is named four times in nine
lines. Elizabethan schoolboys were
taught Latin partly through Caesar's
Commentaries (Baldwin, *School*, 1.125
and *passim*; and see Spencer, 37),
where Caesar always calls himself
'Caesar'. Too much can be made of
Caesar using 'Caesar' as if he 'collabo-
rates in his own deification' (Palmer,
Characters, 37). True, Caesar speaks
about himself more than any other
character does; but then he is also more
spoken about (as Coriolanus in the
later play). All the main characters
speak more of Caesar than themselves
(see Introduction, pp. 41–2).
turned gives full attention, and
possibly because of deafness thought to
accompany epilepsy (Temkin, 246–54)

9 remember.] *Rowe;* remember, *F*   11 SD *Music.*] *this edn; Musick; and the Procession moves. /
Capell; not in F*

SOOTHSAYER

Beware the Ides of March.

CAESAR   What man is that?

BRUTUS   A soothsayer bids you beware the Ides of March.

CAESAR

Set him before me. Let me see his face.   20

CASSIUS   Fellow, come from the throng. Look upon Caesar.

CAESAR

What sayst thou to me now? Speak once again.

SOOTHSAYER   Beware the Ides of March.

CAESAR

He is a dreamer. Let us leave him. Pass.   *Sennet.*

Exeunt all but Brutus and Cassius.

CASSIUS

Will you go see the order of the course?   25

BRUTUS   Not I.

CASSIUS   I pray you, do.

18, 19, 23 Beware . . . March. the 15th of that month (for the Roman calendar, see Introduction, pp. 16–22). Plutarch dates the warning 'long time afore'. The mysterious cry from the crowd, triply repeated, is dramatically sharp. Brutus' first speech in the play is ill-omened.

24 He . . . Pass. a superbly decisive line ('pure gold', Granville-Barker, 81): even so early in the scene, however, all auditors and readers know it to be one of Caesar's gravest errors of judgement. Caesar's metrically perfect line follows a short one (23), suggesting a brief pause.

dreamer attention to this 'dream', as to Calphurnia's (2.2.2–3), would have saved Caesar's life and changed the history of the world. Close behind the pragmatic action of the play is a rich hinterland of metaphysical experiences – to be expected in a play called

A Midsummer Night's Dream, less so in an account of the *realpolitik* of Caesar's assassination. Later Cinna, too, tells us he had dreamed (3.3.1–2).

SD Sennet a flourish of trumpets

25 the . . . course how the ritual is organized, recalling *speed* (6) and *chase* (8); *course* also suggests where the race is held, and *the order* in which the runners finish. *OED* course *sb.* 32 records the biblical use of the word for the organization of the rota of priestly duties: the unusual linking with *order* to make the rare 'the order of his course' is at Luke, 1.8, in the story about an apparently barren woman, Elizabeth, conceiving (Sohmer, chap. 5). A variant is in Geneva 1560, but Shakespeare's phrase came to KJB through Rheims *NT* (1582). In the Lupercal race there is an undercurrent of priestly function.

24.1 *Exeunt all but*] *Manet F1; Manent F2*

BRUTUS

I am not gamesome. I do lack some part
Of that quick spirit that is in Antony.
Let me not hinder, Cassius, your desires;   30
I'll leave you.

CASSIUS

Brutus, I do observe you now of late.
I have not from your eyes that gentleness
And show of love as I was wont to have.
You bear too stubborn and too strange a hand   35
Over your friend, that loves you.

BRUTUS   Cassius,

Be not deceived. If I have veiled my look,
I turn the trouble of my countenance
Merely upon myself. Vexed I am

28–9 Brutus, in this his third speech in the play, shows faulty judgement, both in detaching himself from an important Roman ritual where Antony is central to Caesar, and considering Antony as too light (see 2.1.164, 180–2).

28 **gamesome** sportive, enjoying such a race, with a suggestion of not being serious

29 **quick** lively, with a suggestion of volatile superficiality

34 **show** declaration: more than appearance

35 **stubborn** a metaphor from riding, suggesting firm control, the 'hard rein' of *KL* 3.1.27
strange distant; again, through *hand*, linked with the control of a horse

36 **friend, that loves** F2 reads 'friends that love': but Plutarch tells of recent personal rivalry for promotion between the two (Appendix, p. 325). Caesar preferred Brutus: a first hint of parallels with *Oth*, written soon after. In *JC*, behind the severe action of public duty and virtue, is an unexpectedly warm experience of love

and friendship (see Introduction, p. 8).

37–9 **If ... myself.** Set off by Cassius' *I do observe* (32) and *from your eyes* (33), significant shared images from the mechanics of sight, over nearly forty lines, culminate in Cassius' *I your glass* of 68. Such rhetorical craft does much to strengthen the sense of mutual need of the speakers for each other, at the start of this long dialogue, one of the core passages of the play. The sense is: 'If both my glance and my manner have seemed cold and unreachable, it is because I have been entirely (*Merely*) occupied with my own problems: I have deliberately kept myself to myself.' The intensity of private, hidden conflict isolates him. In this he is like Prince Hamlet, already probably in Shakespeare's mind (see Introduction, pp. 49, 60). Plutarch records the cause as less moral dilemma than responsibility for his family name, and for friends (Appendix, p. 335).

39 **Vexed** vexèd

Of late with passions of some difference,   40
Conceptions only proper to myself
Which give some soil, perhaps, to my behaviours.
But let not therefore my good friends be grieved
(Among which number, Cassius, be you one)
Nor construe any further my neglect   45
Than that poor Brutus, with himself at war,
Forgets the shows of love to other men.

CASSIUS

Then, Brutus, I have much mistook your passion,
By means whereof this breast of mine hath buried
Thoughts of great value, worthy cogitations.   50
Tell me, good Brutus, can you see your face?

BRUTUS

No, Cassius; for the eye sees not itself
But by reflection, by some other things.

CASSIUS   'Tis just,
And it is very much lamented, Brutus,   55

---

40 **passions** strong feelings (literally suf-
ferings) but, as with Hamlet and King
Lear, not in the body's organs, but the
mind (*conceptions*).
  difference disagreement, conflict. Cf.
MV 4.1.166, 'the difference / That
holds this present question in the
court'.
41 **proper** belonging only to a person; *only*,
proper and *to myself* have triple force
42 **soil** stain; also solution, explanation
(*OED sb.* 5; cf. *Son* 69.14, 'The soil is
this'); and possibly an older sense of
absolution (*OED v.*[2] 1). Brutus,
expressing his sense of his own
isolation, like Hamlet articulates rich
complexities.
45 **construe** cònstrue: expound, construe a meaning of
46 **poor ... war** He has been deficient
(*poor*) because, torn between love of
Caesar and belief in freedom, he has

been self-absorbed.
49–50 **By ... Thoughts** Because I mis-
understood your suffering (*passion*) I
kept my thoughts to myself. With passions in the mind, and thoughts in the
breast, the body is disordered.
50 **worthy** of great value: stronger than
today's usage (as is its opposite,
'naughty', of no value); parallel to *worthiness*, 57
52–8 **the ... shadow** In a roughly similar
relationship, Ulysses' exchange with
Achilles, *TC* 3.3.95–111, written close
in time to this passage, elaborates this
familiar thought from Cicero
(Dolman, fol. E6[v]; Dent, E231a; and
cf. Sir John Davies, *Nosce Teipsum*
(i.e. Know Thyself) 1599, stanza 47,
'Mine eyes ... nor see my face ...';
and Scott).
53 The stress is on *other*.
54 **just** true

52–3] *Rowe; F lines Cassius: / reflection, / things. /*

That you have no such mirrors as will turn
Your hidden worthiness into your eye,
That you might see your shadow: I have heard
Where many of the best respect in Rome
(Except immortal Caesar) speaking of Brutus, 60
And groaning underneath this age's yoke,
Have wished that noble Brutus had his eyes.

BRUTUS

Into what dangers would you lead me, Cassius,
That you would have me seek into myself
For that which is not in me? 65

CASSIUS

Therefore, good Brutus, be prepared to hear.
And since you know you cannot see yourself
So well as by reflection, I your glass
Will modestly discover to yourself
That of yourself which you yet know not of. 70
And be not jealous on me, gentle Brutus.
Were I a common laughter, or did use

58 **shadow** reflection, as *VA* 161, 'Narcissus . . . died to kiss his shadow in the brook.' *R2* 4.1.276–302 is a classic exposition, ('The shadow of your sorrow hath destroy'd / The shadow of your face'). That is also in a context of questioned self-knowledge in a dramatic challenge to existing rule. Richard adumbrates Brutus' particular version of the essentially tragic conflict between inner world and public statecraft which begins to occupy Shakespeare from about this time (see Introduction, pp. 51–2, 142–3). *Shadow* also carries a sense of out of the light, as Brutus' look has been *veiled* (37).

59 **best respect** highest rank; 'the noblest men and best citizens' (Plutarch, Appendix, p. 335)

60 **immortal Caesar** and thus beyond Romans of even the *best respect*.

Cassius first comes to the point, and first mentions Caesar, in an ambiguous sarcastic aside. He reflects how most Romans see Caesar.

62 **had his eyes** could see the yoke, sharing the sight of *many*

66 **Therefore** as to that. Cassius is not simply ignoring Brutus' significant three lines: again (as in 24) the metrically perfect line after a short line suggests a pause.

69 **modestly discover** disclose without exaggeration

71 **jealous on** suspicious of
gentle primarily 'noble', as in 'gently born'

72 **laughter** laughing-stock. F is clear enough – that everyone laughed at him. Q5 and editors since Rowe emended to 'laugher' (i.e. jester) or even 'lover' (Cam[1]), though that would

58–9 *Rowe; F lines* shadow: / heard, / Rome, / Laugher *Q5, Rowe*   63] *Rowe; F lines* you / Cassius? /   72 laughter]

To stale with ordinary oaths my love
To every new protester; if you know
That I do fawn on men, and hug them hard,   75
And after scandal them; or if you know
That I profess myself in banqueting
To all the rout, then hold me dangerous.

Flourish, and shout.

BRUTUS

What means this shouting? I do fear the people
Choose Caesar for their king.

CASSIUS   Ay, do you fear it?   80

involve unique compositorial misreading in *JC*'s clean text. *Laughter* is the first of four different kinds of untrustworthiness, expressed in the next lines in brief cameos. These Cassius says are not true of him, and are beneath the nobility of Brutus. In each case they imply patrician superiority, for all the conspirators' claim to act for all Rome. Cf. 4.3.49 and n.

72–3 **did use / To** were in the habit of

73 **ordinary** 'commonplace; perhaps also suggesting bibulous familiarity, an *ordinary* being a tavern' (Oxf¹)

74 **protester** 'One who makes a protestation or solemn affirmation' (*OED* protester 1, citing this first). Cassius' point is wider than the amatory; it is devaluation of response to something important. As each idea passes, he sharpens the distinction between the terms, here *stale* and *protester*.

75 **fawn** at root an animal, physical gesture: cf. *Luc* 421, 'As the grim lion fawneth o'er his prey'.
    hug The word appears late in the sixteenth century; *OED* hug *v.* and *sb.*

76 **scandal** revile: a recent reimport from Latin (*OED v.* 2b, citing this first) with a strong religious sense of offence, from the Greek of Galatians, 5.11, also in the Latin Vulgate and Rheims *NT*, 'the scandal of the cross' in a context of being 'called unto liberty' (5.13).

Hamlet also opposes a 'noble substance' with defamation, 'to his own scandal' (*Ham* 1.4.38). In Cassius' mind, after the physicality of *fawn* and *hug*, the word extends distinction.

77 **profess myself** make profession of friendship. The hint of the religious sense of declaration of personal faith ties with *protester*: the F2 and subsequent Folios' omission of *myself* supports that.
    banqueting luxurious indulgence, carousing: as a verbal noun in Coverdale (1535) at Job, 1.5; and in Rheims *NT* (1582) and later KJB (1611) at 1 Peter, 4.3: 'riotousness, desires, excess of wine, banketings, potations, and unlawful services of idols'

78 **rout** rabble: the word devalues *profess myself*. Cam¹ quotes Moulton, 190, 'All through the conversation between Brut. and Cass. the shouting of the mob reminds us [or rather forewarns us; J.D.W.] of the sc[ene] going on in the Capitol.'

78.1 *Flourish* a fanfare signalling an event
    shout Brutus and Cassius comment as if they are standing outside a theatre, like the new Globe, in which dramatic events are happening. Underscoring their perverse, patrician isolation, *rout* (78) suggests their superiority to the crowd which even now Caesar is pleasing.

77 myself] *Om.F2*   79–80] *Rowe; F lines* Showting? / *Caesar* / King / it?

Then must I think you would not have it so.

BRUTUS

I would not, Cassius, yet I love him well.
But wherefore do you hold me here so long?
What is it that you would impart to me?
If it be aught toward the general good, 85
Set honour in one eye, and death i'th' other,
And I will look on both indifferently.
For let the gods so speed me as I love
The name of honour more than I fear death.

CASSIUS

I know that virtue to be in you, Brutus, 90
As well as I do know your outward favour.
Well, honour is the subject of my story.
I cannot tell what you and other men
Think of this life; but for my single self
I had as lief not be as live to be 95
In awe of such a thing as I myself.
I was born free as Caesar, so were you;
We both have fed as well, and we can both
Endure the winter's cold as well as he.
For once, upon a raw and gusty day, 100

85–9 **If . . . death.** Brutus appears inconsistent (*indifferently* = impartially). His conclusion is that he will put above personal safety honour, to him 'nobleness of mind, scorn of meanness, magnanimity' (Johnson). This, for the highest good, will be his even in death. Cf. *1H4* 1.3.195–208: 'but the steady tone differs from Hotspur's extravagance' (Oxf[1]). Plutarch (see Appendix, p. 335).

88 **gods . . . speed** echoing 'God speed', i.e. make prosper

91 **favour** appearance, countenance, particularly in late-sixteenth-century use

92 **honour . . . story** The *story* in the next thirty-six lines shows that for Cassius *honour* means, as more commonly, personal esteem, reputation.

95 **lief** soon, with wordplay on 'love'. 'I would as soon be dead.'

96 **such . . . myself** a human being like me

97 **I . . . Caesar** See Plutarch (Appendix, p. 334), for Cassius' personal choler, 'hating Caesar privatlie'.

98 **fed as well** enjoyed physical pleasures

100–28 **For . . . girl.** Cassius now extends his earlier sketches to fuller short stories, vivid with bodily sense, and again with a sharp distinction; this time between anything extraordinary in Caesar and common humanity, best exemplified in Cassius himself. Cassius' scorn produces nothing to Caesar's detriment.

100 **gusty** *OED* first cites 'gust' (*sb.*[1]) in *Tit* 5.3.69, and 'gusty' (*a.*[1]) not till 1600.

The troubled Tiber chafing with her shores,
Caesar said to me, 'Dar'st thou, Cassius, now
Leap in with me into this angry flood
And swim to yonder point?' Upon the word,
Accoutred as I was, I plunged in   105
And bade him follow; so indeed he did.
The torrent roared, and we did buffet it
With lusty sinews, throwing it aside,
And stemming it with hearts of controversy.
But ere we could arrive the point proposed   110
Caesar cried, 'Help me, Cassius, or I sink!'
I, as Aeneas, our great ancestor,
Did from the flames of Troy upon his shoulder
The old Anchises bear, so from the waves of Tiber
Did I the tired Caesar: and this man   115
Is now become a god, and Cassius is
A wretched creature, and must bend his body
If Caesar carelessly but nod on him.
He had a fever when he was in Spain,

101 **chafing with** fretting against: cf. *KL*
4.6.21; *WT* 3.3.87.
her See 1.1.45n.
104 **swim** Plutarch records Caesar saving
his own life by swimming strongly,
even with a pile of books held up with
one hand (*Caesar*, 74–5); and see
Suetonius, 64 (Rolfe, 1.85).
105 **Accoutred** equipped, attired. The
word was new. *OED* gives *MV* 3.4.63,
'accoutred like young men', as first
use. It cannot here mean wearing
armour, just fully dressed, perhaps for
a special occasion.
plunged plungèd
107 **buffet** *OED* v. 1b records first use
here in the sense of beat back, contend
with.
108 **sinews** technically, what attach
muscle to bone; but standing for
strength: cf. *Cor* 5.6.45.
109 **stemming** making headway against.

OED stem *v.*³ records first use of the
verb in this frequent sense in *3H6*
2.6.36.
controversy controvèrsy; competi-
tive dispute: struggle against the flood
110 **arrive the point** a Latin form, omitting the preposition after a verb of
motion; see Abbott, 198.
112–14 **as . . . bear** Virgil,11.721ff., gives
the account of Aeneas rescuing his
father Anchises from burning Troy,
familiar to Elizabethans as an example
of filial piety. The reference is pointed,
as Aeneas founded Rome.
117 **creature** someone beneath, an
instrument; recent in this sense (*OED*
creature 5); cf. 1.1.1 and n.
bend his body make a bow
118 **nod on** more condescending than
'nod at'
119 **fever** Plutarch gives the exact contrary: Caesar, though 'leane, white and

And when the fit was on him I did mark   120
How he did shake. 'Tis true, this god did shake:
His coward lips did from their colour fly,
And that same eye, whose bend doth awe the world,
Did lose his lustre: I did hear him groan:
Ay, and that tongue of his that bade the Romans   125
Mark him, and write his speeches in their books,
'Alas,' it cried, 'give me some drink, Titinius',
As a sick girl. Ye gods, it doth amaze me
A man of such a feeble temper should
So get the start of the majestic world   130

soft skinned, and often subject to headache, and otherwise to the falling sickness', fought 'always with his disease, travelling continually ... and commonly lying abroad in the field' (*Caesar*, 66).

122 **coward ... fly** Dent, C773, records the familiar version, 'a coward changes colour', with the sense of colour draining from a face: Cassius' inversion, the lips flying from their colour, allows the ambiguity of cowardly soldiers flying the 'colours', the battlefield ensign, a use first recorded in the 1590s (*OED* colour *sb.*[1] 7). See *TNK* 5.1.113–14 for similar reversal of an expected construction.

123 **bend** in the sense of formidable gaze, 'inclination of the eye in any direction' (*OED* bend *sb.*[4] 3, citing only here).
   awe terrify; *OED* awe *v.* 1, 'control ... by ... fear', records a recent (1599) reuse in *MA* 2.3.250.

124 **his** The neuter 'its' (as for an object, *eye*) did not arrive until later. It is not found e.g. in KJB (1611). The ambiguity is pleasing, of Caesar losing his own lustre.
   lustre a sixteenth-century import from Latin

126 **books** Cassius is inventing: no collections of Caesar's speeches survive, though Plutarch (*Caesar*, 60)

compares Caesar as orator favourably with Cicero, and Suetonius records Caesar saying 'that men should take heed when they spoke with him and should regard what he said as laws' (Rolfe, 1.101.) Cf. *2H6* 4.7.6–14.

127 **'Alas,'** The quotation marks, not in F, indicate Cassius' imitation of Caesar's groan.
   Titinius As Cassius continues his imitation, the name fits well with the squeaking high 'i' sounds in 'it cried give me ... drink ... sick girl'. Titinius does not appear in Plutarch more than as 'one of Cassius chiefest frendes' (Appendix, p. 357), until the scene of Cassius' death; in this play until 4.2.02, speaking first at 4.2.236.

128 **amaze** in the sense of greatly astonish, recent: *OED* *v.*[4] cites first *VA* (1593) 634.

129 **temper** physical condition; but also, newly, mental constitution, like the later-nineteenth-century 'temperament'. *OED* *sb.* 9 gives *KJ* 5.2.40 as first use.

130 **get ... of** have priority of position in: 'so getting the *palm* of victory' (Oxf[1]); recent in this sense (*OED* start *sb.*[2] 6, first use 1580)
   majestic *OED* majestic *a.* b cites this as first use; from Latin.

And bear the palm alone.   *Shout. Flourish.*
BRUTUS   Another general shout?
I do believe that these applauses are
For some new honours that are heaped on Caesar.
CASSIUS
Why, man, he doth bestride the narrow world
Like a colossus, and we petty men   135
Walk under his huge legs and peep about
To find ourselves dishonourable graves.
Men at some time are masters of their fates.
The fault, dear Brutus, is not in our stars
But in ourselves, that we are underlings.   140
'Brutus' and 'Caesar': what should be in that 'Caesar'?
Why should that name be sounded more than yours?
Write them together: yours is as fair a name:
Sound them, it doth become the mouth as well.
Weigh them, it is as heavy: conjure with 'em,   145

131 **palm** leaf or branch as symbol of victory
SD There is no need to reverse F's
order. Both shout and flourish signal
the offer and refusal of the crown.
132 **applauses** acclamations: another
recent word from Latin, uncommon in
the plural. Bate (*Tit* 1.1.234) notes that
Foxe 'translates Latin "*cum applausi
populi*" as "with the rejoycing triumph
of the people"'.
134 **bestride** *OED* bestride *v.* 2, in the
figurative sense of straddle over, first
recorded here
135 **colossus** a huge statue: the most
famous in the ancient world was the
bronze statue of Apollo at Rhodes, one
of the Seven Wonders of the World. It
was said, almost certainly wrongly, to
straddle the harbour: Cassius once
again makes a sketch (see 72n).
136–7 **peep ... graves** can only spend
our lives feebly looking for appropriate
places to die as bondmen
138–40 **Men ... underlings.** a central
conflict in a play dominated by one
colossus (135), Julius Caesar – whether

Brutus and Cassius, as individuals, but
supposedly representing the republic,
can control circumstances; see also
Brutus at 4.3.216–19. 'By the play's
end they recognize defeat by a prevail-
ing destiny' (Oxf[1]).
139–40 **not ... ourselves** 'The stars,
potent as they are, cannot compel, for
the human will remains free' (Cam[1]).
141–2 'The name Caesar, in fact, until
Julius had made it famous, was an
insignificant name in history, but
Brutus – why, it was the greatest name
in Roman annals' (Kittredge; and see
Doran).
142–6 Again Cassius makes quick alternatives – celebrating (*sounded*), writing,
speaking (*sound*), weighing in the
mouth, making spells (*conjure*). Cassius
always uses his rhetoric self-con-
sciously, aware of what will best *become*
[flatter] *the mouth*, like an actor trying
variations at rehearsal, appropriate for
such a theatrically self-conscious play.
145 **conjure** cònjure: pronounce as spells
to raise the dead

172

'Brutus' will start a spirit as soon as 'Caesar'.
Now in the names of all the gods at once,
Upon what meat doth this our Caesar feed
That he is grown so great? Age, thou art shamed!
Rome, thou hast lost the breed of noble bloods!   150
When went there by an age, since the great flood,
But it was famed with more than with one man?
When could they say, till now, that talked of Rome,
That her wide walks encompassed but one man?
Now is it Rome indeed, and room enough,   155
When there is in it but one only man.
O, you and I have heard our fathers say

146 **start a spirit** raise a spirit: ironical – neither name can be successful. Cf. *1H4* 3.1.52–5, where Hotspur punctures Glendower's claim to 'call spirits from the vasty deep'.

147 **names . . . once** 'Spirits could only be raised in the name of a god' (Cam[1]) – following Cassius' train of thought depends on that.

148 **meat** food in general

149 **great** ambiguous, suggesting bodily size from his feeding, and having a cognomen like Pompey's: cf. *LLL* 5.2.547–54.

150–60 In high dramatic blank verse, Cassius is creating a pattern of emphases contrasting *Rome* and *one man*, introduced by the assonance of *bloods* and *flood*.

150 **breed** ability to generate, and stock **noble bloods** men of rank, and of spirit – Cassius is emphasizing plurality; but such loss makes an unusual lament for a republican.

151 **the great flood** Genesis, 6–8: the Septuagint, the Greek version of the Hebrew scriptures, was widely known in the ancient world. Cassius' references, however, from *colossus* in 135 above, are to pagan matters, so the

great flood here may be the classical analogue, whereby, in Greek mythology, Zeus sent a universal flood, and only Deucalion and Pyrrha were saved. See Ovid, 1.187ff. Shakespeare mentions Deucalion as a figure of ultimate distance in time in *Cor* 2.1.102 and *WT* 4.3.423.

152 **famed with** renowned for: *OED* famed *ppl. a.* 2 gives as first use *3H6* 2.1.156.

154 **wide walks** There is no need to amend F to 'walls' as Rowe later in 1709 and most editors since: Shakespeare called walks 'wide' at *Tit* 2.1.114, and never walls. See 3.2.238 for Caesar's bequest of *all his walks*: Rome was – and is – famous for its gardens for leisure. Tracts of forest land (*OED* walks *sb.*[1] 10) 'encompassing' the city are not difficult to visualize, and there lurks in Cassius' phrase an image of many ordinary strollers around the wide city, contrasting with *one only man* (156) inside a room.

155 **Rome . . . room** Elizabethans rhymed 'Rome' with both 'doom' (*Luc* 715) and 'roam' (*1H6* 3.1.51). Kittredge noted, 'Here (as often) the pun expresses contempt.'

154 walks] *(Walkes); walls Rowe*

There was a Brutus once that would have brooked
Th'eternal devil to keep his state in Rome
As easily as a king.   160

BRUTUS

That you do love me, I am nothing jealous:
What you would work me to, I have some aim:
How I have thought of this and of these times
I shall recount hereafter. For this present,
I would not, so with love I might entreat you,   165
Be any further moved. What you have said
I will consider: what you have to say
I will with patience hear, and find a time
Both meet to hear and answer such high things.
Till then, my noble friend, chew upon this: 170

158–60 **There . . . king** A true republican
like the founding Brutus would have
endured an ultimate of horror as the
price of keeping his position as easily as
a more obviously privileged king would
do. He seems to muddy the clear waters
of the republican hatred of a monarch.

158 **a Brutus once** Lucius Junius Brutus,
by tradition the founder of the Roman
Republic about 509 BC: Plutarch
names him an ancestor of Marcus
Brutus. Lucius Junius Brutus was so
honoured for his defeat of the
Tarquins, especially Tarquinus
Superbus (traditionally thought to
have been the last king in Rome) that a
statue of brass was set up in the Capitol
(Plutarch, *Brutus*, 82; and see *Luc*
1807–55, and 1.3.146 below).
brooked tolerated, endured

159 **eternal** perpetual: in Shakespeare
linked with abhorrence, as in *Oth*
4.2.130, Emilia's 'some eternal villain'.
Johnson's emendation reduces the
force of the epithet to cliché.

161–174 Brutus in his characteristic balanced sentences (see his funeral oration, 3.2.12–47) has none of Cassius'
more devious painting of pictures

(until perhaps 'had rather be a villager'
at 171). He concentrates wholly on the
two of them there, at that time present.
They are the centre of a system of verb
tenses also embracing past (*have
thought, have said* and so on) and future
(*shall recount, will consider* and so on).

161 **nothing jealous** not at all mistrustful:
OED jealous *a.* 5b cites this as first use.

162 **work me to** bring me into (*OED*
work *v.* 7): cf. *H8* 2.2.44.
aim conjecture, guess (*OED* aim *sb.* 1
cites this); also in a later sense, necessary here, intention (*OED* aim *sb.* 5,
not until 1625)

164 **I . . . hereafter** Brutus is speaking as
if he were formally ending a letter; he
is distancing himself.
this present this immediate time

165 **so . . . you** so I might beg you, out of
our love

166 **moved** urged; also with a sense of
carried willingly

169 **meet** fitting
high things very significant matters

170 **chew** ruminate; but also with the
sense of 'devise or plan deliberately'
(*OED* chew *v* 3d, with first citation *H5*
2.2.56)

159 eternal] infernal *(Johnson)*

Brutus had rather be a villager
Than to repute himself a son of Rome
Under these hard conditions as this time
Is like to lay upon us.

CASSIUS   I am glad
That my weak words have struck but thus much show   175
Of fire from Brutus.

Enter CAESAR *and his train.*

BRUTUS

The games are done, and Caesar is returning.

CASSIUS

As they pass by, pluck Caska by the sleeve,
And he will, after his sour fashion, tell you
What hath proceeded worthy note today.   180

BRUTUS

I will do so: but look you, Cassius,
The angry spot doth glow on Caesar's brow,
And all the rest look like a chidden train:
Calphurnia's cheek is pale, and Cicero

171 **villager** a recent coinage; a village would be meagre compared with the great city. Cf. *AYL* 3.3.60, 'as a walled town is more worthier than a village'.

173 **these** one might expect 'those'; in so referring to the present not the future, Brutus is keeping his distance.

175 **struck . . . show** Cassius' pleasure is grudging – or tactful – at this stage: the spark from the flint may be only a *show*; but it is at least there.

176.1 'There is no music this time; Caes. is angry' (Cam[1]). Since we are told in 285 that Murellus and Flavius have been *put to silence*, it is likely that they do not here enter at the end of Caesar's train.

178 **sleeve** 'togas had no sleeves' (Cam[1]); but Shakespeare also had London in

mind. A toga covered the body except the right arm: *cloak* at 214 and *doublet* at 264 do suggest another mental image, strengthened by reference to the Peacham drawing (see Bate, *Tit*, 39–43). Cassius' *pluck* and *sleeve* necessarily suggest a slight, almost furtive, gesture: he does not say 'take Caska by the arm'. Such carefulness suggests a watchful and oppressive regime, as do the anonymity of Caska's reply at 1.3.41, the caution in the greetings at 1.3.131–6, the note thrown in at a window (1.2.144–5, 2.1.36–7) and the muffling of the conspirators at night.

180 **worthy note** worthy of note

182 **The angry spot** the mark of anger

183 **chidden** scolded; *OED* gives first use to *TC* 2.2.45.

174–6 I . . . Brutus.] (*Walker*); F lines words / *Brutus.* /   177–8] *Rowe*; F lines done / returning / by, / Sleeue, /

Looks with such ferret and such fiery eyes   185
As we have seen him in the Capitol
Being crossed in conference by some senators.

CASSIUS
Caska will tell us what the matter is.

CAESAR   Antonio.

ANTONY   Caesar.   190

CAESAR
Let me have men about me that are fat,
Sleek-headed men, and such as sleep a-nights.
Yond Cassius has a lean and hungry look:
He thinks too much: such men are dangerous.

ANTONY
Fear him not, Caesar, he's not dangerous.   195
He is a noble Roman, and well given.

CAESAR
Would he were fatter! But I fear him not:
Yet if my name were liable to fear
I do not know the man I should avoid
So soon as that spare Cassius. He reads much,   200
He is a great observer, and he looks
Quite through the deeds of men. He loves no plays

185 **ferret** red, with suggestions of small, fierce and narrowed
187 **crossed in conference** opposed in debate
189 **Antonio** perhaps suggests intimacy: see 3–6n.
191–213 In spite of Caesar's apparent anger at the recent events, to which Brutus has pointed, in his twenty lines to Antony he concentrates sardonically on the character of Cassius, noting that Cassius separates himself, and was not present in the Forum. Shakespeare has expanded remarks in Plutarch in each of three lives: *Caesar*, *Brutus* and *Antonius* (Appendix, pp. 325, 334 and 367.

195–6 There is detectable a tone not only of dismissal of Cassius, but also of patronizing Caesar. Antony's speech, almost his first, expresses a misjudgement of Cassius that parallels Brutus later (3.1.231–53).
196 **well given** well disposed
198 **if ... fear** if the title of Caesar endowed the liability to fear. The conditional is more elevated than arrogant.
200 **spare** lean, almost meagre
201–2 **looks ... men** sees hidden motives
202–3 **loves ... Antony** This puts positively what Brutus (28–9) dismissed as superficial in Antony. Cassius would be better if he loved plays and attended

189 Antonio] *(Antonio)*; Antonius *Pope*

As thou dost, Antony; he hears no music.
Seldom he smiles, and smiles in such a sort
As if he mocked himself and scorned his spirit   205
That could be moved to smile at anything.
Such men as he be never at heart's ease
Whiles they behold a greater than themselves,
And therefore are they very dangerous.
I rather tell thee what is to be feared   210
Than what I fear: for always I am Caesar.
Come on my right hand, for this ear is deaf,
And tell me truly what thou think'st of him.   *Sennet.*
                                    Exeunt Caesar and his train.

CASKA   You pulled me by the cloak. Would you speak
with me?   215

BRUTUS

Ay, Caska, tell us what hath chanced today
That Caesar looks so sad.

CASKA   Why, you were with him, were you not?

---

to music. Music, in Platonic theory, symbolized the harmony in nature and man. 'The man that hath no music in himself . . . Is fit for treasons, stratagems, and spoils' (*MV* 5.1.83–5).

204 **Seldom he smiles** The actor Ian Richardson, asked the secret of playing Cassius, said: 'He smiles once, and that's when he says goodbye to Brutus at the end. The rest of the time, stony-faced' (*Independent*, 1 November 1995). See 5.1.120 and n.

212 **deaf**   Shakespeare's   invention, though possibly an accompaniment to epilepsy (see 17n). The man who is always Caesar leaves the scene, as he entered it, fallible. He is also 'turning a deaf ear' to other people's advice.

214–93 Caska speaks only prose, like the Commoners in 1.1. He is thus permitted a knowing comic excess, aligned with the generally subversive mob: the lines of Brutus and Cassius are never far from iambic pentameters, as befits

treason more loftily directed. Caska gives, albeit scornfully, for the first time in the scene an account of what has been happening offstage. Even if elaborated, it is not wholly fanciful. Thus it shares a sense of true history with Murellus' account of the crowds waiting for Pompey, 1.1.38–48. The physicality of Caska's account, full of people doing things, contrasts with Cassius' rhetoric, where responses to him (*a common laughter*, 1.2.72) or Caesar's humanity ('*Help me, Cassius* . . .', 1.2.111) are vivid brief inventions. That contrast is part of the in-and-out movement from history to fiction, all the more surprising in a tragedy, which the Elizabethans, and all before them, had believed could not be fiction. Shakespeare's *RJ* was fiction, and apart from the Turkish material, so will be *Othello*.

214 **cloak** See 178n.

217 **sad** serious

BRUTUS

I should not then ask Caska what had chanced.

CASKA Why, there was a crown offered him; and being 220
offered him, he put it by with the back of his hand,
thus, and then the people fell a-shouting.

BRUTUS What was the second noise for?

CASKA Why, for that too.

CASSIUS

They shouted thrice: what was the last cry for? 225

CASKA Why, for that too.

BRUTUS Was the crown offered him thrice?

CASKA Ay, marry, was't, and he put it by thrice, every
time gentler than other; and at every putting-by, mine
honest neighbours shouted. 230

CASSIUS Who offered him the crown?

CASKA Why, Antony.

BRUTUS

Tell us the manner of it, gentle Caska.

CASKA I can as well be hanged as tell the manner of it. 235
It was mere foolery: I did not mark it. I saw Mark
Antony offer him a crown – yet 'twas not a crown

---

220 **a crown** Plutarch, *Antonius* (see Appendix, p. 368)

221 **put it by** set it aside: Plutarch, *Caesar, Antonius* (see Appendix, pp. 324, 368)

222 **people fell a-shouting** Cf. *LLL* 4.2.58, and *hooted*, 243 below. Caska's tone is possibly of a satirical ballad.

225 **last cry** As in the sources, only two shouts are recorded, at lines 78 and 131. Oxf[1], following Jennens, suggests the third might have been at 146. Cam[2] notes that Caesar's exit at 24, 'the two responses of the crowd, and his re-entry are . . . spaced symmetrically'.

228 **marry** indeed: common Elizabethan use of an oath originally using the name of the Virgin Mary

229 **gentler** more reluctantly: it is not impossible that beneath Caska's prejudice can be seen Caesar's increasing feebleness as the epileptic seizure approaches (McAlindon, 'Numbering', 373).

230 **honest** a recent use: *OED a.* 1c, 'as a vague epithet of appreciation or praise, esp. as used in a patronizing way to an inferior'. So Leonato to Dogberry, 'What would you with me, honest neighbour?' *(MA 3.5.1).*

233 **gentle** noble: possibly ironic

234 **I . . . it.** probably containing proverbial elements (Dent, H130.1 and T85.1). Caska is speaking like a plebeian.

235 **mere** entirely; and cf. 39.
foolery possibly a further hint of a subversive and carnival quality in what Caska is describing

neither, 'twas one of these coronets – and, as I told you, he put it by once; but for all that, to my thinking, he would fain have had it. Then he offered it to him again; then he put it by again; but to my thinking, he was very 240 loth to lay his fingers off it. And then he offered it the third time; he put it the third time by; and still as he refused it the rabblement hooted, and clapped their chopped hands, and threw up their sweaty nightcaps, and uttered such a deal of stinking breath because 245 Caesar refused the crown that it had almost choked Caesar; for he swooned and fell down at it. And for mine own part, I durst not laugh, for fear of opening my lips and receiving the bad air.

CASSIUS

But soft, I pray you: what, did Caesar swoon? 250

CASKA   He fell down in the market-place, and foamed at mouth, and was speechless.

---

237 **coronets** circlets, small crowns: see Foakes, *KL* p. 14. In Plutarch, Caesar was offered 'a Diadeame [crown or headband] wreathed about with laurell' (Appendix, p. 324).

239 **fain** gladly

242 **still as** whenever: *OED* still *adv.* 3d gives first use in 1656.

243–4 **rabblement ... hands** Shakespeare unites two phrases from Plutarch, *Caesar*, 81 (Appendix, p. 324), and *Antonius*, 264 (Appendix, p. 368). The word is a rare late-sixteenth-century intensification of 'rabble' as 'the mob . . . the common, low, or disorderly part of the populace' (*OED* rabble *sb.*[1] 2c and rabblement 1c.

243 **hooted** a scornful word for Plutarch's 'rejoicing . . . joy'

244 **chopped** chapped: cf. *AYL* 2.4.50.
sweaty nightcaps Elizabethan woollen caps, normally for wearing in bed. Percy Macquoid refers to an Act of Parliament of 1571 enjoining

the wearing of woollen caps on Sundays and holy days 'by every person above the age of six years except women and certain specified officials' (Lee & Onions, 2.111): such are the 'statute caps' of *LLL* 5.2.281. But Caska's scornful epithet and noun suggest disgusting humanity in the disarray of poverty or sickness or both, and probably other irregularities as well – Oxf[1] notes an association with cuckoldry: if that is so, then Caska is sexist, suggesting (as with the 'Three or four wenches' of 270 below) that the enthusiasm for Caesar is only a women's matter, and dismissible.

245 **uttered** shouted; emitted
deal lot

246 **had almost** nearly

250 **soft** an imperative exclamation used to hold hasty action or enjoin silence: cf. *TN* 1.5.277, 'Not too fast! Soft, soft!', and 3.1.122 below.

243 hooted] *(*howted*)*

BRUTUS

'Tis very like. He hath the falling sickness.

CASSIUS

No, Caesar hath it not: but you, and I,

And honest Caska, we have the falling sickness.   255

CASKA   I know not what you mean by that, but I am sure
Caesar fell down. If the tag-rag people did not clap him
and hiss him according as he pleased and displeased
them, as they use to do the players in the theatre, I am
no true man.   260

BRUTUS

What said he when he came unto himself?

CASKA   Marry, before he fell down, when he perceived
the common herd was glad he refused the crown, he
plucked me ope his doublet and offered them his throat
to cut. An I had been a man of any occupation, if I   265
would not have taken him at a word, I would I might
go to hell among the rogues. And so he fell. When he
came to himself again, he said, if he had done or said

---

253 *like. He Punctuation is necessary,
because F's lack of it implies that
Brutus, Caesar's friend, did not know
of the epilepsy (*falling sickness*) for a
fact. *Like* = likely.

255 we ... sickness i.e. our fortunes fall
as Caesar's rise

256 mean signify; intend. Caska is showing political caution.

257 tag-rag people the rabble, by reference to rags and tags (torn scraps) of
clothing (see Dent, T10)

259 use are accustomed

261 What ... himself? Brutus is not
concerned with the rabble, or with
Caska being amusing, but with Caesar.

264–5 plucked ... cut Shakespeare
merges into one Plutarch's two different occasions: in *Caesar* (Appendix, p.
323), having offended the Senate, he
offers his throat; and in *Antonius*

(Appendix, p. 368), after the offers of
the crown, he invites the striking-off of
his head.

264 plucked me ope The ethic dative
(Abbott, 220) adds dramatic force to
the action, as does *ope*, unique in
Shakespeare in prose. The moment
is adapted from Plutarch (Appendix,
p. 323).

doublet   North's   rendering   of
Amyot's 'robe'. Doublet implied
either folded or furred, and with
hose suggested a sort of undress,
lacking either a warm cloak or a gown
of office: Caska is scornfully diminishing Caesar; and see 178 above
and n.

265 An if

man ... occupation *mechanical*, as
1.1.3. Caska says he is above such
crude response.

---

253 like. He] like, he *Rowe*; like; he *Theobald*; like he *F*

anything amiss, he desired their worships to think it
was his infirmity. Three or four wenches where I stood   270
cried, 'Alas, good soul', and forgave him with all their
hearts. But there's no heed to be taken of them: if
Caesar had stabbed their mothers, they would have
done no less.

BRUTUS

And after that he came thus sad away.   275

CASKA   Ay.

CASSIUS   Did Cicero say anything?

CASKA   Ay, he spoke Greek.

CASSIUS   To what effect?

CASKA   Nay, an I tell you that, I'll ne'er look you i'th' face   280
again. But those that understood him, smiled at one
another, and shook their heads; but for mine own
part, it was Greek to me. I could tell you more news
too: Murellus and Flavius, for pulling scarves off
Caesar's images, are put to silence. Fare you well.   285
There was more foolery yet, if I could remember it.

CASSIUS   Will you sup with me tonight, Caska?

CASKA   No, I am promised forth.

---

269 **worships** properly, men of high
rank: Caska is imputing to Caesar a
mocking tone.

273 **stabbed** with perhaps a bawdy sense;
Caesar had a reputation for promiscuity.

278 **Greek** Plutarch notes Cicero as an
able orator in Greek (*Cicero*, 136).
Cicero diplomatically, or pedantically,
spoke only to the educated.

283 **Greek to me** proverbial for unintel-
ligible; Dent, G439. Caska did know
Greek, as Plutarch records (Appendix,
p. 329).

284 **scarves** as decorations. Plutarch has
diadems (Appendix, p. 324);
Suetonius (Rolfe, 1.103) mentions
white ribbons, more akin to Flavius'
Disrobe at 1.1.65.

285 **put to silence** comes across to a

modern audience as a sinister
euphemism for 'killed' (like 'termi-
nated'), which *OED* silence *sb.* 1c supports, citing this line. Plutarch says
they were 'deprived . . . of their
Tribune-ships' (Appendix, pp. 325
and 368). See 176.1n.

286 **more foolery** possibly histrionics
from Caesar and Antony, but suggestive of both growing disorder in the
city and Caska's elaborate pose of
detachment

287 **sup** take supper: begins a run of
images of domestic meals which
suggest secret meetings of the conspirators. The shift from *sup* (take
the evening meal) to *dine* (take the mid-
day meal) two lines later suggests the
rapid passage of time.

CASSIUS   Will you dine with me tomorrow?

CASKA   Ay, if I be alive, and your mind hold, and your   290
    dinner worth the eating.

CASSIUS   Good. I will expect you.

CASKA   Do so. Farewell, both.   *Exit.*

BRUTUS

    What a blunt fellow is this grown to be!

    He was quick mettle when he went to school.   295

CASSIUS

    So is he now, in execution

    Of any bold or noble enterprise,

    However he puts on this tardy form.

    This rudeness is a sauce to his good wit,

    Which gives men stomach to digest his words   300

    With better appetite.

BRUTUS   And so it is.

    For this time I will leave you.

    Tomorrow if you please to speak with me

    I will come home to you: or, if you will,

    Come home to me, and I will wait for you.   305

CASSIUS

    I will do so. Till then, think of the world.   *Exit Brutus.*

    Well, Brutus, thou art noble: yet I see

---

290 **if ... alive** with an added sense of political danger

294–5 **blunt ... mettle** Brutus is imperceptive: he misjudges Caska as he misjudges Antony. His image is of an instrument no longer sharp, *quick mettle* being 'lively spirits' and 'living steel'. Cassius' judgement is right in each case.

296 **So ... execution** Caska will be the first to stab Caesar, 3.1.76.

298 **However** notwithstanding that
tardy form affectation of slow-wittedness

299 **rudeness** roughness: like the blunted steel of 294

sauce used to make food palatable
wit intelligence

300 **stomach** inclination

303 **Tomorrow** accelerates the actions of meetings. Brutus, swayed by Caska's account, has stopped holding back.

306 **the world** state of affairs; what you are to Rome. 'The appeal to duty is the strongest that could be addressed to a man like Brutus' (Verity).

307–21 Cassius speaks in soliloquy here, using the intimate *thou*. His thought is directed at Brutus. His flashing rhetoric has changed to a densely equivocal manner.

307 art noble:] *F*; art: Noble *F2*

Thy honourable mettle may be wrought
From that it is disposed. Therefore it is meet
That noble minds keep ever with their likes;   310
For who so firm that cannot be seduced?
Caesar doth bear me hard, but he loves Brutus.
If I were Brutus now, and he were Cassius,
He should not humour me. I will this night
In several hands in at his windows throw,   315
As if they came from several citizens,
Writings all tending to the great opinion

308 **mettle . . . wrought** A *noble* was an Elizabethan gold coin (cf. 3.2.179 and n.). The pun on *mettle* strengthens the alchemical sense: *noble* and *honourable* metals, as gold or silver are, cannot be *wrought* (transmuted) into baser substance: yet Cassius 'sees' that Brutus *may* be so changed. The insight is sinister.

309 **that . . . disposed** that to which it is disposed: for the grammar, see Abbott, 244. The phrase continues the alchemical pun, suggesting both the natural state of the metal, and the human temperament.

309–10 **it . . . likes** 'It is proper that Brutus should keep his nobility of mind intact by remaining always with his equals (and those he prefers)': perhaps also grounded in a proverb (Dent, B393).

310 **keep** *OED v.* 37–41. The richness of senses in this verb permits probable continuation of an alchemical notion, so that it stands here for the natural chemical stability of noble metal.
likes both equals and preferences

311 **seduced** by Caesar, into supporting his supposed wish to be crowned, which is Cassius' declared motive for working on Brutus. Cassius is admitting that he can himself seduce Brutus to his own destructive hatred of Caesar: the question suggests that that is to Cassius a pleasurable challenge.

312 **bear me hard** bears me ill will. This is no fancy; we have heard it

from Caesar's own lips above, 193–209. Plutarch records Caesar's great 'jealousy' (suspicion) of Cassius (Appendix, p. 325).

313–14 **If . . . me**. If we changed places, I should make sure that Cassius could not change my mind about Caesar. But Cassius' density of thought allows *He* to be Caesar, following line 312, in which case the passage means 'Caesar loves Brutus, but if Brutus and I were to change places, his (Caesar's) love should not humour me, should not take hold of my affection, so as to make me forget my principles' (Johnson). But Cassius knows that 'Brutus . . . is the last man in the world to forget principles' (Verity). The passage may come from hints in Plutarch, (Appendix, p. 333), where Brutus is warned of Caesar's 'sweete intisements' and 'tyrannicall favors' to 'weaken his constant minde'. As Cassius holds himself, Caesar and Brutus together in his mind, summing up the scene, he reveals chasms of possible deviousness. The moment anticipates *Oth* 1.3–2.1 (where a storm is used to strikingly similar effect).

314 **humour** *OED v.* 1, comply with, indulge; *LLL* 3.1.13 and 4.2.52 are the first citations. The noun has a full history of physiological and psychological senses, again permitting an alchemical meaning.

315 **several hands** various handwritings

That Rome holds of his name – wherein obscurely
Caesar's ambition shall be glanced at.
And after this, let Caesar seat him sure,   320
For we will shake him, or worse days endure.   *Exit.*

[1.3]   *Thunder and lightning. Enter* CASKA *and* CICERO.

CICERO

Good even, Caska. Brought you Caesar home?
Why are you breathless, and why stare you so?

CASKA

Are you not moved, when all the sway of earth
Shakes like a thing unfirm? O Cicero,
I have seen tempests when the scolding winds   5

318 **obscurely** not clearly
319 **ambition** possibly four syllables
      glanced glancèd: hinted
320 **seat him sure** seat himself securely:
      possibly a riding metaphor (though see
      1.3.1 and n.)
1.3 location: 'Rome. A street' (Capell)
0.1 *Thunder and lightning.* The sudden
      huge noise (made by metal thunder-
      sheets) and lightning (igniting a chemical
      flash) come directly on Cassius' intention
      to *shake*, or *worse days endure.*
      Enter CASKA *and* CICERO. probably
      upstage, and moving down. Caska (19
      below) has a drawn sword.
1   **Brought . . . home?** from the events
      of the Lupercalia. From the first line
      Caesar is still the subject of this vio-
      lently disturbed scene. The question is
      whether he is *home*, and at the moment
      'seated sure' (1.2.320).
2   In the cosmic disturbance, Cicero's
      question is odd. He keeps a cool
      detachment from the wilder rhetoric
      throughout the scene. See 33–5.
3ff. Caska for the first time speaks verse.
      It is hyperbolic and over-emphatic:
      but the rhetoric of apocalyptic cata-
      strophe is to convince Cicero about
      politics, not meteorology.

3   **sway of earth** a rich image. The earth
      seems to *sway* in the storm. Caesar
      holds *sway*, that is, rule (*OED* sway *sb.*
      6a; a recent use). He is feared to be 'all
      the sway of earth', that is, force in one
      direction (*OED* sway *sb.* 3, 4), though
      he now 'Shakes like a thing unfirm' (4).
4   **unfirm** unstable (*OED a.* 2, 4) and
      weak (*OED a.* 3): both senses are used
      here before *OED*'s first citations.
      O Cicero The new character is now
      named. Cicero was a father of humanist
      rhetoric, and much studied (and imi-
      tated) in Elizabethan schools. He has
      already appeared offstage in Caska's
      account of his senatorial circumspec-
      tion, speaking Greek: see 1.2.277–8.
      His entry here is thus as an influential,
      and sceptical, commentator.
5   **I have seen** a rhetorical device, prob-
      ably implying that it is not to be
      believed. Petruchio in *TS* 1.2.195–206
      boasts of similar extravagant experi-
      ences, which are unlikely in that he has
      just for the first time left home.
      scolding angrily reproving, with a sug-
      gestion of brawling. The first of a run of
      images suggesting challenge to appar-
      ently unstoppable natural power. All
      Caska's verbs and verbal nouns indicate

1.3] *Capell*

Have rived the knotty oaks, and I have seen
Th'ambitious ocean swell, and rage, and foam,
To be exalted with the threatening clouds:
But never till tonight, never till now,
Did I go through a tempest dropping fire.   10
Either there is a civil strife in heaven,
Or else the world, too saucy with the gods,
Incenses them to send destruction.

CICERO

Why, saw you anything more wonderful?

CASKA

A common slave – you know him well by sight –   15

immediate conflict, the meteorological
result of Caesar's ambition, and the
destruction of it, so far unintegrated.

6 **rived** split (*OED* rive *v.*[1] 4), but with
now obsolete senses of tear up, cancel
(*OED v.*[1] 1b), as can be applied to
Caesar's rule
  knotty rugged, gnarled; also with a
sense of both ancient, and thus firmly
fixed; perhaps more faintly, perplexing
(*OED* knotty *a.* 2). Cf. *Tem* 1.2.294–6.
  oaks See *Cor* 1.3.16 for oak as a symbol
of victory in war; it is victorious Caesar
who is to be *rived*.

7–8 **ambitious** the key epithet, establishing
  swell, rage, foam and *exalted with* (raised
as high as) as personifications of a monstrous power. Inside the imagery is a
figure, Caesar, who can *swell*, behave
arrogantly (*OED* swell *v.* 9a), *rage* and
  foam – not only in vehement wrath (*OED*
foam *v.* 1) but probably in his epilepsy.

8 **threatening** maintains both Caesar's
power and the posture of revolting
against it.

9 [1]**never . . . now** The repetition fixes in
the dramatic present the onrush of the
political storm mounting in Rome.
Shakespeare has telescoped the
Lupercalia of mid-February, which
has happened in the day, and the Ides
in mid-March which will follow this

night, to great effect.

10 ***tempest dropping fire** F's hyphens
are attractive here, making Caska walk
through fire rather than a tempest; but
they are probably a scribal trait, as at
2.1.117 and 229, and at 3.1.43.

11 **civil . . . heaven** caused by gross disturbance on earth, as in *KL*
1.2.100–12. It is especially located in
the ruler, as expounded in *KL*
3.2.1–24, so the cause is Caesar rather
than the growing conspiracy. Caska
speaks in a climate of scepticism about
this, especially to Cicero; a scepticism
initially shared by Cassius and Brutus.
Oxf[1] notes, however, that the play
'persistently implies that . . . political
subversion really does derange the
whole supernatural order'.

12 **saucy** insolent: *OED* (*a.*[1] 2b) notes, 'In
Shakespeare as a term of serious condemnation', giving first use in *MM*
three years after *JC*.

14 Are you talking about something more
than this ordinary storm?

15–32 Plutarch recounted prodigies pre-
ceding Caesar's murder (Appendix, p.
326). Those, and others, were also
familiar to Elizabethans through Ovid,
from *Metamorphoses*, 15, either studied
in Latin at school or read in Golding's
1567 translation.

8 threatening] *(threatning)*   10 tempest dropping fire] *Rowe;* Tempest-dropping-fire *F*

Held up his left hand, which did flame and burn
Like twenty torches joined; and yet his hand,
Not sensible of fire, remained unscorched.
Besides – I ha'not since put up my sword –
Against the Capitol I met a lion   20
Who glazed upon me and went surly by
Without annoying me. And there were drawn
Upon a heap a hundred ghastly women
Transformed with their fear, who swore they saw
Men, all in fire, walk up and down the streets.   25
And yesterday the bird of night did sit
Even at noonday upon the market-place
Hooting and shrieking. When these prodigies
Do so conjointly meet, let not men say,
'These are their reasons, they are natural':   30
For I believe they are portentous things
Unto the climate that they point upon.

18 **sensible of** sensitive to
   unscorched *OED* gives this as first use.
19 **put up** sheathed
20 **Against** directly in front of
   lion The prodigy is the lion's unnatural
   preoccupation. Not in Plutarch; but in
   Brutus, 94 (Appendix, p. 334), he attributes Cassius' private hatred to Caesar
   keeping the Megarian lions which
   Cassius thought were his. Released,
   they mauled their masters, not the
   enemy. See Introduction, pp. 87–8.
21 **Who** See Abbott, 265.
   glazed Emendation is not needed.
   OED defines 'glaze' (*v*.2) as stare, citing this as first and other much later
   uses. Kittredge gives four citations
   from Middle English and Tudor texts.
   There is an obvious overlap with the
   notion of 'glazed' as glassed. A glassy
   stare fits the lion's odd state of mind
   better than a glare or a gaze.
22 **annoying** injuring. If the prodigies are
   on the side of the coming conspiracy,

then they cause no harm in Rome.
22–3 **drawn . . . heap** huddled in a crowd
   together: cf. *H5* 4.5.18.
23 **ghastly** pallid; full of fear (*OED a*. 3).
   Cf. *Tem* 2.1.30, 'this ghastly looking'.
   These women are not in Plutarch.
24 **Transformed** transformèd
26 **bird of night** usually the screech-owl,
   i.e. in Shakespeare's England, as
   today, the barn owl. *Tit* 2.3.97 and *MA*
   2.3.76–7 make it the raven; and see
   Dent, R33.
28 **prodigies** extraordinary things
30 Such things can be explained sci-
   entifically.
32 **climate** clime, region. Cam¹ glosses
   'Astrol. term = zone of the earth controlled by a particular constellation or
   planet'. And see *Ham* 1.1.121, where
   the word appears as 'climatures' at the
   climax of a fourteen-line account of
   these prodigies before the death of
   Julius Caesar.
   point upon are directed at

21 glazed] *(glaz'd); glare'd Rowe 1709²; gaz'd Q 1691*   28 Hooting] *(Howting)*

CICERO

Indeed it is a strange-disposed time.
But men may construe things after their fashion
Clean from the purpose of the things themselves. 35
Comes Caesar to the Capitol tomorrow?

CASKA

He doth, for he did bid Antonio
Send word to you he would be there tomorrow.

CICERO

Good night then, Caska: this disturbed sky 39
Is not to walk in.

CASKA   Farewell, Cicero.   *Exit Cicero.*

Enter CASSIUS.

CASSIUS

Who's there?

CASKA   A Roman.

CASSIUS   Caska, by your voice.

33 **strange-disposed** strange-disposèd
34–5 An odd remark from Cicero of all people, the arch-rhetorician. Such empiricism from him, however, amplifies the experience of rhetorical collapse which has been set going in the first thirty lines of the play. Coming at this point in the drama, it should make unsafe all the rhetoric of ethical dilemma, as well as hatred, which will move the conspirators to murder Caesar.
34 **construe** cònstrue: see 1.2.45n. Appropriate to this Roman story, the word had associations for Elizabethans of Latin lessons (*OED v.* 3). See, for a comic example, *TS* 3.1.28–30, 40.
35 **Clean** completely without exception (*OED adv.* 5)
   from distant from

purpose effect intended (*OED sb.* 3)
36 Cicero's question is by no means casual or arbitrary after his previous two lines. As he has begun the scene linking Caesar's movements and Caska, so he now suggests a perceived link between Caska's powers of mistaking the signs and Caesar's movements next day.
39 **disturbed** disturbèd
40 **Is not** is unsuitable
41 **Who's there?** So, famously, will *Ham* open, also with the moving figure, Bernardo, challenging the stationary one, though the reverse is more usual. Both scenes establish an atmosphere of serious and growing disorder; and see 31–2 above.
   by your voice emphasizing darkness on a daylight stage, and symbolically appropriate for the conspiracy

39–40 Good . . . in.] *Rowe; F lines Caska:* / in. /

CASKA

Your ear is good. Cassius, what night is this?

CASSIUS

A very pleasing night to honest men.

CASKA

Whoever knew the heavens menace so?

CASSIUS

Those that have known the earth so full of faults.   45
For my part, I have walked about the streets,
Submitting me unto the perilous night,
And thus unbraced, Caska, as you see,
Have bared my bosom to the thunder-stone:
And when the cross blue lightning seemed to open   50
The breast of heaven, I did present myself
Even in the aim and very flash of it.

CASKA

But wherefore did you so much tempt the heavens?
It is the part of men to fear and tremble
When the most mighty gods by tokens send   55
Such dreadful heralds to astonish us.

---

42 **what night** what a night; see Abbott, 86.

is this? F prints the remark as a question, usually emended to exclamation. But the question, without losing the exclamatory sense, carries also a subtler probing of Cassius.

45 an expressive line that excites Cassius, justifying his self-dramatizing defiance of supernatural power. His inviting actions are as superstitious as his defiance, challenging the heavens to single him out. Both he and Caska know, but have not yet articulated, that the power he is challenging is Caesar's.

47 **Submitting me** exposing myself to; see Abbott, 223.

48 **unbraced** unbracèd; unbuttoned. Hamlet, his 'doublet all unbrac'd' (*Ham* 2.1.78), also uses the gesture for

a self-regarding expression of vulnerability. See above, 1.2.178, 263–5.

49 **thunder-stone** the same as thunderbolt; *OED* cites this line. Believed to be an intensely hot solid body in a lightning strike.

50 **cross** forked; zigzag; also hostile (*OED a.* 4)

52 **Even ... aim** at the very point he liked to believe it was aimed at

53–6 Caska prefers to keep his own version of the storm, which does not include forked lightning being aimed solely at Cassius. For Caska, the weather, possibly exaggerated, is filling Rome with strange portents and divine messages.

55 **by tokens** by portents as evidence

56 **astonish** stun. *OED* witnesses to the very strong sense.

42] *Rowe; F lines* good. / this? /

CASSIUS

You are dull, Caska, and those sparks of life
That should be in a Roman you do want
Or else you use not. You look pale, and gaze,
And put on fear, and cast yourself in wonder   60
To see the strange impatience of the heavens.
But if you would consider the true cause
Why all these fires, why all these gliding ghosts,
Why birds and beasts, from quality and kind,
Why old men, fools, and children calculate,   65
Why all these things change from their ordinance
Their natures and preformed faculties
To monstrous quality, why, you shall find
That heaven hath infused them with these spirits
To make them instruments of fear and warning   70
Unto some monstrous state.
Now could I, Caska, name to thee a man
Most like this dreadful night
That thunders, lightens, opens graves and roars

---

57 **dull** stupid: he wants to rouse Caska to his own political excitement.

58 **want** lack

59 **use not** ignore in yourself

60 **put . . . yourself** Cassius moves a step nearer a full sharing of his political view by revealing to Caska that he can see that his emotions in the storm are put on. Having thus got under Caska's guard, he can begin to outline the details of a secret understanding of the single cause of all the disturbance. He behaves like all conspiracy-theorists everywhere: he will presently (79) get Caska to say, as it were, 'It all fits!' to express the revelation of the supposed central truth in his next speech.

64 **from . . . kind** alien to their character and natural disposition. Hamlet in his first speech finds the King 'less than kind' (*Ham* 1.2.65).

65 'So obvious and so numerous are the portents that any dotard, fool or infant can interpret them' (Cam[1]). *Fools* are natural fools, born idiots, as *OED* fool *sb.* 4.

66 **ordinance** what is ordained for them by Providence

67 **preformed** preformèd: previously formed. *OED* cites this as first use (and not again until 1866). There is a sense, too, of innate.

68, 71 **monstrous** unnatural; horribly deformed; as Iago's 'monstrous birth' at *Oth* 1.3.398

71, 73 The short lines indicate pauses, perhaps for thunder.

71 **state** condition, and the Roman state under Caesar's tyranny

74 **opens graves** the first we have heard of this particular portent, though the sense of ghosts about (above, 63) might

57–60 You . . . wonder] *Rowe; F lines Caska: / Roman, / not. / feare, / wonder, /*

189

As doth the lion in the Capitol: 75
A man no mightier than thyself, or me,
In personal action, yet prodigious grown
And fearful, as these strange eruptions are.

CASKA

'Tis Caesar that you mean. Is it not, Cassius?

CASSIUS

Let it be who it is: for Romans now   80
Have thews and limbs like to their ancestors:
But woe the while, our fathers' minds are dead,
And we are governed with our mothers' spirits:
Our yoke and sufferance show us womanish.

CASKA

Indeed, they say the senators tomorrow   85

suggest it: but if this is the work of *a man* (72) then he must be prodigious indeed. It is the mage Prospero, steeping himself for years in esoteric lore instead of governing, who has 'rifted Jove's stout oak' and opened graves, 'wak'd their sleepers . . . and let 'em forth' (*Tem* 5.1.45, 48–9). In *JC* we have seen no signs of anything even approaching that. In his judgement of Caesar, Cassius is showing signs of paranoia.

75 **lion** probably Caska's surly animal in 20–2 above, now thought of as more active as Cassius develops his theme. In the summer of 1599 there were, however, lions across the river from the Globe, at the Tower, and with a light east wind their roaring could have been heard at that theatre, and might have been a feature of riverside London life. Shakespeare may have been thinking of the Capitol as 'Julius Caesar's Tower' (*R3* 3.1.68–71).

77 **prodigious** monstrous and ominous

78 **eruptions** violent outbreaks. Horatio, hearing of the Ghost, thinks it 'bodes some strange eruption to our state' (*Ham* 1.1.69).

79 Kittredge notes 'the studied simplicity' of this, Caska putting on his *tardy form*, as 1.2.298.

80 **Let . . . is** Again like any conspiracy-theorist, Cassius enjoys secrecy, riddling replies, and a sense of danger: as it were, 'I never told you.'

81 **thews** originally customs, habits; then physical good qualities; latterly in the sixteenth century 'bodily proportions, lineaments, or parts, as indicating physical strength' (*OED* thews *sb.*[1] 3b)

82 **while** occasion: *woe the while* is more a general expression of grief (*OED* while *sb.* 6d); almost a sigh, 'heigh-ho!'

83 **with** by

84 **yoke** servitude
   sufferance patient endurance, as *MV* 1.3.105; but also allowing things to continue, as *3H6* 1.1.234, *H5* 2.2.46, *Cor* 3.1.24 and elsewhere. Cassius, as always, implies a grievance at suppression of his own political power.

79] *F lines* meane: / *Cassius?* /

Mean to establish Caesar as a king,
And he shall wear his crown by sea and land
In every place save here in Italy.

CASSIUS

I know where I will wear this dagger then:
Cassius from bondage will deliver Cassius.   90
Therein, ye gods, ye make the weak most strong;
Therein, ye gods, you tyrants do defeat.
Nor stony tower, nor walls of beaten brass,
Nor airless dungeon, nor strong links of iron,
Can be retentive to the strength of spirit: 95
But life being weary of these worldly bars

---

86 **king** Plutarch (Appendix, p. 327) records Decimus Brutus urging Caesar to go to the Senate for this among other reasons. According to prophecy, only with a king as general could Rome defeat the nimble and inventive (and apparently invincible) troops of Parthia (now northern Iran): Caesar was about to lead a campaign against them to avenge the defeat and death of his colleague Marcus Crassus. Ventidius announces this eventual Roman victory in *AC* 3.1.1–5.

87–8 **wear . . . Italy** Plutarch (Appendix, p. 327)

89–115 Cassius' self-dramatization here reaches a height, though the notion of suicide as an escape is present, partly in preparation for Act 5. Unlike Hamlet, who momentarily finds some relief in the thought of suicide (*Ham* 1.2.129–32: in roughly similar words, 3.1.71–6), Cassius has no evident cause for depression, certainly not in the actions of Caesar that we have seen; only in his own feelings of unregarded merit.

90 Four lines of Kyd's *Cornelia* (1594), 4.1.147–50, are close here: 'while Cassius hath one drop of blood . . . What reck I death . . .?'

91, 92 **Therein** by suicide: see Foakes, *KL* 4.6.62–4n.

93 **Nor** neither
walls . . . brass a bizarre notion. The four actualizations of the effects of the abstract tyranny move logically in scale from larger to smaller – tower, walls, dungeon, chains, each noun with a stereotyped epithet except the second, where walls are unexpectedly of brass. Shakespeare links brass and towers in *Son* 64.4 and brass and stone in *Son* 65.1, where the thought is of transience even in apparent imperishability. Similarly *R2* 3.2.168–9, 'As if this flesh which walls about our life / Were brass impregnable'. Job at 6.12 finds his suffering so extreme that he questions whether he should prolong his life: 'Is my strength the strength of stones? or is my flesh of brass?' (Geneva, 1560). Here, however, Cassius' thought is that the strength of the human spirit cannot be held in, even if the body is: thus the image of brass cannot be of a tomb or memorial, as regularly in Shakespeare: *beaten* 'continues the notion of the body being captured but not the spirit: these prison walls are beaten as well by fists' (S.McB.).

95 **be retentive to** hold in

96 **bars** barriers to progress as well as prison-bars

191

Never lacks power to dismiss itself.
If I know this, know all the world besides,
That part of tyranny that I do bear
I can shake off at pleasure.   *Thunder still.*

CASKA   So can I.   100
So every bondman in his own hand bears
The power to cancel his captivity.

CASSIUS

And why should Caesar be a tyrant then?
Poor man, I know he would not be a wolf
But that he sees the Romans are but sheep.   105
He were no lion, were not Romans hinds.
Those that with haste will make a mighty fire
Begin it with weak straws. What trash is Rome?
What rubbish, and what offal? when it serves
For the base matter to illuminate   110
So vile a thing as Caesar? But, O grief,
Where hast thou led me? I perhaps speak this
Before a willing bondman: then I know
My answer must be made. But I am armed

98 **know ... besides** Let everyone else know.

100 **shake off** Cf. *KL* 4.6.35–6, where Gloucester is also renouncing the world in his suicide.
SD *Thunder still.* i.e. all the time. Curiously, the two SDs, at the start of the scene and here, are both cued by *shake* in the text.

101 **bondman** Caska takes up the idea of imprisonment, also from *bondage*, 90, and *bars*, 96, and turns it to the other sense of 'bond', legal contract.

102 **cancel** a legal term for annulling a contract. Shakespeare uses the idea of life as a bond which death terminates in *R3* 4.4.77, *Mac* 3.2.49, *Cym* 5.4.27–8.

103 **tyrant** Plutarch (Appendix, p. 334): 'Cassius even from his cradell could not abide ... tyrans'.

104–5 **wolf ... sheep** Dent, S300, 'He

that makes himself a sheep shall be eaten by the wolf.'

106 **hinds** deer; household servants; rustics

108–11 Vile Caesar is making the people of Rome into no more than debris to start the great blaze of his own glory abroad.

108 **trash** twigs, hedge-cuttings; residue. A more recent sense, 'a worthless or disreputable person' (*OED sb.*¹4.), is only cited first in *Oth* (1604) 5.1.85.

109 **rubbish** debris, waste material from the decay or repair of buildings (*OED sb.* 1)
offal what is valueless and allowed to fall off (off-fall) from preparation of something, like chips of wood

110 **base matter** All Cassius' nouns are of the lowest of materials; not only incidental, but quick expendable fuel.

114 **My ... made** I must pay the penalty.

And dangers are to me indifferent.   115
CASKA
 You speak to Caska, and to such a man
 That is no fleering tell-tale. Hold, my hand.
 Be factious for redress of all these griefs
 And I will set this foot of mine as far
 As who goes farthest.
CASSIUS   There's a bargain made.   120
 Now know you, Caska, I have moved already
 Some certain of the noblest-minded Romans
 To undergo with me an enterprise
 Of honourable dangerous consequence;
 And I do know by this, they stay for me   125
 In Pompey's Porch. For now this fearful night
 There is no stir or walking in the streets;
 And the complexion of the element

115 **indifferent** unimportant (*OED a.*[1] 10, citing this; and cf. 1.2.87)

117 **fleering** laughing scornfully, gibing, sneering
Hold, my hand You have said enough; I offer my hand for you to take.

118–20 **Be . . . farthest.** If you will be active in the faction or party to redress all the grievances you have mentioned, I will be among the leaders.

123 **undergo** undertake

124 **honourable dangerous** F's lack of hyphen usefully allows equal weight to the three polysyllables of the line.

125 **know by this,** Editors usually emend to 'know, by this', that is, at this time. F, however, allows the phrase to refer back to *I have moved*, 121. Cassius refers to his political success in persuading them to meet.

126 **Pompey's Porch** the *porticus pompeianae*, built by Pompey in 55 BC, eleven years before Caesar's assassination, which Plutarch locates there. They were adjacent to the *Theatrum*

Pompei (152), built at the same time, and one of several porticoes intended as shelter for the theatre audience. Shakespeare moves the assassination to the Capitol (though he keeps the statue of Pompey which was there (Plutarch, Appendix, p. 328), needed in his scene of the murder). Making the conspirators first meet alongside a theatre continues the configuration of the previous scene (see 1.2.78.1n.). 'A place of good omen for the plotters since Pompey had been an enemy of Caesar' (Oxf[1]).

128 **complexion . . . element** the disposition of the sky: *complexion* is best thought of as 'combination', the relative proportions of constituents – in bodily terms best observed in the face, a late-sixteenth-century use first in Shakespeare in *MV* (1596) 2.1.1 (*OED* complexion *sb.* 4); *element* = sky (*OED sb.* 10), with a suggestion of 'atmospheric agencies or powers' (*OED sb.* 11) as in *KL* 3.2.16.

124 honourable dangerous] honourable-dang'rous *Capell* 125 know by this,] know, by this *Rowe*

In favour's like the work we have in hand,
Most bloody, fiery and most terrible.   130

Enter CINNA.

CASKA
Stand close awhile, for here comes one in haste.
CASSIUS
'Tis Cinna. I do know him by his gait.
He is a friend. Cinna, where haste you so?
CINNA
To find out you. Who's that? Metellus Cimber?
CASSIUS
No, it is Caska, one incorporate   135
To our attempts. Am I not stayed for, Cinna?
CINNA
I am glad on't. What a fearful night is this?
There's two or three of us have seen strange sights.
CASSIUS
Am I not stayed for? Tell me.
CINNA   Yes, you are.
O Cassius, if you could   140
But win the noble Brutus to our party –

---

129 **favour** countenance or look (*OED sb.*
9); also continues the sense of heavenly
involvement, as in *OED sb.* 1, 'propitious or friendly regard'.
130 **bloody, fiery** so F. There is no need
to emend to 'bloody-fiery' as Dyce and
others do, to save '*fiery* from limping
along without a *most*' (Oxf[1]). *Most
bloody* is the work below; *fiery* is the sky
above; *most terrible* is everything.
131 **close** out of sight, concealed – the
usual sixteenth-century meaning:
'There is nothing so close, it shall not
be opened' (Matthew, 10.26, Tyndale,
NT).

134 **Metellus** as in Plutarch, *Caesar*, 85
(Appendix, p. 328); 'Tullius' in
Brutus, 102 (Appendix, p. 341)
135–6 **incorporate / To** united with
136–42 **Am ... content.** That Cassius
has to repeat his question; that Cinna
after a curt answer immediately
switches to a wish for the support of
Brutus, then is abruptly cut off by
Cassius – these show tensions already in
the conspiracy. Cinna is not as reveren-
tial to Cassius as he expects, and Cassius
wants to be the one to win Brutus.
137 **on't** about it (i.e. Caska being with
them)

129 In favour's] Is favour'd *Capell;* Is Fauors, *F*   130 bloody, fiery] bloody-fiery *(Walker)*   137] *F
lines* on't. /this? /   139–41 Yes ... party –] *Oxf; F lines Cassius / Brutus / To our party /*

CASSIUS

    Be you content. Good Cinna, take this paper
    And look you lay it in the praetor's chair
    Where Brutus may but find it. And throw this
    In at his window. Set this up with wax   145
    Upon old Brutus' statue. All this done,
    Repair to Pompey's Porch, where you shall find us.
    Is Decius Brutus and Trebonius there?

CINNA

    All but Metellus Cimber, and he's gone
    To seek you at your house. Well, I will hie,   150
    And so bestow these papers as you bade me.

CASSIUS

    That done, repair to Pompey's Theatre.   *Exit Cinna.*
    Come, Caska, you and I will yet ere day
    See Brutus at his house. Three parts of him
    Is ours already, and the man entire   155
    Upon the next encounter yields him ours.

CASKA

    O he sits high in all the people's hearts:
    And that which would appear offence in us
    His countenance, like richest alchemy,

142 **Be you content** 'Calm down!'

143 **praetor's chair** Brutus had been made praetor (just below consul) by Caesar shortly before these events; he would sit in the chair, the *sella curulis*, to settle disputes.

144 **may but** cannot but; see Abbott, 128, for 'Brutus alone'.

146 **old Brutus' statue** See 1.2.158n.

147 **Repair** go

148 **Decius** as in North's Plutarch (Appendix, p. 327), following Amyot, but properly Decimus. A man strongly favoured by Caesar, who made him his heir. 'His participation [in the conspiracy] is gross treachery, and carried through most unscrupulously' (Oxf[1]).

150 **hie** go quickly

152 **Pompey's Theatre** See 126n.

157–60 **O . . . worthiness.** This 'impassioned eulogy of Brutus' (Cam[1]) establishes his public status, to colour the dilemmas of the private scene which follows. The alchemical image links with Cassius' comment on him, immediately after his exit, in 1.2.307–11. The character of Caska is largely Shakespeare's invention, from Plutarch's brief notes (Appendix, pp. 329 and 341). Shakespeare makes him impressionable, articulate and, not least in his pose of slowness of uptake, more than a little sly, so his praise of Brutus may be intended to annoy Cassius.

159 **countenance** appearance, in both senses of look and visible support

Will change to virtue and to worthiness. 160
CASSIUS
Him, and his worth, and our great need of him
You have right well conceited. Let us go,
For it is after midnight, and ere day
We will awake him and be sure of him. *Exeunt.*

2[.1] *Enter* BRUTUS *in his orchard.*

BRUTUS What, Lucius, ho?
I cannot by the progress of the stars
Give guess how near to day – Lucius, I say?
I would it were my fault to sleep so soundly.
When, Lucius, when? Awake, I say: what, Lucius! 5

Enter LUCIUS.

LUCIUS Called you, my lord?
BRUTUS
Get me a taper in my study, Lucius.

---

160 **virtue** the modern sense, and, technically (*OED sb.* 9), great value; here presumably as produced by alchemy

162 **conceited** conceived (*OED* conceit *v.* 1, citing here); and expressed fancifully, whimsically (*OED* conceit *v.* 4) – not entirely praise

2.1.0.1 *orchard* more a pleasure garden, as in *MA* 3.1.5–11, than simply an enclosure with fruit trees. The mood suggested is night-time quiet for Brutus' contemplation. This is in contrast to the violent noise and storm, and dangerous exchanges, in the previous scene; and in dramatic preparation for the vigour of the conspiracy in the dark: cf. the calm before the political storm in *2H4* 3.2, 5.1.

1 **Lucius** invented by Shakespeare: throughout the play his – often sleepy

– presence brings out the humanity of Brutus; his normal response to night contrasts with the conspirators' activity in the dark.

2 **progress ... stars** A starlit night is reassuring after the thunderstorm: for Brutus' incapacity, since he lacks an agreed calendar, see 40 and n. below and Introduction, pp. 19–21. For the ability to read time by the stars, see *1H4* 2.1.1–3.

5 **When ... when?** Shakespearean expressions of impatience, as *R2* 1.1.162, 'When, Harry, when?', and *Tem* 1.2.316, 'Come, thou tortoise! when?'; but also suggestive of Brutus' urgently questioning state of mind

7 **Get me** put for me
taper like 'candle', for which it stands here, an older English word (see Introduction, pp. 60–2)

2.1] *Actus Secundus*

When it is lighted, come and call me here.

LUCIUS   I will, my lord.   *Exit.*

BRUTUS

It must be by his death: and for my part   10
I know no personal cause to spurn at him
But for the general. He would be crowned:
How that might change his nature, there's the
    question.
It is the bright day that brings forth the adder,
And that craves wary walking. Crown him that,   15
And then I grant we put a sting in him

10–34 **It . . . shell.** a Hamlet-like medita-
tion on an abstract notion. Here it is
ambition, set going, as with Hamlet, by
uncertainty about a need to do an act of
violence with insufficient or doubtful
evidence. Similarly the soldiers Bates
and Williams, debating with King
Henry V before Agincourt (*H5*
4.1.120–83, written just before *JC*),
consider the adequacy of the cause for
the coming carnage: as does Troilus
throughout *TC*, written just after *JC*
(see e.g. 1.1.92, 'I cannot fight upon
this argument'). In Shakespeare's next
tragedy, and the next play set in Italy,
Othello is made pathetically certain of
his 'cause' for taking life (*Oth* 5.2.1–3).
Unlike the parallel soliloquy by Cassius
in 1.2.307–21 above, Brutus' here presents moral difficulties. Brutus resolves
to act only on the theoretical premise
that Caesar will become tyrannical,
against his own evidence of his friend.
What Caesar truly is has to be 'fashioned', to be *augmented* (30) against the
true *colour* of the groundlessness of the
quarrel with him (28–9).
10 Cam[1] notes the monosyllabic opening,
comparing Hamlet's 'To be or not to
be' (*Ham* 3.1.56) and Macbeth's 'If it
were done when 'tis done, then 'twere
well' (*Mac* 1.7.1). It is noteworthy that
this soliloquy begins with its conclu-

sion, making the speech a rationalization of that.
11 **spurn** a verb of violent power of kick-
ing, as 'spurn in pieces posts of
adamant', *1H6* 1.4.52. See *OED v.*[1] 2.
12 **general** common, collective good
13 **there's   the   question**   a   richly
Shakespearean phrase. 'Question' in
OED's sense *sb.* 3a (not losing an interrogative element, but roughly 'the
basis of a problem') occurs most
frequently in middle-period Shakespeare, most commonly in *Ham*, and
most famously in 'To be or not to be –
that is the question' at *Ham* 3.1.56.
14 'Good can bring forth evil' (and see Rea).
15–17 Brutus' fact of natural history
becomes political danger, but only
with qualifiers diminishing the argument: *craves* ('calls for', *OED* crave *v.*
5), *then I grant, at his will, he may do*.
Those are themselves all dependent on
(a) the possibility of Caesar's being
crowned; (b) the chance that after that
he might turn evil.
15 **Crown him that** Early editors decorated the phrase with punctuation. F,
though compressed, is clear enough,
with *that* as a pronoun: 'make him dangerous as an adder by crowning him,
and then . . .'.
16 **sting** continues the metaphor of *adder*;
as does *serpent's egg*, 32

15 him that,] him – that – *Rowe;* him?– that; – *Steevens*

That at his will he may do danger with.
Th'abuse of greatness is when it disjoins
Remorse from power; and to speak truth of Caesar
I have not known when his affections swayed   20
More than his reason. But 'tis a common proof
That lowliness is young ambition's ladder
Whereto the climber upward turns his face;
But when he once attains the upmost round
He then unto the ladder turns his back,   25
Looks in the clouds, scorning the base degrees
By which he did ascend. So Caesar may.
Then, lest he may, prevent. And since the quarrel
Will bear no colour for the thing he is,
Fashion it thus: that what he is, augmented,   30
Would run to these and these extremities.
And therefore think him as a serpent's egg

17 **danger** damage (*OED sb.* 6, last recorded here)
19 **Remorse** compassion (*OED* remorse *sb.* 3a), with an older sense of conscience (*sb.* 1)
20 **affections swayed** *affections* = feelings, passions. 'Sway' meaning move in a certain direction, in the general sense of rule, is a particularly middle-period Shakespearean use (*OED* sway *sb.* 4). And see above, 1.3.3 and n.
21 **proof** experience
21–7 The image is in Shakespeare's mind, from *R2* on, in condemnation of the destruction caused by political ambition: *R2* 5.1.55–6; *2H4* 3.1.70–1; *TC* 1.3.101–3, 127–34.
22 **lowliness** humility as an affectation to win popularity. Plutarch describes Caesar's early popularity as a cause of his rise (*Caesar*, 60). At *1H4* 3.2.50–2, the King tells how, as Bolingbroke, he had dressed himself 'in such humility / That I did pluck allegiance from men's hearts'. His son did the same.
23 **climber upward** There is no need to

emend F: the climber looks upward at first merely to the rungs ahead. At the top he looks up to the skies.
24 **round** rung
26 **base degrees** '(a) lower rungs (b) ignoble ranks (c) humble folk' (Oxf[1])
27 **So Caesar may**. Cassius, for his own purpose, has declared Caesar to be 'god' and 'king' as fact: 1.2.116, 121, 160. Yet Brutus also has already concluded 'It must be by his death' (10).
28 **prevent** act before; forestall
   quarrel cause of complaint
29 **colour** excuse, as *OED sb.*[1] 12a; 'allegeable ground or reason', as *sb.*[1] 12b, further suggesting manipulation, even rhetorical embellishments, as *sb.*[1] 13
30 **Fashion** transform: *OED v.* 4 cites 220 below. A Shakespearean use, peculiar to 1599, is 'counterfeit, pervert' (*OED v.* 4b), which is not far from Brutus' perhaps unconscious rationalization. We are being shown the effect of Cassius' persuasion.
31 **extremities** '(a) conclusions (b) severities' (Oxf[1])

23 climber upward] climber-upward *Warburton*

Which hatched, would as his kind grow mischievous,
And kill him in the shell.

Enter LUCIUS.

LUCIUS

The taper burneth in your closet, sir.   35
Searching the window for a flint, I found
This paper, thus sealed up, and I am sure
It did not lie there when I went to bed.
Gives him the letter.

BRUTUS

Get you to bed again, it is not day.
Is not tomorrow, boy, the first of March?   40

LUCIUS   I know not, sir.

BRUTUS

Look in the calendar and bring me word.

LUCIUS   I will, sir.   *Exit.*

BRUTUS

The exhalations whizzing in the air
Give so much light that I may read by them.   45
Opens the letter and reads.

---

33 **kind** nature
    mischievous harmful
34 **kill . . . shell** proverbial: Dent, C496
35 **closet** private room; here study
36 **Searching . . . flint** to make a spark to
    light the taper
40 **first** Theobald's emendation of F's
    'first' to 'Ides', almost universally fol-
    lowed, is attractive if no notice is taken
    of the intensity of the conflict over
    Julius Caesar's reform of the calendar
    in 44 BC, and the parallel conflict
    between the rival Julian and Gregorian
    calendars in 1599 as *JC* was being writ-
    ten and first performed (see Intro-
    duction, p.19). Only when *the calendar*
    (i.e. the right one) (42) has been con-

sulted can the fifteen-day discrepancy
be settled, as it is at 59 below.
Shakespeare is writing to the historical
and contemporary moments at once,
something remarkable in itself.
Probably, having recalled Plutarch's
statement that the Senate was to offer
Caesar a crown on the first day of
March (Appendix, p. 335), he is also
making the calendar-shift bring into
prominence the concentration of time,
so marked a feature of the first three
acts.

44 **exhalations** meteors, thought to be
    exhaled from the earth by influence of
    the sun

40 first] Ides *Theobald*

'Brutus, thou sleep'st; awake and see thyself.
Shall Rome, et cetera. Speak, strike, redress.'
'Brutus, thou sleep'st; awake.'
Such instigations have been often dropped
Where I have took them up.   50
'Shall Rome, et cetera.' Thus must I piece it out:
Shall Rome stand under one man's awe? What Rome?
My ancestors did from the streets of Rome
The Tarquin drive, when he was called a king.
'Speak, strike, redress.' Am I entreated   55
To speak and strike? O Rome, I make thee promise,
If the redress will follow, thou receivest
Thy full petition at the hand of Brutus.

Enter LUCIUS.

LUCIUS

Sir, March is wasted fifteen days.   *Knock within.*
BRUTUS

'Tis good. Go to the gate: somebody knocks.   [*Exit Lucius.*]
Since Cassius first did whet me against Caesar   61

47 Brutus, as we learn immediately, is familiar with such messages, and does not bother to *piece it out* (51): but the *et cetera* here allows him to fill it out in 52–6 according to Cassius' manipulation in 1.2.150–61.
47, 55, 57 **redress** rectify, of a wrong (*OED v.*[1] 11)
52 **What Rome?** Rowe's emendation, commonly accepted, distorts Brutus' genuine question, which does not signal a clear republicanism.
53–4 See 1.2.158n
56–8 **O ... Brutus.** the moment when Brutus' mind becomes firm, that Caesar must die: 'Rome will receive all she asks at the hand of Brutus.' His intention is not fixed by the *instiga-*

tions he has been receiving (49), as Plutarch suggests (Appendix, p. 335): they only support his own previous theoretical conclusions.
56 **I ... promise** I promise Rome.
61 **whet me** Cassius has sharpened Brutus as a knife: an acknowledgement by Brutus, at a key moment, that he is Cassius' instrument. Brutus, from this point, begins to speak like Cassius in his preference for the most modern words.
61–2 **Since ... slept.** The pace of the play gives the impression that the night of the storm, when Caska and Cassius agree to call on Brutus (and hence the time of this scene as well), follows directly from the offering of

52 What] What, *Rowe*   60 SD] *Theobald*

I have not slept.
Between the acting of a dreadful thing
And the first motion, all the interim is
Like a phantasma or a hideous dream: 65
The genius and the mortal instruments
Are then in council, and the state of man,
Like to a little kingdom, suffers then
The nature of an insurrection.

Enter LUCIUS.

LUCIUS

Sir, 'tis your brother Cassius at the door,   70
Who doth desire to see you.

BRUTUS   Is he alone?

LUCIUS

No, sir, there are moe with him.

BRUTUS   Do you know them?

the crown to Caesar. Here Brutus implies a considerable gap, necessary for proper weight on his sleeplessness, in Plutarch a long time (Appendix, pp. 335 and 337). As in other plays, so-called 'double time' operates, whereby the onrush of events partly conceals the necessary time for, in *Oth* for example, many supposed adulteries. The effect is of several perspectives at once, allowing great dramatic density.

63–5 Such a torment of mind will afflict the great tragic heroes that follow – Hamlet, Othello, Macbeth, Antony – with madness never far away. For a close parallel see *Mac* 1.3.138–41.

63 **acting** a recent word, and *OED*'s first example (acting *vbl. sb.* 1) though antedated in Nashe's *The Unfortunate Traveller*, 1594 (Nashe, 2.324).

64 **motion** prompting or impulse. Iago refers to 'our raging motions' *(Oth* 1.3.335).

65 **phantasma** phantom, illusion. In this

form, very recent: *OED* gives first use 1598.

66–9 A *genius* is a guardian spirit which conceives and controls action. The *mortal instruments*, the human functions of mind and body, are not immortal like the genius and should simply carry out the bidding of the genius: if they are daring instead to challenge the genius *in council*, then all that can follow is a dreaded *insurrection*, leading to the madness of civil war. The *state of man* is both the individual and the nation: Brutus, like the later tragic heroes, holds in his inner turmoil the condition of the larger world, an integration implied in *nature*. See Introduction, p. 60.

70 **brother** 'Cassius had married Junia, Brutus' sister' (Plutarch, Appendix, p. 333).

72 **moe** a plural form of 'more'

LUCIUS

No, sir, their hats are plucked about their ears
And half their faces buried in their cloaks,
That by no means I may discover them   75
By any mark of favour.

BRUTUS   Let 'em enter.   [*Exit Lucius.*]

They are the faction. O conspiracy,
Sham'st thou to show thy dangerous brow by night,
When evils are most free? O then by day
Where wilt thou find a cavern dark enough   80
To mask thy monstrous visage? Seek none, conspiracy:
Hide it in smiles and affability;
For if thou path, thy native semblance on,
Not Erebus itself were dim enough
To hide thee from prevention.   85

73 **hats** Pope, in his edition of 1723–5, omitted this supposed anachronism, printing 'their — are pluckt . . .' as if the word were some obscenity. Quite apart from the fine dramatic furtiveness of Shakespeare's image, the Romans did wear headgear, as the note in Ard² explains.

75 **discover** identify

76 **favour** See 1.2.91 and n. But the word is ambiguous, also suggesting that Lucius finds them dislikable.

79 **are most free** 'roam unrestrained' (Oxf¹)

82 All the conspirators except Cassius will behave to Caesar in this way. The future Richard III says, 'I can smile, and murder whiles I smile' (*3H6* 3.2.182). Hamlet's discovery, so important that he has to write it down, is 'That one may smile, and smile, and be a villain!' (*Ham* 1.5.108). Iago is 'honest', but only 'seeming so' (*Oth* 1.1.61). Lady Macbeth gives advice: 'look like th'innocent flower, / But be the serpent under't' (*Mac* 1.5.62–3). Such notings of deception are all early in their plays, as springs to tragic action. *Affability*, being easy to be spoken

to, is a suspect quality throughout Shakespeare, culminating in 'smiling, smooth, detested parasites / . . . affable wolves' (*Tim* 3.6.94–5).

83 ***path**, F2's comma, surely correctly, makes the verb intransitive, a recent use: *OED v.* 3, first cited 1598 and here, meaning to pursue one's course. 'If Conspiracy goes on its way in its true appearance, no darkness could hide it, and *prevention* (forestalling) would follow.' A transitive verb, as commonly emended, distorts by suggesting that Conspiracy's *semblance* (appearance) is not true, is not *native*. The shadowy image in *path* is linked to the road to *Erebus*, the dark place under the world through which the shades pass on the way to Hades, a progress also present at *2H4* 2.4.148. The image also shades into *cavern* (80) and *monstrous visage* (81). According to Hesiod (Grant, 111), Erebus was the child of Chaos. A north-country dialect meaning of 'path', a deep cutting, was used to render the Latin *chaos*, the deep gulf of the lower world, as at Luke, 16.26, in the Lindisfarne Gospels (*OED* path *sb.* 2). See Introduction pp.144–6.

76 SD] *Rowe*   78 dangerous] *(*dang'rous)*   83 path,] *F2*; path *F*

Enter the conspirators: CASSIUS, CASKA, DECIUS,
CINNA, METELLUS *and* TREBONIUS.

CASSIUS

I think we are too bold upon your rest.

Good morrow, Brutus. Do we trouble you?

BRUTUS

I have been up this hour, awake all night.

Know I these men that come along with you?

CASSIUS

Yes, every man of them; and no man here   90

But honours you, and every one doth wish

You had but that opinion of yourself

Which every noble Roman bears of you.

This is Trebonius.

BRUTUS   He is welcome hither.

CASSIUS

This, Decius Brutus.

BRUTUS   He is welcome too.   95

CASSIUS

This, Caska. This, Cinna. And this, Metellus Cimber.

BRUTUS   They are all welcome.

What watchful cares do interpose themselves

Betwixt your eyes and night?

CASSIUS   Shall I entreat a word?

They whisper.

DECIUS

Here lies the east. Doth not the day break here?   100

CASKA   No.

85.1 *the conspirators* Shakespeare would
know from Plutarch that there were
more than sixty.
DECIUS See 1.3.148n.

86 **are too bold** 'intrude too presumptu-
ously' (Oxf¹)

87 **Do . . . you?** a social nicety, but *trouble
you* allows (a) cause you inner torment;

(b) include you in the action that is now
irrevocable

94, 95, 97 **welcome** contains some sense
of 'well come'.

98 **watchful** that keep you awake

100–10 not quite the trivial chatter covering
Brutus and Cassius as sometimes
described. Instead, this 'is a fine example

203

CINNA

O pardon, sir, it doth, and yon grey lines
That fret the clouds are messengers of day.

CASKA

You shall confess that you are both deceived.
Here, as I point my sword, the sun arises,   105
Which is a great way growing on the south,
Weighing the youthful season of the year.
Some two months hence, up higher toward the north
He first presents his fire, and the high east
Stands as the Capitol, directly here.   110

BRUTUS [*Comes forward with Cassius.*]

Give me your hands all over, one by one.

CASSIUS

And let us swear our resolution.

BRUTUS

No, not an oath. If not the face of men,

of Shakespeare's ability to make a short passage perform a variety of functions . . . it reminds the audience of the gradual dawning of the day on which Caesar is to be assassinated; it is symbolically appropriate that Caska should point his sword at the Capitol where Caesar is to be stabbed first by Caska; and it is psychologically true that men at moments of suspense often talk of trivialities to keep their minds from the immediate tension' (Sanders).

103 **fret** interlace, also with decorative patterns: cf. *Ham* 2.2.305, 'this majestical roof fretted with golden fire'.

104 **deceived** mistaken

106 **growing** advancing

107 **Weighing** considering

109–10 **high east** due east: Orrell (154–7) points out that the tradition of orienting Elizabethan theatres had special relevance to these lines, written 'about the time when Peter Street was preoccupied with dismantling the Theatre

and setting it up again across the river'. Caska's sword would be pointing upstage and a little to the right – perhaps to the door by which Caesar entered at the beginning of 1.2 – and due east of the Globe was the Tower of London, associated with Julius Caesar (*R3* 3.1.68–74). It is attractive to give Caska the stage action of pointing his sword (105) directly at Brutus, where he stands apart with Cassius.

111 **all over** one and all

113 **No . . . oath.** Brutus overrules Cassius for the first time, 'with an ethical passion very different from Cassius' high-charged prejudice' (Oxf[1]). Brutus' overrulings have serious consequences for the conspirators. Plutarch specifically notes that oaths were never taken (Appendix, p. 337). **face** commonly emended to 'faith', invited by a marginal note in Plutarch at this point, 'The wonderful faith and secresie of the Conspirators of Caesars

111 SD] *this edn*   113 not the face] *F;* that the face *Theobald;* that the Fate *(Warburton);* not the faith *(Thirlby);* not the faiths *(Malone)*

The sufferance of our souls, the time's abuse;
If these be motives weak, break off betimes, 115
And every man hence to his idle bed.
So let high-sighted tyranny range on
Till each man drop by lottery. But if these,
As I am sure they do, bear fire enough
To kindle cowards, and to steel with valour 120
The melting spirits of women: then, countrymen,
What need we any spur but our own cause
To prick us to redress? What other bond
Than secret Romans that have spoke the word
And will not palter? And what other oath, 125
Than honesty to honesty engaged,
That this shall be, or we will fall for it?
Swear priests and cowards, and men cautelous,
Old feeble carrions, and such suffering souls
That welcome wrongs: unto bad causes swear 130
Such creatures as men doubt. But do not stain
The even virtue of our enterprise,

death' (Appendix, p. 337). No emendation is needed. Johnson glossed 'the *countenance*, the *regard*, the *esteem* of the publick; or, *the face of men* may mean, the dejected look of the people'.

114 **sufferance** distress
the time's abuse injury suffered in these times of Caesar's misdeeds and corruption

116 **idle** (a) unoccupied; (b) in which he is inactive; and see 1.1.1n., and 4.3.68 and n.

117 **high-sighted** The image is from falconry: (a) soaring 'above the view of men' as at 1.1.74; (b) striking even the highest.
range roam: *OED v.*[1] 7a, first recorded 1547; extended here to 'soar'

118 **by lottery** by chance as the tyrant 'ranges' – see 4.1.1–6. The word dates only from the later sixteenth century.

these i.e. the list in 113–14

123 **prick** to drive on as with a spur

125 **palter** equivocate, shift, use trickery (*OED v.* 3, in this sense first recorded here). This sixteenth-century word, of unknown origin, first means 'mumble'.

126 **honesty ... engaged** 'pledges of honour interchanged' (Ard[2])

127 **shall ... will** Both have here intensive futurity.
fall die

128 **cautelous** cautious (*OED a.* 2). The word is late sixteenth-century, used in *Cor* 4.1.33 for 'deceitful'. Brutus says it is the weak as well as the crafty who need oaths.

129 **carrions** carcasses, people little better than dead

132 **even** just; that is, level (*OED a.* 10–12)

117 high-sighted tyranny] *Cam*[1]; high-sighted-Tyranny *F*   121 women. Then] women; Then *F2*

Nor th'insuppressive mettle of our spirits,
To think that or our cause or our performance
Did need an oath, when every drop of blood   135
That every Roman bears, and nobly bears,
Is guilty of a several bastardy
If he do break the smallest particle
Of any promise that hath passed from him.

CASSIUS

But what of Cicero? Shall we sound him?   140
I think he will stand very strong with us.

CASKA

Let us not leave him out.

CINNA   No, by no means.

METELLUS

O let us have him, for his silver hairs
Will purchase us a good opinion,
And buy men's voices to commend our deeds.   145
It shall be said his judgement ruled our hands.
Our youths and wildness shall no whit appear,

---

133 **insuppressive** insuppressible, in-
   domitable (*OED*'s first use)
   mettle courage (*OED sb.* 3). The pun
   on 'metal' follows from *stain* and *virtue*,
   the latter also in the sense of physical
   efficacy (*OED* virtue *sb.* 9d, 10).
134 **or . . . or** either . . . or
137 **a . . . bastardy** showing individually
   that his descent is not purely Roman.
   Shakespeare knew the tradition of
   Brutus' own bastardy (3.1.77n.):
   Plutarch glances at it (*Brutus*, 92); and
   we may assume that the hint was generally known.
138 **particle** possibly the culmination of
   a run of alchemical references in
   131–8: *stain, even virtue, insuppressive
   mettle, spirits, performance, drop, bastardy, particle*. (See Nicholl.) Brutus
   wants the highest Roman qualities to

act together to make new gold.
140 **But . . . Cicero?** Brutus' twenty-six-
   line exposition of the high Roman
   ground is wiped out by Cassius'
   change of subject, his impatience
   marked by the jolting rhythm of the
   line. Brutus is momentarily silenced.
   sound him find what he thinks
143–5 **silver . . . buy** W.A. Wright in
   1878 noted the link between *silver, purchase* and *buy*.
147 **youths and wildness** After Metellus'
   simple metaphors, this hendiadys was
   perhaps suggested by Plutarch's 'hot and
   earnest' (Appendix, p. 336 and see
   Introduction, p. 39). *OED* youth 1b suggests newness, novelty, recentness, citing
   MV 3.2.223 as first use.
   no whit none at all (a *whit* is a very
   small amount)

135 oath, when] *Oxf¹;* Oath. When *F*

But all be buried in his gravity.

BRUTUS

O name him not. Let us not break with him,
For he will never follow anything   150
That other men begin.

CASSIUS

Then leave him out.

CASKA   Indeed he is not fit.

DECIUS

Shall no man else be touched but only Caesar?

CASSIUS

Decius, well urged. I think it is not meet
Mark Antony, so well beloved of Caesar,   155
Should outlive Caesar. We shall find of him
A shrewd contriver. And you know his means
If he improve them may well stretch so far
As to annoy us all: which to prevent
Let Antony and Caesar fall together.   160

BRUTUS

Our course will seem too bloody, Caius Cassius,
To cut the head off and then hack the limbs –
Like wrath in death and envy afterwards –

148 **gravity** After *buried*, the wordplay on 'grave' is worthy of Mercutio (*RJ* 3.1.95).
149 **break with him** let him into the secret
151 The half-line may suggest a pause before Cassius replies.
152 **he . . . fit** This, surprising from Caska after 143, illustrates how far Brutus is deferred to.
154 **meet** fitting
155 **Mark   Antony**   In   Plutarch (Appendix, p. 342), Antony's death is discussed after Caesar's assassination, and vetoed by Brutus on the grounds of his usefulness to 'helpe his contry to

recover her libertie', rather than of his unimportance, as below, 164.
157 **shrewd contriver** '(a) astute and able strategist (b) dangerous schemer' (Oxf[1])   Plutarch,   *Antonius*,   264 (Appendix, p. 368).
    his means his capability of action; his access to power
158 **improve** make good use of
159 **annoy** harm
    prevent forestall
163 **wrath . . . envy** emotions too personal for their task, and to be avoided as two of the Seven Deadly Sins; *envy* = malice, malignancy (see 171, 177).

162 limbs –] *Cam²;* Limbes: *F*   163 afterwards –] *Cam²;* afterwards: *F*

For Antony is but a limb of Caesar.
Let's be sacrificers but not butchers, Caius.   165
We all stand up against the spirit of Caesar,
And in the spirit of men there is no blood.
O that we then could come by Caesar's spirit
And not dismember Caesar! But, alas,
Caesar must bleed for it. And, gentle friends,   170
Let's kill him boldly, but not wrathfully:
Let's carve him as a dish fit for the gods,
Not hew him as a carcass fit for hounds.
And let our hearts, as subtle masters do,
Stir up their servants to an act of rage   175
And after seem to chide 'em. This shall make
Our purpose necessary and not envious,
Which so appearing to the common eyes,
We shall be called purgers, not murderers.
And for Mark Antony, think not of him,   180
For he can do no more than Caesar's arm
When Caesar's head is off.
CASSIUS   Yet I fear him,
For in the ingrafted love he bears to Caesar –

165 **sacrificers** Brutus' lofty aim is lowered
   by the technical images of butchery in
   this speech (see Introduction, pp. 54–5).
166–8 **spirit . . . spirit** Inside the wordplay in these three lines (*spirit* as
   influence and soul) is the irony that
   Caesar's spirit, both as ghost and as a
   tyrannical 'Caesarism' in Octavius,
   will be as alive after death as before his
   'dismemberment', and Brutus himself
   will be defeated by it, as he recognizes,
   5.3.94–6.
170 **gentle** with the courteous generosity
   of nobility: a grotesque self-deception
   as well as flattery, considering the
   furtive intrusion of aggrieved men
171–3 Brutus is trying to make the killing
   an aristocratic, 'gentle', thing, in contrast with the crude hacking to death of
   ignoble prey.

174–6 **And . . . 'em.** lines cut on the stage
   from Bell's acting edition (1774) until
   early in the twentieth century, to pre-
   serve an idealization of Brutus; *servants*
   = hands. In *R2* Bolingbroke rebukes
   Exton for murdering Richard (5.6),
   having instigated him to do just that
   (5.4). See also *KJ* 4.2.
174 **hearts** so soon after *carcass* and *hounds*,
   suggests a submerged image of harts,
   subtly driven to enrage the hounds.
176–7 **This . . . necessary** the language
   of tyrants down the ages; *make* = 'make
   to seem'
179 **purgers, not murderers** again the
   language of tyrants; *purgers* = 'sur-
   geons who treat a patient by bleeding'
   (Cam²)
183 **ingrafted** implanted, grafted in: a gar-
   dening term not recorded before 1589

BRUTUS

Alas, good Cassius, do not think of him.
If he love Caesar, all that he can do   185
Is to himself – take thought, and die for Caesar.
And that were much he should, for he is given
To sports, to wildness and much company.

TREBONIUS

There is no fear in him. Let him not die,
For he will live and laugh at this hereafter.   190
Clock strikes.

BRUTUS

Peace! Count the clock.

CASSIUS   The clock hath stricken three.

TREBONIUS

'Tis time to part.

CASSIUS   But it is doubtful yet
Whether Caesar will come forth this day or no,
For he is superstitious grown of late,
Quite from the main opinion he held once   195
Of fantasy, of dreams and ceremonies.
It may be these apparent prodigies,
The unaccustomed terror of this night

---

184 **do . . . him** See Plutarch (Appendix,
p. 344) for this as 'the first fault he did'.
186 **take thought** suffer deep grief, as
Enobarbus's 'Think, and die' at *AC*
3.13.1
187 **much he should** a surprising
amount, even if he did
188 **sports . . . company** as elaborated in
Plutarch (*Antonius*, 257, 261)
189 **no fear** no cause to fear
190.1 The anachronism of a striking
clock in 44 BC is only distressing to
those shut off from imaginative time.
The dramatic action is more 'here
and now' than 'then', and the bell-
notes signal a change from ethical
debate to urgently deciding what to
do, when.

191 **three** See Introduction, pp. 21–2.
194 **superstitious** It is Calphurnia, not
Caesar, who is superstitious in
Plutarch (Appendix, pp. 326–7 and
339; and see 2.2.13–26, 30–1); but
1.2.7–9 shows him politically appearing sensitive to the fictions of *our
elders*.
195 totally altered from his former fixed
beliefs
196 Cassius gives no evidence for this
elaboration: his suggestion is derogatory. *OED ceremony sb.* 5, a portent,
omen (drawn from the performance of
some rite), cites only this and 2.2.13,
said by Calphurnia.
197 **apparent** visible

209

And the persuasion of his augurers,
May hold him from the Capitol today. 200

DECIUS

Never fear that. If he be so resolved
I can o'ersway him: for he loves to hear
That unicorns may be betrayed with trees,
And bears with glasses, elephants with holes,
Lions with toils and men with flatterers. 205
But when I tell him he hates flatterers,
He says he does, being then most flattered.
Let me work.
For I can give his humour the true bent,
And I will bring him to the Capitol. 210

CASSIUS

Nay, we will all of us be there to fetch him.

BRUTUS

By the eighth hour. Is that the uttermost?

199 **persuasion** more than inducement; there is a sense that, to make a climax to Cassius' customary triplet, after *prodigies* and *terror*, the *augurers* are seen as a religious body, as it were 'of the auguring persuasion'; very recent uses (*OED* persuasion 3b)

201–7 Decius' third, and main, speech in this scene (after 100, 153) prepares for his later action of overriding Caesar's surrender to Calphurnia's fears (2.2.58–104). Here he implies, correctly, a special, relaxed, intimacy with Caesar, mixed with scorn for his apparent gullibility. Caesar is like anyone else in enjoying fantastic tales. There is nothing in the speech hurtful to Caesar until the derision of *flatterers* (205).

203 **unicorns** 'The legendary way of capturing this legendary beast was to tempt it to charge and then dodge behind a tree, into which its horn would stick' (Oxf[1]; and see Womersley).

204 **glasses** mirrors: perhaps to dazzle them; or into which they paused to gaze
holes pitfalls

205 **toils** nets: the figurative sense, *OED* toil *sb.*[2] 3, was recent; it leads easily to *men with flatterers*.
flatterers 'dangerous men like dangerous animals can be rendered harmless by the use of cunning' (Sanders).

207 **flattered** flatterèd; the triple reiteration emphasizes the scorn.

208 **Let me work.** Decisive short lines of strong monosyllables are characteristic of this play: see 1.1.53; 1.2.31, 54; 2.1.62 and *passim*. They suggest figuration turning to action (and see Introduction, pp. 131–5).

209 **humour ... bent** disposition the right turn

211 Cassius here is quick not to be left out, but in the event is not present (2.2.107.1–2).

212 'Observe how strongly Shakespeare marks the passage of time up to the moment of Caesar's death; night, dawn (100), eight o'clock (212), nine o'clock (2.4.23), that our suspense may be heightened, and our interest kept upon the strain' (Dowden, 295).
uttermost latest

CINNA

Be that the uttermost, and fail not then.

METELLUS

Caius Ligarius doth bear Caesar hard,

Who rated him for speaking well of Pompey.   215

I wonder none of you have thought of him.

BRUTUS

Now, good Metellus, go along by him.

He loves me well, and I have given him reasons.

Send him but hither and I'll fashion him.

CASSIUS

The morning comes upon's. We'll leave you, Brutus.   220

And, friends, disperse yourselves – but all remember

What you have said, and show yourselves true Romans.

BRUTUS

Good gentlemen, look fresh and merrily.

Let not our looks put on our purposes,

But bear it as our Roman actors do,   225

With untired spirits and formal constancy.

---

214 **Caius Ligarius** properly Quintus Ligarius. After Cicero had made a speech in Ligarius' defence (still extant), Caesar generously pardoned his fighting alongside Pompey. Though a sick man, he joined the conspirators out of hatred of tyranny (Plutarch, Appendix, p. 336).

bear . . .. hard has ill will to

215 **rated** scolded

217 **go . . . him** call on him at his house

219 **fashion** transform

223–4 See 82 above: Brutus is aware of the duplicity he is adopting.

224 **put on** show: acting on stage is here brought right forward. There have been earlier theatrical images: the shouts heard from inside a crowded building in 1.2, for example, or the muffled figures revealing themselves earlier in this scene.

225 **Roman actors** The most skilled, and

most famous, was Quintus Roscius, particularly for comedy. A friend of Cicero, his name became synonymous with Roman, and thus fine, acting, as in *Ham* 2.2.387, 'When Roscius was an actor in Rome' – another filament linking *JC* and *Ham*. Roman actors wore masks, which would certainly conceal *purposes*. Shakespeare thinks of the skills of his own professional company.

226 **untired** steadfastly withstanding adversity. The other meaning of the pun, supported by *put on*, *actors* and *formal*, includes not wearing 'tires' or costumes: the souls are 'naked and undisguised, not assuming a "formal" appearance' (Miles, 124).

formal merely external, in outward appearance (*OED a.* 2c, first recorded 1581); also precise (*OED a.* 8). See Plutarch (Appendix, p. 338).

constancy with *formal*, means not

220] *Rowe; F lines* upon's: / *Brutus,* /

211

And so good morrow to you every one.

Exeunt all but Brutus.

Boy! Lucius! Fast asleep? It is no matter.

Enjoy the honey-heavy dew of slumber.

Thou hast no figures, nor no fantasies   230

Which busy care draws in the brains of men.

Therefore thou sleep'st so sound.

Enter PORTIA.

PORTIA   Brutus, my lord.

BRUTUS

Portia, what mean you? Wherefore rise you now?

It is not for your health thus to commit

Your weak condition to the raw cold morning.   235

PORTIA

Nor for yours neither. Y'have ungently, Brutus,

Stole from my bed: and yesternight at supper

You suddenly arose, and walked about,

Musing, and sighing, with your arms across;

---

slipping out of character as an actor. It also incongruously suggests the one quality which actors in their playing of many roles do not have.

227 **good morrow** marks the end of night.

229 **Enjoy** Brutus has been taken to show sensitive humanity here, as if such kindliness were the true Brutus, and the man who could talk of wanting to *kill ... boldly* and *carve* his friend (171–3) were an aberration.

honey-heavy ... slumber Brutus, beset with *figures* (figments) and *fantasies* (230), lacks such deep, sweet, refreshing sleep. The health of this leads into the entry of Portia as a normal, domestic, connubial figure; properly alongside Brutus in the night, unlike the men who have just left.

230 **figures** imaginings, like *fantasies*

232–308 This episode with Portia, taken in detail from the prose of North's English of Amyot's French of Plutarch's Greek, is given by Shakespeare new poetic form (Appendix, p. 338).

235 **weak condition** Plutarch tells later (Appendix, p. 340) of Portia's constitutional weakness; a hint, like Ligarius' ague, of an effect of conspiracy on ordinary life in Rome. It is sometimes taken on the stage as indicating pregnancy.

236 **ungently** roughly; discourteously

239 **arms across** traditional posture for sad or disturbed thought: Ariel describes the grieving Ferdinand, 'His arms in this sad knot' (*Tem* 1.2.224).

227SD *Exeunt all but*] *Manet F*   229 honey-heavy dew] *Theobald;* hony-heavy-Dew *F*

And when I asked you what the matter was   240
You stared upon me with ungentle looks.
I urged you further: then you scratched your head
And too impatiently stamped with your foot.
Yet I insisted, yet you answered not
But with an angry wafture of your hand   245
Gave sign for me to leave you. So I did,
Fearing to strengthen that impatience
Which seemed too much enkindled, and withal
Hoping it was but an effect of humour,
Which sometime hath his hour with every man.   250
It will not let you eat, nor talk, nor sleep;
And could it work so much upon your shape
As it hath much prevailed on your condition,
I should not know you Brutus. Dear my lord,
Make me acquainted with your cause of grief.   255

BRUTUS

I am not well in health, and that is all.

PORTIA

Brutus is wise, and were he not in health,
He would embrace the means to come by it.

BRUTUS

Why, so I do. Good Portia, go to bed.

PORTIA

Is Brutus sick, and is it physical   260
To walk unbraced and suck up the humours
Of the dank morning? What, is Brutus sick?

244 **Yet . . . yet** still . . . still
245 ***wafture** waving
249 **humour** passing mood
250 **his** its
253 **condition** disposition
254 **know you** recognize you as
257–8 Beginning with the affirmation of his position as 'Brutus', the lines are a hint that she knows he is contemplating political action of some sort.

259 **so I do** suggesting his political commitment, as well as habitual bodily care
260 **physical** healthy
261 **unbraced** unbracèd: unbuttoned, *en déshabille*. Cassius at 1.3.48–9 was *unbraced* in challenge to the *thunderstone*. Portia fears that Brutus in the quiet of his orchard is vulnerable to forces less dramatic, but as deadly. **humours** dampness

245 wafture] *Rowe;* wafter *F*

213

And will he steal out of his wholesome bed
To dare the vile contagion of the night?
And tempt the rheumy and unpurged air   265
To add unto his sickness? No, my Brutus,
You have some sick offence within your mind
Which by the right and virtue of my place
I ought to know of: and upon my knees
I charm you, by my once commended beauty,   270
By all your vows of love, and that great vow
Which did incorporate and make us one,
That you unfold to me, your self, your half,
Why you are heavy – and what men tonight
Have had resort to you: for here have been   275
Some six or seven who did hide their faces
Even from darkness.

BRUTUS   Kneel not, gentle Portia.

PORTIA

I should not need, if you were gentle Brutus.

264–6 **vile ... sickness** Though infections were thought to hang in the air, Portia rather overdoes the dangers of being out of doors in the small hours in a garden in Rome: she is articulating darker fears.

265 **rheumy and unpurged** unpurgèd; air that is both full of and causing watery ill-health, since the heat of the sun has not yet purified it. The word 'rheumy' was new: *OED a.* 3, citing this line first, and nothing again until 1715, Rowe.

267 **sick offence** disordering harm

270 **charm** conjure or entreat by some potent name: *OED v.*[1] 6 gives this as first use. The potent name is multiple: her *beauty*, his *vows of love*, their marriage-*vow*, their physical union. Portia's power of appeal must not be underrated: her claim is as an equal.
beauty Shakespeare earlier used

Portia's reputed beauty as a reference point, at *MV* 1.1.165–6.

271 **that great vow** 'a notable counterweight to Brutus' refusal of an oath with the conspirators' (S.McB.; and see 1.3.135, *incorporate*)

274 **heavy** weighed down with sorrow
what men Portia claims her equality in political matters.

275 **had resort to** visited, with an important sense of habitual action (*OED* resort *sb.* 4a)

277 **Kneel ... Portia.** Brutus does not answer her question. We may assume that he did not intend to do so, until the force of her *constancy* is revealed at 298–300.

278 **gentle Brutus** This word was debased at 169–73, *bleed ... gentle friends ... kill ... carve*. Perhaps Portia senses that, in playing it back to him. Cf. the play on 'gentle' at *TS* 4.3.71.

274 heavy –] *this edn;* heavy: *F*

Within the bond of marriage, tell me, Brutus,
Is it excepted I should know no secrets   280
That appertain to you? Am I your self
But as it were in sort or limitation,
To keep with you at meals, comfort your bed
And talk to you sometimes? Dwell I but in the suburbs
Of your good pleasure? If it be no more,   285
Portia is Brutus' harlot, not his wife.

BRUTUS

You are my true and honourable wife,
As dear to me as are the ruddy drops
That visit my sad heart.

PORTIA

If this were true, then I should know this secret.   290
I grant I am a woman: but withal
A woman that Lord Brutus took to wife.
I grant I am a woman: but withal
A woman well reputed, Cato's daughter.

279–82 The words *bond, excepted, apper-tain, sort* and *limitation* are legal terms (the last phrase means 'only in one way, for a limited period') set off by the narrower legal sense of *bond*. Portia is making the highest claims for herself as wife, far beyond the simple legal basis. Her speech is a development of that in Plutarch (Appendix, p. 338). For a legally-minded Portia much con-cerned with bonds, see *MV* 4.1.220–34.

281 **appertain** belong

283 **keep** keep company (*OED v.* 45)
    comfort bring pleasure to

284 **suburbs** outskirts; in this figurative sense (*OED* suburb 3b), first recorded the same year as *JC*, 1599. Portia's word is vivid, but itself leads on to *har-lot*, found in the brothels of London's suburbs, particularly Southwark, the environs of the Globe theatre. Her question emphasizes how much Rome, the city, is the centre of Brutus'

thoughts: and incidentally how much London may be shaping Shakespeare's Rome.

288–9 a simple figure of the union of lovers, from the obvious movement of blood, which the heart in times of dis-turbance or sorrow particularly needs. Though the metaphor is affecting, Portia cannot visit his heart in the same way that his own blood can; and at issue is the visitation Brutus has just received in his orchard.

290 **this secret** Portia recognizes the comparison.

294 **Cato's daughter** Marcus Porcius Cato was conspicuous for his stern morality. An ally of Pompey, he killed himself rather than fall into Caesar's hands. 'Brutus' Portia' in *MV* 1.1.165–6 is 'Cato's daughter'. Caius Marcius with 'grim looks' at Corioli (*Cor* 1.4.57–62) is 'a soldier / Even to Cato's wish'. Father to Portia, he was also uncle to Brutus.

Think you I am no stronger than my sex   295
Being so fathered and so husbanded?
Tell me your counsels. I will not disclose 'em.
I have made strong proof of my constancy,
Giving myself a voluntary wound,
Here in the thigh. Can I bear that with patience   300
And not my husband's secrets?
BRUTUS   O ye gods,
Render me worthy of this noble wife!   *Knock.*
Hark, hark, one knocks. Portia, go in a while,
And by and by thy bosom shall partake
The secrets of my heart.   305
All my engagements I will construe to thee,
All the character of my sad brows.
Leave me with haste.   *Exit Portia.*

Enter LUCIUS *and* Caius LIGARIUS.

Lucius, who's that knocks?

296 **fathered** as participial adjective, first
  use in *OED*
  husbanded again, first use in *OED* as
  this participial adjective: the word at
  this time means 'cultivated' (first use
  1578) as well as 'provided . . . with a
  husband'. 'The former perhaps allows
  reference to her upbringing, on the
  heels of *fathered*' (S.McB.)
299 **wound** See Plutarch (Appendix, p.
  338); and Introduction, p. 67.
304–7 **thy . . . brows** a scene we do not see:
  nor is it easy to imagine where it could
  have been in 'real' time, given that
  Brutus leaves with Caius Ligarius.
  These words stand for it, imaginatively.
304 **by and by** immediately, as Tyndale,
  NT, at Mark, 1.31, 'the fever forsook
  her by and by' (εὐθύς, *euthus*, 'straight-
  way'). But as Hamlet noticed (*Ham*
  3.2.377), ' "by and by" is easily said':
  we do not know what Portia was told,
  or when. Here she is hustled away lest
  she should meet the arriving visitor.

304, 306 **thy . . . thee** Portia and Brutus
  have said *you* or *your* to each other
  thirty-four times in this seventy-six-
  line exchange, and Portia has used his
  proper name (apart from vocatively)
  three times, as in *is Brutus sick?* (262). It
  is therefore a shock when Brutus in the
  haste of dismissing her suddenly
  switches to *thy* and *thee*, the more affectionate tone for someone intimate: perhaps continuing to exclude her by
  downgrading her status to subordinate.
306 **All . . .thee** I'll explain all that I am
  committed to do.
  construe cònstrue
307 **character . . . brows** all that the
  symbol of my serious face expresses.
  OED charactery 1 records it first in
  1598 in *MW*.
308.1 For Ligarius, see 214n. His solitary
  visit to Brutus in his sickness reverses
  Plu-tarch, where Brutus visits him
  before his dialogue with Portia
  (Appendix, p. 336).

LUCIUS

Here is a sick man that would speak with you.

BRUTUS

Caius Ligarius, that Metellus spake of.   310

Boy, stand aside. Caius Ligarius, how?

LIGARIUS

Vouchsafe good morrow from a feeble tongue.

BRUTUS

O, what a time have you chose out, brave Caius,

To wear a kerchief? Would you were not sick!

LIGARIUS

I am not sick if Brutus have in hand   315

Any exploit worthy the name of honour.

BRUTUS

Such an exploit have I in hand, Ligarius,

Had you a healthful ear to hear of it.

LIGARIUS

By all the gods that Romans bow before,

I here discard my sickness. Soul of Rome,   320

Brave son, derived from honourable loins,

Thou like an exorcist hast conjured up

My mortified spirit. Now bid me run

And I will strive with things impossible,

Yea, get the better of them. What's to do?   325

309–33 In the sick conspirator Shakespeare makes concrete and brings to a
climax the disordering of nature, the
human ill-health, growing in the
scene. The urgent need for a cure
restores the pace of the plot in senses
both political and dramatic.

311 **how?** How are you? Or even, 'Ho!'

312–20 Cf. *2H4* 1.1.136–52.

312 **Vouchsafe** receive graciously; usually, deign to give

313 **brave** worthy, good, noble. The
murder of Caesar is not *brave* in the
sense of courageous.

314 **kerchief** shawl for the head; etymo-

logically, the first syllable (from
French *couvrir*) suggests covering.
The last conspirator perhaps makes
the most theatrical 'discovery' of himself.

321 Brutus' nobility is strengthened by
his high republican ancestry: on the
eve of the assassination, Ligarius
echoes Cassius' first approach to
Brutus at 1.2.157–60.

322–3 **Thou ... spirit** *Thou* is now for
formal address: 'You have both exor-
cized and revived the deadened
(mortifièd) spirit within me.'

BRUTUS

A piece of work that will make sick men whole.

LIGARIUS

But are not some whole that we must make sick?

BRUTUS

That must we also. What it is, my Caius,

I shall unfold to thee as we are going

To whom it must be done.

LIGARIUS   Set on your foot,   330

And with a heart new-fired I follow you,

To do I know not what: but it sufficeth

That Brutus leads me on.   *Thunder.*

BRUTUS   Follow me, then.   *Exeunt.*

[2.2]   *Thunder and lightning. Enter* Julius CAESAR
                in his nightgown.

CAESAR

Nor heaven nor earth have been at peace tonight.

Thrice hath Calphurnia in her sleep cried out,

'Help ho: they murder Caesar.' Who's within?

Enter a Servant.

326 **make ... whole** heal those who suffer under tyranny
329–30 **I ... done** I shall explain on the way to the house of him who will receive the action.
331 **new-fired** 'The heart was the source of life, heat, and courage' (Cam[1]).
333 SD2 The following scene break is, as usual, minimal.
2.2 location: 'Rome. Caesar's house' (Rowe)
0.2 *nightgown* The more modern British 'dressing-gown', often given as a gloss, is less clear.
2–3 **Thrice ... Caesar.'** The scene is close to his source, but Shakespeare has dramatically sharpened Plutarch: 'he heard his wife Calpurnia, being fast a sleepe, weepe and sigh, and put forth many fumbling lamentable speaches. For she dreamed Caesar was slaine, and that she had him in her armes' (Appendix, p. 326). Calphurnia is in the same tradition as Pilate's wife, sending to him 'upon the judgement seat ... saying ... I have suffered many things this day in a dream' (Matthew, 27.19, Geneva 1599).

326] *Rowe; F lines* worke, / whole. /   **2.2]** *Rowe*   1] *Rowe; F lines* Earth, / night: /

SERVANT   My lord?

CAESAR

Go bid the priests do present sacrifice   5
And bring me their opinions of success.

SERVANT   I will, my lord.   *Exit.*

Enter CALPHURNIA.

CALPHURNIA

What mean you, Caesar? Think you to walk forth?
You shall not stir out of your house today.

CAESAR

Caesar shall forth. The things that threatened me   10
Ne'er looked but on my back: when they shall see
The face of Caesar, they are vanished.

CALPHURNIA

Caesar, I never stood on ceremonies,
Yet now they fright me. There is one within,
Besides the things that we have heard and seen,   15
Recounts most horrid sights seen by the watch.
A lioness hath whelped in the streets,

5   **present** immediate
6   **opinions** their judgements on the
    auguries in the entrails of the sacrificed
    beasts
    success what follows, the result (*OED*
    *sb.*1a)
9   'suggests a wife capable of ordering
    "immortal Caesar" about' (Cam¹).
    The two scenes of married couples
    show parallels (the wife's distress in
    the night and alarm at her husband
    going out). The contrasts do not
    diminish Calphurnia, whose dramatic
    situation is different from Portia's.
10 **Caesar shall forth.** See Introduction,
    p. 48.
11–12 **see / The face** Such power of see-
    ing the face recalls Exodus, 33.20, where
    'the Lord' said to Moses, 'Thou canst
    not see my face, for there shall no man
    see me, and live . . . my face shall not be

seen' (Geneva 1560). Shakespeare articulates Caesar's majesty.
12 **vanished** vanishèd
13 **stood on ceremonies** insisted on the
    precise observance of formalities, and
    refused to go on without them (*OED*
    ceremony 3b, first cited 1603).
    'Ceremony' is portent or omen drawn
    from a rite (*OED* 5, both citations from
    this play, here and at 2.1.196).
16 **watch** Night-watchers of a kind were
    first introduced by Augustus: again,
    London is in mind.
17 **whelped** whelpèd
17–24 The list of unsettling phenomena
    (empty graves, heavenly effects, crying
    ghosts, blood falling from the sky)
    overlaps with Horatio's account of the
    disturbances 'A little ere the mightiest
    Julius fell' (*Ham* 1.1.114), also trig-
    gered by the word 'watch' (110).

And graves have yawned and yielded up their dead.
Fierce fiery warriors fight upon the clouds
In ranks and squadrons and right form of war,   20
Which drizzled blood upon the Capitol.
The noise of battle hurtled in the air,
Horses do neigh, and dying men did groan,
And ghosts did shriek and squeal about the streets.
O Caesar, these things are beyond all use,   25
And I do fear them.

CAESAR   What can be avoided
Whose end is purposed by the mighty gods?
Yet Caesar shall go forth, for these predictions
Are to the world in general as to Caesar.

CALPHURNIA
When beggars die there are no comets seen;   30

Shakespeare was probably already thinking of the opening of *Ham*. Such phenomena do not appear in Plutarch (Appendix, p. 326), who does not mention comets and ghosts; but see the lists of portents in Suetonius, *Julius*, 81 (Rolfe, 1.109) and Virgil, *Georgics* (I.466 *sqq*).

18 **yawned** gaped

19 **fight** so F. Grammatically scrupulous editors emend to 'fought'. Calphurnia is, however, reporting effects which are confused between earth and heaven, then and now. The whole point is unusualness: niceness of grammar is inappropriate.

20 **squadrons** square formations: a precise Italian military word, first recorded in English in 1562; the more general use, of a body of men, is recorded from 1579 (*OED sb.* 1, 2).
right . . . war regular battle order

22 **hurtled** clashed with violence and noise

23 **do neigh** F2's 'did' has been almost universally followed by editors for grammatical consistency: but see 19

and n. – the neighing is one of the general features of the phenomenon.

24 **shriek and squeal** Cf. Horatio's 'sheeted dead / Did squeak and gibber' (*Ham* 1.1.114).

25 **beyond all use** extremely unusual

26–7 **What . . . gods?** proverbial (Dent, F83)

28 **Yet . . . forth** Most probably a stage tag: the exact phrase appears in Marlowe, *Massacre* (21, 67–70, 87) as the imperious Duke of Guise goes to his death. It is as likely to be a general commonplace as that Shakespeare at this important point would use an echo of Marlowe on recent Reformation history.

29 **Are to** are as applicable to

30–1 The link between royal figures and the heavens had been strong in the popular mind for many centuries: in the Gospels, the arrival of 'the King of the Jews' is signalled by 'his star' (Matthew, 2.2, Geneva 1599), and 'with the Angel, a multitude of heavenly soldiers' (Luke, 2.13, Geneva 1599). Heavenly fixtures falling out of

19 fight] fought *White*   23 do] did *F2*

The heavens themselves blaze forth the death of princes.

CAESAR

Cowards die many times before their deaths;
The valiant never taste of death but once.
Of all the wonders that I yet have heard,
It seems to me most strange that men should fear,   35
Seeing that death, a necessary end,
Will come when it will come.

Enter Servant.

What say the augurers?

SERVANT

They would not have you to stir forth today.
Plucking the entrails of an offering forth,
They could not find a heart within the beast.   40

CAESAR

The gods do this in shame of cowardice.
Caesar should be a beast without a heart
If he should stay at home today for fear.
No, Caesar shall not. Danger knows full well

---

place mark royal calamity. Plutarch records 'the great comet' which showed bright for a week, then disappeared (Appendix, p. 331).

31 **blaze** proclaim as well as flame

32 proverbial (Tilley, D27; Dent, C774), but also suggested by Plutarch (*Caesar*, 78)

33 **taste of death** experience death. The phrase, unknown before, came from Tyndale's first New Testament (1526), where it translates the Greek of Matthew 16.28: 'some . . . which shall not taste of death, till they have seen the Son of Man come in his kingdom'. From Tyndale in 1534 it passed into almost all sixteenth-century, and later, Bibles. Shakespeare uses the recollection to heighten Caesar's sense of his own particularity.

34–6 Caesar speaks perfect iambic pen-

tameters, as of one pronouncing solemn *sententiae* from his lofty position.

36–7 **Seeing . . . come** proverbial (Dent, N311)

39–40 Plutarch has 'Caesar self' doing the sacrifice (Appendix, p. 326): there is great dramatic value in having the message arrive from outside. The heart signified courage.

44–8 **Danger . . . forth.** Caesar's present high significance is almost matched by his rival, Danger: the whole grandiloquent speech shows his awareness both of his own outstanding military prowess as 'Caesar' and of his immediate vulnerability. The notion of a dangerous elder sibling is deep in Shakespeare before *JC*, from the English history plays to *AYL* (where the elder brother

That Caesar is more dangerous than he.   45
We are two lions littered in one day,
And I the elder and more terrible,
And Caesar shall go forth.

CALPHURNIA   Alas, my lord,
Your wisdom is consumed in confidence.
Do not go forth today. Call it my fear   50
That keeps you in the house, and not your own.
We'll send Mark Antony to the Senate House,
And he shall say you are not well today.
Let me upon my knee prevail in this.

CAESAR

Mark Antony shall say I am not well,   55
And for thy humour I will stay at home.

Enter DECIUS.

Here's Decius Brutus. He shall tell them so.

DECIUS

Caesar, all hail. Good morrow, worthy Caesar,
I come to fetch you to the Senate House.

CAESAR

And you are come in very happy time   60
To bear my greeting to the senators

---

encounters, with the younger, a lioness, 4.3.112–31 – and note the use there of 'hurtling' for conflict, as in 22 above). The idea is strong in *KL*, and in *Tem*.

46 ***We were** F1's 'We heare' 'could be from MS "We[He] are", with "He" imperfectly deleted' RP.

49 **confidence** In the sense, as here, of over-assurance, the word was new (*OED* 4).

52–6 See Plutarch, *Caesar*, 83–4. (Appendix, pp. 326–7)

56 **thy** Caesar's first personal reference to

Calphurnia has this: she 'you's him.

humour temporary mood (*OED sb.* 5). The word is derogatory, as to a woman; *R3* 1.2.227–8, 'Was ever woman in this humour woo'd? / Was ever woman in this humour won?'

58 Decius uses *Caesar* twice in the line, as once in 69, each time with open flattery. His *Caesar, all hail* recalls Judas betraying Caesar with 'Hail master' (Matthew, 26.49, Tyndale, *NT*).

60 **happy** favourable, with good hap or chance

46 are] *Capell;* heare *F*

And tell them that I will not come today.
Cannot is false; and that I dare not, falser.
I will not come today. Tell them so, Decius.

CALPHURNIA

Say he is sick.

CAESAR   Shall Caesar send a lie?   65
Have I in conquest stretched mine arm so far
To be afeard to tell greybeards the truth?
Decius, go tell them Caesar will not come.

DECIUS

Most mighty Caesar, let me know some cause,
Lest I be laughed at when I tell them so.   70

CAESAR

The cause is in my will, I will not come,
That is enough to satisfy the Senate.
But for your private satisfaction,
Because I love you, I will let you know.
Calphurnia here, my wife, stays me at home.   75
She dreamt tonight she saw my statue,
Which, like a fountain with an hundred spouts,
Did run pure blood; and many lusty Romans
Came smiling and did bathe their hands in it.

---

65 **Say . . . sick**. 'Cal. overreaches herself: he had been ready to send that lie by Ant. – a friend of the family; but with this Decius, who moreover can see that he is perfectly well, the matter is different' (Cam[1]). This is her last remark in the play. Unlike Portia, she is not mentioned again after 105 of this scene. **Shall . . . lie?** i.e. shall he be seen to lie? No one in the Senate had seen that he was sick. 'A drastic change from l. 55, from one who professes such constancy' (Oxf[1]).

71 In this fine self-assured line are two words which reverberate with his death through the play: *cause* (see 2.1.10–34) and *will* (3.2.129–59, 232–43).

74 **I love you** Caesar had made Decius his heir (see 1.3.148n). Decius is about to betray him. Judas Iscariot, who was one of Jesus' intimates – he 'kept the bag' (John, 12.6, Tyndale, *NT*) – and betrayed Jesus with 'Hail Master, and kissed him' (Mark, 14.45, Geneva 1599), may be in mind.

76–9 **She . . . it**. Plutarch gives the dream, but of a fallen pinnacle (Appendix, p. 326). The statue running blood, and anticipation of the conspirators bathing their hands in his blood (below, 3.1.105–10), are Shakespeare's.

76 **tonight** last night
   statue statuè

78 **lusty** stalwart

And these she does apply for warnings and portents   80
And evils imminent, and on her knee
Hath begged that I will stay at home today.

DECIUS

This dream is all amiss interpreted.
It was a vision, fair and fortunate.
Your statue spouting blood in many pipes   85
In which so many smiling Romans bathed
Signifies that from you great Rome shall suck
Reviving blood, and that great men shall press
For tinctures, stains, relics and cognizance.
This by Calphurnia's dream is signified.   90

CAESAR

And this way have you well expounded it.

80 Caesar's strongly regular iambic pentameters here break awkwardly to make an alexandrine; perhaps to suggest scorn at Calphurnia's disturbance: or perhaps the second 'and' is a scribal error.
 apply for interpret as
 portents portènts
83–9 The oily speciousness of Decius is well expressed in the frequent high 'e' and 'i' sounds: *This dream is . . . amiss interpreted / It . . . vision* and so on. Where Caesar had the darker *spouts* in 77 above, Decius has here *pipes*. Through Decius' *flattery* (2.1.201–8) 'Caes., taken with the notion of his blood being sacred, doesn't notice that it implies his death no less than Cal.'s interpretation. The Bear is dazzled with the mirror' (Cam[1]).
85–9 The religious nouns in 89 are led up to by the biblical echoes of the reviving blood of the sacrificed Redeemer, as e.g. in Revelation, 1.5, 'Prince of the kings of the earth . . . washed us from our sins in his blood' (Geneva 1559), or, for the drinking of the blood, all the sacramental references throughout

the New Testament – as e.g. 1 Corinthians, 11.25. Strong interpretation of a 'royal' dream by someone particular is also biblical: Genesis, 37, 40–1, and Daniel, 2. See Paster.
88 **Reviving blood** The monarch as both father and nursing mother of the people was a Tudor commonplace: Caesar is here a king.
89 **tinctures . . . relics** 'sacred tokens coloured and stained with the blood of martyrs' (Oxf[1]); also, as Johnson first noticed, with probable overtones of heraldry (with *cognizance*), where *tinctures* and *stains* refer to colours; and to alchemy, where *relics*, *tinctures* and *stains* are found (see Jonson, *Alchemist*, 3.1.144, and *OED* relic 3a, 1656, Ridgley; tincture *sb.* 6). Decius' interpretation of the dream is suspiciously rich with flattering suggestion, of Caesar as saviour, as lord, or as alchemical transformer. All such significances involve his death. The verbal density is increasing asthe tragic event comes closer, as in most Shakespearean tragedies.
 cognizance device worn by a lord's retainers

DECIUS

  I have, when you have heard what I can say.
  And know it now: the Senate have concluded
  To give this day a crown to mighty Caesar.
  If you shall send them word you will not come,   95
  Their minds may change. Besides, it were a mock
  Apt to be rendered, for some one to say,
  'Break up the Senate till another time
  When Caesar's wife shall meet with better dreams.'
  If Caesar hide himself, shall they not whisper,   100
  'Lo, Caesar is afraid'?
  Pardon me, Caesar, for my dear, dear love
  To your proceeding bids me tell you this,
  And reason to my love is liable.

CAESAR

  How foolish do your fears seem now, Calphurnia!   105
  I am ashamed I did yield to them.
  Give me my robe, for I will go.

Enter BRUTUS, Caius LIGARIUS, METELLUS Cimber,
CASKA, TREBONIUS, CINNA *and* PUBLIUS.

And look where Publius is come to fetch me.

93–4 **Senate ... Caesar** a lie, but not too improbable: Plutarch (Appendix, p. 327)
96–7 **mock ... rendered** remark likely to be made; allowing a retort
103 **proceeding** advancement
104 **reason ... liable** in that love for you and for your advancement, my reason, which tells me to be silent, submits to my love
106 **ashamed** ashamèd
107 Perhaps Calphurnia gives him his robe – and leaves the play.
107.2 PUBLIUS mysterious. It has been suggested that this was originally Cassius, largely on the grounds of the

oddity that Caesar first greets someone who is new to us (see Introduction, p. 136). Though the conspirators talked about enlarging their company (2.1.140–52), no such conspirator appears in Plutarch. A fresh figure at this point is, however, dramatically interesting, and Caesar names him twice so that we can get a good look at him. It is realistic that a senior figure should arrive at Caesar's house coincidentally. See 3.1.85–95.
108–27 Caesar's openness and friendliness to all deprives the conspirators of initiative – their strongest remarks are asides.

225

PUBLIUS
   Good morrow, Caesar.
CAESAR   Welcome, Publius.
   What, Brutus, are you stirred so early too?   110
   Good morrow, Caska. Caius Ligarius,
   Caesar was ne'er so much your enemy
   As that same ague which hath made you lean.
   What is't o'clock?
BRUTUS   Caesar, 'tis strucken eight.
CAESAR
   I thank you for your pains and courtesy.   115

Enter ANTONY.

   See, Antony, that revels long a–nights,
   Is notwithstanding up. Good morrow, Antony.
ANTONY
   So to most noble Caesar.
CAESAR   Bid them prepare within.
   I am too blame to be thus waited for.
   Now, Cinna. Now, Metellus. What, Trebonius,   120
   I have an hour's talk in store for you.
   Remember that you call on me today:
   Be near me, that I may remember you.
TREBONIUS
   Caesar, I will. [*aside*] And so near will I be

---

112 **enemy** See 2.1.214 and n.
116 **revels long** Shakespeare needs
   Antony to have authority in the second
   half of the play, so he gives a milder
   version of Plutarch's 'banquets and
   drunken feasts' (*Antonius*, 261).
118 **prepare within** Shakespeare is unspecific about whom, what and where.
   It seems that Caesar's high position
   makes him automatically understood
   in his household, whether referring to

departure (107) or wine (126).
119 **too blame** too blameworthy (*OED*
   blame *v.* 6, citing *1H4* 3.1.177).
   Whether referring to the Senate, or his
   guests' need for wine, the apology is
   simply gracious good manners.
121 **hour's** disyllabic (how-er's)
   talk . . . you matter to discuss with
   you, laid up and waiting
124 **near** 3.1.25–6 shows Trebonius leading Antony away.

124 SD] *Rowe*

That your best friends shall wish I had been further.   125
CAESAR
    Good friends, go in, and taste some wine with me,
    And we, like friends, will straightway go together.
BRUTUS [*aside*]
    That every like is not the same, O Caesar,
    The heart of Brutus earns to think upon.   *Exeunt.*

[2.3]   *Enter* ARTEMIDORUS [*reading a paper*].

ARTEMIDORUS   *Caesar, beware of Brutus. Take heed of*
    Cassius. Come not near Caska. Have an eye to Cinna.
    Trust not Trebonius. Mark well Metellus Cimber. Decius
    Brutus loves thee not. Thou hast wronged Caius Ligarius.
    There is but one mind in all these men, and it is bent   5
    against Caesar. If thou beest not immortal, look about
    you. Security gives way to conspiracy. The mighty gods
    defend thee.

                    Thy lover, Artemidorus.
    Here will I stand till Caesar pass along   10
    And as a suitor will I give him this.
    My heart laments that virtue cannot live
    Out of the teeth of emulation.
    If thou read this, O Caesar, thou mayst live;   14

126–7 'the classic symbol of betrayal: the murderers taking wine with the victim just before the killing' (Sanders). All the conspirators except Cassius are present. For this as the opposite of tyranny, see Introduction, p. 36.

128–9 That being like friends is not the same as being friends grieves my heart. The Latin proverb *Omne simile non est idem.*

129 **earns** yearns, only in the sense of grieves (*OED* earn $v.^3$ 2)

2.3 1–4 Plutarch's 'little bill' contains no names. Shakespeare may have drawn on written sources for the names (Oxf[1]), but he was quite capable of inserting the names for himself.

7 *Security ... conspiracy.* 'Freedom from suspicion leaves the way open for conspiracy' (Ard[2]). *OED* security 2, 'freedom from doubt', first recorded 1597. Cf. *Mac* 3.5.32, 'security / Is mortals' chiefest enemy'.

9 *lover* friend. Cf. Luke, 15.29, 'to make merry with my lovers' (Tyndale, *NT*).

11 **as a suitor** as if I were a petitioner

13 'beyond the bite of envious rivalry' (Oxf[1])

128 SD] *Pope*   **2.3**] *Rowe*   0.1 *reading a paper*] *Rowe*   14 may'st] *Rowe;* mayest *F*

If not, the Fates with traitors do contrive.   *Exit.*

[2.4]   *Enter* PORTIA *and* LUCIUS.

PORTIA

    I prithee, boy, run to the Senate House.
    Stay not to answer me, but get thee gone.
    Why dost thou stay?

LUCIUS   To know my errand, madam.

PORTIA

    I would have had thee there and here again
    Ere I can tell thee what thou shouldst do there.   5
    [*aside*] O constancy, be strong upon my side:
    Set a huge mountain 'tween my heart and tongue.
    I have a man's mind, but a woman's might.
    How hard it is for women to keep counsel.
    [*to Lucius*] Art thou here yet?

LUCIUS   Madam, what should I do?   10
    Run to the Capitol, and nothing else?
    And so return to you, and nothing else?

PORTIA

    Yes, bring me word, boy, if thy lord look well,
    For he went sickly forth; and take good note
    What Caesar doth, what suitors press to him.   15

---

15 **contrive** conspire. Cercigani supports
   a rhyme with *live*, if it is pronounced
   'leeve' in 12 and 14.

2.4 location: 'Rome. Before Brutus' house'
   (Capell)

1–20 Portia's nervousness lifts her from a
   deep concern and its history in 2.1
   (which could soon become tedious) to
   an instant alarm, a valuable raising of
   the dramatic temperature.

1 **Senate House** by the side of the open
   space, the *Forum Romanorum*, adjacent
   to the Capitol

3 **Why ... stay?** What are you waiting
   for?

6 **constancy** determination, resolution
   (*OED* 1b, first cited 1603)

8 See Plutarch, *Brutus*, 100–1
   (Appendix, p. 340): 'she sodainlie
   swounded'.

9 **keep counsel** keep secrets. She has
   been told of the conspiracy as Brutus
   promised (2.1.306–7). Portia had reason to hate Caesar (see Introduction,
   p. 65).

13 **bring me word** In Plutarch, she 'sent
   messenger after messenger' (Appendix, p. 340). 'Her nervous instability
   prepares us ... for her suicide later'
   (Cam[1]).

2.4] *Capell*

Hark, boy, what noise is that?

LUCIUS

I hear none, madam.

PORTIA   Prithee listen well.

I heard a bustling rumour like a fray,

And the wind brings it from the Capitol.

LUCIUS   Sooth, madam, I hear nothing.   20

Enter the Soothsayer.

PORTIA

Come hither, fellow. Which way hast thou been?

SOOTHSAYER   At mine own house, good lady.

PORTIA

What is't o'clock?

SOOTHSAYER   About the ninth hour, lady.

PORTIA

Is Caesar yet gone to the Capitol?

SOOTHSAYER

Madam, not yet. I go to take my stand   25

To see him pass on to the Capitol.

PORTIA

Thou hast some suit to Caesar, hast thou not?

SOOTHSAYER

That I have, lady, if it will please Caesar

To be so good to Caesar as to hear me:

I shall beseech him to befriend himself.   30

---

18 **bustling rumour** 'Bustling' in the sense of agitated is first cited in 1597 (*OED* bustling *ppl. a*); *rumour* (*OED sb.* 5, 6) = outcry, tumult.
fray disturbance

20 **Sooth** in truth

20.1 *the* **Soothsayer** As another recipient of Portia's anxiety, Shakespeare neatly brings in again Plutarch's Soothsayer from above, 1.2.1–24. He has the opposite fear to Portia's, that Caesar will not act to defend himself.

23 **ninth hour** particular for the passing of the hours (the last time-checks were for the conspirators, *three*, 2.1.191, and *eighth hour* 2.1.212); also ominous – not only in that movement towards the assassination, but in the echo of the Gospels' timing of the Crucifixion: Matthew, 27.45, Mark, 15.35, Luke, 23.44, 'at the ninth hour' (Tyndale, *NT*)

PORTIA

Why, knowst thou any harm's intended towards him?

SOOTHSAYER

None that I know will be,

Much that I fear may chance.

Good morrow to you. Here the street is narrow.

The throng that follows Caesar at the heels,   35

Of senators, of praetors, common suitors,

Will crowd a feeble man almost to death.

I'll get me to a place more void, and there

Speak to great Caesar as he comes along.   *Exit.*

PORTIA

I must go in. Ay me, how weak a thing   40

The heart of woman is. O Brutus,

The heavens speed thee in thy enterprise.

Sure the boy heard me. Brutus hath a suit

That Caesar will not grant. O, I grow faint:

Run, Lucius, and commend me to my lord.   45

Say I am merry. Come to me again

And bring me word what he doth say to thee.

Exeunt [*at separate doors*].

32–3 F's short lines are appropriate for a soothsayer's parallel gnomic statements.

36 **praetors** justices of high rank; both Brutus and Cassius were such, Brutus being chief justice, *praetor urbanus*.

38 **void** empty

43–4 **Brutus … grant.** 'An attempt to explain "enterprise", wh. she thinks Lucius has overheard' (Cam[1])

45 **commend** Plutarch (Appendix, p. 340) has Brutus already at Pompey's Porch with the conspirators, waiting for Caesar, receiving one of his men who 'tolde him his wife was a dying'. The point is Brutus' resolution.

31 harm's] (harme's)   40] *Rowe; F lines* in: / thing /   47 SD *at separate doors*] *this edn*

230

3[.1] *Flourish. Enter* CAESAR, BRUTUS, CASSIUS, CASKA,
DECIUS, METELLUS, TREBONIUS, CINNA, ANTONY, LEPIDUS,
ARTEMIDORUS, PUBLIUS, [POPILIUS Lena] *and the* Soothsayer.

CAESAR   The Ides of March are come.
SOOTHSAYER   Ay, Caesar, but not gone.
ARTEMIDORUS   Hail, Caesar. Read this schedule.
DECIUS
Trebonius doth desire you to o'er-read
At your best leisure this his humble suit.   5
ARTEMIDORUS
O Caesar, read mine first, for mine's a suit
That touches Caesar nearer. Read it, great Caesar.

3.1 location: 'Rome. The Capitol' (Rowe)

0.1–3 The last two short scenes were
either soliloquies (2.3 and the end of
2.4) or 'two-handers' (Portia with
Lucius, Portia with the Soothsayer).
Now suddenly the stage, with a
Flourish, is full of fourteen named
men, all but two of whom are immediately identifiable (but see the next
note). It is one of the marks of
Shakespeare's craft that he can make
this tense scene of the assassination so
fluid and at the same time so continually clear.

0.2 LEPIDUS unheralded, and unspeaking.
His true role in the play is later as a
future member of the triumvirate,
mentioned at 3.2.254 and first speaking at 4.1.3. His unexpected presence
overlaps with the unexpected absence
of one of the conspirators, Ligarius,
who was keen to take part, though ill
(2.1.330–3). Ligarius was addressed by
Caesar at 2.2.111–13 as one of those
taking him to the Senate House; he will
be a target of the mob in the last words
of 3.3. Ringler, having suggested (116)
that an abbreviated '*Li.*' or '*Lig.*' was
misread as '*Le.*' or '*Lep.*', later (122)
noted that one actor could play both
parts, leading to confusion about

whom he was playing here. Doubling
of Cassius with Ligarius has also been
proposed.

0.3 *POPILIUS Lena F2 corrects F1 by
including him, as he speaks at line 13.

1–7 The tension in the scene begins at
height, even as the figures sweep on. It
rises further until the killing; and then
continues to rise.

1–2 The . . . gone. Plutarch (Appendix,
p. 326) gives the exchange, with Caesar
'speaking merily to the soothsayer'.

3   schedule scroll; short note

4–5 The suit is neither in Plutarch nor
mentioned again in the play. Decius,
privileged to be close to Caesar,
has moved in swiftly to distract
Caesar from Artemidorus' revealing
schedule (3).

7   Read it Shakespeare's stage picture of
a man at a critical moment holding two
letters, but opening neither, recurs at
KL 5.1.40–53. There, Albany is given
by Edgar, Artemidorus-like, a letter
with secret information, and then by
Edmund written intelligence of the
enemy, on the assumption he will fight
on his, Edmund's, side. Albany's
immediate exit heightens the suspense. In both plays, the moment is
fleeting: reading the letters would,

3.1] *Actus Tertius*   0.3 POPILIUS] *F2*

CAESAR

What touches us ourself shall be last served.

ARTEMIDORUS

Delay not, Caesar, read it instantly!

CAESAR

What, is the fellow mad?

PUBLIUS   Sirrah, give place.   10

CASSIUS

What, urge you your petitions in the street?
Come to the Capitol.

[*Caesar and his followers move upstage.*]

POPILIUS

I wish your enterprise today may thrive.

CASSIUS

What enterprise, Popilius?

POPILIUS   Fare you well.

BRUTUS

What said Popilius Lena?   15

however, be decisive not only for the recipient, but for a nation's, and even the world's, history. Albany, we later learn, has read both, and survives. Caesar reads neither, and dies.

8   **us ourself** the 'royal we'. Tudor audiences would hear grist to the mill of the conspiracy.
served delivered (*OED* serve *v.*[1] 50); but also attended to (*OED* serve *v.*[1] 35)

10   **Sirrah** contemptuous form of 'sir'. Publius' only speech: is Shakespeare giving him something to do in the scene? Or defining him as a figure of authority? As he is not a conspirator, his intervention here must be tinged with irony.
give place get out of the way

12   **Capitol** Since the conspiracy became decisive at 2.1.227, the assassination has been planned for the Capitol (Decius 'will bring him to the Capitol', 2.1.210), though in Plutarch the

Senate meeting and the assassination took place in Pompey's Theatre. In *Ham* 3.2.100–1, Polonius represented an ancient tradition when he 'did enact Julius Caesar' and 'was killed in the Capitol'. Elizabethans wrongly understood 'the Capitol' as the citadel of ancient Rome, where the Senate met (*Cor* 2.1.92, 2.2).

12.1   *Caesar ... upstage.* to, effectively, *the Capitol*, where he begins to settle to hear suits, as he announces in 31–2. No special scenic effect is required: he needs to move only a few paces to establish the new place on stage, though a chair of state (*thy seat*, 34) is not impossible. See 31–2n.

13   in Plutarch (Appendix, p.340)

13, 16   **enterprise** a chilling euphemism, from North's Plutarch (Appendix, p. 340)

15   The short verse line allows a necessary beat of pause.

12 SD] *this edn*

CASSIUS

He wished today our enterprise might thrive.
I fear our purpose is discovered.

BRUTUS

Look how he makes to Caesar. Mark him.

CASSIUS

Caska, be sudden, for we fear prevention.
Brutus, what shall be done? If this be known,   20
Cassius or Caesar never shall turn back,
For I will slay myself.

BRUTUS   Cassius, be constant.

Popilius Lena speaks not of our purposes,
For look, he smiles, and Caesar doth not change.

CASSIUS

Trebonius knows his time: for look you, Brutus,   25
He draws Mark Antony out of the way.

[Exeunt Antony and Trebonius.]

DECIUS

Where is Metellus Cimber? Let him go
And presently prefer his suit to Caesar.

BRUTUS

He is addressed. Press near and second him.

CINNA

Caska, you are the first that rears your hand.   30

---

17 **discovered** discoverèd
18 **makes to** moves towards. It is more than mere crossing of the stage; it implies a dangerous effectiveness.
19 **prevention** being forestalled
21 **turn back** with the suggestion of 'return alive'
22 **slay myself** Cassius' extreme language develops Plutarch, 'a man halfe besides him selfe' (Appendix, p. 328); Shakespeare adds self-dramatization.
Cassius, be constant. 'Brut. is a bet-

ter leader in a crisis than the excitable Cass.' (Cam¹).
24–6 Such stage directions built into the dialogue sharpen the growing sense of theatre in this scene: the assassination has elements of a play-within-the-play.
25 **Trebonius** as in Plutarch, *Brutus*, 101; Decius in *Caesar* 85 (Appendix, pp. 341 and 328).
28 **presently prefer** immediately offer
29 **addressed** prepared

26 SD] *Malone*

CAESAR

Are we all ready? What is now amiss
That Caesar and his Senate must redress?

METELLUS

Most high, most mighty and most puissant Caesar,
Metellus Cimber throws before thy seat
An humble heart –

CAESAR   I must prevent thee, Cimber: 35

These couchings and these lowly courtesies
Might fire the blood of ordinary men,
And turn pre-ordinance and first decree
Into the lane of children. Be not fond

31–2 'Notably ironic' (S.McB.). Caesar's words might suggest that he is settled in a formal position, perhaps a place of authority, even a chair of state. Nothing, however, should interfere with the fluidity of the action over the stage – a fluidity about to become tragically literal.

32 **his Senate** 'royal' arrogance, like that of Cardinal Wolsey, attacked at *H8* 3.2.315 for writing to princes 'Ego et rex meus' ('I and my king')

35 **prevent** forestall; but also a healthy revulsion from such exaggerated unctuousness

36 **couchings** prostrations, lyings-down; Metellus may be overdoing it.
lowly courtesies 'Both (a) humble civilities (courtesies) and (b) low obeisances (curtsies)' (Oxf[1])

38 **pre-ordinance . . . decree** what has been formerly settled as law. Caesar is saying that neither flattery nor emotional appeal will make him override the Roman way of dispensing justice.

39 **lane** a notorious crux. F1's 'lane' is uncorrected in F2 and later Folios. If *lane* is indeed correct, Caesar's thought is of the trivialization of great matters by turning them, through over-acting, into a children's game played casually in the lane – not even

centrally in the market-place, where, in Luke, 7.32, even the complaining children are, whose games are not going right. It is the contemptuously dismissed *ordinary men*, for whom excessive performance might *fire the blood*, who become children in a playground. Caesar's entire speech, 35–48, is crammed with base humdrum life, the opposite of his lofty 'royal' status: *couchings, lowly, lane, fond, thawed, melteth, fools, sweet, low-crooked, base, spaniel, fawning, bend, fawn, spurn, cur.* Moreover, such vocabulary of everyday life was thought to belong to the genre of comedy, as did the matter of a separated or banished brother, as in 44 below (*CE* 1.1.127; *MA* 1.3.36–40; *TN* 1.1.34, 2.4; *AYL* 1.1.1–22, 92). It has to be said that Shakespeare nowhere else links children and such aimless play, though Rosencrantz's scorn for the 'aery of children, little eyases, that cry out on the top of question' (*Ham* 2.2.336–7) links children with excessive performance. Children are always for Shakespeare, and in frequent reference, seriously significant beings. Here in *JC*, however, they thoughtlessly *calculate* (1.3.65). 'Play', which Shakespeare extensively uses throughout the canon in several senses, is only

39 lane] law *Malone (Johnson);* love *(Thirlby);* play *(Mason);* lune *(Macmillan)*

To think that Caesar bears such rebel blood   40
That will be thawed from the true quality
With that which melteth fools – I mean sweet words,
Low-crooked curtsies and base spaniel fawning.
Thy brother by decree is banished.
If thou dost bend and pray and fawn for him   45
I spurn thee like a cur out of my way.
Know, Caesar doth not wrong, nor without cause
Will he be satisfied.

METELLUS

Is there no voice more worthy than my own
To sound more sweetly in great Caesar's ear   50

linked with children at play twice: at *MW* 4.1.10, where 'Master Slender is let the boys leave to play'; and the sinister 'Go, play, boy, play' of *WT* 1.2.187. Shakespeare's dozen references to 'lane' always imply narrowness: here the contrast to the scope of Roman justice. Hulme (210) sees *lane* as a variant pronunciation of 'line' in its obsolete sense of 'rule, canon, precept'. However, in Tyndale, *Obedience* (1528), a book much concerned with secular authority, the word 'law' is at one point printed 'lane' (sig. f.viii.ͬ). If this is a more frequent compositing error than has been noticed, it remains strange that it was uncorrected in later Folios. The overriding point must not be lost sight of – the unreliability of children.

fond foolish: 'don't be so foolish as to imagine'

40 **rebel blood** blood that will turn against him: the seat of the passions, opposed to reason

41 **That** as
thawed ... quality by contrast with Brutus as seen by Cassius, 1.2.307–11: *quality* is excellence as well as property. There may be an alchemical reference, Caesar seeing his own blood as *true*, unlike baser metals.

42 **With** by

42–3 **melteth ... sweet ... spaniel** See Spurgeon, 195–9, for Shakespeare's association of fawning dogs, melting sweets and flatterers.

43 **Low-crooked** crookèd; with body and knee fully bent

44 **Thy brother** Publius Cimber; see 53, 85, 89–93. Plutarch mentions him, without a name, as brother to Metellus (*Caesar*, 85, see Appendix, p. 328; in *Brutus*, 102, see Appendix, p. 341, he is Tullius).
banished banishèd

45 **bend and pray** as to a god

46 **spurn ... cur** Plutarch (*Brutus*, 102): 'Caesar at the first, simplie refused their ... intreaties: but afterwardes ... he violently thrust them from him.'

47–8 The lines as they stand are clear, and remain unchanged through successive Folios. For Ben Jonson's comment, see Introduction, pp. 136–7.

49–51 Metellus casts his mock-humility as a question, partly to sound unjustly wronged, partly to bring other conspirators closer. In Plutarch, 'They all made as though they were intercessors for him, and tooke him by the handes, and kissed his head and brest' (Appendix, p. 341).

43 Low-crooked curtsies] *(Low-crooked-curtsies)*

Julius Caesar

For the repealing of my banished brother?
BRUTUS
    I kiss thy hand, but not in flattery, Caesar,
    Desiring thee that Publius Cimber may
    Have an immediate freedom of repeal.
CAESAR
    What, Brutus?
CASSIUS   Pardon, Caesar: Caesar, pardon.   55
    As low as to thy foot doth Cassius fall
    To beg enfranchisement for Publius Cimber.
CAESAR
    I could be well moved if I were as you:
    If I could pray to move, prayers would move me.
    But I am constant as the northern star,   60
    Of whose true-fixed and resting quality
    There is no fellow in the firmament.
    The skies are painted with unnumbered sparks:
    They are all fire, and every one doth shine;
    But there's but one in all doth hold his place.   65
    So in the world: 'tis furnished well with men,
    And men are flesh and blood, and apprehensive.
    Yet in the number I do know but one
    That unassailable holds on his rank

---

51 **repealing** recalling and restoring
55 **What, Brutus?** words of astonishment
57 **enfranchisement** restoration to citizenship: the banished Bolingbroke in *R2* 3.3.114 starts by asking only for 'enfranchisement'.
58–73 See Introduction, pp. 36–7, 48.
58–9 'This is to claim super-divinity, since even the gods are moved by prayer' (Cam[1]).
59 an elevated *sententia*, concluding the impossible supposition, and making rhetorical play with *moved* from the previous line. Caesar's rhetoric is moving into the highest mode. He is con-

temptuous: 'If like you I were in the low position of expecting change . . .'.
to move to make some action happen: cf. *BCP*, Morning Prayer: 'The Scripture moveth us in sundry places to acknowledge and confess . . .'.
prayers a monosyllable, throwing the stress on the final *me*
60 **northern star** the unmoving Pole Star
61 **resting** *OED* resting *ppl. a.* 2 cites this as the only example of 'remaining stationary'.
67 **apprehensive** capable of apprehension, perceptive, 'sharp'
69 **holds . . . rank** keeps his position

Unshaked of motion. And that I am he   70
Let me a little show it even in this,
That I was constant Cimber should be banished
And constant do remain to keep him so.

CINNA

O Caesar –

CAESAR   Hence! Wilt thou lift up Olympus?

DECIUS

Great Caesar –

CAESAR   Doth not Brutus bootless kneel?   75

CASKA

Speak hands for me!   *They stab Caesar.*

CAESAR

Et tu, Brute? – Then fall, Caesar.   *Dies.*

---

70 **Unshaked of motion** 'Motion was the law of every star but one' (Cam[1]).

74 **Olympus** The mountain home of the gods in Greek mythology, and so making a metaphor for an impossibility; but Caesar's near-last words suggest that he thinks of himself as a god.

75 **Brutus** so dismissing Decius, supposed closest to him, in a word: there is no point in Decius doing anything if even Brutus is *bootless*, i.e. without success.

76 a short verse line, more powerful in its brevity

76 SD In his lives of both Caesar and Brutus, Plutarch's descriptions of the murder are particularly horrible, in the accounts of frenzied hacking and mangling to death, a brutality in which Brutus gave Caesar 'one wounde about his privities' (Appendix, pp. 329 and 341).

77 *Et tu, Brute?* The famous phrase is in Suetonius in Greek καὶ σύ, τεκνον; (*kai su, teknon*) (Rolfe, 1.110) meaning 'and thou, child (or son)?' The Latin *et tu, Brute* ('and

thou, Brutus') is not found in classical writers, and is first recorded only in 1595. The tradition that Brutus was Caesar's natural son is mentioned by Plutarch (see above, 2.1.137n.), by Suetonius (Rolfe 1.69) and by Appian (3.433).

Then fall, Caesar. Though the speakers before the assassination are minor conspirators, Caesar's last attention, in two remarks, is on Brutus, with sudden recognition that they are 'mighty opposites' (*Ham* 5.2.62). '*Then* could be (a) because my dearest friend (even son) has betrayed me; (b) because I must deserve to die if Brutus thinks so. It is of course the play's stroke of genius to limit personal interaction between the two to this inarticulate moment. My guess is that at this moment Brutus knows he is wrong and that all is lost' (RP). Though the moment of such tragic revelation is brief, in the power of the staging it is heightened beyond anything Shakespeare – or any other dramatist in English before him – had yet achieved.

CINNA

Liberty! Freedom! Tyranny is dead!
Run hence, proclaim, cry it about the streets.

CASSIUS

Some to the common pulpits and cry out   80
Liberty, freedom and enfranchisement!

BRUTUS

People and senators, be not affrighted.
Fly not. Stand still. Ambition's debt is paid.

CASKA

Go to the pulpit, Brutus.

DECIUS   And Cassius too.

BRUTUS   Where's Publius?   85

78–9 **Liberty . . . streets.** Plutarch tells in *Caesar*, 87 (Appendix, p. 330) how 'Brutus and his confederates . . . went . . . boldly . . .' (and see Appendix, p. 342). But Shakespeare gives the first words to a minor conspirator, and the moment is sometimes staged so that horror of what they have done makes the conspirators cower and speak feebly, as in John Barton's 1968 production at Stratford. (See Introduction, p. 115. We should note that Cinna's cry is changed by Cassius two lines later, and by Brutus again at 104.) Now, from Cassius and Brutus and others, haste, indecisiveness and impulsive bloodiness dominate the stage until the entry of Antony at 146.1. Such distractedness among the conspirators allows Shakespeare a sudden shock, the bathing in Caesar's blood (105–7). He is able to build steadily towards a long, high dramatic experience, Antony's funeral speeches (3.2.74–243). The strongest speech in the sixty-eight lines from here at 78 to Antony's entry is given to a servant. That is a demonstration of a sort of *enfranchisement* (81), but on the stage is appalled confusion. Cf. the parallel disintegrating effect of achieved lust in *Son* 129: 'perjur'd, murd'rous, bloody,

full of blame, / Savage, extreme, rude, cruel, nŏt to trust; / Enjoy'd no sooner but despised straight, / Past reason hunted . . . Past reason hated'.

80 **pulpits** platforms, with an obvious association for an Elizabethan audience with the more usual sense, implying that Rome, and thus the stage, is about to become a place of preaching. Shakespeare only ever uses the word six times, and five of those uses are in this scene. (The sixth is at 3.2.8 SD.)

83 **Fly not.** Brutus cannot stop what Plutarch records happening: '[Senators] flying filled all the city with marvelous feare and tumult' (Appendix, p. 329).
Ambition's . . . paid. No one else is to be touched; and death was due to Caesar for being ambitious.

85 **Where's Publius?** The question is a standard dramatic trick of Shakespeare to establish immediate high bustle (cf. *RJ* 1.5.1, 'Where's Potpan?'; *Cor* 4.5.3, 'Where's Cotus?'). Here there is the added advantage that the silent, shocked Publius is in any case mysterious (see 2.2.107.2n., and 10n. above). From this it seems that he has no connection with the conspirators.

CINNA

Here, quite confounded with this mutiny.

METELLUS

Stand fast together, lest some friend of Caesar's

Should chance –

BRUTUS

Talk not of standing. Publius, good cheer.

There is no harm intended to your person,   90

Nor to no Roman else. So tell them, Publius.

CASSIUS

And leave us, Publius, lest that the people

Rushing on us, should do your age some mischief.

BRUTUS

Do so, and let no man abide this deed

But we the doers.   95

---

86 **confounded** stunned
   mutiny tumult; but Shakespeare
   always uses the word with most of its
   more usual sense. It had fairly recently
   arrived from French (*OED* mutine *sb.*
   and *a.*[1]). Publius being *confounded* is
   dramatically powerful, and, though he
   entered at the start of 3.1 to help to take
   Caesar to the Senate, his state here is
   not so logically odd as commentators
   have made out. Shakespeare in his
   mature tragedies invariably makes the
   effect of killing someone stupefyingly
   unlike what was fantasized before-
   hand, hinting that Publius was a conspirator: cf. *Ham* 3.3.36–72; *Oth*
   5.2.128ff.; *Mac* 2.2.13–75.
89 **Talk . . . standing.** 'talk not of organizing resistance' (Sanders). 'Any hint
   of civil strife is shocking to Brut.: the
   deed has only to be explained to the
   people and all will be well (cf. ll.
   224–6)' (Cam[1]).
92–3 **leave . . . mischief** In *Brutus*, 103
   (Appendix, p. 343), Plutarch tells how

Brutus 'sent back againe the noble men
that came hither with him' for their
safety. To signify that, Shakespeare
here makes Cassius address Publius.
Cassius' alarm foreshadows the fate of
Cinna (3.3), but also demonstrates an
extraordinary projection. He, Cassius,
has just violently stabbed Caesar to
death; he now righteously warns
Publius of *mischief* from *the people*, as if
they were murderous and he were not.
It is self-delusion.
94 **abide** Hulme, 312–13, shows the
   double sense of 'stay' as opposed to
   leave, and transitively with *this deed* as
   'abide the consequences of, stand by'.
   There is also overlap with 'abye' =
   suffer for (*OED* abide *v.* 17 note; abye
   v. 3. See *MND* 3.2.175, 335). Brutus is
   showing insight into his own future
   suffering and death, perhaps uncon-
   sciously: this is not the moment of glorious freedom towards which he had
   led the conspiracy.

Enter TREBONIUS.

CASSIUS

Where is Antony?

TREBONIUS   Fled to his house amazed.

Men, wives and children stare, cry out and run,

As it were doomsday.

BRUTUS   Fates, we will know your pleasures.

That we shall die we know; 'tis but the time

And drawing days out, that men stand upon.   100

CASKA

Why, he that cuts off twenty years of life

Cuts off so many years of fearing death.

BRUTUS

Grant that, and then is death a benefit.

So are we Caesar's friends that have abridged

His time of fearing death. Stoop, Romans, stoop,   105

And let us bathe our hands in Caesar's blood

96 **amazed** stunned or stupefied, as by a blow (*OED* amazed *ppl. a.* 1)

98 **As** as if; *As 'twere* may be indicated by the lining.

doomsday the biblical Day of Judgement

98–105 **Fates . . . death.** Brutus, picking up *doomsday*, makes a challenge to the forces controlling the destiny of the conspirators: via threadbare commonplaces about the certainty of death, he leads to outrageous self-congratulation. They have done Caesar service by killing him. They deserve kindly treatment by the *Fates*.

98 **Fates . . . pleasures.** 'This Stoic addresses Fate as an Eliz. would address his prince' (Cam[1]).

99–100 **That . . . upon.** Death is certain: we can only live by the present and lengthening the span of life; the first part a proverb (Dent, N311).

101–3 Cf. *Mac* 3.2.22–6.

105–7 **Stoop . . . swords.** This blooding is not in Plutarch, nor in any telling of the story before. Just as Shakespeare alone saw that the inner logic of the old familiar story of King Lear meant that the king went mad, so here he alone sees that Brutus' dislocation of feeling has now pushed him over a borderline. He makes the others share a psychotic act of shocking brutality. The dramatic pressure is now even higher than at the killing: the contrast with all the conspirators' ideals is all too visible. In these moments, Rome has been forced to exchange, for an autocratic *colossus* (1.2.135), the unleashed sway of brutal New Men. Shakespeare's Brutus is very much not that 'mild and philosophical character' which made Pope give lines 105–10 to Caska. What had been a nightmare for Calphurnia (2.2.76–9) is so soon hideous reality. See also Kirschbaum.

103 SP] *F;* Cassius *Pope*   105 SP] *F;* Casca *Pope*

Up to the elbows and besmear our swords.
Then walk we forth even to the market-place,
And waving our red weapons o'er our heads
Let's all cry, 'Peace, Freedom and Liberty.'   110

CASSIUS

Stoop, then, and wash. How many ages hence
Shall this our lofty scene be acted over
In states unborn and accents yet unknown?

BRUTUS

How many times shall Caesar bleed in sport
That now on Pompey's basis lies along,   115
No worthier than the dust?

CASSIUS   So oft as that shall be,
So often shall the knot of us be called
The men who gave their country liberty.

DECIUS

What, shall we forth?

CASSIUS   Ay, every man away.
Brutus shall lead, and we will grace his heels   120

111–13 **How . . . unknown?** Like a trick
with mirrors, this endless reverbera-
tion allows Shakespeare to pitch the
dramatic experience still higher: to
make their actions not just dreadful,
but fixed in fearfulness for ever.
Cassius' self-dramatization spins into
space. He doesn't say, as Cleopatra
does in *AC* 5.2.215–20, that they
may be played once on the stage: he
suggests infinite repetition in uncount-
able *ages*, future countries and
unknown languages, a repetition of
which our present reading or viewing
is one. The effect is dizziness, appropriate to the sudden horror.

114–16 **How . . . dust.** Picking up Cassius'
lofty scene (112), Brutus reduces it to
sport and the carcass of Caesar below
him, now of the value of dust.

115 **Pompey's basis** the base of

Pompey's statue, against which the
body of Caesar lies stretched out; possibly a hint of Caesar being now the
same as Pompey (*OED* basis 9b).
Plutarch gives the irony: 'it seemed,
that the image tooke just revenge of
Pompeys enemie' (Appendix, p. 329).

117 **knot** a small band (of men) (*OED sb.*[1]
18)

119 **What . . . forth?** Decius' question
expresses impatience with the dramat-
ics, and eagerness to begin the work of
public relations.

120 **Brutus shall lead** as in Plutarch
(Appendix, p. 342)

grace Cassius uses this word for the
men who have just butchered Caesar
and bathed in his blood. It is a question
how far they have convinced themselves of the virtue of the act, and how
far the word is cynical.

113 states] *F2;* State *F*   115 lyes] *F2;* lye *F*

With the most boldest and best hearts of Rome.

Enter a Servant.

BRUTUS

Soft, who comes here? A friend of Antony's.

SERVANT

Thus, Brutus, did my master bid me kneel.
Thus did Mark Antony bid me fall down,
And being prostrate thus he bade me say: 125
Brutus is noble, wise, valiant and honest.
Caesar was mighty, bold, royal and loving.
Say I love Brutus and I honour him.
Say I feared Caesar, honoured him and loved him.
If Brutus will vouchsafe that Antony   130
May safely come to him and be resolved
How Caesar hath deserved to lie in death,
Mark Antony shall not love Caesar dead
So well as Brutus living, but will follow
The fortunes and affairs of noble Brutus   135
Thorough the hazards of this untrod state

121.1 The *most boldest* (121) are brought up short by 'a Servant'. Coming almost half-way through the play, it is the turning-point of the action.

122 **Soft** See 1.2.250n.

A friend Plutarch tells how the following day Antony, as consul, sending his son as a pledge, invited the conspirators 'down from the Capitol' (Appendix, pp. 343 and 369).

126 **honest** honourable

127 **royal** noble, generous, as in a king (*OED a.* and *sb.* 9a, citing this line)

128, 129 **Say** The Servant is repeating Antony's imperative. But the word rings with ambivalence – 'just *say* that; it doesn't have to be true' – though 129 is surely correct.

129 **feared** not 'was afraid of', but feeling a mixture of dread and reverence, as

for any rightful authority (*OED fear sb.*[1] 3d)

130 **If** The word makes a 'turn' in the middle of this formally structured speech, with the power of complete reversal of thought found in the 'turn' in a sonnet (usually at the start of the ninth line), which the speech roughly resembles. See Introduction, pp. 63–4.
vouchsafe allow, with an element of condescension

131–2 **be . . . death** be made certain that Caesar deserved to die. This hangs on the *If* at the start of the previous line. Their failure to satisfy that conditional brings Brutus and Cassius to their deaths.

136 **untrod state** unprecedented state of affairs, as well as the constitutional position of Rome

With all true faith. So says my master Antony.

BRUTUS

Thy master is a wise and valiant Roman;
I never thought him worse.
Tell him, so please him come unto this place 140
He shall be satisfied; and by my honour
Depart untouched.

SERVANT   I'll fetch him presently.   *Exit.*

BRUTUS

I know that we shall have him well to friend.

CASSIUS

I wish we may; but yet I have a mind
That fears him much, and my misgiving still 145
Falls shrewdly to the purpose.

Enter ANTONY.

BRUTUS

But here comes Antony. Welcome, Mark Antony.

ANTONY

O mighty Caesar! Dost thou lie so low?

---

140 **so . . . come** if it please him to come.
Shakespeare here for the moment
keeps Brutus with the higher authority, against Plutarch, to allow the play
to change direction against him.

142 **presently** at once. It is, again, the
structured actions of a servant, not the
wild and bloody criers of *liberty* and
freedom (110), which set going the second half of the play.

143 **well to friend** as a good friend: see
Abbott, 133, for this use of 'to'

145 **misgiving** *OED*'s first recorded use
(misgiving *vbl. sb.*)

145–6 **still . . . purpose** (My misgivings)
'always turn out to be unpleasantly
close to the truth' (Ard²).
shrewdly seriously, as well as astutely
(*OED adv.* 5 and 7)

147 Brutus' short sentences (short lines in
F) accompany strong dramatic change,
and allow Antony a pause on his
arrival, which he makes at the exact
mid-point of the play.

148–63 In Plutarch (Appendix, p. 343),
Antony first meets the conspirators
at a Senate meeting next day.
Shakespeare brings him on amid the
blood. These are the first words on
Caesar's death from outside that
group: they make the hinge on which
the play turns. From his first line,
Antony's speech diminishes the conspirators: it combines high personal
grief and lament for what has been lost
– new feelings, which from this point
begin to control the action. Antony has
said only thirty-four words in the play

147] *Pope; F lines Antony: / Antony. /*

Are all thy conquests, glories, triumphs, spoils,
Shrunk to this little measure? Fare thee well.   150
I know not, gentlemen, what you intend,
Who else must be let blood, who else is rank.
If I myself, there is no hour so fit
As Caesar's death's hour, nor no instrument
Of half that worth as those your swords, made rich   155
With the most noble blood of all this world.
I do beseech ye, if you bear me hard,
Now, whilst your purple hands do reek and smoke,
Fulfil your pleasure. Live a thousand years,
I shall not find myself so apt to die.   160
No place shall please me so, no mean of death,
As here by Caesar, and by you cut off,
The choice and master spirits of this age.

BRUTUS

O Antony, beg not your death of us:
Though now we must appear bloody and cruel,   165
As by our hands and this our present act
You see we do, yet see you but our hands

so far (1.2.5, 9–10, 190, 195–6;
2.2.118). Shakespeare has saved him
for this entrance.

149–50 **conquests . . . measure** Possible
written sources for this tragic thought
(Ard², Oxf¹) are hardly necessary. The
four nouns expressing Caesar's
achievements are the first proper
placing in the play of Caesar as a
man of military stature.

152 **let . . . rank** a passionately sarcastic
metaphor of healing the diseased
(*rank*, swollen) by letting blood

156 **most . . . world** a needed superlative
about Caesar, and a quite different
quality of sharing his blood, out of love

157 **ye, if you** Shakespeare reverses the
older pronouns, where 'ye' was nomi-
native and 'you' accusative. The distinction may have been obsolescent:
even so, such reversal hints at

Antony's distress of mind.
hard ill-will

158 **purple . . . reek . . . smoke** These
newly fashionable poetic attributes of
blood suggest that Antony is again sarcastic about the conspirators' illusions:
'purple' for blood is first recorded by
OED (*a.* and *sb.* 2d) only nine years
before *JC*; 'reek', i.e. smoke (*OED v.*[1]
2c), only six years before, in
Shakespeare's own *Luc* 1377; and
'smoke' is not recorded, of blood, in
OED.

159 **Fulfil your pleasure** The phrase is
bitter for the bloodied political murderers who face him; cf. *KL* 3.2.18–19.
Live should I live
a thousand years hyperbole, like
Cassius' *many ages* (111)

161 **mean** means

And this the bleeding business they have done:
Our hearts you see not. They are pitiful,
And pity to the general wrong of Rome –   170
As fire drives out fire, so pity pity –
Hath done this deed on Caesar. For your part,
To you our swords have leaden points, Mark Antony.
Our arms in strength of malice, and our hearts
Of brothers' temper, do receive you in,   175
With all kind love, good thoughts and reverence.

CASSIUS

Your voice shall be as strong as any man's
In the disposing of new dignities.

BRUTUS

Only be patient till we have appeased
The multitude, beside themselves with fear,   180
And then we will deliver you the cause
Why I, that did love Caesar when I struck him,
Have thus proceeded.

ANTONY   I doubt not of your wisdom.

---

169 **pitiful** full of pity
171 **fire . . . fire** proverbial (Dent, F277): the heat of a fire will drive out the smart of a burn. Frequent in Elizabethan poetry for a grander passion driving out a lesser; cf. *Cor* 4.7.54. **pity pity** Pity for Rome drives out pity for Caesar.
173 **leaden** blunt; too heavy to lift
174 **in . . . malice** much emended, though F makes good sense, 'with the same strength as when the intention was to hurt'. The phrases introduced by *arms* and *hearts* are antithetical, as in *hands* and *hearts* above, 166–9. 'Our bloodied arms and our brotherly hearts receive you.' Such separation of a body's parts distinguishes the conspirators' thinking, as Brutus at 2.1.174–8.
176 **reverence** respect

177–8 Cassius' error is only of timing. The *great observer* of 1.2.201 is more politically realistic than Brutus. In exchange for his support, they will give Antony a share of the power. Plutarch (Appendix, p. 343) records the Senate two days later giving Brutus 'and his consorts great prayses . . . severall governments of provinces': *Caesar*, 87 (Appendix, p. 330), has 'Brutus and his confederates' given 'convenient honors', a diplomatic phrase.
177 **voice** both vote and expression of opinion; see *Cor* 2.3 *passim*.
181 **deliver** declare
183 **I doubt not** Antony's irony directly follows his last statement (163): the 'choice and master spirits' have to be wise, of course.

---

170 Rome –] *Ard²*; Rome, *F*   171 pity –] *Ard²*; pitty *F*   174 in . . . malice] *F*; exempt from malice *Pope*; no strength of malice *Capell*; in strength of amity; *(Singer)* unstringed of malice *Oxf*

Let each man render me his bloody hand.
First, Marcus Brutus, will I shake with you.   185
Next, Caius Cassius, do I take your hand.
Now, Decius Brutus, yours. Now yours, Metellus.
Yours, Cinna; and my valiant Caska, yours.
Though last, not least in love, yours good Trebonius.
Gentlemen all: alas, what shall I say?   190
My credit now stands on such slippery ground
That one of two bad ways you must conceit me,
Either a coward or a flatterer.
That I did love thee, Caesar, O 'tis true:
If then thy spirit look upon us now,   195
Shall it not grieve thee dearer than thy death
To see thy Antony making his peace,
Shaking the bloody fingers of thy foes?
Most noble in the presence of thy corse,
Had I as many eyes as thou hast wounds,   200
Weeping as fast as they stream forth thy blood,
It would become me better than to close
In terms of friendship with thine enemies.
Pardon me, Julius! Here wast thou bayed, brave hart.
Here didst thou fall. And here thy hunters stand   205

---

184 **render . . . hand** The transition from *wisdom* (183) to *bloody hand* is shocking: *render* has a dominant sense of 'surrender' (*OED v.* 7, 8). Antony is increasingly confident of the political power the conspirators, blamed for murdering Caesar, have given him.

185–9 The individual affirmations of friendship conceal the dramatic picking-off of Antony's future targets.

188 **my . . . Caska** sarcasm: Caska struck Caesar first, and from behind. Cf. Antony at 5.1.43, 'damned Caska, like a cur, behind'.

189 **good Trebonius** the same: Trebonius lured Antony away from Caesar to enable them to strike.

191 **credit** credibility
slippery ground literally, with Caesar's blood, as much as metaphorical for his precarious credibility

192 **conceit** conceive: *OED v.* 2b gives this as first recorded use, with object and infinitive complement.

195 **thy spirit** the first invocation of the active cause of the rest of the action

199 **Most noble** refers to *thy spirit* (195)

202 **close** unite (*OED v.* 11)

204 **bayed, brave hart** See 4.1.48–9n. *Hart*, of course, puns on 'heart'.

Signed in thy spoil and crimsoned in thy lethe.
O world, thou wast the forest to this hart,
And this indeed, O world, the heart of thee.
How like a deer, strucken by many princes,
Dost thou here lie?   210

CASSIUS
  Mark Antony –
ANTONY   Pardon me, Caius Cassius.
  The enemies of Caesar shall say this:
  Then, in a friend, it is cold modesty.
CASSIUS
  I blame you not for praising Caesar so,
  But what compact mean you to have with us?   215
  Will you be pricked in number of our friends,
  Or shall we on, and not depend on you?
ANTONY
  Therefore I took your hands, but was indeed
  Swayed from the point by looking down on Caesar.
  Friends am I with you all, and love you all,   220
  Upon this hope, that you shall give me reasons
  Why and wherein Caesar was dangerous.

---

206 **Signed ... spoil** 'marked by the cutting-up of the quarry.' Onions (not *OED*) records 'spoil' as a hunting term for division of the quarry to the hounds: but *OED*'s dominant sense is of pillage, plunder.
  crimsoned *OED* crimson *v.* 1 records this as first use; Antony again sarcastically gives fashionable poetic colouring to the brutality of the murderers; see Introduction, pp. 54–5.
  lethe lethè; 'lethee' in F. Capell first proposed a rare noun 'lethe' for a quarry's blood in which huntsmen bathed, and many editors have followed: but the word is not in *OED*. 'Lethe' as a proper name is usually in Shakespeare (e.g. *2H4* 5.2.72) the water of forgetfulness, in Hades. Here the sense must be some fluid of death, possibly from Latin *letum* = death. Antony's difficult phrase is antithetical, as were Brutus' at 174–5 above. The affirmatory marking of the murderers is with what has been pillaged from Caesar, and their brilliant painting is with what carries him to oblivion.

213 **cold modesty** sober moderation
215 **compact** agreement
216 **pricked** marked down, as 4.1.1, 3, 16
221 **Upon this hope** a conditional syntactically placed for casual mention: but as ultimately fatal to the conspirators as the conditional at 130–2

206 lethe] Lethee *F*   209 strucken] *this edn;* stroken *F;* stricken *F2;* strooken *Capell*

BRUTUS

Or else were this a savage spectacle.
Our reasons are so full of good regard
That were you, Antony, the son of Caesar,   225
You should be satisfied.

ANTONY   That's all I seek,
And am moreover suitor that I may
Produce his body to the market-place,
And in the pulpit, as becomes a friend,
Speak in the order of his funeral.   230

BRUTUS

You shall, Mark Antony.

CASSIUS   Brutus, a word with you.
[*aside*] You know not what you do. Do not consent
That Antony speak in his funeral.
Know you how much the people may be moved
By that which he will utter.

BRUTUS   By your pardon: 235
I will myself into the pulpit first,
And show the reason of our Caesar's death.
What Antony shall speak, I will protest
He speaks by leave and by permission;

223 **were this** this would be
224 **regard** consideration; but also continuing *spectacle* (223)
225 **son of Caesar** as rumour said that Brutus himself was: and note Suetonius at 77n. Brutus' reference here is confident, and brutal.
226 **should** must
228–30 **Produce ... funeral** cleverly spoken as if an afterthought, and thus of little importance
230 **order** ceremony
232–3 The broken rhythms indicate Cassius' agitation. Plutarch (Appendix, p. 344) notes this as Brutus' second mistake, after sparing Antony.
234–5 **Know ... utter.** Though there is no interrogative in F, it is possible to read this as an urgent question,

suggesting that Cassius is either asking for factual information, or querying whether Brutus knows what he is doing.
236–7 'Perhaps this is the clearest display in a small compass of Brutus' political weakness, showing (1) his naive conviction that everyone sees situations as he does, (2) his idealistic belief in the obvious rightness of his cause, (3) his conviction that "sovereign reason" prevails in all men, and (4) his blindness concerning the nature of man as a political animal' (Sanders).
237 **our ... death** Brutus' phrase conveys intimacy, as if the murderers were all acting only out of dearest friendship: a further mark of how far Brutus is from reality.
238 **protest** proclaim

And that we are contented Caesar shall   240
Have all true rites and lawful ceremonies,
It shall advantage more than do us wrong.

CASSIUS

I know not what may fall. I like it not.

BRUTUS

Mark Antony, here, take you Caesar's body.
You shall not in your funeral speech blame us,   245
But speak all good you can devise of Caesar,
And say you do't by our permission:
Else shall you not have any hand at all
About his funeral. And you shall speak
In the same pulpit whereto I am going,   250
After my speech is ended.

ANTONY   Be it so.
I do desire no more.

BRUTUS

Prepare the body, then, and follow us.

Exeunt all but Antony.

ANTONY

O pardon me, thou bleeding piece of earth,
That I am meek and gentle with these butchers.   255
Thou art the ruins of the noblest man
That ever lived in the tide of times.
Woe to the hand that shed this costly blood.
Over thy wounds now I do prophesy
(Which like dumb mouths do ope their ruby lips   260
To beg the voice and utterance of my tongue)

252 **I . . . more.** 'He has all he could have
desired – including the unlooked-for
last word' (Cam¹).

254–75 See Introduction, pp. 70–2.

257 **lived** livèd
tide of times stream of history

258 **costly** of great value; causing excessive expenditure

253 SD *Exeunt all but*] *Manet F*

261 **utterance** speech, but with a further
sense of something that is 'utter', an
ultimate extremity: Antony's tongue
will turn wounds to mouths. *OED*
utterance²; cf. Macbeth's 'come, Fate,
into the list, / And champion me to th'
utterance!' (*Mac* 3.1.70–1).

A curse shall light upon the limbs of men:
Domestic fury and fierce civil strife
Shall cumber all the parts of Italy:
Blood and destruction shall be so in use,   265
And dreadful objects so familiar,
That mothers shall but smile when they behold
Their infants quartered with the hands of war:
All pity choked with custom of fell deeds,
And Caesar's spirit, ranging for revenge,   270
With Ate by his side come hot from hell,
Shall in these confines, with a monarch's voice,

262 **limbs** much emended in the eighteenth and nineteenth centuries, unnecessarily; 'limb' covers any organ or part of the body (*OED sb.*[1] 1). Curses alighted on bodies – see *KL* 2.4.158–60, and *Tim* 4.1.21–5. Much of the point of Antony's speech is its strong physicality.

263 **Domestic** national
  civil strife regarded with exceptional horror. *Civil strife* was historically true for the whole Roman Empire between Caesar's death in 44 BC and the battle of Actium in 31, when Augustus finally triumphed. The conspirators, who had killed a supposed *rex*, in the end caused a real *imperator*.

264 **cumber** overwhelm (*OED v.* 1)

268 **quartered** cut into pieces
  with by
  hands continuing the verbal emphasis on hands as separate and evil in this scene, matching the stage picture of eight men with bloodied hands (Antony's have blood from the murderers)

269 **with . . . deeds** because of the familiarity of cruel deeds

270–5 The artifice of rising rhythms, with the forecast of uncontrollable slaughter as revenge, echoes *H5* 1.1.281–8. The release of such beyond-human bloodlust in war is increasingly expressed by Shakespeare with high rhetoric in his mature plays: *H5* 3.3.10–27; *Cor*

2.2.105–20.

270 **Caesar's . . . revenge** the driving principle of the second half of the play, begun with Antony's entrance at the numerical mid-point, 146.1 above.
  ranging roving in search of prey

271 **Ate** Atè: Greek goddess of blind infatuation, daughter of Zeus in Homer, of Strife in Hesiod, and sister of lawlessness; Shakespeare uses her for the stirrer of 'blood and strife', as *KJ* 2.1.63, and *LLL* 5.2.676–7 comically (though shortly before 'the scene begins to cloud', 710). Accompanying *Caesar's spirit*, she will cause blindness: as Caesar's death is avenged, Shakespeare emphasizes the weak eyesight of the two chief conspirators at 4.3.274 and 5.3.21.

272 **these confines** regions of Italy; also enclosure, like the wooden bear-baiting structures where the *dogs* will be *let slip* (273) – the originals of theatres like the Globe. An 'echo' of Cassius' idealized 'unborn . . . unknown' claim at 111–13. But Antony grimly understands the truth of what effects will be re-enacted, in a real world.

272 **monarch's voice** Only a monarch or his representative could cry havoc: cf. *KJ* 2.1.357. What Caesar was murdered for, for supposedly wanting in life a crown, he now has even more powerfully in death.

262 limbs] kind *Hanmer;* line *Warburton;* loins *(Collier);* lives *(Johnson);* times *(Walker)*

Cry havoc and let slip the dogs of war,
That this foul deed shall smell above the earth
With carrion men, groaning for burial.   275

Enter Octavius' Servant.

You serve Octavius Caesar, do you not?
SERVANT   I do, Mark Antony.
ANTONY
Caesar did write for him to come to Rome.
SERVANT
He did receive his letters and is coming,
And bid me say to you by word of mouth –   280
O Caesar!
ANTONY
Thy heart is big: get thee apart and weep.
Passion, I see, is catching, for mine eyes,
Seeing those beads of sorrow stand in thine,
Begin to water. Is thy master coming?   285
SERVANT
He lies tonight within seven leagues of Rome.
ANTONY
Post back with speed and tell him what hath chanced.
Here is a mourning Rome, a dangerous Rome,

---

273 **Cry havoc** signal slaughter and pillage without mercy
let slip unleash
dogs of war the hounds of 'famine, sword and fire' (*H5* 1.Prol. 7–8)
274–5 Cf. *H5* 4.3.100–3.
275 **carrion ... burial** The metaphor finally fixes the animal references in Antony's speeches: from hunted *hart* (204), attacking *dogs* (273), now to the double oxymoron of men who are animal flesh, both dead and groaning to die.
276 **Octavius Caesar** See List of Roles 10n.

281 **O Caesar!** Again it is a servant who has dramatic power in his human response to the body of Caesar, as the drama turns.
282–5 He draws from Antony direct and sympathetic feeling, strikingly absent until now, and doing much to fix an audience on Antony's side.
282 **big** swollen with grief
283 **Passion** sorrow
286 **seven leagues** about twenty-one miles

275.1 *Octavius'*] *Rowe; Octauio's F*   283 catching, for] *F2;* catching from *F*

No Rome of safety for Octavius yet.
Hie hence, and tell him so. Yet stay awhile –   290
Thou shalt not back till I have borne this corpse
Into the market-place. There shall I try
In my oration how the people take
The cruel issue of these bloody men,
According to the which thou shalt discourse   295
To young Octavius of the state of things.
Lend me your hand.   *Exeunt.*

[3.2]   *Enter* BRUTUS *and* CASSIUS *with the* Plebeians.

PLEBEIANS
We will be satisfied: let us be satisfied.
BRUTUS
Then follow me, and give me audience, friends.
Cassius, go you into the other street
And part the numbers:
Those that will hear me speak, let 'em stay here.   5

289 **Rome of safety** also 'room'
290 **Hie** hasten, hurry
292 **try** test
294 **issue** outcome; what *these bloody men*
have done; so also 'deed' as *OED* issue
sb. 8b, citing this line.
296 **young Octavius** He was twenty-
one.
297 **Lend ... hand.** to carry the body
off stage. (In Plutarch, the body was
apparently left where it was: *Antonius*,
265, see Appendix, pp. 368–9). Cf.
'Assist', the last word of *Cor.*
Presumably it was always awkward for
an actor to get a body off stage without
help: Hamlet has to drag Polonius ('I'll
lug the guts . . .', *Ham* 3.4.212). The
bodies of Shakespeare's Roman tragic
heroes, seeming to lack onstage ceremo-
nial persons, cause such calls for aid to
get them off. Cleopatra finds 'we have no
friend . . .', *AC* 4.15.90.

3.2 location: 'Rome. The Forum' (Rowe)
0.1 What is effectively the second half of
the play begins with a strong echo of
the opening. Two men in authority
encounter an unruly crowd. Cam[1]
notes the same 'combination of familiarity and deference' in the commoners,
now called *Plebeians*. Unlike them,
these speak in verse, though often frag-
mented and irregular
1 We insist on sufficient explanation to
enable us to rest content with what you
have done.
3 **Cassius, go** Cassius is given no exit in
F; he is barely present in the scene, and
could exit here, with the others following at 6. He is next heard of (258–9)
galloping out of Rome like a madman,
and we do not see him again until his
entry for the Quarrel scene, 4.3.
4 **part the numbers** divide the throng

3.2] *Rowe*   1 SP] *Cam¹; Ple. F*

Those that will follow Cassius, go with him
And public reasons shall be rendered
Of Caesar's death.   [*Goes into the pulpit.*]

1 PLEBEIAN   I will hear Brutus speak.

2 PLEBEIAN

I will hear Cassius, and compare their reasons
When severally we hear them rendered.   10

                    [*Exeunt Cassius and some of the Plebeians.*]

3 PLEBEIAN

The noble Brutus is ascended. Silence.

BRUTUS

Be patient till the last.

Romans, countrymen and lovers, hear me for my
cause and be silent, that you may hear. Believe me for
mine honour and have respect to mine honour, that you   15
may believe. Censure me in your wisdom and awake
your senses, that you may the better judge. If there be

7   **public** in public; of public policy
7, 10 rendered renderèd
8 SD See 11n and 64n.
10 **severally** separately
11 **ascended** possibly to the upper level
(gallery) of the Globe. In this scene,
the four main movements – Brutus
ascending and descending, Antony
ascending and descending – are covered by the Plebeians. The gallery was,
however, only accessible from the tir-
ing-house. Each move is accompanied
by lines to indicate their notice of
arrival 'above' (see *Tit* 1.1 233.1,
291–5.1). Brutus' ascent at 8 (moved
from F's headnote) allows time for
Third Plebeian's remark here. From
the gallery, moreover, command of a
stage audience would be poorer. Both
Brutus and Antony need to be close to
their hearers. Ascents could be only
upstage to *the public chair*.
12 The short verse line acts as a cadence
to the preparation for Brutus' prose.

13–40 **Romans . . . death.** Plutarch does
not give Brutus' speeches. He does,
however, tell how they were received:
the first, dubiously (Appendix, p. 330);
the second made 'not all contented with
the murther' (Appendix, p. 343). Elsewhere, Plutarch quotes a letter by
Brutus (*Brutus*, 91) to illustrate his
Spartan ('of the Lacedaemonians'),
clipped, spare manner. Brutus' balanced rhetorical style and unemotional
reasonableness here is an attempt to give
full acting weight to a dispassionate
statement (see Introduction, pp. 55–6).
13 **lovers** friends
14 **cause** subject of concern; position
pressed to you; grounds for action: cf.
Oth 5.2.1 and see Introduction, p. 54.
15 **have respect to** bear in mind
16 **Censure** judge
17 **senses** reason, as in 'no one in their
senses' (*OED* sense *sb.* 10). The
rhetorical balance can be heard:
Censure . . . wisdom; senses . . . judge.

8 SD] at 3.2.0.1 *F*   8+ SP] *Cam²;* 1 *Ple. F*   9+ SP] *Cam²;* 2. *F*   10 SD] not in *F*   11+ SP]
Cam²; 3. *F*

any in this assembly, any dear friend of Caesar's, to him
I say, that Brutus' love to Caesar was no less than his.
If then that friend demand why Brutus rose against   20
Caesar, this is my answer: not that I loved Caesar less,
but that I loved Rome more. Had you rather Caesar
were living, and die all slaves, than that Caesar were
dead, to live all freemen? As Caesar loved me, I weep
for him; as he was fortunate, I rejoice at it; as he was   25
valiant, I honour him: but as he was ambitious, I slew
him. There is tears, for his love; joy, for his fortune;
honour, for his valour; and death, for his ambition.
Who is here so base, that would be a bondman? If any,
speak, for him have I offended. Who is here so rude,   30
that would not be a Roman? If any, speak, for him have
I offended. Who is here so vile, that will not love his
country? If any, speak, for him have I offended. I pause
for a reply.

ALL   None, Brutus, none.

BRUTUS   Then none have I offended. I have done no more   35
to Caesar, than you shall do to Brutus. The question
of his death is enrolled in the Capitol: his glory not
extenuated, wherein he was worthy, nor his offences
enforced, for which he suffered death.

                                                            40

Enter Mark ANTONY *with* CAESAR*'s body.*

Here comes his body, mourned by Mark Antony, who,
though he had no hand in his death, shall receive the

---

24 *freemen F's 'Free-men' suggests
    freed slaves.
27 There is tears See Abbott, 335, for
    singular verb and plural subject.
30 rude barbarous
37 question why his death was necessary

38 enrolled recorded: perhaps Brutus
    means Plutarch's meeting of the
    Senate the day after Caesar was
    killed (Appendix, p. 343).
39 extenuated diminished; undervalued
40 enforced stressed

24 freemen] *(*Free-men*)*

benefit of his dying, a place in the commonwealth, as
which of you shall not? With this I depart, that as I slew
my best lover for the good of Rome, I have the same   45
dagger for myself, when it shall please my country to
need my death.   [*Comes down.*]

ALL   Live Brutus, live, live.

1 PLEBEIAN

Bring him with triumph home unto his house.

2 PLEBEIAN

Give him a statue with his ancestors.

3 PLEBEIAN   50

Let him be Caesar.

4 PLEBEIAN   Caesar's better parts

Shall be crowned in Brutus.

1 PLEBEIAN

We'll bring him to his house with shouts and clamours.

BRUTUS

My countrymen.

2 PLEBEIAN   Peace, silence, Brutus speaks.

1 PLEBEIAN

Peace ho.

BRUTUS   55

Good countrymen, let me depart alone,
And, for my sake, stay here with Antony:

---

43 **a . . . commonwealth** wholly vague;
something like the rights of a free
Roman, with the silent implication
that such rights were not possible
under Caesar

47 SD allows the Plebeians to cover his exit
and re-entry 'below'

51–2 Brutus has killed his best friend to
prevent *Caesar* being crowned. So
badly has he misjudged Rome that

after hearing a couple of speeches the
people want to crown Brutus as
Caesar, ending the republic anyway. If
Brutus heard these lines, he would
have known that his position was
doubtful: yet he still handed the occasion over to Antony. It is likely that he
did not 'hear' them, if he was offstage
'coming down'.

47 SD] *Capell*   51+ SP] *Cam²;* 4. *F*   53] *Capell; F lines* House, / clamors. /

Do grace to Caesar's corpse and grace his speech
Tending to Caesar's glories, which Mark Antony,
By our permission, is allowed to make.   60
I do intreat you, not a man depart
Save I alone, till Antony have spoke.   *Exit.*

1 PLEBEIAN

Stay ho, and let us hear Mark Antony.

3 PLEBEIAN

Let him go up into the public chair.
We'll hear him. Noble Antony, go up.   65

ANTONY

For Brutus' sake I am beholding to you.
[*Goes into the pulpit.*]

4 PLEBEIAN

What does he say of Brutus?

3 PLEBEIAN   He says, for Brutus' sake
He finds himself beholding to us all.

4 PLEBEIAN

'Twere best he speak no harm of Brutus here.

1 PLEBEIAN

This Caesar was a tyrant.

3 PLEBEIAN   Nay, that's certain.   70
We are blest that Rome is rid of him.

2 PLEBEIAN

Peace, let us hear what Antony can say.

---

58 **grace … grace** further misjudgement, and in the careful elegance of
Brutus' instruction to the people to get
on in his absence with honouring
Caesar's corpse and hearing Antony
courteously. Though foolish, however, it is magnanimous.
59 **Tending … glories** Brutus
confidently, but in fatal error,
announces Antony's subject.
62 SD Here Brutus significantly leaves

alone (Cassius exits at 10.1, but see also
2 and n.), still confident in his course,
and believing that he is on top of the
situation. It is an ironic departure.
Some 200 lines after this exit, we are
told of his flight fom Rome. We do not
meet him again until the quarrel scene.
64 **public chair** as in Plutarch
(Appendix, p. 347), 'the chair or pulpit
for orations'
66, 68 **beholding** indebted

66 SD] *Globe*

ANTONY
You gentle Romans.

ALL   Peace ho, let us hear him.

ANTONY
Friends, Romans, countrymen, lend me your ears:
I come to bury Caesar, not to praise him.   75
The evil that men do lives after them:
The good is oft interred with their bones.
So let it be with Caesar. The noble Brutus
Hath told you Caesar was ambitious:
If it were so, it was a grievous fault,   80
And grievously hath Caesar answered it.
Here, under leave of Brutus and the rest
(For Brutus is an honourable man;
So are they all, all honourable men)

---

73 **gentle** technically, nobly-born; i.e. as
Romans. Plutarch calls this audience 'a
multitude of rakehells of all sortes'
(Appendix, p. 343). In his three words
of getting silence Antony has already
overtaken Brutus' appeal, which had
been his cautious 'Be patient till the
last' (12).

74–252 We are right to see the brilliance of
this dramatic writing as Shakespeare's
own. As with Brutus' oration, Plutarch
gives only the spirit of Antony's
speeches. 'Such was the light timber
from which Sh. framed one of his finest
and most famous scenes' (Cam[1]).
Plutarch twice mentions the powerful
effect of Antony displaying Caesar's
blood-stained robe (*Brutus*, 105;
Antonius, 265; see Appendix, pp. 344
and 369). In *Caesar* he does not mention
speeches by Antony. Caesar's will is read
by persons unspecified (Appendix,
p. 330). In *Brutus*, 104 (Appendix,
pp. 343–4) Brutus approves of Antony's
proposal that the will be read (not by
him), overruling Cassius. Antony's
specific stirring of the crowd comes later
(*Brutus*, 104–5, see Appendix, p. 344).
Plutarch notes that Antony's style was

'called Asiatik, which carried the best
grace and estimation at that time',
though he, Plutarch, finds it 'full of
ostentation, foolishe braverie, and vaine
ambition' (*Antonius*, 255).

74 **Friends** Stressing this first, against
Brutus' more formal *Romans* (13),
allows immediate warmth, and thus
access to their hearts. He is 'the "plain
blunt man" in sad perplexity' (Cam[1]).
His movement from the personal to the
national is reinforced by expansion:
Friends (one syllable), *Romans* (two syllables), *countrymen* (three syllables).

75 **not to praise** immediately contradict-
ing Brutus' introduction of him
(58–60), because at this moment the
crowd are on the conspirators' side.
Part of Antony's skill in manipulation
is in being gradual.

76–7 proverbial (Tilley, T619; Dent,
Appendix C)

77 **interred** interrèd

79 **ambitious** here, and throughout, with
four syllables

80 **If** Antony again suggests doubt; cf.
1–2. 3.1.130, 221–2.

81 **answered** paid the penalty for

82 **under leave** by permission

257

Come I to speak in Caesar's funeral.   85
He was my friend, faithful and just to me;
But Brutus says, he was ambitious,
And Brutus is an honourable man.
He hath brought many captives home to Rome,
Whose ransoms did the general coffers fill.   90
Did this in Caesar seem ambitious?
When that the poor have cried, Caesar hath wept:
Ambition should be made of sterner stuff.
Yet Brutus says, he was ambitious,
And Brutus is an honourable man.   95
You all did see, that on the Lupercal
I thrice presented him a kingly crown,
Which he did thrice refuse. Was this ambition?
Yet Brutus says, he was ambitious,
And sure he is an honourable man.   100
I speak not to disprove what Brutus spoke,
But here I am to speak what I do know.
You all did love him once, not without cause:
What cause withholds you then to mourn for him?
O judgement, thou art fled to brutish beasts   105
And men have lost their reason. Bear with me.
My heart is in the coffin there with Caesar,
And I must pause till it come back to me.

1 PLEBEIAN

Methinks there is much reason in his sayings.

2 PLEBEIAN

If thou consider rightly of the matter,   110

89 **captives** Cf. 1.1.34–5 and n.
90 **general coffers** the state's money-chests
96 **Lupercal** See 1.1.68 and n.; 1.2.25.
105–6 **O . . . reason**. See Wilson, 36, for a defence of this remark against Jonson's supposed mockery, citing in support Hamlet's 'O God! a beast

that wants discourse of reason / would have mourned longer' (*Ham* 1.2.150–1).
105 **brutish** perhaps a pun on Brutus, dehumanizing him
108 **pause** Genuine emotion allows him at the same time to test reaction: he is skilful enough to know that the break in his speech will be to his advantage.

105 art] *F2;* are *F*

Caesar has had great wrong.
3 PLEBEIAN   Has he, masters?
I fear there will a worse come in his place.
4 PLEBEIAN
Mark ye his words? He would not take the crown;
Therefore 'tis certain he was not ambitious.
1 PLEBEIAN
If it be found so, some will dear abide it.   115
2 PLEBEIAN
Poor soul, his eyes are red as fire with weeping.
3 PLEBEIAN
There's not a nobler man in Rome than Antony.
4 PLEBEIAN
Now mark him; he begins again to speak.
ANTONY
But yesterday the word of Caesar might
Have stood against the world. Now lies he there,   120
And none so poor to do him reverence.
O masters! If I were disposed to stir
Your hearts and minds to mutiny and rage,
I should do Brutus wrong, and Cassius wrong,
Who (you all know) are honourable men.   125
I will not do them wrong. I rather choose
To wrong the dead, to wrong myself and you,
Than I will wrong such honourable men.

111 ***Has he masters?** F2's punctuation
112 proverbial, that change is seldom for the better (Tilley, B332)
115 **dear abide** suffer dearly for; cf. 3.1.94 and n.
116 **Poor soul** Perhaps Second Plebeian was written as a woman's part: see 1.2.270–2, and Introduction, pp. 134–5. 'The crowd all through ignore principles and care only for persons – now Pompey, now Caesar, now Brutus,

now Antony' (Verity).
red as fire proverbial (Dent, F248); but *fire* is an appropriate element for the mood that is developing.
117 Third Plebeian specializes in instant adulation: it was he, or she, who wanted Brutus to be Caesar in line 51.
121 'The meanest man is now too high to do reverence to Caesar' (Johnson).
123 **mutiny and rage** See Plutarch, (Appendix, p.344), for the phrase.

111–12 Has . . . place.] Capell; *one line F*   111 H'as he,] *F2;* Ha's hee *F*   113 Mark] Marke *F. fol. ll I^r catchword;* Mark'd *F fol. ll I^v*

But here's a parchment, with the seal of Caesar.
I found it in his closet. 'Tis his will.   130
Let but the commons hear this testament –
Which, pardon me, I do not mean to read –
And they would go and kiss dead Caesar's wounds,
And dip their napkins in his sacred blood,
Yea, beg a hair of him for memory,   135
And, dying, mention it within their wills,
Bequeathing it as a rich legacy
Unto their issue.

4 PLEBEIAN

We'll hear the will. Read it, Mark Antony.

ALL

The will, the will. We will hear Caesar's will.   140

ANTONY

Have patience, gentle friends. I must not read it.
It is not meet you know how Caesar loved you.
You are not wood, you are not stones, but men:
And being men, hearing the will of Caesar,
It will inflame you, it will make you mad.   145
'Tis good you know not that you are his heirs,
For if you should, O what would come of it?

4 PLEBEIAN

Read the will, we'll hear it, Antony.
You shall read us the will, Caesar's will.

ANTONY

Will you be patient? Will you stay awhile?   150
I have o'ershot myself to tell you of it.
I fear I wrong the honourable men

---

130 **closet** See 2.1.35n.
133–5 **kiss ... memory** treat him as a
holy martyr, create sacred relics, either
dipping handkerchiefs in the blood of a
martyr or asking for a hair plucked from
the head. Plutarch (Appendix, p. 330)
notes that in his funeral he was to be

honoured 'as a god'.
142 **meet** fitting, proper
143 **wood ... stones** Contrast Murellus
at 1.1.36–7.
146–7 all strong monosyllables
149 **shall** must; cf. *Cor* 3.1.89–90.
151 **o'ershot myself** said too much

260

Whose daggers have stabbed Caesar: I do fear it.

4 PLEBEIAN

They were traitors: honourable men?

ALL

The will, the testament.   155

2 PLEBEIAN

They were villains, murderers. The will, read the will.

ANTONY

You will compel me then to read the will?
Then make a ring about the corpse of Caesar,
And let me show you him that made the will.
Shall I descend? And will you give me leave?   160

ALL

Come down.

2 PLEBEIAN   Descend.

[*Antony comes down from the pulpit.*]

3 PLEBEIAN   You shall have leave.

4 PLEBEIAN   A ring.

Stand round.

1 PLEBEIAN   Stand from the hearse, stand from the body.

2 PLEBEIAN

Room for Antony, most noble Antony.

ANTONY

Nay, press not so upon me. Stand far off.   165

ALL

Stand back. Room, bear back.

---

153 **stabbed Caesar** The words of reality, which Antony has held off until
now, are the trigger of getting his audience to do something about it – at first
only the small movement of encircling
the corpse.

160 **Shall I descend?** Antony is making
them cause the actions: he can do this best
by being close to them. His entry among

them and the repeated calls for playing
room echo the medieval popular drama,
as in Chambers, *Mediaeval*, 2.276.

163 **hearse** bier or coffin (*OED sb.* 5, citing this); whatever Caesar's body was
on when he was carried in at 40.1

165 ***far** F's 'farre', also in *WT* 1.2.109,
4.4.423, can suggest 'farther' (Abbott,
478). Here a monosyllable is needed.

161 SD] *Rowe*   165 far] farre *F*

ANTONY

If you have tears, prepare to shed them now.
You all do know this mantle. I remember
The first time ever Caesar put it on.
'Twas on a summer's evening in his tent,   170
That day he overcame the Nervii.
Look, in this place ran Cassius' dagger through:
See what a rent the envious Caska made:
Through this, the well-beloved Brutus stabbed,
And as he plucked his cursed steel away,   175
Mark how the blood of Caesar followed it,
As rushing out of doors to be resolved
If Brutus so unkindly knocked or no;
For Brutus, as you know, was Caesar's angel.
Judge, O you gods, how dearly Caesar loved him.   180
This was the most unkindest cut of all:

168–87 See Plutarch, *Brutus*, 105, and *Antonius*, 265 (Appendix, pp. 344 and 369).

168 **mantle** cloak

170 **a summer's evening** Antony did not join Caesar in Gaul until three years later. This is a fiction about himself and Caesar, like those of Cassius' 'memories' in 1.2.100–15, 119–28. Antony's tone is of apparently artless charm, building the personal link: but everything he says about the cloak is made up.

171 **overcame the Nervii** a famous victory (at which Antony was not present) lavishly celebrated in Rome. North's marginal note to Plutarch reads, 'Nervii, the stoutest warriors of all the Belgae' (North, 773). Caesar had shown conspicuous bravery in rescuing his men. Antony's choice of occasion is pointed but risky. 'Sh. would imagine many of Caes.'s veterans in the Forum' (Cam¹) – who might recognize Antony's untruth.

173 **envious** malicious (*OED a.* 2): see 2.1.163 and n. As he intends, it is hard to recall that he did not see the murder: but we did, so he must be carefully

unspecific.

174–8 from Antony, an unexpectedly baroque conceit, following *Luc* 1734–6, about another Brutus withdrawing a knife, and blood following. This climax, just after Lucrece has stabbed herself, is the moment when this Brutus (Lucius Junius) is first named. Antony needs to begin by making the horror personal, almost domestic, to wind up the effect over the next dozen lines to the words *treason* (190) and the final *traitors* (195 *et seq.* and 183), increasingly pointing to Brutus' betrayal of love.

175 **cursed** cursèd

178 **unkindly** cruelly; and against nature ('kind'), as in Hamlet's 'less than kind' (*Ham* 1.2.65)

179 **angel** a minister of loving offices (*OED* 1d): again high-flown, heightening the betrayal, for angels do not *stab* (182). Brutus is being made the specific murderer. Like *noble* (1.2.307), with which it was associated, an *angel* was an Elizabethan gold coin.

181 **most unkindest** as 178; and see Abbott, 11.

For when the noble Caesar saw him stab,
Ingratitude, more strong than traitor's arms,
Quite vanquished him: then burst his mighty heart;
And in his mantle muffling up his face,   185
Even at the base of Pompey's statue,
Which all the while ran blood, great Caesar fell.
O what a fall was there, my countrymen!
Then I, and you, and all of us fell down,
Whilst bloody treason flourished over us.   190
O, now you weep, and I perceive you feel
The dint of pity: these are gracious drops.
Kind souls, what weep you when you but behold
Our Caesar's vesture wounded? Look you here,
Here is himself, marred as you see with traitors.   195

1 PLEBEIAN
O piteous spectacle!

2 PLEBEIAN   O noble Caesar!

3 PLEBEIAN
O woeful day!

4 PLEBEIAN   O traitors, villains!

---

184 **burst** Caesar would not have had enough blood left from all the wounds for such an event (Alan Smith). Antony's conceit is of grief: by Brutus Caesar's heart was broken.
185 **in his mantle** as Plutarch (Appendix, p. 329)
186 **statue** statuè
187 **ran blood** perhaps as Pompey showed sympathy, even with a former enemy. The effect does not need to be explainable: it is very telling.
   great Caesar fell a powerful verbal effect. *Caesar* has had almost no epithet through the many uses of his name in Antony's speech since he began at 74: only *dead Caesar's wounds* at 133, and *the noble Caesar* at 182. Now *great Caesar fell*, the rhythm clinched with the monosyllabic heavy

stress of *fell*, especially strong after the unusual delaying phrases *in . . . face* (185), *Even . . . statue* (186) and *Which . . . blood* (187).
190 **flourished** triumphed; also made flourishes, swaggered
192 **dint** mark, impression from a blow
193 **Kind** unlike Brutus (178, 181)
   what how much
194 **vesture wounded** Antony removes the mantle, disclosing Caesar's body: the phrase is perhaps more than a conceit (as in *MND* 5.1.145, Prologue's bathetic '*Thisby's mantle slain*') and now carries a sense of Caesar's skin.
194–5 **here . . . himself** Brutus the traitor is dismissed: Caesar's stabbed corpse is suddenly present, a reality that is dramatically explosive.

263

1 PLEBEIAN
   O most bloody sight!
2 PLEBEIAN   We will be revenged!
ALL
   Revenge! About! Seek! Burn! Fire! Kill! Slay!
   Let not a traitor live!
ANTONY   Stay, countrymen.   200
1 PLEBEIAN
   Peace there, hear the noble Antony.
ALL
   We'll hear him, we'll follow him, we'll die with him!
ANTONY
   Good friends, sweet friends, let me not stir you up
   To such a sudden flood of mutiny:
   They that have done this deed are honourable.   205
   What private griefs they have, alas, I know not,
   That made them do it: they are wise and honourable
   And will no doubt with reasons answer you.
   I come not, friends, to steal away your hearts.
   I am no orator, as Brutus is,   210
   But, as you know me all, a plain blunt man
   That love my friend, and that they know full well
   That gave me public leave to speak of him.

199–200 **Revenge!** ... **live!** See Plutarch, *Brutus*, 105 (Appendix, p. 344).

199 **About!** Set about it!

202 SP *Though Second Plebeian (198) uses the plural, the triple plural is more likely to be collective.

203–23 Antony apparently lowers the tension in twenty-one lines of renewed irony, to make it build even higher, all enclosed in the word *mutiny* (204, 223).

206 **private griefs** reducing the elevated principles of the conspirators to personal grudge

208 **with reasons** suggesting that none have yet been given, and effectively devaluing any that might be given

210 **no ... is** an outrageous reversal. The rhetorical 'modesty topos' (disclaiming ability in speaking before demonstrating it) is used for the theatrical effect of causing, through *a tongue* (221), an explosion of violence. Of the 115 words to the end of the speech, only seventeen are not monosyllables, and seven of those are repeated proper nouns. See Introduction, pp. 72–3.

213 **public leave** permission to speak publicly

199 SP] *Collier ; 2.F*

For I have neither wit, nor words, nor worth,
Action, nor utterance, nor the power of speech   215
To stir men's blood. I only speak right on:
I tell you that which you yourselves do know,
Show you sweet Caesar's wounds, poor poor dumb
          mouths,
And bid them speak for me. But were I Brutus,
And Brutus Antony, there were an Antony   220
Would ruffle up your spirits and put a tongue
In every wound of Caesar that should move
The stones of Rome to rise and mutiny.

ALL

We'll mutiny.

1 PLEBEIAN   We'll burn the house of Brutus.

3 PLEBEIAN

Away then, come, seek the conspirators.   225

ANTONY

Yet hear me, countrymen, yet hear me speak.

214 *wit F2 is surely right, for *wit* (intellectual cleverness), as well as starting a run of alliteration, begins a list of the whole technique of good oratory, followed by *words* (fluency), *worth* (authority), *action* (gesture), *utterance* (eloquence), all leading to stirring *power* (see Kittredge). 'Writ' was kept by Johnson and Malone and other editors for 'penned or premeditated oration'.

216 **right on** straight on (cf. *LC* 26)

218–19 Antony, 'no orator, as Brutus is', the 'plain blunt man' (211–12), creates a baroque conceit. He expects his hearers to notice the oratory, controlled by the verbs *Show* and *bid*. *Poor poor* is the rhetorical device of *epizeuxis*, a repeated word with nothing intervening, specifically set aside for appeals to extreme passion. *Dumb mouths* (cf. 3.1.260–1) is *oxymoron*, two contraries linked. The phrase *poor poor dumb mouths* chimes. Inside the conceit, which itself is a form of *prosopopoeia* (where an absent person is given life and action), is the Elizabethan notion that a victim's wounds bled afresh in the presence of the murderer (see *R3* 1.2.55–61). That murderer is immediately identified in *were I Brutus*.

219–20 **Brutus . . . Antony** an exhilarating rhetorical trick, repeating and enlarging the linking of opposites by *syneciosis*, to appeal beyond Brutus' command of rhetoric

221 **ruffle up** stir to rage

223 **stones** an echo of Luke, 19.40. At Christ's entry into Jerusalem, the Pharisees told him to rebuke 'the whole multitude of the disciples' for their enthusiasm; he replied, 'if these should hold their peace, the stones would cry' (Geneva 1599). The conceit suddenly goes beyond decoration to cause action in *rise* and *mutiny*.

214 wit] *F2;* writ *F*

ALL

Peace ho, hear Antony, most noble Antony.

ANTONY

Why, friends, you go to do you know not what.
Wherein hath Caesar thus deserved your loves?
Alas, you know not. I must tell you then.   230
You have forgot the will I told you of.

ALL

Most true. The will, let's stay and hear the will.

ANTONY

Here is the will, and under Caesar's seal.
To every Roman citizen he gives,
To every several man, seventy-five drachmas.   235

2 PLEBEIAN

Most noble Caesar, we'll revenge his death.

3 PLEBEIAN

O royal Caesar!

ANTONY   Hear me with patience.

ALL   Peace ho.

ANTONY

Moreover, he hath left you all his walks,
His private arbours and new-planted orchards,
On this side Tiber. He hath left them you   240
And to your heirs for ever: common pleasures
To walk abroad and recreate yourselves.
Here was a Caesar: when comes such another?

1 PLEBEIAN

Never, never. Come, away, away.

---

231 **the will** Again, Antony momentarily
lowers the excitement in order to raise
it still higher.
235 **several** distinct, individual
seventy-five drachmas Equivalence
in modern currency is both impossible
and irrelevant: the dramatic force is in
the sense of generosity. See Plutarch

(Appendix, pp. 330, 344 and 370.
237 **royal Caesar** both munificent
and king; only moments ago, in 70,
a tyrant
238 **walks** as in Plutarch (Appendix,
p. 344)
241 **pleasures** pleasure grounds

We'll burn his body in the holy place,   245
And with the brands fire all the traitors' houses.
Take up the body.

2 PLEBEIAN

Go fetch fire.

3 PLEBEIAN   Pluck down benches.

4 PLEBEIAN   Pluck down forms, windows, anything.   250

Exit Plebeians [with the body].

ANTONY

Now let it work. Mischief, thou art afoot:
Take thou what course thou wilt.

Enter Servant.

How now, fellow?

SERVANT

Sir, Octavius is already come to Rome.

ANTONY

Where is he?

SERVANT   He and Lepidus are at Caesar's house.

ANTONY

And thither will I straight to visit him.   255
He comes upon a wish. Fortune is merry
And in this mood will give us anything.

SERVANT

I heard him say Brutus and Cassius

245 **burn . . . place** Plutarch (Appendix, pp. 330 and 344); and see Appian (Bullough, 5.159)

246 **fire . . . houses** Plutarch records attempts to lynch the conspirators and burn their houses (Appendix, pp. 330 and 344).

250 **forms** benches (*OED* form *sb.* 17) or window frames (*OED* 19a)
windows shutters

251 **Mischief** discord; harm, evil (*OED* 2a, 2c)

254 **Lepidus** in Plutarch, a powerful and decisive close friend of Caesar (Appendix, p. 330). See 3.1.0.2n.

256 **upon a wish** as I want. In *Brutus*, 106–7 (Appendix, p. 345), Plutarch writes that Octavius' arrival was the last thing Antony wanted, as he was managing matters on his own to his own advantage.

258–9 **Brutus . . . Rome** Their 'departure' in Plutarch was later. Shakespeare gets dramatic force out of

250.1 *with the body*] *not in F*

Are rid like madmen through the gates of Rome.

ANTONY

Belike they had some notice of the people   260

How I had moved them. Bring me to Octavius.   *Exeunt.*

[**3.3**]   *Enter* CINNA *the poet, and after him the* Plebeians.

CINNA

I dreamt tonight that I did feast with Caesar,

And things unluckily charge my fantasy.

I have no will to wander forth of doors,

Yet something leads me forth.

1 PLEBEIAN   What is your name?   5

2 PLEBEIAN   Whither are you going?

3 PLEBEIAN   Where do you dwell?

4 PLEBEIAN   Are you a married man or a bachelor?

2 PLEBEIAN   Answer every man directly.

1 PLEBEIAN   Ay, and briefly.   10

4 PLEBEIAN   Ay, and wisely.

3 PLEBEIAN   Ay, and truly, you were best.

CINNA   What is my name? Whither am I going? Where do

I dwell? Am I a married man or a bachelor? Then to

answer every man, directly and briefly, wisely and   15

truly: wisely I say, I am a bachelor.

2 PLEBEIAN   That's as much as to say they are fools that

marry. You'll bear me a bang for that, I fear. Proceed,

directly.

---

speeding up: they go on the instant, riding *like madmen* – and the news at third hand gives distance.

3.3 location: 'Rome. A street' (Capell)

0.1. CINNA *the poet* Gaius Helvius Cinna, whom Catullus admired; (Plutarch, Appendix, p. 344)

1 **tonight** last night

2 **unluckily ... fantasy** 'ominously oppress my imagination' (Oxf[1]).

Plutarch records the dream as 'marvelous straunge and terrible' (Appendix, p. 331). Cf. Sinfield, 24–8.

5–35 **What . . . him!** Cf. *2H6* 4.2.

18 **bear me a bang** suffer a blow from me

19, 23 **directly** The mildness of this poet's wordplay, and the fact that he is both answering and proceeding

3.3] *Capell*   5+ SP] *Cam²;* 1. *F*   6+ SP] *Cam²;* 2. *F*   7+ SP] *Cam²;* 3. *F*   8+ SP] *Cam²;* 4. *F*

CINNA   Directly, I am going to Caesar's funeral.   20
1 PLEBEIAN   As a friend or an enemy?
CINNA   As a friend.
2 PLEBEIAN   That matter is answered directly.
4 PLEBEIAN   For your dwelling, briefly.
CINNA   Briefly, I dwell by the Capitol.   25
3 PLEBEIAN   Your name, sir, truly.
CINNA   Truly, my name is Cinna.
1 PLEBEIAN   Tear him to pieces, he's a conspirator.
CINNA   I am Cinna the poet, I am Cinna the poet.
4 PLEBEIAN   Tear him for his bad verses, tear him for his   30
    bad verses.
CINNA   I am not Cinna the conspirator.
4 PLEBEIAN   It is no matter, his name's Cinna. Pluck but
    his name out of his heart and turn him going.
3 PLEBEIAN   Tear him, tear him!   [*They set upon him.*]   35
ALL   Come, brands, ho! Firebrands! To Brutus', to
    Cassius', burn all! Some to Decius'   house, and
    some to Casca's, some to Ligarius'! Away, go!
                    Exeunt all the Plebeians [dragging off Cinna].

directly, are charming. 'He uses the Plebeians' aggressive series of adverbs to structure the rhetoric of his replies' (RP). He is thus appallingly out of key with the thugs attacking him.

28 **Tear him** from Plutarch (*Caesar*, 88, 'dispatched'; *Brutus*, 106 'torne . . . in pieces', see Appendix, pp. 331 and 345). There are in the heart of the play two frenzied gang-attacks. The first killed Caesar, who was said to have had some guilt; the second victim is innocent. In each case the victim's name is made crucial: see 1.2.141–9. As the first frenzy commented on Brutus and Cassius, so does this on Antony. He has released 'lions' who turn on Romans, not their enemies, like

Cassius' Megarian lions (see 1.3.20n).
33–4 **Pluck . . . heart** a violent physical action for what has been metaphorical in, e.g., 2.1.167. As elsewhere in Shakespeare, disturbing imagery rises into horrific action. Cf. *KJ*, where earlier images of heat, of iron and of sickness suddenly coalesce in 4.1 to onstage hot irons '*and* Executioners' and the boy Arthur's cry, 'Must you with hot irons burn out both my eyes?' (4.1.39) (Pettet, 136).
34 **turn him going** not so much 'send him away' as 'send him where he was going', i.e. to join the mangled Caesar
35 **Tear him** Prudish staging should not conceal the horror of the action in the imperative verb.

38 SD *dragging off Cinna*] *Ard²*

4.1   *Enter* ANTONY, OCTAVIUS *and* LEPIDUS.

ANTONY

These many, then, shall die; their names are pricked.

OCTAVIUS

Your brother too must die; consent you, Lepidus?

LEPIDUS

I do consent.

OCTAVIUS   Prick him down, Antony.

LEPIDUS

Upon condition Publius shall not live,

Who is your sister's son, Mark Antony.   5

4.1 location: 'Antony's house' (Rowe). The last words of 3.2 are Antony's 'Bring me to Octavius', which suggests going to Caesar's house (as at 255). Now at 7 Antony sends Lepidus there to fetch the will, so editors have located this first scene of Act 4 in 'Antony's house'. This does not affect the fluidity of performance, as in the rush of events the discrepancy is not noticeable, and one patch of Globe stage will do as well as another; the point is where things are not literally, but dramatically. The first words show not someone's 'house', but Antony's obvious authority, Octavius' menace and Lepidus' doggy nature – he can be told 'Fetch!'

0.1 Though F starts a new act here, there is good sense in thinking of this scene as '3.4' (Jones, *Form*, 77).
OCTAVIUS his first appearance. He has been imminent at two key moments: immediately after Antony's soliloquy (3.1.275); and after the mob have left Antony to riot (3.2.253).
LEPIDUS stronger in Plutarch than in Shakespeare. Historically, Antony and Octavius were bitter rivals after Caesar's death. Their armies fought. They then made a threefold agreement with Lepidus (Plutarch, Appendix, pp. 347 and 370–1).

4.1] *Actus Quartus*

1 **These ... pricked.** Plutarch (Appendix, pp. 347 and 371). Spoken as the inflamed mob, after naming the five main conspirators, is rushing off with Cinna's body.
pricked marked with a pinprick through the list

2 **Your brother** Lucius Aemilius Paulus had been consul. He supported Brutus and declared Lepidus a public enemy for joining Antony after the assassination of Caesar. When the triumvirate was formed, Lepidus put him at the head of the proscription list, but in fact he escaped, perhaps with Lepidus' connivance.

4 **Publius** Plutarch (Appendix, p. 347) mentions a Publius Silicius who was proscribed. Antony had no nephew of this name, and this is hardly the Publius of 3.1.85–93. For an unknown reason Shakespeare invented this nephew instead of Lucius Caesar (*Antonius*, 268 – 'his Uncle by his mother'; Lepidus killed 'his owne brother, Paulus', see Appendix, p. 371). Brutal politics override close human ties: the scene shows Antony's harsh dismissal of Lepidus from effectiveness in the triumvirate. The following scene, 4.2, and much of the rest of the play, will be about human links falling to pieces.

ANTONY

He shall not live. Look, with a spot I damn him.
But, Lepidus, go you to Caesar's house:
Fetch the will hither, and we shall determine
How to cut off some charge in legacies.

LEPIDUS

What, shall I find you here?   10

OCTAVIUS

Or here, or at the Capitol.   *Exit Lepidus.*

ANTONY

This is a slight unmeritable man,
Meet to be sent on errands: is it fit,
The threefold world divided, he should stand
One of the three to share it?

OCTAVIUS   So you thought him,   15
And took his voice who should be pricked to die
In our black sentence and proscription.

ANTONY

Octavius, I have seen more days than you;
And though we lay these honours on this man
To ease ourselves of diverse slanderous loads,   20

---

6 **with ... him** I condemn him with a mark, a stain: cf. *Tim* 5.4.33–5.

9 **cut ... legacies** Antony had won the mob with the promises in Caesar's will. Cynically he now sets out to make cuts in that expenditure.

12 **unmeritable** unable to claim merit: *OED* first records in *R3*, 1594, in *JC* here (as 1601), and not again until 1797

14 **threefold ... divided** both 'the Empire of Rome amonge them selves' (Plutarch, Appendix, p. 347) and Europe, Africa and Asia. Octavius in *AC* 4.6.5, hoping to defeat Antony, looks to universal peace in 'the three-nooked world'. The idea probably comes from medieval maps centred on Jerusalem, where Asia, Europe and

Africa were the three parts: *OED* nook *sb.* 3 and 4.

16 **his voice** his vote and his recommendation

17 **black sentence** sentence of death
    proscription declaration of outlawry and confiscation of property; used by this triumvirate to get funds, as well as rid themselves of personal and political enemies: Plutarch, *Antonius* 268, see Appendix, p. 371.

18 **more days** Antony, says Plutarch (*Antonius*, 269), was the most feared of the triumvirs, 'being elder then Caesar'. In 44 BC he was about forty, twice as old as Octavius.

20 **diverse ... loads** various accusations we might bear

20 slanderous] *(sland'rous)*

He shall but bear them as the ass bears gold,
To groan and sweat under the business,
Either led or driven, as we point the way:
And having brought our treasure where we will,
Then take we down his load and turn him off,   25
Like to the empty ass, to shake his ears
And graze in commons.

OCTAVIUS   You may do your will;
But he's a tried and valiant soldier.

ANTONY
So is my horse, Octavius, and for that
I do appoint him store of provender.   30
It is a creature that I teach to fight,
To wind, to stop, to run directly on,
His corporal motion governed by my spirit,
And, in some taste, is Lepidus but so:
He must be taught, and trained, and bid go forth;   35
A barren-spirited fellow; one that feeds

21–7 He . . . commons Shakespeare, in the plays written around this time, can pack the lines with suggestive metaphors which flash in the onward rush of thought ('Thinks thou the fiery fever will go out / With titles blown from adulation', *H5* 4.1.249–50; 'these but the trappings and the suits of woe', *Ham* 1.2.86; 'if his occulted guilt / Do not itself unkennel', *Ham* 3.2.78–9). Antony here takes seven lines to develop a simple analogy of an ass. The effect is of steamrollering: nothing can stop the superior weight of Antony's words. The point is the lack of feeling: Lepidus is so unimportant that Antony can't be bothered to rouse his audience, as he has done so superlatively in the scene just gone.

21 ass bears gold not in fact proverbial. Dent, A360, 'The ass, though laden with gold, still eats thistles', refers in its examples before *JC* to avarice, not here relevant (Muir, 9–10).

22 See *Ham* 3.1.77 for almost the same phrase with an unexpected end.

23 point indicate; appoint

26–7 shake . . . commons The everyday picture clinches the dismissal. With work over, the ass Lepidus put out on common land is even rather lovable.

29–34 five lines for a simple simile of training a war-horse. The methodical detail suggests a more personal relationship than with the ass, with Antony firmly on top.

32 wind wheel about: rhymes with 'blind'

34 taste measure

36–9 one . . . fashion Lepidus does not live in the real world, but fills his head with curiosities, artificial things and imitations, which he makes his own only when they have been worn out by everyone else and are long out of fashion. The only difficulty in the lines is the sudden compression of thought after the longer-paced similes of the ass and the horse. Eighteenth-century

On objects, arts and imitations
Which, out of use and staled by other men,
Begin his fashion. Do not talk of him
But as a property. And now, Octavius,   40
Listen great things. Brutus and Cassius
Are levying powers. We must straight make head.
Therefore let our alliance be combined,
Our best friends made, our means stretched,
And let us presently go sit in counsel,   45
How covert matters may be best disclosed,
And open perils surest answered.

OCTAVIUS

Let us do so: for we are at the stake
And bayed about with many enemies,

editors emended wildly, even following Theobald in making in 37 a
ridiculous Spoonerism, 'abject orts',
supposed to mean 'rejected scraps'.
Lepidus is even feebler in *AC* 2.7,
written seven years later.

40 **property** in a sense dating only from
1598, simply a means to an end, appur-
tenance, but still with the older theatrical sense of a stage accessory (*OED
sb.* 4, 3). All the meanings as Antony
uses the word express contempt. Cf.
TN 4.2.87; *KJ* 5.2.70.

41 **Listen** hear, attend to: see Abbott,
199.

42 **powers** Plutarch records the joy with
which Brutus and Cassius viewed their
'great armies' (*Brutus*, 109).
straight make head immediately
raise a force

44 *Our best friends made* means securing
other allies; *our means stretched* is
extending their joint resources.
Antony is expressing the extremity in
which they find themselves. The
defective metre of the line has caused

emendation (beginning with F2) and
discussion. The simplest solution is
to think that the end of the line
was dropped – it might have been
'*stretched* to the full' or something
similar.

45 **presently** at once

46 **covert . . . disclosed** hidden things
brought to light

47 **answered** answerèd; managed, or
responded to

48–9 **stake . . . about** In bear-baiting, at
the time an entertainment in wooden
structures similar to the theatres, the
bear was tied to a stake and the dogs
attacked freely, as they *bayed* the bear
about: *bayed* means 'barked with a deep
voice', and 'driven to bay', i.e. driven
to defend itself at close quarters
(*OED* bay *v.*[1] 5, 6; *sb.*[4] 3). Cf. *Mac*
5.7.1–2, shortly before Macbeth's
death, 'They have tied me to a stake; I
cannot fly / But bear-like I must fight
the course.' The image implies immediate danger.

38 staled] (stal'de) 44 our means stretched] our best meanes stretcht out *F2;* our best means
stretcht *Johnson;* our best means stretch'd *Capell;* our meinies stretched *Oxf* 45 counsel]
(Councell)

And some that smile have in their hearts, I fear,   50
Millions of mischiefs.   *Exeunt.*

[4.2]   *Drum. Enter* BRUTUS, LUCILIUS *and the army.*
         TITINIUS *and* PINDARUS *meet them.*

BRUTUS
    Stand ho.
LUCILIUS
    Give the word, ho, and stand.
BRUTUS
    What now, Lucilius, is Cassius near?
LUCILIUS
    He is at hand, and Pindarus is come
    To do you salutation from his master.   5
BRUTUS
    He greets me well. Your master, Pindarus,
    In his own change, or by ill officers,
    Hath given me some worthy cause to wish
    Things done, undone: but if he be at hand

---

50 **smile** 'That one may smile and smile
and be a villain' is Hamlet's discovery
(*Ham* 1.5.108; and see above, 2.1.82
and n.); but it was proverbial (Dent,
F16). In Chaucer's *Knight's Tale*
the temple of Mars contains 'The
smylere with the knyf under the
cloke' (l. 1999). The young and reticent Octavius has a sharper political
sense than the older and voluble
Antony.

51 **mischiefs** injuries to inflict

4.2 location: 'Camp near Sardis. Before
Brutus' tent' (Rowe)

0.1–2 LUCILIUS ... TITINIUS ...
PINDARUS See List of Roles 22n., 23n.,
32n. In the rapid 'placing' on stage,
Brutus addresses Lucilius several times
by name, and Pindarus, but ignores the
important Titinius. Perhaps Titinius'

entry should be at 30 below.

2 **Give the word** pass on the command
3 **is Cassius near?** Plutarch tells how
Brutus asked Cassius to come to
Sardis, and went out to meet him
(Appendix, p. 348).

6 **He ... well.** He sends me greetings by
a good man. 'Brutus is always courteous to ... subordinates' (Kittredge).

7 either changing on his own, or
influenced by bad subordinates.
Warburton's usually-adopted emendation to 'charge', seems unnecessary:
change is supported by the *hot friend,
cooling* of 19 below.

8 **worthy** substantial

9 **Things done, undone** Cf. Plutarch:
'Nowe, as it commonly hapneth ...
there ranne tales and complaints
betwixt them' (Appendix, p. 349).

4.2] *Rowe*   7 change] charge *Warburton*

I shall be satisfied.

PINDARUS   I do not doubt   10
But that my noble master will appear
Such as he is, full of regard and honour.

BRUTUS
He is not doubted. A word, Lucilius,
How he received you: let me be resolved.

LUCILIUS
With courtesy and with respect enough,   15
But not with such familiar instances
Nor with such free and friendly conference
As he hath used of old.

BRUTUS   Thou hast described
A hot friend, cooling. Ever note, Lucilius,
When love begins to sicken and decay   20
It useth an enforced ceremony.
There are no tricks in plain and simple faith:
But hollow men, like horses hot at hand,
Make gallant show and promise of their mettle:

                                        Low march within.

But when they should endure the bloody spur,   25
They fall their crests, and like deceitful jades

---

10 **shall** must
   be satisfied receive satisfaction, i.e.
   full explanation; cf. 3.2.1 and n.
12 **regard** respect
13 **A word** 'Aside', which eighteenth-
   century editors add, does not appear as
   an SD in printed plays until long after
   F. In any case, Brutus is turning to
   Lucilius from Pindarus, and the
   phrase is natural.
14 **resolved** put out of doubt
16 **familiar instances** marks of intimacy
17 **conference** conversation
20–1 Cf. *Tim* 1.2.15–18: 'ceremony was
   but devis'd at first / To set a gloss on
   faint deeds ... / But where there is
   true friendship, there needs none'.

23 **hollow** insincere, false; with an obvious
   element of lacking substance. Apparently the source of T.S. Eliot's title
   for his poem of 1925 (Williamson, 154)
   hot at hand lively at the start (*OED*
   hand *sb.* 25c). Cf. Tilley, H732, 'Soon
   hot, soon cold.'
24.1 *Low march within.* 'drums faintly
   heard from the tiring house to denote
   the approaching army' (Cam[1])
25 **endure** show their ability to endure
26 **crests** The crest is the ridge of a
   horse's neck. *VA* 272 and 297 show a
   high crest as a mark of distinction.
   jades horses ill-conditioned, worn
   out, ill-tempered or of inferior breed:
   the word is contemptuous

26 crests] Crest *F2*

Sink in the trial. Comes his army on?

LUCILIUS

They mean this night in Sardis to be quartered.
The greater part, the horse in general,
Are come with Cassius.

Enter CASSIUS *and his powers.*

BRUTUS   Hark, he is arrived.   30
March gently on to meet him.

CASSIUS

Stand ho.

BRUTUS

Stand ho. Speak the word along.

1 SOLDIER

Stand.

2 SOLDIER

Stand.   35

3 SOLDIER

Stand.

CASSIUS

Most noble brother, you have done me wrong.

BRUTUS

Judge me, you gods; wrong I mine enemies?
And if not so, how should I wrong a brother?

---

27 **Sink . . . trial** fail when put to the test
28 **Sardis** See 4.3.3n.
29 **horse in general** main body of cavalry
30 SD 'Quite a stirring spectacle: massed troops with ensigns flying, sharp words of command passing down the line, and two generals between whom trouble is brewing' (Cam¹). Theatre managements at the end of the twentieth century have difficulty paying 'massed troops': but the remark is stimulating. For *powers*, cf. *Ham* 4.4.9.

31 **gently** with dignity, in response to the *Low march* (24.1)
34–6 *1 . . . 2 . . . 3 . . . F has a simply repeated '*Stand.*', passing the word along the line. One speaker could be Lucilius.
37 Cassius sets the feeling high from the start. Plutarch writes that they avoided quarrelling before their troops, but 'went into a litle chamber together' (Appendix, p. 349).
39 **should** could I imaginably

34–6 SPs] *Cam²; not in F*

CASSIUS

Brutus, this sober form of yours hides wrongs,   40

And when you do them –

BRUTUS   Cassius, be content.

Speak your griefs softly. I do know you well.

Before the eyes of both our armies here,

Which should perceive nothing but love from us,

Let us not wrangle. Bid them move away: 45

Then in my tent, Cassius, enlarge your griefs

And I will give you audience.

CASSIUS   Pindarus,

Bid our commanders lead their charges off

A little from this ground.

BRUTUS

Lucilius, do you the like, and let no man   50

Come to our tent till we have done our conference.

Let Lucius and Titinius guard our door.

Exeunt all but Brutus and Cassius.

[4.3]

CASSIUS

That you have wronged me doth appear in this:

40 **sober form** grave demeanour: exasperating to the excited Cassius

41 **content** calm, quiet (*OED a.* 1b: all three citations are from Shakespeare, including this line)

42 'i.e. we are old friends and needn't shout at each other' (Cam[1]).

46 **enlarge** give free expression to
griefs grievances

47 **I . . . audience** a promise to listen, but to Cassius surely offensively formal

48 **charges** troops

50 **Lucilius** following F, which also has '*Lucius*' at 52. Editors since White, following Craik, have transposed these

two names here: but F can easily stand. Lucilius has the authority to be in command: he appears again for Brutus in battle (5.4.7–25). Lucius, as his servant, would naturally guard Brutus.

50–1 **let . . . conference** The instruction has overtones of assignation, and keeps the feeling strong: something personal and compelling is about to take place between the two of them alone.

4.3. location: 'Camp near Sardis. Brutus's tent' (Theobald). The new scene was first numbered here by

50–2 Lucilius . . . Lucius] Lucius . . . Lucilius *(White, Craik)*   52 SD *Exeunt all but*] *Manet* F
4.3] *Pope*

You have condemned and noted Lucius Pella
For taking bribes here of the Sardians;
Wherein my letters, praying on his side
Because I knew the man, was slighted off.   5

BRUTUS
You wronged yourself to write in such a case.

CASSIUS
In such a time as this it is not meet
That every nice offence should bear his comment.

BRUTUS
Let me tell you, Cassius, you yourself
Are much condemned to have an itching palm,   10
To sell and mart your offices for gold
To undeservers.

CASSIUS   I, an itching palm?

Pope, on the grounds that Brutus and Cassius now go to a different place, i.e. inside the tent. The change is unnecessary, effected simply by the exit of soldiers. Here '4.3' has become standard, and to number lines through from the previous scene could lead to confusion.

   This Quarrel scene, to Johnson 'universally celebrated', to Coleridge (1.16) showing Shakespeare's 'genius . . . superhuman', is made of two distinct quarrels in Plutarch (Appendix, pp. 349 and 350). It reveals Caesar's spirit at work. It enlarges and deepens our understanding of Brutus and Cassius, which is artistically satisfying in the development of the drama. Their reconciliation brings them anew to our sympathy.

2 **condemned and noted** North's phrase from Plutarch (Appendix, p. 350); *noted*, means branded with disgrace.
Lucius Pella 'a defamed person'

directly from Plutarch (Appendix, p. 350)

3 **Sardians** inhabitants of Sardis, ancient capital of Lydia in Asia Minor (*OED sb.* 1 dates first 1598); their king was Croesus.

5 **was** See Abbott, 333, for the very frequent plural subjects with singular verbs.
slighted off disregarded; dismissed

8 Cf. Plutarch (Appendix, p. 350): not 'to take thinges at the worst'.
nice unimportant, trivial (*OED a.* 10b, citing only *RJ* 5.2.18 and here)
bear his comment be subject to criticism

10 **condemned to have** blamed for having
itching palm 'streak of covetousness' (Sanders). Plutarch contrasts Cassius' extreme covetousness and cruelty to the Rhodians with Brutus' clemency to the Lycians (*Brutus*, 113).

11 **mart** market, traffic in
offices positions of trust

4–5 letters, . . . man,] *Malone;* Letters, . . . man *F;* Letter, . . . man *F2*

You know that you are Brutus that speaks this,
Or, by the gods, this speech were else your last.
BRUTUS

The name of Cassius honours this corruption,   15
And chastisement doth therefore hide his head.
CASSIUS

Chastisement?
BRUTUS

Remember March, the Ides of March remember:
Did not great Julius bleed for justice' sake?
What villain touched his body, that did stab   20
And not for justice? What, shall one of us,
That struck the foremost man of all this world
But for supporting robbers: shall we now
Contaminate our fingers with base bribes,
And sell the mighty space of our large honours   25
For so much trash as may be grasped thus?
I had rather be a dog and bay the moon
Than such a Roman.
CASSIUS   Brutus, bait not me.

13–16 The use of the names is significantly different. Cassius says that
Brutus speaks in the certainty of his
untouchability as a patrician with the
highest reputation, and as a friend of
Cassius. Brutus says that because corruption is associated with the name of
Cassius, it has a spurious respecta-
bility, making punishment of anybody
impossible.

20–1 **What . . . justice?** 'Which of us was
so villainous as to stab for any other
cause but justice?' (Oxf[1])

23 **But . . . robbers** Plutarch (Appendix,
p. 350): 'Brutus . . . aunswered . . .
they slue Julius Caesar . . . a favorer
and suborner of all them that did robbe
and spoyle, by his countenaunce and
authoritie.' This is the first we hear of
this charge, and it is quite contrary to

2.1.18–21, where Brutus, first brood-
ing on the need for Caesar to die,
specifically says he has not known of
any corrupt behaviour in him. Even
the ideals the conspirators once had are
now becoming tainted.

25 **mighty . . . honours** the high offices
we hold. Brutus' rising grandilo-
quence (67–9) is perhaps to conceal his
weak position (69–71).

26 **trash** See 1.3.108n.; only recently
(*OED* gives 1592) used for money; cf.
Oth 3.3.161.
   grasped graspèd
   thus probably accompanied by a
   scornful gesture of grasping

27 **dog . . . moon** proverbial for something useless (Dent, D449)

28 **bait** unnecessarily emended to 'bay'
by Theobald and succeeding editors:

27–8 bay . . . bait] baite . . . baite *F2;* bay . . . bay *Theobald*

I'll not endure it. You forget yourself
To hedge me in. I am a soldier, I,   30
Older in practice, abler than yourself
To make conditions.

BRUTUS

Go to, you are not, Cassius.

CASSIUS   I am.

BRUTUS

I say you are not.

CASSIUS

Urge me no more. I shall forget myself.   35
Have mind upon your health. Tempt me no farther.

BRUTUS

Away, slight man!

CASSIUS

Is't possible?

BRUTUS   Hear me, for I will speak.

Must I give way and room to your rash choler?
Shall I be frighted when a madman stares?   40

CASSIUS

O ye gods, ye gods, must I endure all this?

F is clear. Cassius is picking up the reference to *dog* (27) to think of dogs set on to harass a bear (*OED* bait *v.*[1] 2, citing *2H6* 5.1.148; and see above, 4.1.48–9 and n.) and at the same time of Brutus angling to trap him into losing control by means of *bait*.

29 **endure** put up with

30 **hedge me in** limit my freedom

31 **Older in practice** Plutarch records Cassius as older and better experienced (Appendix, p. 355): but *practice* has unhappy senses (this is the earliest recorded) of scheming trickery, machination, even conspiracy (*OED* 6a). Cf. 87.

32 **make conditions** arrange matters; but again *conditions* suggests qualifications (*OED* condition *sb.* 5)

33 Brutus responds to the slights of *Older* and *abler*, and lets the negatives of *practice* and *conditions* pass him by. Both men are, after all, equal conspirators.

35 **Urge** provoke

36 **health** welfare
   Tempt Rather than simply provoke, it is here test, put to trial (as in Matthew, 6.13, 'Lead us not into temptation', Tyndale, *NT*).

37 **slight** of no importance

38 **will speak** won't be prevented from speaking

39 **room** and 'Rome'
   rash choler impetuous anger. Plutarch records Cassius as 'hot, chollerick, and cruell' (Appendix, p. 348).

BRUTUS

All this? Ay, more: fret till your proud heart break.
Go show your slaves how choleric you are,
And make your bondmen tremble. Must I budge?
Must I observe you? Must I stand and crouch   45
Under your testy humour? By the gods,
You shall digest the venom of your spleen
Though it do split you; for, from this day forth,
I'll use you for my mirth, yea for my laughter,
When you are waspish.

CASSIUS   Is it come to this?   50

BRUTUS

You say you are a better soldier:
Let it appear so. Make your vaunting true
And it shall please me well. For mine own part,
I shall be glad to learn of noble men.

CASSIUS

You wrong me every way: you wrong me, Brutus.   55
I said an elder soldier, not a better.
Did I say better?

BRUTUS   If you did, I care not.

---

42 **Fret ... break.** The sense of these
six words enlarges as Brutus says
them. *Fret*, i.e. chafe and be vexed, is
more trivial: *your proud heart break*
puts the feeling on a different scale
altogether: a heart breaks from something larger than fretting, even more
a *proud heart*. There is perhaps a
deeper image of a musical instrument,
with frets so abused that the
heart[strings] break. Brutus is a
scholastic rhetorician: Antony does
not speak like this.

44 **budge** probably flinch, conjectured
in *OED* (*v.*[1] 1b), citing this first: it
could simply be move from one's
place (*OED v.*[1] 1, and *MV* 2.2.20–1).
Brutus' other verbs, *observe*, *stand*,

crouch (45), suggest larger movement than flinching: he could be
saying that he doesn't need to shift
his ground just because Cassius is
hot-tempered.

45 **observe** watch closely, with the additional sense of pay court to

46 **testy humour** irritable nature

47 **shall** must

47–8 **digest ... you** swallow your own
poisonous sudden ill-temper though it
burst you asunder

49–50 **I'll ... waspish** 'The coldness
and superiority of this reveal the
worst side of Brut.'s character' (Cam[1]).
Cf. 1.2.72

54 **learn of** learn about or learn from:
both are wounding.

55] *Rowe; F lines* way: / *Brutus:* /

CASSIUS

When Caesar lived he durst not thus have moved me.

BRUTUS

Peace, peace, you durst not so have tempted him.

CASSIUS

I durst not?   60

BRUTUS

No.

CASSIUS

What, durst not tempt him?

BRUTUS   For your life you durst not.

CASSIUS

Do not presume too much upon my love:

I may do that I shall be sorry for.

BRUTUS

You have done that you should be sorry for.   65

There is no terror, Cassius, in your threats:

For I am armed so strong in honesty

That they pass by me as the idle wind,

Which I respect not. I did send to you

For certain sums of gold, which you denied me,   70

For I can raise no money by vile means:

By heaven, I had rather coin my heart

And drop my blood for drachmas, than to wring

From the hard hands of peasants their vile trash

---

59 **durst not** would not have dared

67 **I ... honesty** a Hamlet-like understanding of his position, without Hamlet's complexity of nature and situation. Indeed, 'Brutus' priggish claim to self-sufficiency here is reminiscent of Caesar in 2.2 and 3.1' (RP).

68 **idle** inconsequential, careless, unregarding; worthless (*OED a.* 2); see 1.1.1n. and 2.1.116n.

69–75 **I ... indirection.** His self-praised *honesty* (67) becomes valueless, as he reveals his inability to stoop to extor-

tion, while berating Cassius for not handing over to him the fruits of Cassius' own extortion. Thus Brutus deceives himself into wanting a clean conscience and the dirty money.

69 **respect** consider

72 **coin** turn into money

73 **drop** let fall in drops

73–4 **wring ... trash** Plutarch records that Cassius raised money 'with great evil will of the people' (Appendix, p. 348).

282

By any indirection. I did send   75
To you for gold to pay my legions,
Which you denied me: was that done like Cassius?
Should I have answered Caius Cassius so?
When Marcus Brutus grows so covetous,
To lock such rascal counters from his friends,   80
Be ready gods with all your thunderbolts,
Dash him to pieces!
CASSIUS   I denied you not.
BRUTUS
    You did.
CASSIUS   I did not. He was but a fool
    That brought my answer back. Brutus hath rived my
        heart.
    A friend should bear his friend's infirmities,   85
    But Brutus makes mine greater than they are.
BRUTUS
    I do not, till you practise them on me.
CASSIUS
    You love me not.
BRUTUS   I do not like your faults.
CASSIUS
    A friendly eye could never see such faults.
BRUTUS
    A flatterer's would not, though they do appear   90
    As huge as high Olympus.
CASSIUS
    Come, Antony, and young Octavius, come,

---

75 **indirection** crooked means; but ironically accurate for Brutus' own reception of the money from the *peasants*
80 **rascal** mean, wretched (*OED sb.* and
  a. 2, a recent use)
  counters paltry amounts; small change
82 **Dash** break, with violence; 'dash in
  pieces' is a biblical phrase, e.g. Hosea,
  10.14 (Geneva 1560).

I . . . not. In Plutarch (Appendix,
p. 348), Cassius 'gave him the thirde
parte of his totall summe'.
84 **rived** broken; violently split
87 **practise them** make them operate
90–1 'Reminiscences of earlier scenes begin
  to accumulate; 2.1.207–9; 3.1.74.' (RP).
92–106 **Come . . . Cassius.** Mistakes
  in the handling of the military

283

Revenge yourselves alone on Cassius,
For Cassius is a-weary of the world:
Hated by one he loves, braved by his brother,   95
Checked like a bondman; all his faults observed,
Set in a notebook, learned and conned by rote
To cast into my teeth. O I could weep
My spirit from mine eyes! There is my dagger,
And here my naked breast: within, a heart   100
Dearer than Pluto's mine, richer than gold.
If that thou beest a Roman, take it forth.
I that denied thee gold will give my heart.
Strike as thou didst at Caesar: for I know,
When thou didst hate him worst, thou lov'dst him
        better   105
Than ever thou lov'dst Cassius.
BRUTUS   Sheathe your dagger:
Be angry when you will, it shall have scope:
Do what you will, dishonour shall be humour.

---

organization are ignored by Cassius as he directs all attention to his own emotional state, which, for all its exaggeration, is no more than self-pity. So, with higher art, will Cleopatra try to prevent Antony from going to Rome for a while in *AC* 1.3.

95 **braved** defied

96 **Checked** rebuked

97 **conned by rote** studied (or learned by heart) by mechanical repetition

99 **spirit** vital spirits (*OED sb.* 16); and probably essence (*OED sb.* 21), though first recorded 1610

101 **Pluto** the god of the nether world, and thus of gold and silver mines: even in classical times, often overlapping with Plutus, god of riches, who, in *AW* 5.3.101, as an alchemist, is able to turn base metal into gold. See Introduction, pp. 125–6, for the tendency of the copy for *JC* to use 'o' endings for 'u', which might make the original Plutus here.

Yet Cassius is at the height of rhetorical gesturing, and the chime of 'o' and 'i' sounds in 'Pluto's mine, richer than gold' might have appeal.

103 **denied ... heart** I, that am accused of denying gold, will in reality give my heart.

106 **Than ... Cassius** His climax is the all-too-human cry 'you never loved me', with its implication 'if you did, you would never speak to me like that'. And, of course, 'you really loved someone else more': which is also Cleopatra's complaint in *AC* 1.3.

107 **it ... scope** Your anger shall have free play.

108 **dishonour ... humour** I shall take your insults as no more than your capricious whim. Also possibly a sense of Brutus agreeing not to demur even at dishonourable conduct.

O Cassius, you are yoked with a lamb
That carries anger as the flint bears fire,   110
Who, much enforced, shows a hasty spark
And straight is cold again.

CASSIUS   Hath Cassius lived
To be but mirth and laughter to his Brutus,
When grief and blood ill-tempered vexeth him?

BRUTUS
When I spoke that, I was ill-tempered too.   115

CASSIUS
Do you confess so much? Give me your hand.

BRUTUS
And my heart too.

CASSIUS   O Brutus!

BRUTUS   What's the matter?

CASSIUS
Have you not love enough to bear with me,
When that rash humour which my mother gave me
Makes me forgetful?

BRUTUS   Yes, Cassius, and from henceforth   120

---

109 **yoked** yokèd
  lamb a sudden surreal image of
  impossible matching (yoking implies
  an ox, here with a lamb): Brutus is out
  of his element – surely honourably
110 **carries** conveys
  anger The subject is not military
  achievement, but high emotions: the
  argument is now entirely on Cassius'
  terms.
  flint proverbial (Dent, F371: 'In the
  coldest flint there is hot fire'). The
  point is the reverse: Brutus' inability to
  maintain emotion at Cassius' level, an
  impossibility as striking as an intermit-
  tently angry lamb.
111 **enforced** enforcèd
112 **straight** immediately
112–14 **Hath . . . him?** Do I only matter
  to my Brutus when my fits of crying

and bad temper (which I cannot help)
amuse him in bad moments? Cassius is
becoming possessive: Brutus is not
allowed to be his own man. He is still
upset by Brutus' *mirth* and *laughter*
more than sixty lines ago (49).
114 **ill-tempered** having the 'humours'
  or elements badly 'tempered' or mixed
  (*OED* ill-tempered *a*., citing this
  first). See McAlindon, *Tragic*, 79.
117 **What's the matter?** a question
  which does Brutus honour – he is completely outside Cassius' emotional
  world; also a sense of 'what is the subject, the matter in hand?'
119 **rash humour** sudden, hasty nature
  my . . . me not in Plutarch; a
  Shakespearean underlining of Cassius'
  solipsistic 'bear with me, I cannot help
  it'

285

When you are over-earnest with your Brutus,
He'll think your mother chides, and leave you so.

Enter a Poet, [LUCILIUS *and* TITINIUS].

POET

Let me go in to see the generals.
There is some grudge between 'em; 'tis not meet
They be alone.

LUCILIUS　　　　　　You shall not come to them.　　　　　125

POET

Nothing but death shall stay me.

CASSIUS

How now? What's the matter?

POET

For shame, you generals, what do you mean?
Love and be friends, as two such men should be,
For I have seen more years, I'm sure, than ye.　　　　130

---

121 **over-earnest** Brutus' euphemism for Cassius' 'impossible' outbursts
122 **think ... chides** Brutus plays along with the 'it was your mother's fault' idea with cool detachment
leave you so leave it at that
122.1 *Enter a* Poet in Plutarch (Appendix, p. 349) a Cynic philosopher, Marcus Phaonius (properly Favonius), once a friend of Cato
124 **meet** proper, fit
126 **stay** hinder, restrain
129–30 He is quoting Homer, *Iliad*, 1.259, as Plutarch explains (Appendix, p. 349): 'the verses which old Nestor sayd ... / My lords, I pray you harken both to mee, / For I have seene moe yeares than suchye three. Cassius fel a laughing at him: but Brutus thrust him out of the chamber, and called him dogge, and counterfeate Cynick.' Early in Book 1 of the *Iliad*, the quarrel between Agamemnon and Achilles is a dispute almost disastrous to the Greeks.

Achilles, sulking in selfish anger, for a long time refuses to fight. Old and respected Nestor tries, and fails, to get the disputants to see their folly, saying 'Listen to me. You are both my juniors.' Nestor is described by Homer as 'that master of the courteous word ... the clear-voiced orator ... whose speech ran sweeter than honey off his tongue' (Rieu, 29–30). Shakespeare picks up Plutarch's unspoken point, that such a quarrel between Brutus and Cassius will bring long-range disaster, possibly also seeing Cassius as the self-regarding Achilles: and then makes it dramatically un-solemn, with the breaking-in not of a philosopher but a *Poet* speaking an absurd couplet instead of Nestor's honey. The lightening of the tone is welcome – the incident should get laughs in performance – especially in preparation for the news of Portia's death. Yet the force of the warning is not lost dramatically.

122.1 LUCILIUS *and* TITINIUS] *Rowe*

CASSIUS

Ha, ha, how vildly doth this cynic rhyme.

BRUTUS

Get you hence, sirrah; saucy fellow, hence.

CASSIUS

Bear with him, Brutus, 'tis his fashion.

BRUTUS

I'll know his humour when he knows his time.
What should the wars do with these jigging fools?   135
Companion, hence.

CASSIUS   Away, away, be gone.   *Exit Poet.*

BRUTUS

Lucilius and Titinius, bid the commanders
Prepare to lodge their companies tonight.

CASSIUS

And come yourselves, and bring Messala with you
Immediately to us.   [*Exeunt Lucilius and Titinius.*]

BRUTUS [*Calls.*]   Lucius! A bowl of wine.   140

CASSIUS

I did not think you could have been so angry.

---

131 **vildly** a once-fashionable variant of 'vilely', like 'vild' common 1590–1650: Cassius is being up-to-date.
cynic Plutarch says that Marcus Phaonius is a 'counterfeate ... Philosopher (Appendix, p. 349). Cynics were extreme in contempt of enjoyment, and Cassius' word *cynic* is itself contemptuous. The word was recent in Cassius' sense in English (1596, *OED sb.* 2). *Cynic* is Greek for 'dog-like', hence Plutarch's Brutus 'called him dogge' (Appendix, p. 349).

132 **sirrah** contemptuous form of 'sir'
saucy fellow stronger than in modern usage

134 I'll put up with his self-indulgent eccentricities when he knows the right

time for them. Brutus spills on to the Poet some of his feeling about Cassius.

135 **jigging** contemptuous for empty, metrically-thumping verse, from the jerky, even vulgar, dance called a jig; cf. Marlowe, *I Tamburlaine*, Prologue, 1–6, similarly contrasting 'war' and 'jigging'.

136 **Companion** derisive, as one might say 'matey'

137 **commanders** like *wars* two lines above, one of the first mentions of impending large-scale conflict in the play. Shakespeare wrote *JC* in the middle of a sequence of plays where war is important.

138 **lodge** prepare billets for

140 SD1] *Rowe*   SD2] *this edn*

287

BRUTUS

    O Cassius, I am sick of many griefs.

CASSIUS

    Of your philosophy you make no use

    If you give place to accidental evils.

BRUTUS

    No man bears sorrow better. Portia is dead.   145

CASSIUS

    Ha? Portia?

BRUTUS

    She is dead.

CASSIUS

    How scaped I killing when I crossed you so?

    O insupportable and touching loss!

    Upon what sickness?

BRUTUS   Impatient of my absence,   150

    And grief that young Octavius with Mark Antony

    Have made themselves so strong – for with her death

    That tidings came – with this she fell distract,

    And, her attendants absent, swallowed fire.

CASSIUS

    And died so?

BRUTUS   Even so.

CASSIUS   O ye immortal gods!   155

143–4 You should be above evils brought by chance. Plutarch records of Brutus that 'he loved Platoes sect best' (*Brutus*, 90). Discussion of whether or not these trite lines refer specifically to Brutus being a Stoic (which he was not: see Introduction, p. 52n.) have obscured the sheer cheek of such a remark coming from Cassius.

145 **No ... dead** Brutus' dignity in the two statements puts steel into the long exchange with Cassius. 'The odd blend of stark grief and Stoic pride ... is the play's most dramatic demonstra-tion of constancy as repression of pain' (Miles, 144).

149 **touching** grievous

150 **Impatient** Contrast Portia's ability to 'bear ... with patience' (2.1.300) when Brutus is with her.

152 **her death** news of her death

154 **swallowed fire** For accounts of Portia's death, see Introduction, pp. 137–43. Just as Portia's was the first blood spilled in the play (2.1.298–300) so the horror contained in these two words prepares for the tragic violence to come.

Enter LUCIUS *with wine and tapers.*

BRUTUS

Speak no more of her: give me a bowl of wine.
In this I bury all unkindness, Cassius.   *Drinks.*

CASSIUS

My heart is thirsty for that noble pledge.
Fill, Lucius, till the wine o'er-swell the cup.   159
I cannot drink too much of Brutus' love.   [*Exit Lucius.*]

Enter TITINIUS *and* MESSALA.

BRUTUS

Come in, Titinius. Welcome, good Messala.
Now sit we close about this taper here
And call in question our necessities.

CASSIUS

Portia, art thou gone?

BRUTUS   No more, I pray you.

Messala, I have here received letters   165
That young Octavius and Mark Antony
Come down upon us with a mighty power,
Bending their expedition toward Philippi.

MESSALA

Myself have letters of the selfsame tenor.

BRUTUS

With what addition?   170

155.1 For F's *Boy* see Introduction, p. 137.
159–60 Cassius' apparent warmth does not conceal his continued self-absorption.
162 **taper** candle; see 2.1.7n.
163 **call in question** discuss
168 **expedition** force; speed
   toward Philippi Philippi is in Thrace, across the Dardanelles and 200 miles north-northwest from

Sardis in Asia Minor where Brutus and Cassius are. The dramatic point is that Octavius and Antony 'Come down upon us', and the story, as everyone knew, will end at Philippi. The phrase, like the Poet's quotation from Homer, points to the coming end. From now, the play is aimed at Philippi.

169 **tenor** purport

155.1 LUCIUS] *Capell; Boy F*   160 SD] *Globe*   161] *Rowe; F lines Titinius: / Messala: /*   169 tenor] *(Tenure)*

289

MESSALA

    That by proscription and bills of outlawry

    Octavius, Antony and Lepidus

    Have put to death an hundred senators.

BRUTUS

    Therein our letters do not well agree.

    Mine speak of seventy senators that died   175

    By their proscriptions, Cicero being one.

CASSIUS

    Cicero one?

MESSALA   Cicero is dead,

    And by that order of proscription.

    Had you your letters from your wife, my lord?

BRUTUS

    No, Messala.   180

MESSALA

    Nor nothing in your letters writ of her?

BRUTUS

    Nothing, Messala.

MESSALA   That methinks is strange.

BRUTUS

    Why ask you? Hear you aught of her in yours?

MESSALA

    No, my lord.

BRUTUS

    Now, as you are a Roman, tell me true.   185

MESSALA

    Then like a Roman bear the truth I tell,

    For certain she is dead, and by strange manner.

---

171 **proscription** See 4.1.17n.

173 **an hundred** Plutarch reports 200 (*Brutus*, 108, see Appendix, p. 347) or 300 (*Antonius*, 269).

182 **Nothing, Messala.** Brutus is one of Shakespeare's authoritative characters

who says things once only. In 156 he has said 'Speak no more of her.' There is no problem here. Brutus means what he says.

185 **tell me true** Messala must tell what he knows as *a Roman*, and that is that.

177–8 ²Cicero . . . proscription.] *one line F*   183] *Rowe; F lines* you? / yours? /

BRUTUS

  Why, farewell, Portia: we must die, Messala:

  With meditating that she must die once

  I have the patience to endure it now.   190

MESSALA

  Even so great men great losses should endure.

CASSIUS

  I have as much of this in art as you,

  But yet my nature could not bear it so.

BRUTUS

  Well, to our work alive. What do you think

  Of marching to Philippi presently?   195

CASSIUS

  I do not think it good.

BRUTUS   Your reason?

CASSIUS   This it is:

  'Tis better that the enemy seek us,

  So shall he waste his means, weary his soldiers,

  Doing himself offence, whilst we, lying still,

  Are full of rest, defence and nimbleness.   200

BRUTUS

  Good reasons must of force give place to better:

  The people 'twixt Philippi and this ground

  Do stand but in a forced affection,

  For they have grudged us contribution.

  The enemy, marching along by them,   205

  By them shall make a fuller number up,

  Come on refreshed, new-added and encouraged;

---

191 **Even so** indeed, yes; just like that

192–3 'I am as well trained as you in Stoical theory, but I couldn't bear to put it into practice like this'; but also, a meaning shared only between Cassius and Brutus, 'I thought *I* was a good hypocrite, but how can you bear to act in a moment like this?' (Miles, 145).

194 **alive** with the living; concerning us now

197–210 **'Tis . . . back**. Shakespeare follows Plutarch (Appendix, pp. 354–5) in the opposing strategies, Cassius being for restraint and Brutus for one decisive battle.

199 **offence** harm

201 **of force** necessarily

204 **contribution** supplies

207 **new-added** reinforced

From which advantage shall we cut him off
If at Philippi we do face him there,
These people at our back.

CASSIUS   Hear me, good brother.   210

BRUTUS

Under your pardon. You must note beside
That we have tried the utmost of our friends,
Our legions are brimful, our cause is ripe.
The enemy increaseth every day;
We, at the height, are ready to decline.   215
There is a tide in the affairs of men
Which, taken at the flood, leads on to fortune:
Omitted, all the voyage of their life
Is bound in shallows and in miseries.
On such a full sea are we now afloat,   220
And we must take the current when it serves,
Or lose our ventures.

CASSIUS   Then with your will go on.
We'll along ourselves, and meet them at Philippi.

---

211 Under ... pardon. Brutus' 'solemn obstinacy' (Kittredge) while overruling Cassius' interruption with heavy courtesy recalls 3.1.235, where Brutus, beginning *By your pardon*, insists that Antony be allowed to speak at Caesar's funeral. Both overrulings prove disastrous.

216–22 There is ... ventures. Such aphorisms about seizing the moment are widespread, as e.g. Chaucer, *Troilus and Cressida*, 2.281–7. Attempts to fix an Elizabethan school-book 'source', like Cato's *Distichs*, 2.26 (Kittredge), though of interest, are not necessary. Dent lists proverbs on taking the time and tide (T283, 312, 313, 323, 334). London's south-bank theatres were on a tidal river: crossing the Thames to reach the new Globe without a muddy walk from the boat would mean taking

the tide *at the flood* (Sohmer, who suggests that the first performance of *JC*, opening the Globe, was timed for an exceptional spring tide, which would give these lines additional force).

222 ventures specifically, in the context of the *tide*, merchant venturing, investment in cargoes; more generally, enterprises. The idea of 'good aventure' surrounds Pandarus' words to Criseide – see 216–22n.
Then ... on. F's lack of commas strengthens the sense of doing as Brutus wishes.
with your will as you wish
223 along a metrically clumsy word in the line, a monosyllable being needed: *them* could refer to the reluctant *people* on the way to Philippi (210), so a word of directed force like 'march' might apply: or even a simple 'on'.

222–3 Then ... Philippi.] Capell; F lines along / Philippi. /   222 Then ... will] Then, ... will, *Ard²*

BRUTUS
> The deep of night is crept upon our talk,
> And nature must obey necessity, 225
> Which we will niggard with a little rest.
> There is no more to say.

CASSIUS   No more. Good night.
> Early tomorrow will we rise, and hence.

Enter LUCIUS.

BRUTUS
> Lucius. My gown.   [*Exit Lucius.*]
>   Farewell, good Messala.
> Good night, Titinius. Noble, noble Cassius, 230
> Good night, and good repose.

CASSIUS   O my dear brother,
> This was an ill beginning of the night.
> Never come such division 'tween our souls.
> Let it not, Brutus.

Enter LUCIUS *with the gown.*

BRUTUS   Everything is well.

CASSIUS
> Good night, my lord.

BRUTUS   Good night, good brother. 235

TITINIUS, MESSALA
> Good night, Lord Brutus.

BRUTUS   Farewell, every one.
>   *Exeunt* [*Cassius, Titinius and Messala*].

---

226 **niggard . . . rest** fob off with only a short sleep

228.1 following F: a good servant, Lucius is alert to people leaving. There is no need to move the SD until after Brutus has said his name.

229 short lines indicate a pause after 'gown'

231 **brother** brother-in-law, as at 2.1.70

229 SD *Q 1691*   236 SD *Cassius . . . Messala*] *Q 1691*

234 **Let it not** Cassius modifies his impersonal *Never come*, to make *division* Brutus' responsibility.

235 **my lord** unexpected, and on the surface respectful: but again placing the weight on Brutus

good brother Brutus quietly restores the balance

Give me the gown. Where is thy instrument?

LUCIUS

Here in the tent.

BRUTUS   What, thou speak'st drowsily?

Poor knave, I blame thee not; thou art o'erwatched.

Call Claudio and some other of my men.   240

I'll have them sleep on cushions in my tent.

LUCIUS

Varrus and Claudio!

Enter VARRUS *and* CLAUDIO.

VARRUS

Calls my lord?

BRUTUS

I pray you, sirs, lie in my tent and sleep.

It may be I shall raise you by and by   245

On business to my brother Cassius.

VARRUS

So please you, we will stand and watch your pleasure.

BRUTUS

I will not have it so: lie down, good sirs.

It may be I shall otherwise bethink me.

Look, Lucius, here's the book I sought for so: 250

---

237 **Give ... gown.** In the whole play, Brutus' scenes of relaxed night-time intimacy are not with his wife, but his young servant. Shakespeare, as so often in his tragedies, lowers the dramatic tension towards the end of Act 4, in order then to raise it at compelling speed to the play's climax. Theatrically, Brutus' unbuttoned appreciation of Lucius, of music and of his reading, is too relaxed: something is about to happen.

239 **knave** boy: not derogatory
   o'erwatched over-tired with staying up, on 'watch'

240–2 **Claudio ... Varrus** Shakespeare's inventions; see List of Roles 27–8n., and Introduction, p. 125.

245 **raise** rouse

247 **watch your pleasure** stay awake and alert for anything you want us to do

249 Brutus is saying that he may in the end not need to use them, so they may as well get some sleep.

250 **book** Plutarch stresses Brutus' wakeful, industrious habits, and at night 'if he had any leysure left him, he would read some booke till the third watche of the night' (Appendix, p. 350).

247] *Rowe; F lines* stand / pleasure. /   248 will] *F2;* will it *F*

I put it in the pocket of my gown.

LUCIUS

I was sure your lordship did not give it me.

BRUTUS

Bear with me, good boy, I am much forgetful.

Canst thou hold up thy heavy eyes awhile

And touch thy instrument a strain or two? 255

LUCIUS

Ay, my lord, an't please you.

BRUTUS It does, my boy.

I trouble thee too much, but thou art willing.

LUCIUS

It is my duty, sir.

BRUTUS

I should not urge thy duty past thy might.

I know young bloods look for a time of rest. 260

LUCIUS

I have slept, my lord, already.

BRUTUS

It was well done, and thou shalt sleep again.

I will not hold thee long. If I do live,

I will be good to thee. *Music, and a song.*

This is a sleepy tune: O murderous slumber! 265

Layest thou thy leaden mace upon my boy

---

251 **gown** See 2.2.0.2n.
254 **heavy** with sleep
255 **strain** tune
260 **look for** require
264 **SD** so F, though, since no words are given, probably a melody on a lute. The eighteenth-century tradition of putting here the two six-line stanzas of 'Orpheus with his lute' from *H8* 3.1.3–14 is superficially attractive: words and music to soothe an overworn high person (Brutus; the Queen) with a disturbing entry about to hap-

pen (the Ghost; Wolsey and Campeius). Here Lucius, however, is more likely to fall asleep in mid-strum than mid-warble.
265 **murderous slumber** 'Because it is "the death of each day's life" [*Mac* 2.2.38]' (Macmillan)
266 **leaden mace** The bailiff or his sergeant arrested offenders (cf. *Ham* 5.2.328–9, 'this fell sergeant Death / Is strict in his arrest') by touching them with his rod; *leaden* because of the weight of sleep.

265 murderous] (Murd'rous)

That plays thee music? Gentle knave, good night:
I will not do thee so much wrong to wake thee.
If thou dost nod, thou break'st thy instrument;
I'll take it from thee; and, good boy, good night.   270
Let me see, let me see: is not the leaf turned down
Where I left reading? Here it is, I think.

Enter the Ghost *of Caesar.*

How ill this taper burns. Ha! Who comes here?
I think it is the weakness of mine eyes
That shapes this monstrous apparition.   275
It comes upon me: art thou any thing?
Art thou some god, some angel, or some devil,
That mak'st my blood cold, and my hair to stare?
Speak to me what thou art.

GHOST

Thy evil spirit, Brutus.

BRUTUS   Why com'st thou?   280

268 Brutus, so often admired for his quiet thoughtfulness in not waking a sleeping boy, murdered his best friend Caesar – as Caesar within four lines reminds him.

271 **leaf turned down** A supposed 'fault' of Shakespeare's anachronisms (Brutus would read from a scroll, not a codex with leaves). Shakespeare needs the book to move attention closer in, from Lucius to something in Brutus' hand, for the full effect of the Ghost's entry.

272.1 As in *Ham* (1.1.39), the Ghost's first entry comes on the fringes of military action at a moment of relaxed un-watchfulness. Plutarch (Appendix, p. 332) wrote, 'the ghost that appeared unto Brutus shewed plainly, that the goddes were offended with the murther of Caesar': he does not say it was Caesar's ghost. Valerius Maximus' *Facta et dicta memorabilia* (1.8.8) tells that Caesar's figure 'of more than mortal stature' haunted Cassius before the battle of Philippi, and the tradition

grew that the murdered man's spirit was seeking revenge (see Introduction, pp. 78–9). At the end of the play (5.5.17) Brutus identifies it. The later academic play *Caesar's Revenge* (anon., 1607) makes the Ghost explain from the first that he is Caesar (Bullough, 5.199, 209).

273 **ill ... burns** Plutarch writes of 'the lampe that waxed very dimme' (Appendix, p. 332). 'It was a common superstition that lights burned dim, or blue, in the presence of a ghost or evil spirit' (Ard²), as in *R3* 5.3.180, 'The lights burn blue.'

275 **monstrous apparition** As Hamlet experiences (*Ham* 1.4.39–44 and *passim*), a likeness is not immediately clear – it may be a devil: *monstrous*, both abnormal and 'of a wonderfull greatnes, and dreedfull looke' (Plutarch, Appendix, p. 332).

278 **stare** stand on end

280 **Thy ... Brutus.** as in Plutarch (Appendix, p. 351)

GHOST

  To tell thee thou shalt see me at Philippi.

BRUTUS

  Well: then I shall see thee again?

GHOST

  Ay, at Philippi.

BRUTUS

  Why, I will see thee at Philippi then: *[Exit Ghost.]*
  Now I have taken heart thou vanishest.   285
  Ill spirit, I would hold more talk with thee.
  Boy, Lucius, Varrus, Claudio, sirs, awake!
  Claudio!

LUCIUS

  The strings, my lord, are false.

BRUTUS

  He thinks he still is at his instrument.   290
  Lucius, awake.

LUCIUS

  My lord?

BRUTUS

  Didst thou dream, Lucius, that thou so cried'st out?

LUCIUS

  My lord, I do not know that I did cry.

BRUTUS

  Yes, that thou didst. Didst thou see anything?   295

LUCIUS

  Nothing, my lord.

BRUTUS

  Sleep again, Lucius. Sirrah Claudio,

282–4 **shall . . . will** *Shall* is futurity; *will*
  is intention.
285 **taken . . . vanishest** Momentarily
  Brutus tries to persuade himself it was
  imagination.

286 **Ill spirit** as Plutarch, (Appendix,
  p. 332), 'I am thy ill angell, Brutus'.
  more talk as Hamlet wants, *Ham*
  1.4.44–57
289 **false** gone out of tune

284 SD] *Rowe*   297–8 Sleep . . . awake!] *one line F*

Fellow, thou, awake!

VARRUS   My lord?

CLAUDIO   My lord?

BRUTUS

Why did you so cry out, sirs, in your sleep?

BOTH

Did we, my lord?

BRUTUS   Ay. Saw you anything?   300

VARRUS

No, my lord, I saw nothing.

CLAUDIO   Nor I, my lord.

BRUTUS

Go and commend me to my brother Cassius.
Bid him set on his powers betimes before
And we will follow.

BOTH   It shall be done, my lord.   *Exeunt.*

5.1   *Enter* OCTAVIUS, ANTONY *and their army.*

OCTAVIUS

Now, Antony, our hopes are answered.
You said the enemy would not come down,
But keep the hills and upper regions.
It proves not so: their battles are at hand.
They mean to warn us at Philippi here,   5
Answering before we do demand of them.

ANTONY

Tut, I am in their bosoms and I know

---

303 **set ... before** advance his forces:
betimes, first thing, early in the
morning
5.1 location: 'The plains of Philippi' (Rowe)
1   **answered** answerèd
4   **battles** forces
5   **warn** challenge
    at Philippi here Shakespeare neces-
sarily telescopes locations and histori-

cal events far apart to focus on the climactic encounter, first signalled
at 4.3.168. Brutus and Cassius met at
Sardis early in 42 BC: the Battle of
Philippi was about nine months later.
6   responding to our challenge before we
have issued it
7   **in their bosoms** knowing their
secrets

5.1] *Actus Quintus.*

Wherefore they do it: they could be content
To visit other places, and come down
With fearful bravery, thinking by this face   10
To fasten in our thoughts that they have courage.
But 'tis not so.

Enter a Messenger.

MESSENGER   Prepare you, generals:
The enemy comes on in gallant show.
Their bloody sign of battle is hung out,
And something to be done immediately.   15

ANTONY
Octavius, lead your battle softly on,
Upon the left hand of the even field.

OCTAVIUS
Upon the right hand I. Keep thou the left.

ANTONY
Why do you cross me in this exigent?   19

OCTAVIUS
I do not cross you: but I will do so.   *March.*

8–12 **they . . . so** They would like to be in different positions, from which they could with frightening courage and show make surprise attacks, to convince us by such a show how courageous they are. But I know it is not like that.

10 **fearful** must mean causing, not feeling, fear
   bravery Brutus' army, according to Plutarch, had 'bravery [splendour] and rich furniture . . . silver and gilt . . . bravery of armor, and weapon' (Appendix, p. 352): but 'courage' must be in the word as well.
   face front

11 **fasten . . . thoughts** persuade us

14 **bloody . . . battle** In Plutarch (Appendix, p. 354) 'the signall of battell was set out . . . which was an arming scarlet coate'; i.e. a vest of rich material embroidered with heraldic devices.

16 **softly** slowly, warily, as in the modern 'Softlee, softlee, catchee monkey.'

17–18 **left hand . . . right hand** The 'right of the line' is the traditional position of honour. In Plutarch, the dispute is between Cassius and Brutus (Appendix, p. 355). Shakespeare wants to show rivalry between Antony and Octavius.

19, 20 **cross** contradict; oppose

19 **exigent** critical moment

20 I am not just being perverse. I will do what I say.

Drum. Enter BRUTUS, CASSIUS *and their army*
[: LUCILIUS, TITINIUS, MESSALA *and others*].

BRUTUS
They stand, and would have parley.
CASSIUS
Stand fast, Titinius. We must out and talk.
OCTAVIUS
Mark Antony, shall we give sign of battle?
ANTONY
No, Caesar, we will answer on their charge.
Make forth, the generals would have some words.   25
OCTAVIUS [*to a commander*]
Stir not until the signal.
BRUTUS
Words before blows: is it so, countrymen?
OCTAVIUS
Not that we love words better, as you do.
BRUTUS
Good words are better than bad strokes, Octavius.
ANTONY
In your bad strokes, Brutus, you give good words.   30
Witness the hole you made in Caesar's heart,
Crying, 'Long live! Hail, Caesar!'
CASSIUS   Antony,
The posture of your blows are yet unknown;
But, for your words, they rob the Hybla bees

20.1 *Drum* effective in creating atmosphere at the start of the battle scenes
24 **answer ... charge** counter whenever they attack
25 **Make forth** come forward; and see McAlindon, 'Numbering', 383.
27 **Words before blows** the primitive tradition of 'flyting', exchanging insults before battle, common in Elizabethan and earlier literature

33 **posture ... blows** how you will strike (*OED* posture *sb*. 2b, 3). *OED*'s first citation of 'posture' in a military sense (*sb*. 2b, 3) is 1625; the first record of the word in any sense at all is Bacon, 1605. A singluar noun, it commands a plural verb. Cassius is speaking the latest jargon (see Introduction, pp. 60–2).
34 **Hybla** in Sicily, famous for honey

20.2 LUCILIUS ... *others*] *not in* F

And leave them honeyless.

ANTONY   Not stingless too?   35

BRUTUS

O yes, and soundless too.
For you have stol'n their buzzing, Antony,
And very wisely threat before you sting.

ANTONY

Villains! You did not so, when your vile daggers
Hacked one another in the sides of Caesar.   40
You showed your teeth like apes, and fawned like
    hounds,
And bowed like bondsmen, kissing Caesar's feet;
Whilst damned Caska, like a cur, behind
Struck Caesar in the neck. O you flatterers!

CASSIUS

Flatterers? Now, Brutus, thank yourself.   45
This tongue had not offended so today
If Cassius might have ruled.

OCTAVIUS

Come, come, the cause. If arguing makes us sweat,
The proof of it will turn to redder drops:
Look, I draw a sword against conspirators.   50
When think you that the sword goes up again?
Never till Caesar's three and thirty wounds

---

35 **honeyless** *OED*'s first citation.
Cassius sneers at Antony's words in the
light of his declaration of friendship
immediately after the assassination.
stingless Antony retorts that he was
surely effective in his funeral oration.

36 **soundless** *OED*'s first citation

39–44 Antony's picture of Caesar hypocrit-
ically *Hacked* without warning and from
behind is coloured by debasing images of
animals and slaves in grotesque action.

41 **showed your teeth** grinned
fawned See 3.1.42–3n.

43 **damned** damnèd

46 **had not** would not have

47 **Cassius . . . ruled** that Antony should
be killed, at 2.1.154–6
ruled prevailed

48 **the cause** the real business

49 **proof** trial

51 **goes up** into the scabbard

52 **three and thirty** Plutarch has 'three
and twenty', with . . . '23 wounds' . . .
in the margin (Appendix, p. 329). The
reason for Shakespeare's change is not
known. Thirty-three is traditionally
the age of Christ at his death (Sohmer,
chaps. 11 and 14).

41] *Rowe; F lines* Apes, / Hounds, /   teeth] *F3;* teethes *F*

Be well avenged, or till another Caesar
Have added slaughter to the sword of traitors.

BRUTUS

Caesar, thou canst not die by traitors' hands   55
Unless thou bring'st them with thee.

OCTAVIUS   So I hope.
I was not born to die on Brutus' sword.

BRUTUS

O, if thou wert the noblest of thy strain,
Young man, thou couldst not die more honourable.

CASSIUS

A peevish schoolboy, worthless of such honour,   60
Joined with a masquer and a reveller.

ANTONY

Old Cassius still.

OCTAVIUS   Come, Antony, away.
Defiance, traitors, hurl we in your teeth.
If you dare fight today, come to the field;
If not, when you have stomachs.   65

Exeunt Octavius, Antony and army.

CASSIUS

Why now, blow wind, swell billow and swim bark.
The storm is up and all is on the hazard.

BRUTUS

Ho, Lucilius, hark, a word with you.

53–4 **or ... slaughter** until I too fall
   victim
58 **if** even if
   strain lineage
60 **peevish** silly, rather than irritable: cf.
   AYL 3.5.109, ''Tis but a peevish boy'.
62 **Old Cassius still.** Antony's three
   words are stronger than they look; in
   saying both 'ever the same scornful
   Cassius' and 'elderly Cassius' he is
   reducing the fiery revolutionary that
   Cassius likes to see himself as to an

older man set in his ways.
65 **stomachs** inclination; valour (*OED*
   stomach *sb.* 8a)
66–7 imagery which heightens the sense of
   approaching climax of the action; the
   heavens themselves register disturbance. Momentarily seen in *Ham*
   5.2.269, 'the heaven to earth'; extended
   through *KL*, from 3.2.1 on; visible in
   Mac 5.5.51–2, 'Blow wind, come wrack'.
66 **bark** sailing ship
67 **on the hazard** at stake

66] *Rowe; F lines* billow, / Barke: /

LUCILIUS
    My lord.   [*Brutus speaks apart to Lucilius.*]
CASSIUS
    Messala.
MESSALA   What says my general?
CASSIUS   Messala,   70
    This is my birthday: as this very day
    Was Cassius born. Give me thy hand, Messala:
    Be thou my witness that against my will
    (As Pompey was) am I compelled to set
    Upon one battle all our liberties.   75
    You know that I held Epicurus strong
    And his opinion: now I change my mind
    And partly credit things that do presage.
    Coming from Sardis, on our former ensign
    Two mighty eagles fell and there they perched,   80
    Gorging and feeding from our soldiers' hands,
    Who to Philippi here consorted us:
    This morning are they fled away and gone,
    And in their steads do ravens, crows and kites
    Fly o'er our heads and downward look on us   85

---

71 **birthday** Plutarch (Appendix, p. 354)
tells of Cassius' behaviour before the
battle.
as . . . day See Abbott, 114, for redundant 'as' in expressions of time; but
Cassius' whole phrase is redundant –
he has already said it is his birthday.
74 **(As Pompey was)** Shakespeare follows Plutarch closely in Cassius'
speech, even to this parenthesis
(Appendix, p. 354). Before Pharsalus,
Pompey wished to avoid battle, but his
inexperienced troops were impatient,
causing disaster. The reference is ominous for Cassius.
set stake; in Plutarch, 'jeopard'
(Appendix, p. 354)

75 **all our** of all of us
76 **Epicurus** 'The Epicureans did not
believe in omens, for they thought that
the gods were not interested in human
affairs' (Ard[2]). Plutarch, who mentions that Cassius was an Epicurean
(*Brutus*, 116), also notes him praying to
the gods for aid (*Brutus*, 119) and
attending to 'certain unlucky signs'
(Appendix, pp. 351–4).
79 **former ensign** foremost standard;
Plutarch (Appendix, p.352)
80 **fell** swooped
84 **ravens, crows and kites** birds of ill
omen before a battle, being scavengers
and eaters of carrion

69 SD] *Rowe*   70–1 [2]Messala . . . day] *Pope; one line F*

As we were sickly prey: their shadows seem
A canopy most fatal, under which
Our army lies, ready to give up the ghost.
MESSALA
Believe not so.
CASSIUS   I but believe it partly,
For I am fresh of spirit and resolved   90
To meet all perils very constantly.
BRUTUS [*Comes forward.*]
Even so, Lucilius.
CASSIUS   Now, most noble Brutus,
The gods today stand friendly, that we may,
Lovers in peace, lead on our days to age.
But since the affairs of men rest still incertain,   95
Let's reason with the worst that may befall.
If we do lose this battle, then is this
The very last time we shall speak together.
What are you then determined to do?
BRUTUS
Even by the rule of that philosophy   100

---

86 **As** as if
86–8 **their … ghost** a powerful image
which suddenly transforms the
shadows of the downward-looking
birds into something material and concrete, a *canopy*. For Shakespeare that
word has usually sinister associations,
of some rich formal covering (which can
include the firmament) contrasted with
doom; see especially *Cor* 4.5.38–42,
where it is 'I' th' city of kites and crows'.
(Cf. Grandpre in *H5* 4.2.38–55.) 'Like
Caesar, Cassius is "superstitious grown
of late" (2.1.194)' (Sohmer, chap. 17).
87 **fatal** presaging death
88 **give up the ghost** an Anglo-Saxon
phrase; see e.g. Mark, 15.37, in
Tyndale, *NT* and all subsequent sixteenth-century versions, and KJB.
92 SD *clarifies Brutus having finished

giving instructions to Lucilius
93 **stand** may they stand (subjunctive)
94 **Lovers** dear friends, as at 3.2.13
95 **rest** remain
still always
96 **reason … befall** not quite the
proverb that Dent (W912) makes it, 'It
is good to fear the worst.' Rather,
Cassius is saying that they should set
out actively to consider whatever *worst*
may happen.
99 **determined** determinèd
100 **that philosophy** not Stoicism, as
so often glossed, though the following lines, 103–7, recount the central
tenets of that. Brutus preferred
'Platoes sect' (Plutarch, *Brutus*, 90).
Brutus' death shows the soldier over-
coming the philosopher. See Maxwell;
MacCallum, 237, n. 1; Miles, 125–7.

92 SD] *this edn*   95 rest] *Rowe;* rests *F*

By which I did blame Cato for the death
Which he did give himself – I know not how,
But I do find it cowardly and vile,
For fear of what might fall, so to prevent
The time of life – arming myself with patience   105
To stay the providence of some high powers
That govern us below.

CASSIUS   Then, if we lose this battle,
You are contented to be led in triumph
Thorough the streets of Rome?

BRUTUS

No, Cassius, no: think not, thou noble Roman,   110
That ever Brutus will go bound to Rome.
He bears too great a mind. But this same day
Must end that work the Ides of March begun;

101 **Cato** Portia's father: see 2.1.294 and
n. Shakespeare gathers the threads of
reference as he approaches the climax
of the play. After Pompey's cause was
lost, Cato, an enemy of Caesar, took his
own life. His son, Portia's brother,
fights with Brutus and is killed in the
battle, proclaiming his father's name:
below, 5.4.2–6.1.

104 **fall** befall

104–5 **prevent / The time** anticipate the
natural end

105–7 **arming . . . below** In the elevated
thought there may be a faint echo of
Ephesians, 6, in Tyndale, *NT* and subsequent versions, and being 'strong in
the Lord' in fighting evil, where
'armour' enables to 'stand stedfast'
against 'power'. Brutus is perhaps
becoming a little more active against
the providence . . .

106 **stay** await; but also stand one's
ground, be steadfast (*OED vb.*[1] 7b);
and rely upon (*OED vb.*[2] 3b)
some in the sense of 'any there may
be'. In Plutarch, the difference
between the generals is sharper.
Cassius says 'The gods graunt us, O

Brutus, that this day we may win the
field' (Appendix, p. 354). Brutus
admits that he has previously condemned Cato's suicide 'touching the
gods . . . but being now in the middest
of the daunger, I am of a contrary
mind. For if it be not the will of
God . . .' (Appendix, p. 354).

108 **triumph** unlikely; triumphs were
strictly controlled, and only granted
for victory over external enemies.
Shakespeare, however, begins his *JC*
with the offence caused by Caesar's
irregular triumph over Pompey's sons
in a civil war.

110 **No, Cassius, no** Brutus' contradiction, implying suicide, necessitates a
distinction between killing oneself
when faced with assumed dangers
from a political enemy (as Cato did),
and not suffering captivity.

112–18 **But . . . made** following Plutarch
closely (Appendix, p. 354)

113 **Ides of March** Again Shakespeare is
gathering the threads; Plutarch has
Brutus saying that he gave up his life
for his country 'in the Ides of Marche'
(Appendix, p. 354).

110] *Rowe; F lines* no: / Romane, /

And whether we shall meet again, I know not: 115
Therefore our everlasting farewell take:
For ever and for ever farewell, Cassius.
If we do meet again, why, we shall smile;
If not, why then this parting was well made.

CASSIUS

For ever and for ever farewell, Brutus:
If we do meet again, we'll smile indeed;   120
If not, 'tis true this parting was well made.

BRUTUS

Why then, lead on. O that a man might know
The end of this day's business ere it come:
But it sufficeth that the day will end,   124
And then the end is known. Come ho, away.   *Exeunt.*

[5.2]   *Alarum. Enter* BRUTUS *and* MESSALA.

BRUTUS

Ride, ride, Messala, ride, and give these bills
Unto the legions on the other side.   *Loud alarum.*

---

115 **everlasting farewell** They do not
meet again.
120 **smile indeed** Plutarch reported that
'Cassius fell a laughing' (Appendix,
p. 354). Ian Richardson further noted
that a unique smile from Cassius at this
moment electrified an audience. Cf.
1.2.204n.
122–3 **that ... business** Even at the first
performance of *JC*, the audience at
the Globe would know the end:
Shakespeare is again playing with perspectives, as at 3.1.111–18.
5.2 location: 'The field of battle' (Capell).
(No scene-change in F, of course. It is
important to keep the flow of action
without break.)
0.1 *Alarum* originally a call to arms
(Italian *all'arme*), then with drum or
trumpet added; 'A technical term

for offstage noises during battle
sequences' (Craik, *H5* 3.0.33.1n.)
Enter BRUTUS Irwin Smith finds sixteen points in Shakespeare where
characters immediately re-enter, and
twenty-four more where only alarms
and excursions intervene.
1–2 **bills ... side** Plutarch (Appendix,
p. 355) tells of Brutus sending 'litle
billes', that is, dispatches, 'to the
Colonells and Captaines of private
bandes', but keeping the legions in
ignorance, leading to great disorder
and scattering.
2 **the other side** of the army. It was poor
communications over the field that led
to the defeat of Brutus' army.
2 SD *Loud alarum* technically, only used
for special effects, and unknown elsewhere in the middle of dialogue: but

5.2] *Capell*

Let them set on at once, for I perceive
But cold demeanour in Octavius' wing,
And sudden push gives them the overthrow.   5
Ride, ride, Messala. Let them all come down.   *Exeunt.*

[5.3]   *Alarums. Enter* CASSIUS *and* TITINIUS.

CASSIUS

O look, Titinius, look, the villains fly:
Myself have to mine own turned enemy:
This ensign here of mine was turning back;
I slew the coward and did take it from him.

TITINIUS

O Cassius, Brutus gave the word too early,   5
Who having some advantage on Octavius
Took it too eagerly: his soldiers fell to spoil,
Whilst we by Antony are all enclosed.

Shakespeare needs here a sudden dramatic development of urgency. Hinman (1.298–300) speculates F compositors misreading 'Low alarum' in Shakespeare's hand.

4   **cold** timorous
5   **overthrow** as indeed happened; but Brutus' troops impetuously squandered the victory.
6   **them** the legions to whom Brutus sends Messala
     come down attack by surprise, from the hills where they have waited (5.1.2–3)
5.3 location: 'Another part of the field' (Capell)
     Plutarch (Appendix, pp. 355–9) describes the battle at length, gives a good deal of detail. Shakespeare follows him closely, and it is instructive to watch the playwright selecting, emphasizing and adding. At the start of this scene Shakespeare shows that Cassius was

defeated because of Brutus' unclear battle signals, items in the wealth of Plutarch's detail that are a large page apart in North. Shakespeare ignores, among much else, Plutarch's vivid mention of the supposed killing of Octavius. He adds as his own invention Cassius killing his own fleeing standard-bearer.

1   **villains** his own men
3–4 Cassius points presumably to the body of a standard-bearer. *Ensign* or 'ancient' is a (fairly lowly) rank, as in *1H4* 4.2.24, 'ancients, corporals . . .', and 34, 'more dishonourable ragged than an old-fac'd ancient', and from *2H4* 2.4.65, Ancient Pistol. Cassius took the standard from the body – and presumably gave it to another soldier, as he cannot spend the rest of his life holding it; Plutarch says 'he stucke it fast at his feete' (Appendix, p. 357).

4 Octavius] *Pope; Octauio's F*   5.3] *Capell*

Enter PINDARUS.

PINDARUS

    Fly further off, my lord, fly further off,

    Mark Antony is in your tents, my lord: 10

    Fly, therefore, noble Cassius, fly far off.

CASSIUS

    This hill is far enough. Look, look, Titinius,

    Are those my tents where I perceive the fire?

TITINIUS

    They are, my lord.

CASSIUS   Titinius, if thou lovest me,

    Mount thou my horse and hide thy spurs in him,   15

    Till he have brought thee up to yonder troops

    And here again, that I may rest assured

    Whether yond troops are friend or enemy.

TITINIUS

    I will be here again, even with a thought.   *Exit.*

CASSIUS

    Go, Pindarus, get higher on that hill;   20

    My sight was ever thick: regard, Titinius,

    And tell me what thou not'st about the field.

                           [Exit Pindarus.]

9–11 The emphatic repetitions indicate extreme urgency. Pindarus, Cassius' slave from Parthia (the modern northern Iran) has been momentarily present as a messenger from Cassius to Brutus, at 4.2.4, 6, 10–12: but this is his scene. It is marked by his precipitate entry here, his killing of his master and his mysterious exit from the play. Shakespeare follows Plutarch closely, but the touches of high colour, like these desperate repetitions, belong to the playwright.

11 **far** either the comparative farther, or the simplified speech of a foreign slave. Pindarus in excitement has a trick of simple repetition which supports the latter.

12 **This hill** where we have got to; a hill in dramatic imagination

19 **with a thought** as quick as thought: Shakespearean (*AC* 4.14.9–10; *Tem* 4.1.164) and proverbial (Dent, T240)

21 **My . . . thick** Cf. Plutarch (Appendix, p. 357): 'his sight was verie bad'; cf. 3.1.271n.

22 **what thou not'st** what you observe

22.1 *F has no SD, but Pindarus has to be *above* three lines later: *Exit*, if indeed needed here, should give him time to go up the back stairs to the gallery of the stage: equally, he may simply stand upstage.

11 far] *(*farre*)*   22 SD] *Hanmer*

This day I breathed first. Time is come round;
And where I did begin, there shall I end.
My life is run his compass. Sirrah, what news?   25

PINDARUS (*above*)
O my lord!

CASSIUS
What news?

PINDARUS
Titinius is enclosed round about
With horsemen, that make to him on the spur,
Yet he spurs on. Now they are almost on him.   30
Now, Titinius. Now some light: O, he lights too.
He's ta'en. (*Shout.*) And hark, they shout for joy.

CASSIUS
Come down, behold no more:
O, coward that I am, to live so long,
To see my best friend ta'en before my face.   35

Enter PINDARUS.

Come hither, sirrah.
In Parthia did I take thee prisoner,
And then I swore thee, saving of thy life,
That whatsoever I did bid thee do,
Thou shouldst attempt it. Come now, keep thine oath.   40
Now be a free man, and with this good sword
That ran through Caesar's bowels, search this bosom.

23–5 **This . . . compass.** Cassius in meditative mode will be unhurried, giving Pindarus time to get to whatever position is best.

23 **day . . . first** my birthday
breathed breathèd

25 **his compass** its full circle
Sirrah variant of 'sir', usually to inferiors; sometimes dismissive, as in

3.1.10, 4.3.132; here more familiar

28 **enclosed** enclosèd

29 **make to him** make towards him

29–31 See 11n.

31 **light** alight, dismount

32, 35 **ta'en** taken, pronounced 'tane'

38 **swore thee** made thee swear

42 **search** probe

32] Pope; F lines Showt. / ioy. /   36–7] Pope; one line F

> Stand not to answer: here, take thou the hilts,
> And when my face is covered, as 'tis now,
> Guide thou the sword – Caesar, thou art revenged   45
> Even with the sword that killed thee.
> [*Pindarus kills him.*]

PINDARUS

> So, I am free; yet would not so have been
> Durst I have done my will. O Cassius!
> Far from this country Pindarus shall run,   49
> Where never Roman shall take note of him.   [*Exit.*]

Enter TITINIUS *and* MESSALA.

MESSALA

> It is but change, Titinius: for Octavius
> Is overthrown by noble Brutus' power,
> As Cassius' legions are by Antony.

TITINIUS

> These tidings will well comfort Cassius.

MESSALA

> Where did you leave him?

TITINIUS   All disconsolate,   55

> With Pindarus his bondman, on this hill.

MESSALA

> Is not that he that lies upon the ground?

TITINIUS

> He lies not like the living. O, my heart!

---

43 **Stand not** don't wait, or hesitate
   hilts handles of the sword; see
   5.5.28 n.
46.1 *as Plutarch (Appendix, p. 358).
   He explains that Cassius 'slue him
   selfe with the same sworde, with the
   which he strake Caesar' (Appendix,
   p. 331).
48 **Durst I** had I dared; Pindarus would

rather not have got his freedom that
way.
50 **take note of** notice
51 **change** exchange of fortunes in war
54 **comfort** encourage, strengthen, in the
   Latinate sense common in the English
   Bible, as in John, 14 (Tyndale, *NT* and
   subsequent versions)

46 SD] *F2*   47] *Rowe; F lines* free, / Yet . . . beene /   50 SD] *Rowe*

MESSALA

Is not that he?

TITINIUS   No, this was he, Messala,

But Cassius is no more. O setting sun: 60

As in thy red rays thou dost sink tonight,

So in his red blood Cassius' day is set.

The sun of Rome is set. Our day is gone:

Clouds, dews and dangers come: our deeds are done.

Mistrust of my success hath done this deed.   65

MESSALA

Mistrust of good success hath done this deed.

O hateful Error, Melancholy's child,

Why dost thou show to the apt thoughts of men

The things that are not? O Error, soon conceived,

Thou never com'st unto a happy birth   70

But kill'st the mother that engendered thee.

TITINIUS

What, Pindarus? Where art thou, Pindarus?

MESSALA

Seek him, Titinius, whilst I go to meet

---

60 **O setting sun** proleptic: 'When the sun later tonight sets in red rays, so . . .'. At 109 it is three o'clock, with a further fight due *ere night*. A literal reading makes Cassius die here in the setting sun. Not so. The vivid image is of the setting of *Cassius' day* (62).

63 **sun . . . set** Titinius in his poetic hyperbole also registers the end of their cause. The old Rome has gone for ever.

64 **Clouds . . . dangers** all threatening natural phenomena. Though Titinius was not present in the violent storms in which the conspiracy was conceived (1.3), he registers its end in nature's hostility. *Clouds* bring darkness; *dews* are hostile, as at 2.1.260ff.; when *day is gone*, night's *dangers* follow.

65 **Mistrust . . . success** fear of my mission's outcome; *success* means result, good or bad

67–71 **O . . . thee.** The personification of error was rich in significance to Elizabethans, often with cause and effect seen as parent and offspring. Thus Spenser's epic *The Faerie Queene* opens with the Red Cross Knight defeating the hideous monster Error, a 'dam' with 'a thousand young ones' (*FQ*, 1.1.15).

67 **Melancholy's child** Non-existent evils are the offspring of depressed, even suicidal, thoughts.

68 **apt** impressionable

71 **the mother** the melancholy mind; here Cassius

71 engendered] *(engendred)*

The noble Brutus, thrusting this report
Into his ears. I may say thrusting it: 75
For piercing steel and darts envenomed
Shall be as welcome to the ears of Brutus
As tidings of this sight.
TITINIUS   Hie you, Messala,
And I will seek for Pindarus the while.   [*Exit Messala.*]
Why didst thou send me forth, brave Cassius? 80
Did I not meet thy friends, and did not they
Put on my brows this wreath of victory
And bid me give it thee? Didst thou not hear their
    shouts?
Alas, thou hast misconstrued everything.
But hold thee, take this garland on thy brow; 85
Thy Brutus bid me give it thee, and I
Will do his bidding. Brutus, come apace,
And see how I regarded Caius Cassius.
By your leave, gods. This is a Roman's part.
Come, Cassius' sword, and find Titinius' heart. 90
Dies.

74–8 **thrusting . . . sight** The powerful
image haunts with suggestions of
Ham: 'thrusting . . . into his ear(s)'
(1.5.62–3); 'the point envenom'd'
(5.2.313); 'welcome . . . tidings of this
sight' (1.2.159–253). Cf. *AC* 2.5.24–5.
'Thrusting this report / Into his ears'
looks forward, too, to Iago's strategy.
76 **darts** arrows
    envenomed envenomèd
78 **Hie you** hurry, hasten
79 **the while** meanwhile
80 **brave** noble
82 **wreath** in Plutarch given to Titinius

(Appendix, p. 358); it is Shakespeare's
extension to have it intended for
Cassius. The *corona obsidionalis*, made
of the grass of the battlefield, was given
by an army to those who had saved it
(Weinstock, 148).
84 **thou . . . everything** a fair epitaph for
Cassius as, in a villainous way, also for
Iago
89 **a Roman's part** suicide: as Horatio,
Ham 5.2.333, 'antique Roman'.
Shakespeare gives Titinius a graver
ending than he had in Plutarch, 'cursing himself' (*Brutus*, 89).

79 SD] *Q 1691*

Alarum. Enter BRUTUS, MESSALA, Young CATO,
STRATO, VOLUMNIUS [*and* LUCILIUS].

BRUTUS
Where, where, Messala, doth his body lie?
MESSALA
Lo yonder, and Titinius mourning it.
BRUTUS
Titinius' face is upward.
CATO   He is slain.
BRUTUS
O Julius Caesar, thou art mighty yet.
Thy spirit walks abroad and turns our swords   95
In our own proper entrails.   *Low alarums.*
CATO   Brave Titinius.
Look whe'er he have not crowned dead Cassius.
BRUTUS
Are yet two Romans living such as these?
The last of all the Romans, fare thee well:
It is impossible that ever Rome   100
Should breed thy fellow. Friends, I owe more tears
To this dead man than you shall see me pay.
I shall find time, Cassius: I shall find time.
Come therefore, and to Thasos send his body.
His funerals shall not be in our camp,   105

90.2 **Young** CATO Portia's brother
90.3 **STRATO, VOLUMNIUS** friends of
Brutus (Plutarch, Appendix, pp.
361–2): silent until 5.5 below, but con-
tributing to the mourning group
93 **Titinius . . . upward** He is clearly not
mourning Cassius.
94 Caesar was mighty before his death;
his continuing power after death is the
controlling idea of the second half of
the play, re-stated as the end
approaches.

96 **proper** belonging to us (French
propre); here with *own* for emphasis
97 **whe'er** whether
99–101 **The . . . fellow** almost word-for-
word Plutarch (Appendix, p. 358);
impossible because Rome has changed
and new empire-builders have taken
over.
104 *****Thasos** as in Plutarch; an island near
Philippi. F has '*Tharsus*', assimilating
to Tarsus in Asia Minor, the birthplace
of St Paul.

104 Thasos] *Tharsus F;* Thassos *Theobald*

313

Lest it discomfort us. Lucilius, come,
And come, young Cato: let us to the field.
Labio and Flavio set our battles on.
'Tis three o'clock; and, Romans, yet ere night,   109
We shall try fortune in a second fight.   *Exeunt.*

[**5.4**]   *Alarum. Enter* BRUTUS, MESSALA, [Young] CATO,
                    LUCILIUS *and* FLAVIUS.

BRUTUS

Yet, countrymen: O yet, hold up your heads!
                    [*Exit fighting, followed by Messala and Flavius.*]

CATO

What bastard doth not? Who will go with me?
I will proclaim my name about the field.
I am the son of Marcus Cato, ho!
A foe to tyrants and my country's friend.   5

106 **discomfort** discourage; cf. 54 and n.
108 **Labio and Flavio** Their existence
on stage depends on a non-existent
comma. F has no comma in this line,
so *set . . . on* ('are in command of our
forces') is a statement. Some editors
add a comma, making it Brutus' order
to these two to be in command: they
thus have to bring them on at the start
of 5.4 in square brackets. (They are,
one might say, punctuationally
dependent.) The battle scenes are
crowded enough with new named
soldiers, one might think, to avoid
putting on stage two more non-
speaking parts, though 'FLAVIUS' is
among the silent soldiers entering at
5.4.1. In Plutarch (Appendix, p. 361)
they are respectively Brutus'
lieutenant ('Labio') and his captain of
pioneers ('Flavius'). Their Italian
names in the play (usually emended
to 'Labeo and Flavius') are further
evidence of the italic 'o'/'u' confu-

sion in the copy; see Introduction,
p. 125.
    battles armies
109–10 Cf. Plutarch, *Brutus*, 126. The
second battle of Philippi was twenty
days later.
110 SD See 5.4.0.1n.
5.4 location: 'Another part of the field'
(Capell)
0.1 *Alarum. Enter . . .* In the rapid movements on an open stage, formal exits
and re-entries are technicalities. There
is no need to emend F, as Capell and
many editors after have done. The first
sixteen lines of this scene are excep-
tionally active and rapid. *Alarum* is
significant evidence of renewed
fighting.
1.1 *Flavius does not speak, nor appear
again: Messala is silent until 5.5.54.
2   **What . . . not?** Who is so base-born
not to?
4   **Marcus Cato** See Introduction, p.65,
and Plutarch (Appendix, p. 360).

5.4] Capell   0.1 *Enter* BRUTUS] *Enter fighting, soldiers of both armies; then Brutus;* / Capell   Young]
Dyce   1 SD] Cam²

314

I am the son of Marcus Cato, ho!

Enter Soldiers *and fight.*

LUCILIUS

And I am Brutus, Marcus Brutus, I!

Brutus, my country's friend: know me for Brutus!

[*Young Cato is killed.*]

O young and noble Cato, art thou down?   10

Why, now thou diest as bravely as Titinius,

And mayst be honoured, being Cato's son.

1 SOLDIER

Yield, or thou diest.

LUCILIUS   Only I yield to die.

There is so much that thou wilt kill me straight:

Kill Brutus and be honoured in his death.

1 SOLDIER

We must not: a noble prisoner!   15

Enter ANTONY.

2 SOLDIER

Room, ho! Tell Antony, Brutus is ta'en.

1 SOLDIER

I'll tell the news. Here comes the general.

Brutus is ta'en, Brutus is ta'en, my lord.

ANTONY

Where is he?

---

7 ***Brutus** In Plutarch, Lucilius imper-
sonates Brutus to relieve some pressure on him, as Sir Walter Blunt does
the King in *1H4* 5.3.1–21, fatally. F's
SP two lines below needed raising to
this line (see Introduction, p. 129).

12 **Only ... die.** I yield only to die; see
Abbott, 420.

13 **There ... much** Hanmer and many
following editors add '(*Offering
money*)'. One can see why, but it is

forced. Lucilius means that as he is the
great Brutus, there is so much to be
gained by his death that the Soldier
should kill him immediately, gaining
his own honour.

14 **be ... death** You will have the honour
of having killed great Brutus.

15.1 The large Globe stage allows Antony
to register his presence, and be unno-
ticed by the soldiers holding Lucilius.
There is no need to adjust F's SD.

7 SP] *Macmillan; before 9F*   8 SD] *not in F*   17 the news] *Q1;* thee newes *F*

LUCILIUS

Safe, Antony; Brutus is safe enough.
I dare assure thee that no enemy
Shall ever take alive the noble Brutus.
The gods defend him from so great a shame!
When you do find him, or alive or dead,
He will be found like Brutus, like himself.   25

ANTONY

This is not Brutus, friend, but, I assure you,
A prize no less in worth. Keep this man safe;
Give him all kindness. I had rather have
Such men my friends than enemies. Go on,
And see whe'er Brutus be alive or dead,   30
And bring us word unto Octavius' tent
How everything is chanced.   *Exeunt.*

5.5 *Enter* BRUTUS, DARDANIUS, CLITUS, STRATO
and VOLUMNIUS.

BRUTUS

Come, poor remains of friends, rest on this rock.

21–8 **I . . . kindness.** Shakespeare makes dramatic speech directly from Plutarch (Appendix, p. 361): 'I had rather have suche men my frendes, as this man here, then enemies'. Lucilius served one of Brutus' friends for the rest of his life.

30 ***whe'er** whether, though F's 'where' makes sense, implying a comma after *be* – 'where Brutus be, alive or dead'

32 **is chanced** has happened, with the sense of turned out, probably unexpectedly

5.5 location: 'Another part of the field' (Pope)

0.1 Dardanius and Clitus were friends of Brutus (Plutarch, Appendix, pp.

361–2); Strato was a Greek rhetorician. Shakespeare's instinct to gather previously unknown figures to the 'poor remains of friends' (1) is sound, on the heels of Antony's triumph.

1 **rock** No property is necessary; an audience can understand the presence of a rock without it having to be formally visible. A stage rock, though mentioned in Henslowe's inventory of Shakespeare's rival company, the Admiral's at the Rose Theatre, is most unlikely to have been brought on now in the rapid swirl of the action, just for five men to perch on – or lean against, as in Plutarch (Appendix, p. 361).

30 whe'er] *(where)*   5.5] *Capell*

CLITUS

Statilius showed the torchlight, but, my lord,
He came not back. He is or ta'en or slain.

BRUTUS

Sit thee down, Clitus. Slaying is the word.
It is a deed in fashion. Hark thee, Clitus.   [*Whispers.*]   5

CLITUS

What, I, my lord? No, not for all the world.

BRUTUS

Peace, then. No words.

CLITUS   I'll rather kill myself.

BRUTUS

Hark thee, Dardanius.   [*Whispers.*]

DARDANIUS   Shall I do such a deed?

CLITUS

O Dardanius!

DARDANIUS

O Clitus!   10

CLITUS

What ill request did Brutus make to thee?

DARDANIUS

To kill him, Clitus. Look, he meditates.

CLITUS

Now is that noble vessel full of grief,
That it runs over even at his eyes.

BRUTUS

Come hither, good Volumnius, list a word.   15

---

2   **Statilius** as in Plutarch (Appendix, p. 362), he was sent on night reconnaissance, and the torch (the reference indicates stage darkness) was to be a signal that all was well: he was killed.

3   **or . . . or** either . . . or

7   **Peace** hold your peace; keep quiet

13 **vessel** as in *WT* 3.3.21–2, 'a vessel of like sorrow, / So fill'd and so becoming'. The word, though primarily suggesting a container overflowing, echoes New Testament use for special people, as 'he is a chosen vessel' (Acts, 9.15) and 'the weaker vessel' (1 Peter, 3.7) (Geneva 1599).

15 **list a word** listen for a moment

5 SD] *Rowe*   8 SD] *Capell*

VOLUMNIUS
    What says my lord?
BRUTUS   Why this, Volumnius:
    The ghost of Caesar hath appeared to me
    Two several times by night: at Sardis once,
    And this last night, here in Philippi fields:
    I know my hour is come.
VOLUMNIUS   Not so, my lord.   20
BRUTUS
    Nay, I am sure it is, Volumnius.
    Thou seest the world, Volumnius, how it goes.
    Our enemies have beat us to the pit.   *Low alarums.*
    It is more worthy to leap in ourselves
    Than tarry till they push us. Good Volumnius,   25
    Thou knowst that we two went to school together:
    Even for that our love of old, I prithee
    Hold thou my sword-hilts while I run on it.
VOLUMNIUS
    That's not an office for a friend, my lord.
    Alarum still.
CLITUS
    Fly, fly, my lord, there is no tarrying here.   30
BRUTUS
    Farewell to you; and you; and you, Volumnius.
    Strato, thou hast been all this while asleep:
    Farewell to thee too, Strato. Countrymen:

---

17 **The ... Caesar** clearly identifying
the apparition at 4.3.273–84 (Appendix, pp. 351 and 332.
18 **several** different
23 **pit** into which a hunted animal would
be driven. A strongly biblical word for
a grave, and for the Hebrew *sheol*, the
underworld, as Job, 17.16, 'They shall
go down into the bottom of the pit'
(Geneva 1560).

26 **school together** childhood friends; in
Plutarch, more like graduate students
reading philosophy together (Appendix, p. 362)
28 **sword-hilts** a heavy sword would
have cross-barred hilts
29 **office** proper function, service
32 **asleep** and so has not heard Brutus'
appeals to Clitus, Dardanius and
Volumnius

33 to ... Countrymen] *Cam²;* to thee, to Strato, Countrymen *F*

318

My heart doth joy that yet in all my life
I found no man but he was true to me.   35
I shall have glory by this losing day
More than Octavius and Mark Antony
By this vile conquest shall attain unto.
So fare you well at once, for Brutus' tongue
Hath almost ended his life's history: 40
Night hangs upon mine eyes: my bones would rest,
That have but laboured to attain this hour.
Alarum. Cry within, 'Fly, fly, fly.'

CLITUS

Fly, my lord, fly!

BRUTUS   Hence; I will follow.
                    [*Exeunt Clitus, Dardanius and Volumnius.*]
I prithee, Strato, stay thou by thy lord.
Thou art a fellow of a good respect: 45
Thy life hath had some smatch of honour in it.
Hold then my sword, and turn away thy face,
While I do run upon it. Wilt thou, Strato?

STRATO

Give me your hand first. Fare you well, my lord.

BRUTUS

Farewell, good Strato –   [*Runs on his sword.*]
                    Caesar, now be still.

                                        50

34–8 dramatic, poetic paraphrase of Plutarch (Appendix, p. 362)
38 **vile** paltry – to him, as suffering defeat; ominous for the republican Rome he tried to restore
39 **at once** instantly; all together
41 **Night hangs** the sense both that he sees no future, and that his eyes will shortly see nothing; perhaps a literal sense as well, recalling the Brutus of 2.1
41–2 **my . . . hour** a reference both to the painful effort, without anything else

(*but laboured*), of reaching this hour, and that the point of the toil has been to *attain* this rest. The thought is not Stoic, for Brutus is not saying that death is no calamity.
45 **respect** reputation
46 **smatch** relish
50–1 **Caesar . . . will.** The spirit of Caesar, like the ghost in revenge tragedy, is able to rest when his murderer is dead – as Hamlet promises when revenge is sworn: 'Rest, rest, perturbed spirit!' (*Ham* 1.5.182).

43 SD2] *Capell*   50 SD] *Rowe*

319

I killed not thee with half so good a will.   *Dies.*

Alarm. Retreat. Enter ANTONY, OCTAVIUS, MESSALA,
LUCILIUS *and the army.*

OCTAVIUS

What man is that?

MESSALA

My master's man. Strato, where is thy master?

STRATO

Free from the bondage you are in, Messala,
The conquerors can but make a fire of him: 55
For Brutus only overcame himself,
And no man else hath honour by his death.

LUCILIUS

So Brutus should be found. I thank thee, Brutus,
That thou hast proved Lucilius' saying true.

OCTAVIUS

All that served Brutus, I will entertain them.   60
Fellow, wilt thou bestow thy time with me?

STRATO

Ay, if Messala will prefer me to you.

OCTAVIUS

Do so, good Messala.

MESSALA

How died my master, Strato?

STRATO

I held the sword and he did run on it.   65

51.1 *Retreat* the signal for pursuit to
cease
52 **What ... that?** i.e. Brutus' friend
Strato. Afterwards, as Plutarch tells,
he was treated with distinction by
Octavius (Appendix, p. 363). His
new speaking presence in twenty-
odd lines at the end of the play eases
the action towards Octavius and

Antony, where the historical future
lies.
53 SP MESSALA also afterwards a friend
of Octavius, who made him one of his
generals
55 **but** only
56 **only** alone
60 **entertain** take them into my service

MESSALA

Octavius, then take him to follow thee,
That did the latest service to my master.

ANTONY

This was the noblest Roman of them all:
All the conspirators save only he
Did that they did in envy of great Caesar.   70
He only, in a general honest thought
And common good to all, made one of them.
His life was gentle, and the elements
So mixed in him that nature might stand up
And say to all the world, 'This was a man!'   75

OCTAVIUS

According to his virtue let us use him,
With all respect and rites of burial.
Within my tent his bones tonight shall lie,
Most like a soldier, ordered honourably.

68–75 Antony's generous epilogue does much to lift him above his ruthlessness earlier in the play. He shows magnanimity and wisdom in separating Brutus from his fellow-conspirators. Shakespeare has found the elements of this speech in many parts of Plutarch, even from the opening paragraphs of the *Life* (*Brutus*, 90).

70 **envy of** ill-will towards

71–2 '(1) he alone was motivated by concern with the public good; (2) he joined them only because he was so motivated' (RP).

73 **gentle** noble; and see above, 3.2.73 and n., 140.

73–4 **elements / So mixed** air, earth, fire and water so tempered together in the 'humours' that they made someone of outstanding 'temperament'

75 **'This was a man!'** a humanist ideal; not a god, as the emperor Caesar was

hailed: see above, 3.1.58–9n. and *Ham* 1.2.187–8

78 **my tent** magnanimity, not arrogant division from Antony. Octavius, though severe, acknowledges the worth of enemies with generous fulness; see him on the death of Antony, *AC* 5.1.14–48.

79 **Most … soldier** as Hamlet, carried by 'four captains … like a soldier' (*Ham* 5.2.387–8), and Coriolanus (*Cor* 5.6.149), 'Help, three of the chiefest soldiers; I'll be one.' These formal exits allow for drums to beat ('The soldier's music', *Ham* 5.2.391) as the body is carried off; and so perhaps here.

ordered honourably with all honourable observance. Shakespeare transfers Brutus' final honours (Plutarch, Appendix, p. 363) from Antony to Octavius.

71 He only,] He, onely *F*

So call the field to rest, and let's away,   80
To part the glories of this happy day.   *Exeunt omnes.*

FINIS

---

80 **call ... rest** command to trumpets
81 **part** share out
81 SD In September 1599, after the play
finished, Thomas Platter reported (see
Introduction, p. 12) that 'they danced
together admirably and exceedingly
gracefully'. Is this any more strange
than the modern tradition of the
'curtain call', itself a repeated dance?
In present-day Britain, applause and
curtain-calls can be shockingly per-
functory, but in theatres in mainland
Europe they can continue for many
minutes, an experience as curiously
satisfying as any stage dance.

APPENDIX

PLUTARCH'S *LIVES OF THE NOBLE GRECIANS AND ROMANES*

The following extracts are taken from Sir Thomas North's translation of Plutarch's *Lives* (1579); page references are to Bullough; modern i and u replace j and v.

THE LIFE OF JULIUS CAESAR

... All these thinges were purposed to be done, but tooke no effecte. But, the ordinaunce of the kalender, and reformation of the yeare, to take away all confusion of time, being exactly calculated by the Mathematicians, and brought to perfection, was a great commoditie unto all men. ... But the chiefest cause that made him mortally hated, was the covetous desire he had to be called king ... (pp. 79–80)

... But he sitting still in his majesty, disdaining to rise up unto them when they came in, as if they had bene private men, aunswered them: that his honors had more neede to be cut of, then enlarged. This did not onely offend the Senate, but the common people also, to see that he should so lightly esteeme of the Magistrates of the common wealth: insomuch as every man that might lawfully goe his way, departed thence very sorrowfully. Thereupon also Caesar rising, departed home to his house, and tearing open his doblet coller, making his necke bare, he cried out alowde to his frendes, that his throte was readie to offer to any man that would come and cut it. Notwithstanding, it is reported, that afterwardes to excuse this folly, he imputed it to his disease, saying, that their wittes are not perfit which have his disease of the falling evill, when standing of their feete they speake to the common people, but are soone troubled with a trembling of their body, and a sodaine dimnes and guidines. But that was not true. For he would have risen up to the Senate, but Cornelius Balbus one of his frendes (but rather a flatterer) would not let him, saying: what, doe you not remember that you are Caesar, and will you not let them reverence you, and doe their dueties? Besides these occasions and offences, there followed also his shame and reproache, abusing the Tribunes of the people in this sorte. At that time, the feast Lupercalia was celebrated, the which in olde time men say was the feast of sheapheards or heard men, and is much like unto the feast of the Lycaeians in Arcadia. But howesoever it is, that day there are divers noble mens sonnes, young men, (and some of them Magistrats them selves that governe then) which run naked through the city, striking in sport them they meete in their way, with leather thonges, heare and all on, to make them geve place. And many noble women, and gentle women also, goe of purpose to stand in their way, and doe put forth their handes to be striken, as schollers hold them out to their schoolemaster, to be striken with the ferula: perswading them selves that being with childe, they shall have good deliverie, and also being barren, that it will make them to conceive with child. Caesar sate to beholde that sport upon the pulpit for orations, in a chayer of gold, apparelled in triumphing manner. Antonius, who was Consull at that time, was one of them that ranne this holy course. So when he came into the market place, the people made a lane for him to runne at libertie, and he came to Caesar, and presented him a Diadeame wreathed about with laurell. Whereuppon there rose a certaine crie of rejoycing, not very great, done onely by a few, appointed for the purpose. But when Caesar refused the Diadeame, then all the people together made an outcrie of joy. Then Antonius offering it him againe, there was a second shoute of joy, but yet of a few. But when Caesar refused it againe the second time, then all the whole people showted. Caesar having made this proofe, found that the people did not like of it, and thereuppon rose out of his chayer, and commaunded the crowne to be caried unto Jupiter in the Capitoll. After that, there were set up images of Caesar in the city with Diadeames upon their heades, like kinges. Those, the two Tribunes, Flavius and Marullus, went and pulled downe: and furthermore, meeting with them that first saluted Caesar as king, they committed them to prison. The people followed them rejoycing at it, and called them Brutes: bicause of Brutus, who had in old time driven the kings out of Rome, & that brought the kingdom of one person, unto the government of the Senate and people. Caesar was so offended withall, that he deprived Marullus and Flavius of their Tribuneshippes, and accusing them, he spake also against the people, and called them Bruti, and Cumani, to witte, beastes, and fooles. Hereupon the people went straight unto Marcus Brutus, who from his father came of the first Brutus, and by his mother, of the house of the Servilians, a noble house as any was in Rome, and was also nephew and sonne in law of Marcus Cato. Notwithstanding, the great honors and favor Caesar shewed unto him, kept him backe that of him selfe alone, he did not conspire nor consent to depose him of his kingdom. For Caesar did not onely save his life, after the battell of Pharsalia when Pompey fled, and did at his request also save many more of his frendes besides: but furthermore, he put a marvelous confidence in him. For he had already preferred him to the Praetorshippe for that yeare, and furthermore was appointed to be Consul, the fourth yeare after that, having through Caesars frendshippe, obtained it before Cassius, who likewise made sute for the same: and Caesar also, as it is reported, sayd in this contention, in deede Cassius hath alleaged best reason, but yet shall he not be chosen before Brutus. Some one day accusing Brutus while he practised this conspiracy, Caesar would not heare of it, but clapping his hande on his bodie, told them, Brutus will looke for this skinne: meaning thereby, that Brutus for his vertue, deserved to rule after him, but yet, that for ambitions sake, he woulde not shewe him selfe unthankefull nor dishonorable. Nowe they that desired chaunge, and wished Brutus only their Prince and Governour above all other: they durst not come to him them selves to tell him what they woulde have him to doe, but in the night did cast sundrie papers into the Praetors seate where he gave audience, and the most of them to this effect. Thou sleepest Brutus, and art not Brutus in deede. Cassius finding Brutus ambition sturred up the more by these seditious billes, did pricke him forwarde, and egge him on the more, for a private quarrell he had conceived against Caesar: the circumstance whereof, we have sette downe more at large in Brutus life. Caesar also had Cassius in great gelouzie, and suspected him much whereuppon he sayed on a time to his frendes, what will Cassius doe, thinke ye? I like not his pale lookes. An other time when Caesars frendes complained unto him of Antonius, and Dolabella, that they pretended some mischiefe towardes him: he aunswered them againe, as for those fatte men and smooth comed heades, quoth he, I never reckon of them: but these pale visaged and carian leane people, I feare them most, meaning Brutus and Cassius. Certainly, destenie may easier be fore-seene, then avoyded: considering the straunge & wonderfull signes that were sayd to be seene before Caesars death. For, touching the fires in the element, and spirites running up and downe in the night, and also these solitarie birdes to be seene at noone dayes sittinge in the great market place: are not all these signes perhappes worth the noting, in such a wonderfull chaunce as happened. But Strabo the Philosopher wryteth, that divers men were seene going up and downe in fire: and further-more, that there was a slave of the souldiers, that did cast a marvelous burning flame out of his hande, insomuch as they that saw it, thought he had bene burnt, but when the fire was out, it was found he had no hurt. Caesar selfe also doing sacrifice unto the goddes, found that one of the beastes which was sacrificed had no hart: and that was a straunge thing in nature, how a beast could live without a hart. Furthermore, there was a certaine Soothsayer that had geven Caesar warning long time affore, to take heede of the day of the Ides of Marche, (which is the fifteenth of the moneth) for on that day he shoulde be in great daunger. That day being come, Caesar going unto the Senate house, and speak-ing merily to the Soothsayer, tolde him, the Ides of Marche be come: so be they, softly aunswered the Soothsayer, but yet are they not past. And the very day before, Caesar supping with Marcus Lepidus, sealed certaine letters as he was wont to do at the bord: so talke falling out amongest them, reasoning what death was best: he preventing their opinions, cried out alowde, Death unlooked for. Then going to bedde the same night as his manner was, and lying with his wife Calpurnia, all the windowes and dores of his chamber flying open, the noyse awooke him, and made him affrayed when he saw such light: but more, when he heard his wife Calpurnia, being fast a sleepe, weepe and sigh, and put forth many fumbling lamentable speaches. For she dreamed that Caesar was slaine, and that she had him in her armes. Others also doe denie that she had any suche dreame, as amongest other, Titus Livius wryteth, that it was in this sorte. The Senate having set upon the toppe of Caesars house, for an ornament and setting foorth of the same, a cer-taine pinnacle: Calpurnia dreamed that she sawe it broken downe, and that she thought she lamented and wept for it. Insomuch that Caesar rising in the morning, she prayed him if it were possible, not to goe out of the dores that day, but to adjorne the session of the Senate, untill an other day. And if that he made no reckoning of her dreame, yet that he woulde searche further of the Soothsayers by their sacrifices, to knowe what should happen him that day. Thereby it seemed that Caesar like-wise did feare and suspect somewhat, bicause his wife Calpurnia untill that time, was never geven to any feare or supersticion: and then, for that he saw her so troubled in minde with this dreame she had. But much more afterwardes, when the Soothsayers having sacrificed many beastes one after an other, tolde him that none did like them: then he determined to sende Antonius to adjorne the session of the Senate. But in the meane time came Decius Brutus, surnamed Albinus, in whom Caesar put such confidence, that in his last will and testament he had appointed him to be his next heire, and yet was of the conspiracie with Cassius and Brutus: he fearing that if Caesar did adjorne the session that day, the conspiracie woulde out, laughed the Soothsayers to scorne, and reproved Caesar, saying: that he gave the Senate occasion to mislike with him, and that they might thinke he mocked them, considering that by his commaundement they were assembled, and that they were readie willingly to graunt him all thinges, and to proclaime him king of all the provinces of the Empire of Rome out of Italie, and that he should weare his Diadeame in all other places, both by sea and land. And further-more, that if any man should tell them from him, they should departe for that present time, and returne againe when Calpurnia shoulde have better dreames: what would his enemies and ill willers say, and how could they like of his frendes wordes? And who could perswade them otherwise, but that they would thinke his dominion a slaverie unto them, and tirannicall in him selfe? And yet if it be so, sayd he, that you utterly mislike of this day, it is better that you goe your selfe in person, and saluting the Senate, to dismisse them till an other time. Therewithall he tooke Caesar by the hand, and brought him out of his house. Caesar was not gone farre from his house, but a bondman, a straunger, did what he could to speake with him: and when he sawe he was put backe by the great prease and multitude of people that followed him, he went straight unto his house, and put him selfe into Calpurniaes handes to be kept, till Caesar came backe againe, telling her that he had great matters to imparte unto him. And one Artemidorus also borne in the Ile of Gnidos, a Doctor of Rethoricke in the Greeke tongue, who by meanes of his profession was verie familliar with certaine of Brutus confederates, and therefore knew the most parte of all their practises against Caesar: came & brought him a litle bill wrytten with his owne hand, of all that he ment to tell him. He marking howe Caesar received all the supplications that were offered him, and that he gave them straight to his men that were about him, pressed neerer to him, and sayed: Caesar, reade this memoriall to your selfe, and that quickely, for they be matters of great waight and touche you neerely. Caesar tooke it of him, but coulde never reade it, though he many times attempted it, for the number of people that did salute him: but holding it still in his hande, keeping it to him selfe, went on withall into the Senate house. Howbeit other are of opinion, that it was some man else that gave him that memoriall, and not Artemidorus, who did what he could all the way as he went to geve it Caesar, but he was alwayes repulsed by the people. For these things, they may seeme to come by chaunce: but the place where the murther was prepared, and where the Senate were assembled, and where also there stoode up an image of Pompey dedicated by him selfe amongest other ornamentes which he gave unto the Theater: all these were manifest proofes that it was the ordinaunce of some god, that made this treason to be executed, specially in that verie place. It is also reported, that Cassius (though otherwise he did favour the doctrine of Epicurus) beholding the image of Pompey, before they entred into the action of their traiterous enterprise: he did softely call upon it, to aide him. But the instant daunger of the present time, taking away his former reason, did sodainly put him into a furious passion, and made him like a man halfe besides him selfe. Now Antonius, that was a faithfull frende to Caesar, and a valliant man besides of his handes, him, Decius Brutus Albinus entertained out of the Senate house, having begon a long tale of set purpose. So Caesar comming into the house, all the Senate stoode up on their feete to doe him honor. Then parte of Brutus companie and confederates stoode rounde about Caesars chayer, and parte of them also came towardes him, as though they made sute with Metellus Cimber, to call home his brother againe from banishment: and thus prosecuting still their sute, they followed Caesar, till he was set in his chayer. Who, denying their petitions, and being offended with them one after an other, bicause the more they were denied, the more they pressed upon him, and were the earnester with him: Metellus at length, taking his gowne with both his handes, pulled it over his necke, which was the signe geven the confederates to sette apon him. Then Casca behinde him strake him in the necke with his sword, howbeit the wounde was not great nor mortall, bicause it seemed, the feare of such a develishe attempt did amaze him, and take his strength from him, that he killed him not at the first blowe. But Caesar turning straight unto him, caught hold of his sword, and held it hard: and they both cried out, Caesar in Latin: O vile traitor Casca, what doest thou? And Casca in Greeke to his brother, brother, helpe me. At the beginning of this sturre, they that were present, not knowing of the conspiracie were so amazed with the horrible sight they sawe: that they had no power to flie, neither to helpe him, not so much, as once to make any outcrie. They on thother side that had conspired his death, compassed him in on everie side with their swordes drawen in their handes, that Caesar turned him no where, but he was striken at by some, and still had naked swords in his face, and was hacked and mangeled amonge them, as a wilde beaste taken of hunters. For it was agreed among them, that every man should geve him a wound, bicause all their partes should be in this murther: and then Brutus him selfe gave him one wounde about his privities. Men reporte also, that Caesar did still defende him selfe against the rest, running everie waye with his bodie: but when he sawe Brutus with his sworde drawen in his hande, then he pulled his gowne over his heade, and made no more resistaunce, and was driven either casually, or purposedly, by the counsell of the conspirators, against the base whereupon Pompeys image stoode, which ranne all of a goare bloude, till he was slaine. Thus it seemed, that the image tooke just revenge of Pompeys enemie, being throwen downe on the ground at his feete, and yelding up his ghost there, for the number of wounds he had upon him. For it is reported, that he had three and twenty wounds apon his body: and divers of the conspirators did hurt them selves, striking one body with so many blowes. When Caesar was slaine, the Senate (though Brutus stood in the middest amongest them as though he would have sayd somwhat touching this fact) presently ran out of the house, and flying, filled all the city with marvelous feare and tumult. Insomuch as some did shut to their dores, others forsooke their shops & warehouses, and others ranne to the place to see what the matter was:

and others also that had seene it, ran home to their houses againe. But Antonius and Lepidus, which were two of Caesars chiefest frends, secretly conveying them selves away, fled into other mens houses, and forsooke their owne. Brutus and his confederats on thother side, being yet hotte with this murther they had committed, having their swordes drawen in their hands, came all in a troupe together out of the Senate, and went into the market place, not as men that made countenaunce to flie, but otherwise boldly holding up their heades like men of corage, and called to the people to defende their libertie, and stayed to speake with every great personage whome they met in their way. Of them, some followed this troupe, and went amongest them, as if they had bene of the conspiracie, and falsely chalenged parte of the honor with them: among them was Caius Octavius, and Lentulus Spinther. But both of them were afterwards put to death, for their vaine covetousnes of honor, by Antonius, and Octavius Caesar the younger: and yet had no parte of that honor for the which they were put to death, neither did any man beleve that they were any of the confederates, or of counsell with them. For they that did put them to death, tooke revenge rather of the will they had to offend, then of any fact they had committed. The next morning, Brutus and his confederates came into the market place to speake unto the people, who gave them such audience, that it seemed they neither greatly reproved, nor allowed the fact: for by their great silence they showed, that they were sory for Caesars death, and also that they did reverence Brutus. Nowe the Senate graunted generall pardonne for all that was paste, and to pacifie every man, ordained besides, that Caesars funeralls shoulde bee honored as a god, and established all thinges that he had done: and gave certaine provinces also, and convenient honors unto Brutus and his confederates, whereby every man thought all things were brought to good peace & quietnes againe. But when they had opened Caesars testament, and found a liberall legacie of money, bequeathed unto every citizen of Rome, and that they saw his body (which was brought into the market place) al bemangled with gashes of swordes : then there was no order to keepe the multitude and common people quiet, but they plucked up formes, tables, and stooles, and layed them all about the body, & setting them a fire, burnt the corse. Then when the fire was well kindled, they tooke the firebrandes, and went unto their houses that had slaine Caesar, to set them a fire. Other also ranne up and downe the citie to see if they could meete with any of them, to cut them in peeces: howbeit they could meete with never a man of them, bicause they had locked them selves up safely in their houses. There was one of Caesars frends called Cinna, that had a marvelous straunge & terrible dreame the night before. He dreamed that Caesar bad him to supper, & that he refused, and would not goe: then that Caesar tooke him by the hand, and led him against his will. Now Cinna hearing at that time, that they burnt Caesars body in the market place, notwithstanding that he feared his dreame, and had an agew on him besides: he went into the market place to honor his funeralls. When he came thither, one of meane sorte asked what his name was? He was straight called by his name. The first man told it to an other, and that other unto an other, so that it ranne straight through them all, that he was one of them that murdered Caesar: (for in deede one of the traitors to Caesar, was also called Cinna as him selfe) wherefore taking him for Cinna the murderer, they fell upon him with such furie, that they presently dispatched him in the market place. This sturre and furie made Brutus and Cassius more affrayed, then of all that was past, and therefore within fewe dayes after, they departed out of Rome: and touching their doings afterwards, and what calamity they suffered till their deathes, we have wrytten it at large, in the life of Brutus. Caesar dyed at six and fifty yeres of age: and Pompey also lived not passing foure yeares more then he. So he reaped no other frute of all his raigne & dominion, which he had so vehemently desired all his life, and pursued with such extreame daunger: but a vaine name only, and a superficiall glory, that procured him the envy and hatred of his contrie. But his great prosperitie and good fortune that favored him all his life time, did continue afterwards in the revenge of his death, pursuing the murtherers both by sea & land, till they had not left a man more to be executed, of al them that were actors or counsellers in the conspiracy of his death. Furthermore, of all the chaunces that happen unto men upon the earth, that which came to Cassius above all other, is most to be wondered at. For he being overcome in battell at the jorney of Philippes, slue him selfe with the same sworde, with the which he strake Caesar. Againe, of signes in the element, the great comet which seven nightes together was seene very bright after Caesars death, the eight night after was never seene more. Also the brightnes of the sunne was darkened, the which all that yeare through rose very pale, and shined not out, whereby it gave but small heate: therefore the ayer being very clowdy & darke, by the weakenes of the heate that could not come foorth, did cause the earth to bring foorth but raw and unrype frute, which rotted before it could rype. But above all, the ghost that appeared unto Brutus shewed plainly, that the goddes were offended with the murther of Caesar. The vision was thus: Brutus being ready to passe over his army from the citie of Abydos, to the other coast lying directly against it, slept every night (as his manner was) in his tent, and being yet awake, thinking of his affaires: (for by reporte he was as carefull a Captaine, and lived with as litle sleepe, as ever man did) he thought he heard a noyse at his tent dore, & looking towards the light of the lampe that waxed very dimme, he saw a horrible vision of a man, of a wonderfull greatnes, and dreadfull looke, which at the first made him marvelously afraid. But when he sawe that it did him no hurt, but stoode by his bedde side, and sayd nothing: at length he asked him what he was. The image aunswered him: I am thy ill angell, Brutus, and thou shalt see me by the citie of Philippes. Then Brutus replied againe, and sayd: Well, I shall see thee then. Therewithall, the spirit presently vanished from him. After that time Brutus being in battell neere unto the citie of Philippes, against Antonius and Octavius Caesar, at the first battell he wan the victorie, and overthrowing all them that withstoode him, he drave them into young Caesars campe, which he tooke. The second battell being at hand, this spirit appeared again unto him, but spake never a word. Thereuppon Brutus knowing he should dye, did put him selfe to all hazard in battell, but yet fighting could not be slaine. So seeing his men put to flight and overthrowen, he ranne unto a litle rocke not farre of, and there setting his swordes point to his brest, fell upon it, and slue him selfe, but yet as it is reported, with the helpe of his frend, that dispatched him. (Pp. 80–9)

THE END OF CAESARS LIFE

THE LIFE OF MARCUS BRUTUS

... Now there were divers sortes of Praetorshippes at Rome, and it was looked for, that Brutus or Cassius would make sute for the chiefest Praetorshippe, which they called the Praetorshippe of the citie: bicause he that had that office, was as a Judge to minister justice unto the citizens. Therfore they strove one against the other, though some say that there was some litle grudge betwext them for other matters before, and that this contencion did sette them further out, though they were allyed together. For Cassius had maried Junia, Brutus sister. Others say, that this contencion betwext them came by Caesar himselfe, who secretly gave either of them both hope of his favour. So their sute for the Praetorshippe was so followed and laboured of either partie, that one of them put an other in sute of lawe. Brutus with his vertue and good name contended against many noble exploytes in armes, which Cassius had done against the Parthians. So Caesar after he had heard both their objections, he told his frendes with whom he consulted about this matter: Cassius cause is the juster, sayd he, but Brutus must be first preferred. Thus Brutus had the first Praetorshippe, and Cassius the second: who thanked not Caesar so much for the Praetorshippe he had, as he was angrie with him for that he had lost. But Brutus in many other thinges tasted of the benefite of Caesars favour in any thing he requested. For if he had listed, he might have bene one of Caesars chiefest frendes, and of greatest authoritie and credit about him. Howebeit Cassius frendes did disswade him from it (for Cassius and he were not yet reconciled together sithence their first contencion and strife for the Praetorship) and prayed him to beware of Caesars sweete intisements, and to flie his tyrannicall favors: the which they sayd Caesar gave him, not to honor his vertue, but to weaken his constant minde, framing it to the bent of his bowe. Now Caesar on the other side did not trust him overmuch, nor was not without tales brought unto him against him: howebeit he feared his great minde, authority, & frends. Yet on the other side also, he trusted his good nature, & fayer condicions. For, intelligence being brought him one day, that Antonius and Dolabella did conspire against him: he aunswered, that these fat long heared men made him not affrayed, but the leane and whitely faced fellowes, meaning that, by Brutus and Cassius. At an other time also when one accused Brutus unto him, and bad him beware of him: What, sayd he againe, clapping his hand on his brest: thinke ye that Brutus will not tarie till this bodie dye? Meaning that none but Brutus after him was meete to have suche power as he had. And surelie, in my opinion, I am perswaded that Brutus might in dede have come to have bene the chiefest man of Rome, if he could have contented him selfe for a time and have bene next unto Caesar, & to have suffred his glorie and authoritie, which he had gotten by his great victories, to consume with time. But Cassius being a chollericke man, and hating Caesar privatlie, more then he did the tyrannie openlie: he incensed Brutus against him. It is also reported, that Brutus coulde evill away with the tyrannie, and that Cassius hated the tyranne: making many complayntes for the injuries he had done him, and amongest others, for that he had taken away his Lyons from him. Cassius had provided them for his sportes, when he should be Aedilis, and they were found in the citie of Megara, when it was wonne by Calenus, and Caesar kept them. The rumor went, that these Lyons did marvelous great hurt to the Magarians. For when the citie was taken, they brake their cages where they were tied up, and turned them loose, thinking they would have done great mischiefe to the enemies, and have kept them from setting uppon them: but the Lyons contrarie to expectacion, turned upon them selves that fled unarmed, & did so cruelly tare some in peces, that it pitied their enemies to see them. And this was the cause, as some do report, that made Cassius conspire against Caesar. But this holdeth no water. For Cassius even from his cradell could not abide any maner of tyrans, as it appeared when he was but a boy, & went unto the same schoole that Faustus, the sonne of Sylla did. And Faustus bragging among other boyes, highly boasted of his fathers kingdom: Cassius rose up on his feete, and gave him two good whirts on the eare. Faustus governors would have put this matter in sute against Cassius: But Pompey woulde not suffer them, but caused the two boyes to be brought before him, and asked them howe the matter came to passe. Then Cassius, as it is wrytten of him, sayd unto the other: goe to Faustus, speake againe and thou darest, before this noble man here, the same wordes that made me angrie with thee, that my fistes may walke once againe about thine eares. Suche was Cassius hotte stirring nature. But for Brutus, his frendes and contrie men, both by divers procurementes, and sundrie rumors of the citie, and by many bills also, did openlie call and procure him to doe that he did. For, under the image of his auncester Junius Brutus, that drave the kinges out of Rome, they wrote: O, that it pleased the goddes thou wert now alive, Brutus: and againe, that thou wert here amonge us nowe. His tribunall (or chaire) where he gave audience duringe the time he was

Praetor, was full of suche billes: Brutus, thou art a sleepe, and art not Brutus in deede. And of all this, Caesars flatterers were the cause: who beside many other exceeding and unspeakeable honors they dayly devised for him, in the night time they did put Diadeames uppon the heades of his images, supposinge thereby to allure the common people to call him kinge, in steade of Dictator. Howebeit it turned to the contrarie, as we have wrytten more at large in Julius Caesars life. Nowe when Cassius felt his frendes, and did stirre them up against Caesar: they all agreed and promised to take parte with him, so Brutus were the chiefe of their conspiracie. For they told him, that so high an enterprise and attempt as that, did not so muche require men of manhoode, and courage to drawe their swordes: as it stoode them uppon to have a man of suche estimacion as Brutus, to make everie man boldlie thinke, that by his onelie presence the fact were holie, and just. If he tooke not this course, then that they shoulde goe to it with fainter hartes, and when they had done it, they shoulde be more fearefull: bicause everie man woulde thinke that Brutus woulde not have refused to have made one with them, if the cause had bene good and honest. Therefore Cassius considering this matter with him selfe, did first of all speake to Brutus, since they grewe straunge together for the sute they had for the Praetorshippe. So when he was reconciled to him againe, and that they had imbraced one an other: Cassius asked him if he were determined to be in the Senate house, the first day of the moneth of Marche, bicause he heard say that Caesars frendes shoulde move the counsell that day, that Caesar shoulde be called king by the Senate. Brutus aunswered him, he would not be there. But if we be sent for sayd Cassius: howe then? For my selfe then sayd Brutus, I meane not to holde my peace, but to withstande it, and rather dye then lose my libertie. Cassius being bolde, and taking holde of this worde: why, quoth he, what Romane is he alive that will suffer thee to dye for the libertie? What, knowest thou not that thou art Brutus? Thinkest thou that they be cobblers, tapsters, or suche like base mechanicall people, that wryte these billes and scrowles which are founde dayly in thy Praetors chaire, and not the noblest men and best citizens that doe it? No, be thou well assured, that of other Praetors they looke for giftes, common distribucions amongst the people, and for common playes, and to see fensers fight at the sharpe, to shew the people pastime: but at thy handes, they specially require (as a due det unto them) the taking away of the tyranny, being fully bent to suffer any extremity for thy sake, so that thou wilt shew thy selfe to be the man thou art taken for, and that they hope thou art. Thereuppon he kissed Brutus, and imbraced him: and so each taking leave of other, they went both to speake with their frendes about it. Nowe amongest Pompeys frendes, there was one called Caius Ligarius, who had bene accused unto Caesar for taking parte with Pompey, and Caesar discharged him. But Ligarius thanked not Caesar so muche for his discharge, as he was offended with him for that he was brought in daunger by his tyrannicall power. And therefore in his hearte he was alway his mortall enemie, and was besides verie familiar with Brutus, who went to see him beinge sicke in his bedde, and sayed unto him: O Ligarius, in what a time art thou sicke! Ligarius risinge uppe in his bedde, and taking him by the right hande, sayed unto him: Brutus, sayed he, if thou hast any great enterprise in hande worthie of thy selfe, I am whole. After that time they beganne to feele all their acquaintaunce whome they trusted, and layed their heades together consultinge uppon it, and did not onelie picke out their frendes, but all those also whome they thought stowt enough to attempt any desperate matter, and that were not affrayed to loase their lives. For this cause they durst not acquaint Cicero with their conspiracie, although he was a man whome they loved dearelie, and trusted best: for they were affrayed that he being a coward by nature, and age also having increased his feare, he woulde quite turne and alter all their purpose, and quenche the heate of their enterprise, the which speciallie required hotte and earnest execucion, seeking by perswasion to bring all thinges to suche safetie, as there should be no perill. Brutus also did let other of his frendes alone, as Statilius Epicurian, and Faonius, that made profession to followe Marcus Cato. Bicause that having cast out wordes a farre of, disputing together in Philosophie to feele their mindes: Faonius aunswered, that civill warre was worse then tyrannicall government usurped against the lawe. And Statilius tolde him also, that it were an unwise parte of him, to put his life in daunger, for a sight of ignoraunt fooles and asses. Labeo was present at this talke, and maintayned the contrarie against them both. But Brutus helde his peace, as though it had bene a doubtfull matter, and a harde thing to have decided. But afterwardes, being out of their companie, he made Labeo privie to his intent: who verie readilie offered him selfe to make one. And they thought good also to bring in an other Brutus to joyne with him, surnamed Albinus: who was no man of his handes him selfe, but bicause he was able to bring good force of a great number of slaves, and fensers at the sharpe, whome he kept to shewe the people pastime with their fighting, besides also that Caesar had some trust in him. Cassius and Labeo tolde Brutus Albinus of it at the first, but he made them no aunswere. But when he had spoken with Brutus him selfe alone, and that Brutus had tolde him he was the chiefe ring-leader of all this conspiracie: then he willinglie promised him the best aide he coulde. Furthermore, the onlie name and great calling of Brutus, did bring on the most of them to geve consent to this conspiracie. Who having never taken othes together, nor taken or geven any caution or assuraunce, nor binding them selves one to an other by any religious othes: they all kept the matter so secret to them selves, and coulde so cunninglie handle it, that notwithstanding the goddes did reveale it by manifest signes and tokens from above, and by predictions of sacrifices: yet all this woulde not be beleved. Nowe Brutus, who knewe verie well that for his sake all the noblest, valliantest, and most couragious men of Rome did venter their lives, waying with him selfe the greatnesse of the daunger: when he was out of his house, he did so frame and facion his countenaunce and lookes, that no man coulde discerne he had any thing to trouble his minde. But when night came that he was in his owne house, then he was cleane chaunged. For, either care did wake him against his will when he woulde have slept, or else oftentimes of him selfe he fell into suche deepe thoughtes of this enterprise, casting in his minde all the daungers that might happen: that his wife lying by him, founde that there was some marvelous great matter that troubled his minde, not beinge wont to be in that taking, and that he coulde not well determine with him selfe. His wife Porcia (as we have tolde you before) was the daughter of Cato, whome Brutus maried being his cosin, not a maiden, but a younge widowe after the death of her first husbande Bibulus, by whome she had also a younge sonne called Bibulus, who afterwardes wrote a booke of the actes and jeastes of Brutus, extant at this present day. This young Ladie being excellentlie well seene in Philosophie, loving her husbande well, and being of a noble courage, as she was also wise: bicause she woulde not aske her husbande what he ayled before she had made some proofe by her selfe, she tooke a litle rasor suche as barbers occupie to pare mens nayles, and causinge all her maydes and women to goe out of her chamber, gave her selfe a greate gashe withall in her thigh, that she was straight all of a goare bloode, and incontinentlie after, a vehement fever tooke her, by reason of the payne of her wounde. Then perceiving her husbande was marvelouslie out of quiet, and that he coulde take no rest: even in her greatest payne of all, she spake in this sorte unto him I being, O Brutus, (sayed she) the daughter of Cato, was maried unto thee, not to be thy beddefellowe and companion in bedde and at borde onelie, like a harlot: but to be partaker also with thee, of thy good and evill fortune. Nowe for thy selfe, I can finde no cause of faulte in thee touchinge our matche: but for my parte, howe may I showe my duetie towardes thee, and howe muche I woulde doe for thy sake, if I can not constantlie beare a secret mischaunce or griefe with thee, which requireth secrecy and fidelity? I confesse, that a womans wit commonly is too weake to keepe a secret safely: but yet, Brutus, good educacion, and the companie of vertuous men, have some power to reforme the defect of nature. And for my selfe, I have this ben-efit moreover: that I am the daughter of Cato, & wife of Brutus. This notwithstanding, I did not trust to any of these things before: untill that now I have found by experience, that no paine nor griefe whatsoever can overcome me. With those wordes she shewed him her wounde on her thigh, and tolde him what she had done to prove her selfe. Brutus was amazed to heare what she sayd unto him, and lifting up his handes to heaven, he besought the goddes to geve him the grace he might bring his enterprise to so good passe, that he might be founde a husband, wor-thie of so noble a wife as Porcia: so he then did comfort her the best he coulde. Now a day being appointed for the meeting of the Senate, at what time they hoped Caesar woulde not faile to come: the conspirators determined then to put their enterprise in execucion, bicause they might meete safelie at that time without suspicion, and the rather, for that all the noblest and chiefest men of the citie woulde be there. Who when they should see suche a great matter executed, would everie man then set to their handes, for the defence of their libertie. Furthermore, they thought also that the appointment of the place where the counsell shoulde be kept, was chosen of purpose by divine providence, and made all for them. For it was one of the porches about the Theater, in the which there was a certaine place full of seates for men to sit in, where

also was set up the image of Pompey, which the citie had made and con-
secrated in honor of him: when he did beawtifie that parte of the citie
with the Theater he built, with divers porches about it. In this place was
the assembly of the Senate appointed to be, just on the fifteenth day of
the moneth of March, which the Romanes call, Idus Martias: so that it
seemed some god of purpose had brought Caesar thither to be slaine,
for revenge of Pompeys death. So when the day was come, Brutus went
out of his house with a dagger by his side under his long gowne, that no
bodie sawe nor knewe, but his wife onelie. The other conspirators were
all assembled at Cassius house, to bring his sonne into the market place,
who on that day did put on the mans gowne, called Toga Virilis: and
from thence they came all in a troupe together unto Pompeys porche,
looking that Caesar woulde straight come thither. But here is to be
noted, the wonderfull assured constancie of these conspirators, in so
daungerous and waightie an enterprise as they had undertaken. For
many of them being Praetors, by reason of their office, whose duetie is
to minister justice to everie bodie: they did not onelie with great quiet-
nesse and curtesie heare them that spake unto them, or that pleaded
matters before them, and gave them attentive eare, as if they had had
no other matter in their heades: but moreover, they gave just sentence,
and carefullie dispatched the causes before them. So there was one
among them, who being condemned in a certaine summe of money,
refused to pay it, and cried out that he did appeale unto Caesar. Then
Brutus casting his eyes uppon the conspirators, sayd, Caesar shall not
lette me to see the lawe executed. Notwithstanding this, by chaunce
there fell out many misfortunes unto them, which was enough to have
marred the enterprise. The first and chiefest was, Caesars long tarying,
who came verie late to the Senate: for bicause the signes of the sacrifices
appeared unluckie, his wife Calpurnia kept him at home, and the
Soothsayers bad him beware he went not abroade. The seconde cause
was, when one came unto Casca being a conspirator, and taking him by
the hande, sayd unto him: O Casca, thou keptest it close from me, but
Brutus hath tolde me all. Casca being amazed at it, the other went on
with his tale, and sayd: why, howe nowe, howe commeth it to passe thou
art thus riche, that thou doest sue to be Aedilis? Thus Casca being
deceived by the others doubtfull wordes, he tolde them it was a
thowsand to one, he blabbed not out all the conspiracie. An other

Senator called Popilius Laena, after he had saluted Brutus and Cassius more frendlie then he was wont to doe: he rounded softlie in their eares, and told them, I pray the goddes you may goe through with that you have taken in hande, but withall, dispatche I reade you, for your enterprise is bewrayed. When he had sayd, he presentlie departed from them, and left them both affrayed that their conspiracie woulde out. Nowe in the meane time, there came one of Brutus men post hast unto him, and tolde him his wife was a dying. For Porcia being verie carefull and pensive for that which was to come, and being too weake to away with so great and inward griefe of minde: she coulde hardlie keepe within, but was frighted with everie litle noyse and crie she hearde, as those that are taken and possest with the furie of the Bacchantes, asking every man that came from the market place, what Brutus did, and still sent messenger after messenger, to knowe what newes. At length, Caesars comming being prolonged as you have heard, Porciaes weakenesse was not able to holde out any lenger, and thereuppon she sodainlie swounded, that she had no leasure to goe to her chamber, but was taken in the middest of her house, where her speache and sences failed her. Howbeit she soone came to her selfe againe, and so was layed in her bedde, and tended by her women. When Brutus heard these newes, it grieved him, as it is to be presupposed: yet he left not of the care of his contrie and common wealth, neither went home to his house for any newes he heard. Nowe, it was reported that Caesar was comming in his litter: for he determined not to stay in the Senate all that day (bicause he was affrayed of the unluckie signes of the sacrifices) but to adjorne matters of importaunce unto the next session, and counsell holden, faining him selfe not to be well at ease. When Caesar came out of his litter: Popilius Laena, that had talked before with Brutus and Cassius, and had prayed the goddes they might bring this enterprise to passe: went unto Caesar, and kept him a long time with a talke. Caesar gave good eare unto him. Wherefore the conspirators (if so they shoulde be called) not hearing what he sayd to Caesar, but conjecturing by that he had tolde them a litle before, that his talke was none other but the verie discoverie of their conspiracie: they were affrayed everie man of them, and one looking in an others face, it was easie to see that they all were of a minde, that it was no tarying for them till they were apprehended, but rather that they should kill them selves with their owne handes. And when Cassius and certeine other clapped their handes on their swordes under their gownes to draw them: Brutus marking the countenaunce and gesture of Laena, and considering that he did use him selfe rather like an humble and earnest suter, then like an accuser: he sayd nothing to his companion (bicause there were many amongst them that were not of the conspiracie) but with a pleasaunt countenaunce encouraged Cassius. And immediatlie after, Laena went from Caesar, and kissed his hande: which shewed plainlie that it was for some matter concerning him selfe, that he had held him so long in talke. Nowe all the Senators being entred first into this place or chapter house where the counsell should be kept: all the other conspirators straight stoode about Caesars chaire, as if they had had some thing to have sayd unto him. And some say, that Cassius casting his eyes upon Pompeys image, made his prayer unto it, as if it had bene alive. Trebonius on thother side, drewe Antonius atoside, as he came into the house where the Senate sate, and helde him with a long talke without. When Caesar was come into the house, all the Senate rose to honor him at his comming in. So when he was set, the conspirators flocked about him, & amongst them they presented one Tullius Cimber, who made humble sute for the calling home againe of his brother that was banished. They all made as though they were intercessors for him, and tooke him by the handes, and kissed his head and brest. Caesar at the first, simplie refused their kindnesse and intreaties: but afterwardes, perceiving they still pressed on him, he violently thrust them from him. Then Cimber with both his hands plucked Caesars gowne over his shoulders, and Casca that stoode behinde him, drew his dagger first, and strake Caesar upon the shoulder, but gave him no great wound. Caesar feeling him selfe hurt, tooke him straight by the hande he held his dagger in, and cried out in Latin: O traitor, Casca, what doest thou? Casca on thother side cried in Graeke, and called his brother to helpe him. So divers running on a heape together to flie uppon Caesar, he looking about him to have fledde, sawe Brutus with a sworde drawen in his hande readie to strike at him: then he let Cascaes hande goe, and casting his gowne over his face, suffered everie man to strike at him that woulde. Then the conspirators thronging one upon an other bicause everie man was desirous to have a cut at him, so many swords and daggers lighting upon one bodie, one of them hurte an other, and among them Brutus caught a blowe on his hande, bicause he would make one

in murdering of him, and all the rest also were every man of them bloud-
ied. Caesar being slaine in this maner, Brutus standing in the middest
of the house, would have spoken, and stayed the other Senators that
were not of the conspiracie, to have tolde them the reason why they had
done this facte. But they as men both affrayd and amazed, fled one upon
anothers necke in haste to get out at the dore, and no man followed
them. For it was set downe, and agreed betwene them, that they should
kill no man but Caesar onely, and should intreate all the rest to looke to
defend their libertie. All the conspirators, but Brutus, determining
upon this matter, thought it good also to kill Antonius, bicause he was
a wicked man, and that in nature favored tyranny: besides also, for that
he was in great estimation with souldiers, having bene conversant of
long time amongest them: and specially, having a mind bent to great
enterprises, he was also of great authoritie at that time, being Consul
with Caesar. But Brutus would not agree to it. First, for that he sayd it
was not honest: secondly, bicause he told them there was hope of
chaunge in him. For he did not mistrust, but that Antonius being a
noble minded and coragious man (when he should knowe that Caesar
was dead) would willingly helpe his contry to recover her libertie, having them an example unto him, to follow their corage and vertue. So
Brutus by this meanes saved Antonius life, who at that present time disguised him selfe, and stale away. But Brutus & his consorts, having their
swords bloudy in their handes, went straight to the Capitoll, perswading the Romanes as they went, to take their libertie againe. Now, at the
first time when the murther was newly done, there were sodaine out-
cryes of people that ranne up & downe the citie, the which in deede did
the more increase the feare and tumult. But when they saw they slue no
man, neither did spoyle or make havock of any thing: then certaine of
the Senators, & many of the people imboldening them selves, went to
the Capitoll unto them. There a great number of men being assembled
together one after another: Brutus made an oration unto them to winne
the favor of the people, and to justifie that they had done. All those that
were by, sayd they had done well, and cryed unto them that they should
boldly come downe from the Capitoll. Whereuppon, Brutus and his
companions came boldly downe into the market place. The rest followed in trowpe, but Brutus went formost, very honorably compassed
in round about with the noblest men of the citie, which brought him

from the Capitoll, thorough the market place, to the pulpit for orations. When the people saw him in the pulpit, although they were a multitude of rakehells of all sortes, and had a good will to make some sturre: yet being ashamed to doe it for the reverence they bare unto Brutus, they kept silence, to heare what he would say. When Brutus began to speake, they gave him quiet audience: howbeit immediately after, they shewed that they were not all contented with the murther. For when another called Cinna would have spoken, and began to accuse Caesar: they fell into a great uprore among them, and marvelously reviled him. Insomuch that the conspirators returned againe into the Capitol. There Brutus being affrayd to be beseeged, sent back againe the noble men that came thither with him, thinking it no reason, that they which were no partakers of the murther, should be partakers of the daunger. Then the next morning the Senate being assembled, and holden within the temple of the goddesse Tellus, to wete the earth: and Antonius, Plancus, and Cicero, having made a motion to the Senate in that assembly, that they should take an order to pardon and forget all that was past, and to stablishe friendship and peace againe: it was decreed, that they should not onely be pardoned, but also that the Consuls should referre it to the Senate what honors should be appoynted unto them. This being agreed upon, the Senate brake up, and Antonius the Consul, to put them in hart that were in the Capitoll, sent them his sonne for a pledge. Upon this assurance, Brutus and his companions came downe from the Capitoll, where every man saluted and imbraced eche other, among the which, Antonius him selfe did bid Cassius to supper to him: and Lepidus also bad Brutus, and so one bad another, as they had friend-ship and acquaintance together. The next day following, the Senate being called againe to counsell, did first of all commend Antonius, for that he had wisely stayed and quenched the beginning of a civill warre: then they also gave Brutus and his consorts great prayses, and lastly they appoynted them severall governments of provinces. For unto Brutus, they appoynted Creta: Africk, unto Cassius: Asia, unto Trebonius: Bithynia, unto Cimber: and unto the other Decius Brutus Albinus, Gaule on this side the Alpes. When this was done, they came to talke of Caesars will and testament, and of his funeralls and tombe. Then Antonius thinking good his testament should be red openly, and also that his body should be honorably buried, and not in hugger mugger, least the people might thereby take occasion to be worse offended if they did otherwise: Cassius stowtly spake against it. But Brutus went with the motion, & agreed unto it: wherein it seemeth he committed a second fault. For the first fault he did was, when he would not consent to his fellow conspirators, that Antonius should be slayne: and therefore he was justly accused, that thereby he had saved and strengthened a stronge & grievous enemy of their conspiracy. The second fault was, when he agreed that Caesars funeralls should be as Antonius would have them: the which in deede marred all. For first of all, when Caesars testament was openly red amonge them, whereby it appeared that he bequeathed unto every Citizen of Rome, 75. Drachmas a man, and that he left his gardens and arbors unto the people, which he had on this side of the river of Tyber, in the place where now the temple of Fortune is built: the people then loved him, and were marvelous sory for him. Afterwards when Caesars body was brought into the market place, Antonius making his funerall oration in praise of the dead, according to the auncient custom of Rome, and perceiving that his wordes moved the common people to compassion: he framed his eloquence to make their harts yerne the more, and taking Caesars gowne all bloudy in his hand, he layed it open to the sight of them all, shewing what a number of cuts and holes it had upon it. Therewithall the people fell presently into such a rage and mutinie, that there was no more order kept amongest the common people. For some of them cryed out, kill the murtherers: others plucked up formes, tables, and stalles about the market place, as they had done before at the funeralls of Clodius, and having layed them all on a heape together, they set them on fire, and thereuppon did put the bodye of Caesar, and burnt it in the middest of the most holy places. And furthermore, when the fire was thoroughly kindled, some here, some there, tooke burning fire brands, and ranne with them to the murtherers houses that had killed him, to set them a fire. Howbeit the conspirators foreseeing the daunger before, had wisely provided for them selves, and fled. But there was a Poet called Cinna, who had bene no partaker of the conspiracy, but was alway one of Caesars chiefest friends: he dreamed the night before, that Caesar bad him to supper with him, and that he refusing to goe, Caesar was very importunate with him, and compelled him, so that at length he led him by the hand into a great darke place, where being marvelously affrayd, he was driven to follow him in spite of his hart. This dreame put him all night into a fever, and yet notwithstanding, the next morning when he heard that they caried Caesars body to buriall, being ashamed not to accompany his funerals: he went out of his house, and thrust him self into the prease of the common people that were in a great uprore. And bicause some one called him by his name, Cinna: the people thinking he had bene that Cinna, who in an oration he made had spoken very evill of Caesar, they falling upon him in their rage, slue him outright in the market place. This made Brutus and his companions more affrayd, then any other thing, next unto the chaunge of Antonius. Wherefore they got them out of Rome, and kept at the first in the citie of Antium, hoping to returne againe to Rome, when the furie of the people were a litle asswaged. The which they hoped would be quickly, considering that they had to deale with a fickle and unconstant multitude, easye to be caried, and that the Senate stoode for them: who notwithstanding made no enquiery of them that had torne poore Cinna the Poet in peeces, but caused them to be sought for and apprehended, that went with fire brands to set fire of the conspirators houses. The people growing weary now of Antonius pride and insolency, who ruled all things in manner with absolute power: they desired that Brutus might returne againe, and it was also looked for, that Brutus would come him selfe in person to playe the playes which were due to the people, by reason of his office of Praetorship. But Brutus understanding that many of Caesars souldiers which served under him in the warres, and that also had lands and houses given them in the cities where they lay, did lye in wayte for him to kill him, and that they dayly by small companies came by one and by one into Rome: he durst no more returne thither, but yet the people had the pleasure and pastyme in his absence, to see the games and sportes he made them, which were sumptuouslie set foorth and furnished with all thinges necessarie, sparing for no cost. For he had bought a great number of straunge beastes, of the which he would not geve one of them to any frende he had, but that they shoulde all be employed in his games: and went him selfe as farre as Byzantium, to speake to some players of comedies and musitions that were there. And further he wrote unto his friends for one Canutius an excellent player, that whatsoever they did, they should intreate him to play in these playes: For, sayd he, it is no reason to compell any Graecian, unles he will come of his owne good will. Moreover, he wrote also unto Cicero, and earnestly prayed him in any case to be at these playes. Now the state of Rome standing in these termes, there fell out an other chaunge and alteracion, when the younge man Octavius Caesar came to Rome. He was the sonne of Julius Caesars Nece, whome he had adopted for his sonne, and made his heire, by his last will and testament. But when Julius Caesar his adopted father was slayne, he was in the citie of Apollonia, where he studied tarying for him, bicause he was determined to make warre with the Parthians: but when he heard the newes of his death, he returned againe to Rome, where to begin to curry favor with the common people, he first of all tooke upon him his adopted fathers name, & made distribution amonge them of the money which his father had bequeathed unto them. By this meanes he troubled Antonius sorely, and by force of money, got a great number of his fathers souldiers together, that had served in the warres with him. And Cicero him selfe, for the great malice he bare Antonius, did favor his proceedings. But Brutus marvelously reproved him for it. ... Now, the citie of Rome being devided in two factions, some taking part with Antonius, other also leaning unto Octavius Caesar, and the souldiers making portsale of their service to him that would give most: Brutus seeing the state of Rome would be utterly overthrowen, he determined to goe out of Italy, and went a foote through the contry of Luke, unto the citie of Elea, standing by the sea. There Porcia being ready to depart from her husband Brutus, and to returne to Rome, did what she could to dissemble the griefe and sorow she felt at her hart: but a certaine paynted table bewrayed her in the ende, although untill that time she alwayes shewed a constant and pacient mind. The devise of the table was taken out of the Greeke stories, howe Andromachè accompanied her husband Hector, when he went out of the citie of Troy to goe to the warres, and how Hector delivered her his litle sonne, and how her eyes were never of him. Porcia seeing this picture, and likening her selfe to be in the same case, she fell a weeping: and comming thither oftentymes in a day to see it, she wept still. Acilius one of Brutus friendes perceiving that, rehearsed the verses Andromachè speaketh to this purpose in Homer:

> Thou Hector art my father, and my mother, and my brother,
> And husband eke, and [all] in all: I mind not any other.

Then Brutus smyling, aunswered againe: but yet (sayd he) I can not for my part say unto Porcia, as Hector aunswered Andromachè in the same place of the Poet:

> Tush, meddle thou with weying dewly owt
> Thy mayds their task, and pricking on a clowt. [*Iliad*, vi]

For in deede, the weake constitution of her body, doth not suffer her to performe in shew, the valliant acts that we are able to doe: but for corage and constant minde, she shewed her selfe as stowt in the defence of her contry, as any of us. Bibulus, the sonne of Porcia, reporteth this story thus ... (pp. 93–107)

... So Brutus preparing to goe into Asia, newes came unto him of the great chaunge at Rome. For Octavius Caesar was in armes, by commaundement and authoritie from the Senate, against Marcus Antonius. But after that he had driven Antonius out of Italy, the Senate then began to be affrayd of him: bicause he sued to be Consul, which was contrary to the law, and kept a great army about him, when the Empire of Rome had no neede of them. On the other side, Octavius Caesar perceiving the Senate stayed not there, but turned unto Brutus that was out of Italy, and that they appoynted him the government of certaine provinces: then he began to be affrayd for his part, and sent unto Antonius to offer him his friendship. Then comming on with his armye neare to Rome, he made him selfe to be chosen Consul, whether the Senate would or not, when he was yet but a strippling or springal of twenty yeare old, as him selfe reporteth in his own commentaries. So when he was Consul, he presently appoynted Judges to accuse Brutus and his companions, for killing of the noblest person in Rome, and chiefest Magistrate, without law or judgement: and made L. Cornificius accuse Brutus, and M. Agrippa, Cassius. So, the parties accused were condemned, bicause the Judges were compelled to give such sentence. The voyce went, that when the Herauld (according to the custom after sentence given) went up to the chaier or pulpit for orations, & proclaymed Brutus with a lowd voyce, summoning him to appeare in person before the Judges: the people that stoode by sighed openly, and the noble men that were present honge downe their heads, & durst not speake a word. Among them, the teares fell from Publius Silicius eyes: who shortly after, was one of the proscripts or outlawes appoynted to be slayne. After that, these three Octavius Caesar, Antonius, and Lepidus, made an agreement betwene them selves, and by those articles devided the provinces belonging to the Empire of Rome amonge them selves, and did set up billes of proscription and outlary, condemning two hundred of the noblest men of Rome to suffer death, and among that number, Cicero was one... (p. 108)

... Now Cassius would have done Brutus as much honor, as Brutus did unto him: but Brutus most commonly prevented him, and went first unto him, both bicause he was the elder man, as also for that he was sickly of bodye. And men reputed him commonly to be very skilfull in warres, but otherwise marvelous chollerick and cruell, who sought to rule men by feare, rather then with lenitie: and on the other side he was too familiar with his friends, and would jest too brodely with them. But Brutus in contrary manner, for his vertue and valliantnes, was well-beloved of the people and his owne, esteemed of noble men, and hated of no man, not so much as of his enemies: bicause he was a marvelous lowly and gentle person, noble minded, and would never be in any rage, nor caried away with pleasure and covetousnes, but had ever an upright mind with him, and would never yeeld to any wronge or injustice, the which was the chiefest cause of his fame, of his rising, and of the good will that every man bare him: for they were all perswaded that his intent was good. For they did not certainly beleve, that if Pompey him selfe had overcome Caesar, he would have resigned his authoritie to the law: but rather they were of opinion, that he would still keepe the soverainty and absolute government in his hands, taking onely, to please the people, the title of Consul or Dictator, or of some other more civill office. And as for Cassius, a hot, chollerick, & cruell man, that would often-tymes be caried away from justice for gayne: it was certainly thought that he made warre, and put him selfe into sundry daungers, more to have absolute power and authoritie, then to defend the libertie of his contry... (pp. 109–10)

... Now whilest Brutus and Cassius were together in the citie of Smyrna: Brutus prayed Cassius to let him have some part of his money whereof he had great store, bicause all that he could rappe and rend of his side, he had bestowed it in making so great a number of shippes, that by meanes of them they should keepe all the sea at their commaundement. Cassius friendes hindered this request, and earnestly disswaded him from it: perswading him, that it was no reason that Brutus should have the money which Cassius had gotten together by sparing, and leavied with great evill will of the people their subjects, for him to bestowe liberally uppon his souldiers, and by this meanes to winne their good willes, by Cassius charge. This notwithstanding, Cassius gave him the thirde parte of his totall summe... (p. 111)

... About that tyme, Brutus sent to praye Cassius to come to the citye of Sardis, and so he did. Brutus, understanding of his comming, went to meete him with all his friendes. There, both their armies being armed, they called them both Emperors. Nowe, as it commonly hapneth in great affayres betwene two persons, both of them having many friends, and so many Captaines under them: there ranne tales and complaints betwixt them. Therefore, before they fell in hand with any other matter, they went into a litle chamber together, and bad every man avoyde, and did shut the dores to them. Then they beganne to powre out their complaints one to the other, and grew hot and lowde, earnestly accusing one another, and at length fell both a weeping. Their friends that were without the chamber hearing them lowd within, and angry betwene them selves, they were both amased, and affrayd also lest it would grow to further matter: but yet they were commaunded, that no man should come to them. Notwithstanding, one Marcus Phaonius, that had bene a friend and follower of Cato while he lived, & tooke upon him to counterfeate a Philosopher, not with wisedom and discretion, but with a certaine bedlem and frantick motion: he would needes come into the chamber, though the men offered to keepe him out. But it was no boote to let Phaonius, when a mad moode or toye tooke him in the head: for he was a hot hasty man, & sodaine in all his doings, and cared for never a Senator of them all. Now, though he used this bold manner of speeche after the profession of the Cynick Philosophers, (as who would say, doggs) yet this boldnes did no hurt many times, bicause they did but laugh at him to see him so mad. This Phaonius at that time, in despite of the doorekeepers, came into the chamber, and with a certaine scoffing & mocking gesture which he counterfeated of purpose, he rehearsed the verses which old Nestor sayd in Homer:

> My Lords, I pray you harken both to mee,
> For I have seene moe yeares than suchye three.

Cassius fel a laughing at him: but Brutus thrust him out of the chamber, & called him dogge, and counterfeate Cynick. Howbeit his comming in brake their strife at that time, and so they left eche other. The selfe same night Cassius prepared his supper in his chamber, and Brutus brought his friendes with him. So when they were set at supper, Phaonius came to sit downe after he had washed. Brutus tolde him alowd, no man sent for him, and bad them set him at the upper end: meaning in deede at the lower ende of the bed. Phaonius made no ceremonie, but thrust in amongest the middest of them, and made all the companye laugh at him: so they were merry all supper tyme, and full of their Philosophie. The next daye after, Brutus, upon complaynt of the Sardians, did condemne and noted Lucius Pella for a defamed person, that had bene a Praetor of the Romanes, and whome Brutus had given charge unto: for that he was accused and convicted of robberie, and pilferie in his office. This judgement much misliked Cassius: bicause he him selfe had secretly (not many dayes before) warned two of his friends, attainted and convicted of the like offences, and openly had cleered them: but yet he did not therefore leave to employ them in any manner of service as he did before. And therefore he greatly reproved Brutus, for that he would shew him selfe so straight and seveare in such a tyme, as was meeter to beare a litle, then to take thinges at the worst. Brutus in contrary manner aunswered, that he shoulde remember the Ides of Marche, at which tyme they slue Julius Caesar: who nether pilled nor polled the contrye, but onely was a favorer and suborner of all them that did robbe and spoyle, by his countenaunce and authoritie. And if there were any occasion whereby they might honestly sette aside justice and equitie: they should have had more reason to have suffered Caesars friendes, to have robbed and done what wronge and injurie they had would, then to beare with their owne men. For then sayde he, they could but have sayde they had bene cowards: and nowe they may accuse us of injustice, beside the paynes we take, and the daunger we put our selves into. And thus may we see what Brutus intent and purpose was. But as they both prepared to passe over againe, out of Asia into Europe: there went a rumor that there appeared a wonderfull signe unto him. Brutus was a carefull man, and slept very litle, both for that his dyet was moderate, as also bicause he was continually occupied. He never slept in the day tyme, and in the night no lenger, then the tyme he was driven to be alone, and when every bodye els tooke their rest. But nowe whilest he was in warre, and his heade ever busily occupied to thinke of his affayres, and what would happen: after he had slumbered a litle after supper, he spent all the rest of the night in dispatching of his waightiest causes, and after he had taken order for them, if he had any leysure left him, he would read some booke till the third watche of the night, at what tyme the Captaines, pety Captaines and Colonells, did use to come unto him. So, being ready to goe into Europe, one night very late (when all the campe tooke quiet rest) as he was in his tent with a litle light, thinking of waighty matters: he thought he heard one come in to him, and casting his eye towards the doore of his tent, that he saw a wonderfull straunge and monstruous shape of a body comming towards him, and sayd never a word. So Brutus boldly asked what he was, a god, or a man, and what cause brought him thither. The spirit aunswered him, I am thy evill spirit, Brutus: and thou shalt see me by the citie of Philippes. Brutus beeing no otherwise affrayd, replyed againe unto it: well, then I shall see thee agayne. The spirit presently vanished away: and Brutus called his men unto him, who tolde him that they heard no noyse, nor sawe any thinge at all. Thereuppon Brutus returned agayne to thinke on his matters as he did before: and when the daye brake, he went unto Cassius, to tell him what vision had appeared unto him in the night. Cassius beeing in opinion an Epicurian, and reasoning thereon with Brutus, spake to him touching the vision thus. In our secte, Brutus, we have an opinion, that we doe not alwayes feele, or see, that which we suppose we doe both see and feele: but that our senses beeing credulous, and therefore easily abused (when they are idle and unoccupied in their owne objects) are induced to imagine they see and conjecture that, which they in truth doe not. For, our minde is quicke and cunning to worke (without eyther cause or matter) any thinge in the imagination whatsoever. And therefore the imagination is resembled to claye, and the minde to the potter: who without any other cause than his fancie and pleasure, chaungeth it into what facion and forme he will. And this doth the diversitie of our dreames shewe unto us. For our imagination doth uppon a small fancie growe from conceit to conceit, altering both in passions and formes of thinges imagined. For the minde of man is ever occupied, and that continuall moving is nothing but an imagination. But yet there is a further cause of this in you. For you being by nature given to melancholick discoursing, and of late continually occupied: your wittes and sences having bene overlabored, doe easilier yeelde to such imaginations. For, to say that there are spirits or angells, and if there were, that they had the shape of men, or such voyces, or any power at all to come unto us: it is a mockerye. And for myne owne parte, I would there were suche, bicause that we shoulde not onely have souldiers, horses, and shippes, but also the ayde of the goddes, to guide and further our honest and honorable attempts. With these words Cassius did somewhat comfort and quiet Brutus. When they raysed their campe, there came two Eagles that flying with a marvelous force, lighted uppon two of the foremoste enseignes, and alwayes followed the souldiers, which gave them meate, and fedde them, untill they came neare to the citie of Philippes: and there one daye onely before the battell, they bothe flewe awaye... (pp. 114–17)

... For, Octavius Caesar could not followe him bicause of his sicknes, and therefore stayed behind: whereuppon they had taken his army, had not Antonius ayde bene, which made such wonderful speede, that Brutus could scant beleve it. So Caesar came not thether of ten daies after: & Antonius camped against Cassius, and Brutus on thother side against Caesar. The Romanes called the valley betweene both campes, the Philippian fields: and there were never seene two so great armies of the Romanes, one before the other, ready to fight. In truth, Brutus army was inferior to Octavius Caesars, in number of men: but for bravery and rich furniture, Brutus army farre excelled Caesars. For the most part of their armors were silver and gilt, which Brutus had bountifully given them: although in all other things he taught his Captaines to live in order without excesse. But for the bravery of armor, & weapon, which souldiers should cary in their hands, or otherwise weare upon their backes: he thought that it was an encoragement unto them that by nature are greedy of honor, & that it maketh them also fight like devills that love to get, and be affrayd to lose: bicause they fight to keepe their armor and weapon, as also their goods and lands. Now when they came to muster their armies, Octavius Caesar tooke the muster of his army within the trenches of his campe, & gave his men onely a litle corne, and five silver Drachmas to every man to sacrifice to the gods, & to pray for victory. But Brutus skorning this miserie and niggardlines, first of all mustered his armie, and did purifie it in the fields, according to the manner of the Romanes: and then he gave unto every band a number of weathers to sacrifice, and fiftie silver Drachmas to every souldier. So that Brutus and Cassius souldiers were better pleased, and more coragiously bent to fight at the daye of the battell, then their enemies souldiers were. Notwithstanding, being busily occupied about the ceremonies of this purification, it is reported that there chaunced certaine unlucky signes unto Cassius. For one of his Sergeaunts that caried the roddes before him, brought him the garland of flowers turned backwards, the which he should have worne on his head in the tyme of sacrificing. Moreover it is reported also, that at another tyme before, in certaine sportes and triumphe where they caried an image of Cassius victorie of cleane gold, it fell by chaunce, the man stumbling that caried it. And yet further, there were seene a marvelous number of fowles of praye, that feede upon dead carkasses: and beehives also were founde, where bees were gathered together in a certaine place within the trenches of the campe: the which place the Soothsayers thought good to shut out of the precinct of the campe, for to take away the superstitious feare and mistrust men would have of it. The which beganne somewhat to alter Cassius minde from Epicurus opinions, and had put the souldiers also in a marvelous feare. Thereuppon Cassius was of opinion not to trye this warre at one battell, but rather to delay tyme, and to drawe it out in length, considering that they were the stronger in money, and the weaker in men and armors. But Brutus in contrary manner, did alway before, and at that tyme also, desire nothing more, then to put all to the hazard of battell, assoone as might be possible: to the ende he might either quickely restore his contry to her former libertie, or rid him forthwith of this miserable world, being still troubled in following and mainteyning of such great armies together. But perceiving that in the dayly skirmishes and byckerings they made, his hem were alway the stronger, and ever had the better: that yet quickned his spirits againe, and did put him in better hart. And furthermore, bicause that some of their owne men had already yelded them selves to their enemies, and that it was suspected moreover divers others would doe the like: that made many of Cassius friendes, which were of his minde before, (when it came to be debated in counsell whether the battell shoulde be fought or not) that they were then of Brutus minde. But yet was there one of Brutus friendes called Atellius, that was against it, and was of opinion that they should tary the next winter. Brutus asked him what he should get by tarying a yeare lenger? If I get nought els, quoth Attellius agayne, yet have I lived so much lenger. Cassius was very angry with this aunswer: and Atellius was maliced and esteemed the worse for it of all men. Thereuppon it was presently determined they should fight battell the next daye. So Brutus all supper tyme looked with a cheerefull countenaunce, like a man that had good hope, and talked very wisely of Philosophie, and after supper went to bed. But touching Cassius, Messala reporteth that he supped by him selfe in his tent with a fewe of his friendes, and that all supper tyme he looked very sadly, and was full of thoughts, although it was against his nature: and that after supper he tooke him by the hande, and holding him fast (in token of kindnes as his manner was) tolde him in Greeke: Messala, I protest unto thee, and make thee my witnes, that I am compelled against my minde and will (as Pompey the great was) to jeopard the libertie of our contry, to the hazard of a battel. And yet we must be lively, and of good corage, considering our good fortune, whome we shoulde wronge too muche to mistrust her, although we followe evill counsell. Messala writeth, that Cassius having spoken these last wordes unto him, he bad him farewell, and willed him to come to supper to him the next night following, bicause it was his birth day. The next morning by breake of day, the signall of battell was set out in Brutus and Cassius campe, which was an arming scarlet coate: and both the Chiefetaines spake together in the middest of their armies. There Cassius beganne to speake first, and sayd: the gods graunt us, O Brutus, that this day we may winne the field, and ever after to live all the rest of our life quietly, one with another. But sith the gods have so ordeyned it, that the greatest & chiefest things amongest men are most uncertaine, and that if the battell fall out otherwise to daye then we wishe or looke for, we shall hardely meete againe: what art thou then determined to doe, to flye, or dye? Brutus aunswered him, being yet but a young man, and not overgreatly experienced in the world: I trust, (I know not how) a certaine rule of Philosophie, by the which I did greatly blame and reprove Cato for killing of him selfe, as being no lawfull nor godly acte, touching the gods, not concerning men, valliant, not to give place and yeld to divine providence, and not constantly and paciently to take whatsoever it pleaseth him to send us, but to drawe backe, and flie: but being nowe in the middest of the daunger,

I am of a contrary mind. For if it be not the will of God, that this battell fall out fortunate for us: I will looke no more for hope, neither seeke to make any new supply for warre againe, but will rid me of this miserable world, and content me with my fortune. For, I gave up my life for my contry in the Ides of Marche, for the which I shall live in another more glorious worlde. Cassius fell a laughing to heare what he sayde, and imbracing him, come on then sayde he, let us goe and charge our enemies with this mynde. For eyther we shall conquer, or we shall not neede to feare the Conquerors. After this talke, they fell to consultacion amonge their friendes for the ordering of the battell. Then Brutus prayed Cassius he might have the leading of the right winge, the which men thought was farre meeter for Cassius: both bicause he was the elder man, and also for that he had the better experience. But yet Cassius gave it him, and willed that Messala (who had charge of one of the warrelikest legions they had) shoulde be also in that winge with Brutus. So Brutus presently sent out his horsemen, who were excellently well appoynted, and his footemen also were as willing and readye to give charge. Nowe Antonius men did cast a trenche from the marishe by the which they laye, to cutte of Cassius way to come to the sea: and Caesar, at the least his armye, styrred not. As for Octavius Caesar him selfe, he was not in his campe, bicause he was sicke. And for his people, they litle thought the enemies would have given them battell, but onely have made some light skirmishes to hinder them that wrought in the trenche, and with their darts and slings to have kept them from finishing of their worke: but they taking no heede to them that came full upon them to give them battell, marvelled much at the great noyse they heard, that came from the place where they were casting their trenche. In the meane tyme Brutus that led the right winge, sent litle billes to the Colonells and Captaines of private bandes, in the which he wrote the worde of the battell: and he him selfe riding a horse backe by all the trowpes, did speake to them, and incoraged them to sticke to it like men. So by this meanes very fewe of them understoode what was the worde of the battell, and besides, the moste parte of them never taryed to have it tolde them, but ranne with greate furie to assayle the enemies: whereby through this disorder, the legions were marvelously scattered and dispersed one from the other. For first of all, Messalaes legion, and then the next unto them, went beyond the left winge of the enemies, and did nothing, but glawnsing by them, overthrewe some as they went, and so going on further, fell right upon Caesars campe, out of the which (as him selfe writeth in his commentaries) he had bene conveyed away a litle before, thorough the counsell and advise of one of his friendes called Marcus Artorius: Who dreaming in the night, had a vision appeared unto him, that commaunded Octavius Caesar should be caried out of his campe. Insomuch as it was thought he was slayne, bicause his lytter (which had nothing in it) was thrust through & through with pykes and darts. There was great slaughter in this campe. For amongest others, there were slayne two thowsand Lacedaemonians, who were arrived but even a litle before, comming to ayde Caesar. The other also that had not glaunsed by, but had given a charge full upon Caesars battell: they easily made them flie, bicause they were greatly troubled for the losse of their campe, and of them there were slayne by hand, three legions. Then being very earnest to followe the chase of them that fled, they ranne in amongest them hand over head into their campe, & Brutus among them. But that which the conquerors thought not of, occasion shewed it unto them that were overcome: & that was, the left wing of their enemies left naked, & ungarded of them of the right wing, who were strayed too far of, in following of them that were overthrowen. So they gave a hot charge upon them. But notwithstanding all the force they made, they coulde not breake into the middest of their battell, where they founde men that received them, and valliantlie made head against them. Howbeit they brake and overthrewe the left wing where Cassius was, by reason of the great disorder among them, and also bicause they had no intelligence how the right wing had sped. So they chased them beating them into their campe, the which they spoyled, none of both the Chieftaines being present there. For Antonius, as it is reported, to flie the furie of the first charge, was gotten into the next marish: and no man coulde tell what became of Octavius Caesar, after he was caried out of his campe. Insomuche that there were certaine souldiers that shewed their swords bloodied, & sayd that they had slaine him, and did describe his face, and shewed what age he was of. Furthermore the voward, and the middest of Brutus battell, had alreadie put all their enemies to flight that withstoode them, with great slaughter: so that Brutus had conquered all of his side, and Cassius had lost all on the other side. For nothing undid them, but that Brutus went not to helpe Cassius, thinking he had overcome them, as him selfe had done: and Cassius on the other side taried not for Brutus, thinking he had bene overthrowen, as him selfe was. And to prove that the victorie fell on Brutus side, Messala confirmeth it: that they wanne three Eagles, and divers other ensignes of their enemies, and their enemies wanne never a one of theirs. Now Brutus returning from the chase, after he had slaine and sacked Caesars men: he wondred muche that he coulde not see Cassius tent standing up high as it was wont, neither the other tentes of his campe standing as they were before, bicause all the whole campe had bene spoiled, and the tentes throwen downe, at the first comming in of the enemies. But they that were about Brutus, whose sight served them better, tolde him that they sawe a great glistering of harnes, and a number of silvered targets, that went & came into Cassius campe, and were not (as they tooke it) the armors, nor the number of men that they had left there to gard the campe: and yet that they saw not such a number of dead bodies, and great overthrow, as there should have bene, if so many legions had bene slaine. This made Brutus at the first mistrust that which had hapned. So he appointed a number of men to keepe the campe of his enemie which he had taken, and caused his men to be sent for that yet followed the chase, and gathered them together, thinking to leade them to aide Cassius, who was in this state as you shall heare. First of all he was marvelous angrie, to see how Brutus men ranne to geve charge upon their enemies, and taried not for the word of the battell, nor commaundement to geve charge: and it grieved him beside, that after he had overcome them, his men fell straight to spoyle, and were not carefull to compasse in the rest of the enemies behinde. But with tarying too long also, more then through the valliantnesse or foresight of the Captaines his enemies: Cassius founde him selfe compassed in with the right wing of his enemies armie. Whereuppon his horsemen brake immediatly, and fled for life towardes the sea. Furthermore, perceiving his footemen to geve ground, he did what he could to kepe them from flying, and tooke an ensigne from one of the ensigne bearers that fled, and stucke it fast at his feete: although with much a do he could scant keepe his owne gard together. So Cassius him selfe was at length compelled to flie, with a few about him, unto a litle hill, from whence they might easely see what was done in all the plaine: howebeit Cassius him selfe sawe nothing, for his sight was verie bad, saving that he saw (and yet with much a doe) how the enemies spoiled his campe before his eyes. He sawe also a great troupe of horsemen, whom Brutus sent to aide him, and thought that they were his enemies that followed him: but yet he sent Titinnius, one of them that was with him, to goe and know what they were. Brutus horsemen sawe him comming a farre of, whom when they knewe that he was one of Cassius chiefest frendes, they showted out for joy: and they that were familiarly acquainted with him, lighted from their horses, and went and imbraced him. The rest compassed him in rounde about a horsebacke, with songs of victorie and great rushing of their harnes, so that they made all the field ring againe for joy. But this marred all. For Cassius thinking in deede that Titinnius was taken of the enemies, he then spake these wordes: desiring too much to live, I have lived to see one of my best frendes taken, for my sake, before my face. After that, he gotte into a tent where no bodie was, and tooke Pyndarus with him, one of his freed bondmen, whom he reserved ever for suche a pinche, since the cursed battell of the Parthians, where Crassus was slaine, though he notwithstanding scaped from that overthrow: but then casting his cloke over his head, & holding out his bare neck unto Pindarus, he gave him his head to be striken of. So the head was found severed from the bodie: but after that time Pindarus was never seene more. Wherupon, some tooke occasion to say, that he had slaine his master without his commaundement. By & by they knew the horsemen that came towards them, & might see Titinnius crowned with a garland of triumphe, who came before with great speede unto Cassius. But when he perceived by the cries and teares of his frends which tormented them selves, the misfortune that had chaunced to his Captaine Cassius, by mistaking: he drew out his sword, cursing him selfe a thowsand times that he had taried so long, and so slue him selfe presentlie in the fielde. Brutus in the meane time came forward still, and understoode also that Cassius had bene overthrowen: but he knew nothing of his death, till he came verie neere to his campe. So when he was come thither, after he had lamented the death of Cassius, calling him the last of all the Romanes, being unpossible that Rome should ever breede againe so noble & valliant a man as he: he caused his bodie to be buried, and sent it to the citie of Thassos, fearing least his funerals within the campe should cause great disorder. Then he called his souldiers together, & did encorage them againe. And when he saw that they had lost all their cariage, which they could not brooke well: he promised everie man of them two thowsand Drachmas in recompence. After his souldiers had heard his Oration, they were al of them pretily cheered againe, wondering much at his great liberalitie, and waited upon him with great cries when he went his way, praising him, for that he only of the foure Chieftaines, was not overcome in battell. And to speake the trueth, his deedes shewed that he hoped not in vaine to be conqueror. For with fewe legions, he had slaine and driven all them away, that made head against him: and yet if all his people had fought, and that the most of them had not outgone their enemies to runne to spoyle their goods: surely it was like enough he had slaine them all, and had left never a man of them alive. There were slaine of Brutus side, about eight thowsand men, counting the souldiers slaves, whom Brutus called Brigas: and of the enemies side, as Messala wryteth, there were slaine as he supposeth, more then twise as many moe... (pp. 117–24)

... For the day before the last battell was geven, verie late in the night, came Clodius, one of his enemies into his campe, who told that Caesar hearing of the overthrow of his armie by sea, desired nothing more then to fight a battell before Brutus understoode it. Howebeit they gave no credit to his words, but despised him so muche, that they would not vouchsafe to bring him unto Brutus, bicause they thought it was but a lye devised, to be the better welcome for this good newes. The selfe same night, it is reported that the monstruous spirit which had appeared before unto Brutus in the citie of Sardis, did now appeare againe unto him in the selfe same shape and forme, and so vanished away, and sayd never a word... (p. 127)

... Then sodainly, one of the chiefest Knightes he had in all his armie called Camulatius, and that was alway marvelously esteemed of for his valliantnes, untill that time: he came hard by Brutus a horsebacke, and roade before his face to yeeld him selfe unto his enemies. Brutus was marvelous sorie for it, wherefore partely for anger, and partely for feare of greater treason and rebellion, he sodainly caused his armie to marche, being past three of the clocke in the after noone. So in that place where he him selfe fought in person, he had the better: and brake into the left wing of his enemies, which gave him way, through the helpe of his horsemen that gave charge with his footemen, when they saw the enemies in a maze, and affrayed. Howbeit the other also on the right wing, when the Captaines would have had them to have marched: they were affraid to have bene compassed in behinde, bicause they were fewer in number then their enemies, and therefore did spred them selves, and leave the middest of their battell. Wherby they having weakened them selves, they could not withstande the force of their enemies, but turned taile straight, and fled. And those that had put them to flight, came in straight upon it to compasse Brutus behinde, who in the middest of the conflict, did all that was possible for a skilfull Captaine and valliant souldier: both for his wisedom, as also for his hardinesse, for the obtaining of victorie. But that which wanne him the victorie at the first battell, did now lose it him at the seconde. For at the first time, the enemies that were broken and fled, were straight cut in peeces: but at the seconde battell, of Cassius men that were put to flight, there were fewe slaine: and they that saved them selves by speede, being affrayed bicause they had bene overcome, did discourage the rest of the armie when they came to joyne with them, & filled all the army with feare & disorder. There was the sonne of M. Cato slaine, valliantly fighting amongst the lustie youths. For, notwithstanding that he was verie wearie, and over-harried, yet would he not therefore flie, but manfully fighting and laying about him, telling alowde his name, and also his fathers name, at length he was beaten downe amongest many other dead bodies of his enemies, which he had slaine rounde about him. So there were slaine in the field, all the chiefest gentlemen and nobilitie that were in his armie: who valliantlie ranne into any daunger, to save Brutus life. Amongest them there was one of Brutus frendes called Lucilius, who seeing a troupe of barbarous men making no reckoning of all men else they met in their way, but going all together right against Brutus, he determined to stay them with the hazard of his life, and being left behinde, told them that he was Brutus: and bicause they should beleve him, he prayed them to bring him to Antonius, for he sayd he was affrayed of Caesar, and that he did trust Antonius better. These barbarous men being very glad of this good happe, and thinking them selves happie men: they caried him in the night, and sent some before unto Antonius, to tell him of their comming. He was marvelous glad of it, and went out to meete them that brought him. Others also understanding of it, that they had brought Brutus prisoner: they came out of all parts of the campe to see him, some pitying his hard fortune, & others saying, that it was not done like him selfe so cowardlie to be taken alive of the barbarous people, for feare of death. When they came neere together, Antonius stayed a while, bethinking him selfe how he should use Brutus. In the meane time Lucilius was brought to him, who stowtly with a bold countenaunce sayd. Antonius, I dare assure thee, that no enemie hath taken, nor shall take Marcus Brutus alive: and I beseech God keepe him from that fortune. For wheresoever he be found, alive or dead: he will be found like him selfe. And nowe for my selfe, I am come unto thee, having deceived these men of armes here, bearing them downe that I was Brutus: and doe not refuse to suffer any torment thou wilt put me to. Lucilius wordes made them all amazed that heard him. Antonius on the other side, looking upon all them that had brought him, sayd unto them: my companions, I thinke ye are sorie you have failed of your purpose, & that you thinke this man hath done you great wrong: but I doe assure you, you have taken a better bootie, then that you followed. For, in steade of an enemie, you have brought me a frend: and for my parte, if you had brought me Brutus alive, truely I can not tell what I should have done to him. For, I had rather have suche men my frendes, as this man here, then enemies. Then he embraced Lucilius, and at that time delivered him to one of his frendes in custodie, and Lucilius ever after served him faithfullie, even to his death. Nowe Brutus having passed a litle river, walled in on either side with hie rockes, and shadowed with great trees, being then darke night, he went no further, but stayed at the foote of a rocke with certaine of his Captaines and frends that followed him: and looking up to the firmament that was full of starres, sighing, he rehearsed two verses, of the which Volumnius wrote the one, to this effect:

> Let not the wight from whom this mischiefe went
> (O Iove!) escape without dew punishment.

And sayth that he had forgotten the other. Within a litle while after, naming his frendes that he had seene slaine in battell before his eyes, he fetched a greater sigh then before: specially, when he came to name Labio, and Flavius, of the which the one was his Lieutenant, and the other, Captaine of the pioners of his campe. In the meane time, one of the companie being a thirst, and seeing Brutus a thirst also: he ranne to the river for water, and brought it in his sallet. At the selfe same time they heard a noyse on the other side of the river. Whereupon Volumnius tooke Dardanus, Brutus servaunt with him, to see what it was: and returning straight againe, asked if there were any water left. Brutus smiling, gentlie tolde them all was dronke, but they shall bring you some more. Thereuppon he sent him againe that went for water before, who was in great daunger of being taken by the enemies, and hardly scaped, being sore hurt. Furthermore, Brutus thought that there was no great number of men slaine in battell, and to know the trueth of it, there was one called Statilius, that promised to goe through his enemies (for otherwise it was impossible to goe see their campe) and from thence if all were well, that he woulde lift up a torche light in the ayer, and then returne againe with speede to him. The torche light was lift up as he had promised, for Statilius went thither. Nowe Brutus seeing Statilius tarie long after that, and that he came not againe, he sayd: if Statilius be alive, he will come againe. But his evill fortune was suche, that as he came backe, he lighted in his enemies hands, and was slaine. Now, the night being farre spent, Brutus as he sate bowed towards Clitus one of his men, and told him somewhat in his eare, the other aunswered him not, but fell a weeping. Thereupon he proved Dardanus, and sayd somewhat also to him: at length he came to Volumnius him selfe, & speaking to him in Graeke, prayed him for the studies sake which brought them acquainted together, that he woulde helpe him to put his hande to his sword, to thrust it in him to kill him. Volumnius denied his request, and so did many others: and amongest the rest, one of them sayd, there was no tarying for them there, but that they must needes flie. Then Brutus rising up, we must flie in deede sayd he, but it must be with our hands, not with our feete. Then taking every man by the hand, he sayd these words unto them with a cheerefull countenance. It rejoyceth my hart that not one of my frends hath failed me at my neede, and I do not complaine of my fortune, but only for my contries sake: for, as for me, I thinke my selfe happier than they that have overcome, considering that I leave a perpetuall fame of our corage and manhoode, the which our enemies the conquerors shall never attaine unto by force nor money, neither can let their posteritie to say, that they being naughtie and unjust men, have slaine good men, to usurpe tyrannical power not pertaining to them. Having sayd so, he prayed everie man to shift for them selves, and then he went a litle aside with two or three only, among the which Strato was one, with whom he came first acquainted by the studie of Rethoricke. He came as neere to him as he coulde, and taking his sword by the hilts with both his hands, & falling downe upon the poynt of it, ran him selfe through. Others say, that not he, but Strato (at his request) held the sword in his hand, & turned his head aside, and that Brutus fell downe upon it: and so ranne him selfe through, and dyed presently. Messala, that had bene Brutus great frend, became afterwards Octavius Caesars frend. So, shortly after, Caesar being at good leasure, he brought Strato, Brutus frende unto him, and weeping sayd: Caesar, beholde, here is he that did the last service to my Brutus. Caesar welcomed him at that time, and afterwards he did him as faithfull service in all his affaires, as any Graecian els he had about him, untill the battell of Actium. It is reported also, that this Messala him selfe aunswered Caesar one day, when he gave him great praise before his face, that he had fought valliantlie, and with great affection for him, at the battell of Actium: (notwithstanding that he had bene his cruell enemy before, at the battell of Philippes, for Brutus sake) I ever loved, sayd he, to take the best and justest parte. Now, Antonius having found Brutus bodie, he caused it to be wrapped up in one of the richest cote armors he had. Afterwards also, Antonius understanding that this cotearmor was stollen, he put the theefe to death that had stollen it, & sent the ashes of his bodie unto Servilia his mother. And for Porcia, Brutus wife: Nicolaus the Philosopher, and Valerius Maximus doe wryte, that she determining to kill her selfe (her parents and frendes carefullie looking to her to kepe her from it) tooke hotte burning coles, and cast them into her mouth, and kept her mouth so close, that she choked her selfe. There was a letter of Brutus found wrytten to his frendes, complayning of their negligence, that his wife being sicke, they would not helpe her, but suffred her to kill her selfe, choosing to dye, rather then to languish in paine. Thus it appeareth, that Nicolaus knewe not well that time, sith the letter (at the least if it were Brutus letter) doth plainly declare the disease and love of this Lady, and also the maner of her death.

THE COMPARISON OF DION WITH BRUTUS

To come nowe to compare these two noble personages together, it is certaine that both of them having had great gifts in them (& specially Dion) of small occasions they made them selves great men: & therfore Dion of both deserveth chiefest praise. For, he had no cohelper to bring him unto that greatnesse, as Brutus had of Cassius: who doubtlesse was not comparable unto Brutus, for vertue and respect of honor, though otherwise in matters of warre, he was no lesse wise and valliant then he. For many doe impute unto Cassius, the first beginning and originall of all the warre and enterprise: and sayd it was he that did encourage Brutus, to conspire Caesars death. Where Dion furnished him selfe with armor, shippes and souldiers and wanne those frendes and companions also that did helpe him, to prosecute his warre. Nor he did not as Brutus, who rose to greatnesse by his enterprises, and by warre got all his strength and riches. But he in contrarie maner, spent of his owne goods to make warre for the libertie of his contrie and disbursed of his owne money, that should have kept him in his banishment. Furthermore, Brutus and Cassius were compelled of necessity to make warres, bicause they coulde not have lived safelie in peace, when they were driven out of Rome: for that they were condemned to death, and pursued by their enemies. And for this cause therefore they were driven to hazard them selves in warre, more for their owne safetie, then for the libertie of their contrie men. Whereas Dion on the other side, living more merily and safelie in his banishment, then the tyranne Dionysius him selfe that had banished him: did put him selfe to that daunger, to deliver Sicile from bondage. Nowe the matter was not a like unto the Romanes, to be delivered from the government of Caesar: as it was for the Syracusans, to be ridde of Dionysius tyrannie. For Dionysius denyed not, that he was not a tyranne, having filled Sicile with suche miserie and calamitie. Howebeit Caesars power and government when it came to be established, did in deede much hurt at his first entrie and beginning unto those that did resist him: but afterwardes, unto them that being overcome had received his government, it seemed he rather had the name and opinion onely of a tyranne, then otherwise that he was so in deede. For there never followed any tyrannicall nor cruell act, but contrarilie, it seemed that he was a mercifull Phisition, whom God had ordeyned of speciall grace to be Governor of the Empire of Rome, and to set all thinges againe at quiet stay, the which required the counsell and authoritie of an absolute Prince. And therefore the Romanes were marvelous sorie for Caesar after he was slaine, and afterwardes would never pardon them that had slaine him. On the other side, the cause why the Syracusans did most accuse Dion, was: bicause he did let Dionysius escape out of the castell of Syracusa, and bicause he did not overthrow and deface the tombe of his father. Furthermore, towching the warres: Dion alway shewed him selfe a Captaine unreprovable, having wiselie and skilfullie taken order for those things, which he had enterprised of his owne head and counsell: and did amende the faults others committed, and brought things to better state then he found them. Where it seemeth, that Brutus did not wisely to receive the second battell: considering his rest stoode upon it. For, after he had lost the battell, it was unpossible for him ever to rise againe: & therefore his hart failed him, and so gave up all, and never durst strive with his evill fortune as Pompey did, considering that he had present cause enough in the field to hope of his souldiers, and being beside a dreadfull Lorde of all the sea over. Furthermore, the greatest reproache they could object against Brutus, was: that Julius Caesar having saved his life, and pardoned all the prisoners also taken in battell, as many as he had made request for, taking him for his frende, and honoring him above all his other frends: Brutus notwithstanding had imbrued his hands in his blood, wherewith they could never reprove Dion. For on the contrarie side, so long as Dion was Dionysius frende and kinseman, he did alway helpe him to order and governe his affaires. But after he was banished his contrie, and that his wife was forciblie maried to an other man, and his goodes also taken from him: then he entred into just and open warres against Dionysius the tyranne. But in this poynt, they were contrarie together. For wherein their chiefest praise consisted, to witte, in hating of tyrannes and wicked men: it is most true that Brutus desire was most sincere of both. For having no private cause of complaint or grudge against Caesar, he ventred to kill him, onely to set his contrie againe at libertie. Where if Dion had not received private cause of quarrell against Dionysius: he woulde never have made warre with him. The which Plato proveth in his Epistells, where is plainlie seene: that Dion being driven out of the tyrans Court against his will, and not putting him selfe to voluntarie banishment, he drave out Dionysius. Furthermore, the respect of the common wealth caused Brutus, that before was Pompeys enemie, to become his frende, and enemie unto Caesar, that before was his frend: only referring his frendshippe and enmitie, unto the consideracion of justice and equitie. And Dion did many things for Dionysius sake and benefit, all the while he trusted him: and when he beganne to mistrust him, then for anger he made warre with him. Wherefore all his frendes did not beleve, but after he had driven out Dionysius, he would stablish the government to him selfe, flattering the people with a more curteous and gentle title then the name of a tyranne. But for Brutus, his verie enemies them selves confessed, that of all those that conspired Caesars death, he only had no other ende and intent to attempt his enterprise, but to restore the Empire of Rome againe, to her former state & government. And furthermore, it was not all one thing to deale with Dionysius, as it was to have to doe with Julius Caesar. For no man that knew Dionysius, but would have despised him, considering that he spent the most parte of his time in drinking, dycing, and in haunting lewde womens company. But to have undertaken to destroy Julius Caesar, and not to have shroncke backe for feare of his great wisedom, power, and fortune, considering that his name only was dreadfull unto everie man, and also not to suffer the kings of Parthia and India to be in rest for him: this could not come but of a marvelous noble minde of him, that for feare never fainted, nor let fall any part of his corage. And therfore, so sone as Dion came into Sicilia, many thowsands of men came and joyned with him, against Dionysius. But the fame of Julius Caesar did set up his frends againe after his death, and was of suche force, that it raised a young stripling, Octavius Caesar, (that had no meanes nor power of him selfe) to be one of the greatest men of Rome: and they used him as a remedie to encounter Antonius malice and power. And if men will say, that Dion drave out the tyran Dionysius with force of armes, and sundrie battells: and that in contrarie maner Brutus slue Caesar, being a naked man, and without gard: then doe I aunswere againe, that it was a noble parte, and of a wise Captaine, to choose so apt a time and place, to come uppon a man of so great power, and to finde him naked without his gard. For he went not sodainlie in a rage, and alone, or with a small companie, to assaile him: but his enterprise was long time before determined of, and that with divers men, of all the which, not a man of them once fayled him: but it is rather to be thought, that from the beginning he chose them honest men, or else that by his choyse of them, he made them good men. Whereas Dion, either from the beginning made no wise choyse in trusting of evill men, or else bicause he could not tell how to use them he had chosen: of good men he made them become evill, so that neither the one nor the other coulde be the parte of a wise man. For Plato him selfe reproveth him, for that he had chosen suche men for his frendes, that he was slaine by them, and after he was slaine, no man woulde then revenge his death. And in contrarie maner, of the enemies of Brutus, the one (who was Antonius) gave his bodie honorable buriall: and Octavius Caesar the other, reserved his honors and memories of him. For at Millayne, (a citie of Gaule on Italie side) there was an image of his in brasse, verie like unto him: the which Caesar afterwardes passing that way, behelde verie advisedly, for that it was made by an excellent workeman, and was verie like him, and so went his way. Then he stayed sodainly againe, and called for the Governors of the citie, and before them all tolde them, that the citizens were his enemies, and traitors unto him, bicause they kept an enemie of his among them. The Governors of the citie at the first were astonied at it, and stowtlie denyed it: and none of them knowing what enemie he ment, one of them looked on an other. Octavius Caesar then turning him unto Brutus statue, bending his browes, sayd unto them: this man you see standing up here, is he not our enemie? Then the Governors of the citie were worse affrayed then before, & could not tel what answere to make him. But Caesar laughing, and commending the Gaules for their faithfulnes to their frendes, even in their adversities: he was contented Brutus image should stand still as it did. (Pp. 128–35)

THE LIFE OF MARCUS ANTONIUS

... For it is reported that Caesar aunswered one that did accuse Antonius and Dolabella unto him for some matter of conspiracie: tushe said he, they be not those fat fellowes and fine comed men that I feare, but I mistrust rather these pale and leane men, meaning by Brutus and Cassius, who afterwards conspired his death, and slue him. Antonius unwares afterwards, gave Caesars enemies just occasion and culler to doe as they did: as you shall heare. The Romanes by chaunce celebrated the feast called Lupercalia, & Caesar being apparelled in his triumphing robe, was set in the Tribune where they use to make their orations to the people, and from thence did behold the sport of the runners. The manner of this running was this. On that day there are many young men of noble house, and those specially that be chiefe Officers for that yeare: who running naked up & downe the citie annointed with the oyle of olyve, for pleasure do strike them they meete in their way, with white leather thongs they have in their hands. Antonius being one amonge the rest that was to ronne, leaving the auncient ceremonies & old customes of that solemnitie: he ranne to the Tribune where Caesar was set, and caried a laurell crowne in his hand, having a royall band or diademe wreathed about it, which in old time was the auncient marke and token of a king. When he was come to Caesar, he made his fellow ronners with him lift him up, & so he did put this laurell crowne upon his head, signifying thereby that he had deserved to be king. But Caesar making as though he refused it, turned away his heade. The people were so rejoyced at it, that they all clapped their hands for joy. Antonius againe did put it on his head: Caesar againe refused it, and thus they were striving of and on a great while together. As oft as Antonius did put this laurell crowne unto him, a fewe of his followers rejoyced at it: & as oft also as Caesar refused it, all the people together clapped their hands. And this was a wonderfull thing, that they suffered all things subjects should doe by commaundement of their kings: & yet they could not abide the name of a king, detesting it as the utter destruction of their liberty. Caesar in a rage rose out of his seate, and plucking downe the choller of his gowne from his necke, he shewed it naked, bidding any man strike of his head that would. This laurel crowne was afterwards put upon the head of one of Caesars statues or images, the which one of the Tribunes pluckt of. The people liked his doing therein so well, that they wayted on him home to his house, with great clapping of hands. Howbeit Caesar did turne them out of their offices for it. This was a good incoragement for Brutus & Cassius to conspire his death, who fel into a consort with their trustiest friends, to execute their enterprise: but yet stood doubtful whether they should make Antonius privy to it or not. Al the rest liked of it, saving Trebonius only. He told them, that when they rode to meete Caesar at his returne out of Spayne, Antonius & he alwaies keping company, & lying together by the way, he felt his mind a farre of: but Antonius finding his meaning, would harken no more unto it, & yet notwithstanding never made Caesar acquainted with this talke, but had faithfully kept it to him self. After that they consulted whether they should kil Antonius with Caesar. But Brutus would in no wise consent to it, saying: that ventring on such an enterprise as that, for the maintenance of law & justice, it ought to be clere from all villanie. Yet they fearing Antonius power, & the authoritie of his office, appointed certain of the conspiracy, that when Caesar were gone into the Senate, and while others should execute their enterprise, they should keepe Antonius in a talke out of the Senate house. Even as they had devised these matters, so were they executed: and Caesar was slaine in the middest of the Senate. Antonius being put in a feare withall, cast a slaves gowne upon him, and hid him selfe. But afterwards when it was told him that the murtherers slue no man els, and that they went onely into the Capitoll: he sent his sonne unto them for a pledge, & bad them boldly come downe upon his word. The selfe same day he did bid Cassius to supper, and Lepidus also bad Brutus. The next morning the Senate was assembled, & Antonius him selfe preferred a lawe that all things past should be forgotten, and that they should appoint provinces, unto Cassius and Brutus: the which the Senate confirmed, and further ordeyned, that they should cancell none of Caesars lawes. Thus went Antonius out of the Senate more praysed, and better esteemed, than ever man was: bicause it seemed to every man that he had cut of all occasion of civill warres, and that he had shewed him selfe a marvelous wise governor of the common wealth, for the appeasing of these matters of so great waight & importance. But nowe, the opinion he conceived of him selfe after he had a litle felt the good will of the people towards him, hoping thereby to make him selfe the chiefest man if he might overcome Brutus: did easily make him alter his first mind. And therefore when Caesars body was brought to the place where it should be buried, he made a funeral oration in commendacion of Caesar, according to the auncient custom of praising noble men at their funerals. When he saw that the people were very glad and desirous also to heare Caesar spoken of, & his praises uttered: he mingled his oration with lamentable wordes, and by amplifying of matters did greatly move their harts and affections unto pitie & compassion. In fine to conclude his oration, he unfolded before the whole assembly the bloudy garments of the dead, thrust through in many places with their swords, & called the malefactors, cruell & cursed murtherers. With these words he put the people into such a fury, that they presently toke Caesars body, & burnt it in the market place, with such tables & fourmes as they could get together. Then when the fire was kindled, they toke firebrands, & ran to the murtherers houses to set them afire, & to make them come out to fight. Brutus therfore & his accomplices, for safety of their persons were driven to fly the city. Then came all Caesars friends unto Antonius, & specially his wife Calpurnia putting her trust in him, she brought the moste part of her money into his house, which amounted to the summe of foure thowsand talents, & furthermore brought him al Caesars bokes & writings, in the which were his memorials of all that he had done & ordeyned. Antonius did daily mingle with them such as he thought good, and by that meanes he created newe officers, made newe Senators, called home some that were banished, and delivered those that were prisoners: and then he sayde that all those thinges were so appoynted and ordeyned by Caesar. Therefore the Romanes mocking them that were so moved, they called them Charonites: bicause that when they were overcome, they had no other helpe but to saye, that thus they were found in Caesars memorials, who had sayled in Charons boate, and was departed. Thus Antonius ruled absolutely also in all other matters, bicause he was Consul, and Caius one of his brethren Praetor, and Lucius the other, Tribune. Now thinges remayning in this state at Rome, Octavius Caesar the younger, came to Rome, who was the sonne of Julius Caesars Nece, as you have heard before, and was left his lawefull heire by will, remayning at the tyme of the death of his great Uncle that was slayne, in the citie of Apollonia. This young man at his first arrivall went to salute Antonius, as one of his late dead father Caesars friendes, who by his last will and testament had made him his heire: and withall, he was presently in hande with him for money and other thinges which were left of trust in his handes, bicause Caesar had by will bequeathed unto the people of Rome, three score and fifteene silver Drachmas to be given to every man, the which he as heire stoode charged withall. Antonius at the first made no reckoning of him, bicause he was very younge: and sayde he lacked witte, and good friendes to advise him, if he looked to take such a charge in hande, as to undertake to be Caesars heire. But when Antonius saw that he could not shake him of with those wordes, and that he was still in hande with him for his fathers goods, but specially for the ready money: then he spake and did what he could against him... (pp. 263–6)

... When he was come into their campe, and that he had all the army at his commaundement: he used Lepidus very curteously, imbraced him, and called him father: and though in deede Antonius did all, and ruled the whole army, yet he alway gave Lepidus the name and honor of the Captaine... (p. 268)

... So Octavius Caesar would not leane to Cicero, when he saw that his whole travail and endevor was onely to restore the common wealth to her former libertie. Therefore he sent certaine of his friends to Antonius, to make them friends againe: and thereuppon all three met together, (to wete, Caesar, Antonius, & Lepidus) in an Iland envyroned round about with a litle river, & there remayned three dayes together. Now as touching all other matters, they were easily agreed, & did devide all the Empire of Rome betwene them, as if it had bene their owne inheritance. But yet they could hardly agree whom they would put to death: for every one of them would kill their enemies, and save their kinsmen and friends. Yet at length, giving place to their gredy desire to be revenged of their enemies, they spurned all reverence of bloud, and holines of friendship at their feete. For Caesar left Cicero to Antonius will, Antonius also forsooke Lucius Caesar, who was his Uncle by his mother: and both of them together suffred Lepidus to kill his owne brother Paulus. (P. 268)

ABBREVIATIONS AND REFERENCES

Unless otherwise stated, the place of publication is London.

ABBREVIATIONS

ABBREVIATIONS USED IN NOTES

*	precedes commentary notes involving readings that are not found in either Q or F
ed., eds	editor, editors
edn	edition
opp.	opposite
SD	stage direction
SP	speech prefix
subst.	substantially
this edn	a reading adopted for the first time in this edition
t.n.	textual notes at the foot of the page
vol.,vols	volume, volumes

SHAKESPEARE'S WORKS AND WORKS PARTLY BY SHAKESPEARE

AC	*Antony and Cleopatra*
AW	*All's Well that Ends Well*
AYL	*As You Like It*
CE	*The Comedy of Errors*
Cor	*Coriolanus*
Cym	*Cymbeline*
Ham	*Hamlet*
1H4	*King Henry IV Part 1*
2H4	*King Henry IV Part 2*
H5	*King Henry V*
1H6	*King Henry VI Part 1*
2H6	*King Henry VI Part 2*
3H6	*King Henry VI Part 3*
H8	*King Henry VIII*
JC	*Julius Caesar*
KJ	*King John*

KL	*King Lear*
LLL	*Love's Labour's Lost*
Luc	*The Rape of Lucrece*
MA	*Much Ado about Nothing*
Mac	*Macbeth*
MM	*Measure for Measure*
MND	*A Midsummer Night's Dream*
MV	*The Merchant of Venice*
MW	*The Merry Wives of Windsor*
Oth	*Othello*
Per	*Pericles*
PP	*The Passionate Pilgrim*
R2	*King Richard II*
R3	*King Richard III*
RJ	*Romeo and Juliet*
Son	*Shakespeare's Sonnets*
STM	*Sir Thomas More*
TC	*Troilus and Cressida*
Tem	*The Tempest*
TGV	*The Two Gentlemen of Verona*
Tim	*Timon of Athens*
Tit	*Titus Andronicus*
TN	*Twelfth Night*
TNK	*The Two Noble Kinsmen*
TS	*The Taming of the Shrew*
VA	*Venus and Adonis*
WT	*The Winter's Tale*

REFERENCES

EDITIONS OF SHAKESPEARE COLLATED

Alexander	*William Shakespeare: The Complete Works*, ed. Peter Alexander (1951)
Ard[1]	*Julius Caesar*, ed. Michael Macmillan (1902)
Ard[2]	*Julius Caesar*, ed. T.S. Dorsch, The Arden Shakespeare (1955)
Bell's	*Julius Caesar* in *Bell's Acting Edition*, 8 vols (1774)
Cam	*Works*, ed. W.G. Clark and W.A. Wright, 9 vols (Cambridge, 1863-6)
Cam[1]	*Julius Caesar*, ed. J. Dover Wilson (Cambridge, 1949)
Cam[2]	*Julius Caesar*, ed. Marvin Spevack (Cambridge, 1988)
Capell	*Comedies, Histories and Tragedies*, ed. Edward Capell, 10 vols (1767–8)

Collier	*Works*, ed. John Payne Collier, 8 vols (1842–4)
Dyce	*Works*, ed. Alexander Dyce, 6 vols (1857)
F or F1	*Comedies, Histories and Tragedies*, The First Folio (1623)
F2	*Comedies, Histories and Tragedies*, The Second Folio (1632)
F3	*Comedies, Histories and Tragedies*, The Third Folio (1664)
Globe	*Works*, ed. W.G. Clark and W.A. Wright (1864)
Hanmer	*Works*, ed. Sir Thomas Hanmer, 6 vols (Oxford, 1743–4)
Hudson	*Works*, ed. H.N. Hudson, 11 vols (Boston, 1851–6)
Hudson[2]	*Works*, ed. H.N. Hudson, 11 vols (Boston, 1880–1)
Jennens	*Julius Caesar*, ed. Charles Jennens (1774)
Johnson	*Plays*, ed. Samuel Johnson, 8 vols (1765)
Kittredge	*Complete Works*, ed. G.L. Kittredge (Boston, 1936)
Malone	*Plays and Poems*, ed. Edmond Malone, 10 vols (1790)
Mason	J.M. Mason, *Comments on the Last Edition of Shakespeare's Plays*, (1785)
Oxf	*William Shakespeare: The Complete Works*, ed. Stanley Wells, Gary Taylor, John Jowett and William Montgomery (Oxford, 1986)
Oxf[1]	*Julius Caesar*, ed. Arthur Humphreys (Oxford, 1984)
Pope	*Works*, ed. Alexander Pope, 6 vols (1723–5)
Pope[2]	*Works*, ed. Alexander Pope, 10 vols (1728)
Q 1691	*Julius Caesar*, quarto
Q1, Q3, Q5	Undated quartos of *Julius Caesar*, late seventeenth and early eighteenth centuries
Riv	*The Riverside Shakespeare*, textual ed. G. Blakemore Evans (Boston, 1974)
Rowe	*Works*, ed. Nicholas Rowe, 6 vols (1709)
Rowe[2]	*Works*, ed. Nicholas Rowe, 9 vols (1714)
Sanders	*Julius Caesar*, ed. Norman Sanders (Harmondsworth, 1967)
Singer	*Dramatic Works*, ed. S.W. Singer (1826)
Steevens	*Plays*, ed. Samuel Johnson and George Steevens, 10 vols (1773)
Steevens[2]	*Plays*, ed. Samuel Johnson and George Steevens, 10 vols (1778)
Theobald	*Works*, ed. Lewis Theobald, 7 vols (1733)
Var	*Julius Caesar*, A New Variorum Edition, ed. H.H. Furness Jr (Philadelphia, 1913)
Verity	*Julius Caesar*, ed. A.W. Verity (Cambridge, 1895)
Walker	W.S. Walker, *A Critical Examination of the Text of Shakespeare*, ed. W.N. Lettsom, 3 vols (1860)
Warburton	*Works*, ed. William Warburton, 8 vols (1747)
White	*Works*, ed. Richard Grant White, 12 vols (1857–66)
Wright	*Julius Caesar*, ed. W.A. Wright (Oxford, 1878)

OTHER WORKS

Abbott	E.A. Abbott, *A Shakespearian Grammar* (1886)
Amyot	Plutarch, trans. Amyot, *Vies des hommes illustres ...* (Paris, 1559)
Antonius	Plutarch, trans. North, 'The Life of Marcus Antonius', in Bullough, vol. 5 (1964), 254–321; and Appendix above
Appian	*Appian's Roman History*, trans. Horace White, 4 vols Loeb Classical Library (1912)
Appian, *History*	Appian of Alexandria, *An Auncient History*, trans. H. Binniman (1578)
Baldwin, *Structure*	T.W. Baldwin, *William Shakespere's Five-Act Structure* (Urbana, Ill., 1947)
Baldwin, *School*	T.W. Baldwin, *William Shakespere's Petty School* (Urbana, Ill., 1943)
Barroll	J. Leeds Barroll, 'Shakespeare and Roman history', *MLR*, 53 (1958), 327–43
Bate, *JC*	Jonathan Bate, 'The cobbler's awl: *Julius Caesar*, 1.i.21-24', *SQ*, 35 (1984), 461–2
Bate, *Tit*	Jonathan Bate, ed., *Titus Andronicus*, Arden 3 (1995)
Beauman	Sally Beauman, *The Royal Shakespeare Company: A History of Ten Decades* (Oxford, 1982)
Beaumont & Fletcher	Beaumont and Fletcher, *The Maid's Tragedy* (1610)
Beerbohm	Max Beerbohm, 'Savonarola' Brown, in *Seven Men* (1919)
Belsey	Catherine Belsey, *The Subject of Tragedy* (1985)
Berry, *Directing*	Ralph Berry, *On Directing Shakespeare* (1977)
Berry, *Anecdotes*	Ralph Berry, *The Methuen Book of Anecdotes* (1992)
Bingham	Madeleine Bingham, ' "The great lover"; The life and art of Beerbohm Tree', *Athenaeum* XX (1979), 86–100
Boecker	A. Boecker, *A Probable Italian Source of Shakespeare's Julius Caesar* (New York, 1913)
Bonjour	Adrien Bonjour, *The Structure of Julius Caesar* (1958)
BCP	*Book of Common Prayer* (1590)
Booth	Michael R. Booth, 'The Meininger Company and English Shakespeare', *SS*, 35 (1982), 13-20
Bowers	Fredson Bowers, 'The copy for Shakespeare's *Julius Caesar*', *South Atlantic Bulletin*, 43 (1978), 23–36
Bracciolini	Poggio Bracciolini, *De fortunae varietate*, in *Opera*, ed. H. Bebelius (1538)
Bradford	Ernle Bradford, *Julius Caesar: The Pursuit of Power* (1984)
Bradley	A.C. Bradley, *Shakespearean Tragedy* (1904)
Brandon	Samuel Brandon, *The Tragicomedy of the Virtuous Octavia*, ed. R.B. McKerrow: Malone Society (1909)

Brockbank	J.P. Brockbank, 'The frame of disorder: *Henry VI*' in *Early Shakespeare*, ed. John Russell Brown and Bernard Harris, *Stratford-upon-Avon Studies* 3 (1961), 73–99
Brooke	Nicholas Brooke, *Shakespeare's Early Tragedies* (1968)
Brutus	Plutarch, trans. North, 'The Life of Marcus Brutus', in Bullough, vol. 5, 90–135; and Appendix above
Bullough	Geoffrey Bullough, *Narrative and Dramatic Sources of Shakespeare*, 8 vols (1964–75)
Burckhardt	Sigurd Burckhardt, *Shakespearean Meanings* (Princeton, 1968)
Caesar	Julius Caesar, *Commentaries*, trans. as *The Conquest of Gaul*, S.A. Handford (Harmondsworth, 1951)
Caesar	Plutarch, trans. North, 'The Life of Julius Caesar', in Bullough, vol. 5, 58–89; and Appendix above
Cercignani	Fausto Cercignani, *Shakespeare's Works and Elizabethan Pronunciation* (Oxford, 1981)
Chambers, *Mediaeval*	E.K. Chambers, *The Mediaeval Stage*, 2 vols (Oxford, 1903)
Chambers, *Stage*	E.K. Chambers, *The Elizabethan Stage*, 4 vols (Oxford, 1923)
Chambers, *Shakespeare*	E.K. Chambers, *William Shakespeare: A Study of Facts and Problems*, 2 vols (Oxford, 1930)
Charlton	H.B. Charlton, *The Senecan Tradition in Renaissance Tragedy* (1921: Manchester, 1946)
Charney	Maurice Charney, *Shakespeare's Roman Plays: The Function of Imagery in the Drama* (Cambridge, Mass., 1961)
Chaucer	Geoffrey Chaucer, *Complete Works*, ed. F.N. Robinson (Oxford, 1933)
Cicero	Cicero, *Selected Letters*, trans. D.R. Shackleton Bailey (1986)
Cicero	Plutarch, trans. North, 'The Life of Marcus Tullius Cicero' in Bullough, vol. 5, 136–40
Coleridge	S.T. Coleridge, 'Notes on the Tragedies of Shakespeare ... *Julius Caesar*', in *Coleridge's Criticism of Shakespeare: a Selection*, edited by R. A. Foakes (1989)
Cook	Juliet Cook, *Shakespeare's Players* (1983)
Coverdale	Miles Coverdale, trans., *The Bible: that is, the holy Scripture ...* (1535)
Craik	G.L. Craik, *The English of Shakespeare* (1857)
Craik	T.W. Craik, ed., *King Henry V*, Arden 3 (1995)
Daniel, *Cleopatra*	Samuel Daniel, *The Tragedy of Cleopatra* (1595), in *The Complete Works*, ed. A.B. Grosart, 5 vols (1885–96)
Daniel, *Octavia*	Samuel Daniel, *A Letter from Octavia to Marcus Antonius* (1598), in *The Complete Works*, ed. A.B. Grosart, 5 vols (1885–96)

Daniel, *Musophilus*	Samuel Daniel, *Musophilus* (1599), in *The Complete Works*, ed. A.B. Grosart, 5 vols (1885–96)
Daniel, *Wars*	Samuel Daniel, *The First Four Books of the Civil Wars*, in *The Complete Works*, ed. A.B. Grosart, 5 vols (1885–96)
Dante	Dante Alighieri, *Inferno*, trans. H.F. Cary, Temple Classics (1919)
David	Richard David, *Shakespeare in the Theatre* (Cambridge, 1978)
Davies, *Microsmos*	John Davies, *Microcosmos*, in *The Works*, ed. A.B. Grosart, 2 vols (1875–8)
Davies, *Nosce*	Sir John Davies, *Nosce teipsum* (1599), in *The Works*, ed. H. Morley, 3 vols (1889)
Dekker	Thomas Dekker, *The Shoemaker's Holiday* (1660), ed. D.J. Palmer (1975)
Dent	R.W. Dent, *Shakespeare's Proverbial Language: An Index* (Berkeley, Cal., 1981)
Dodsley	Robert Dodsley, *Old English Plays*, ed. W.C. Hazlitt, 15 vols (1874–6)
Dolman	John Dolman, trans., *Those five questions which Mark Tully Cicero, disputed in his Manor of Tusculanum* (1561)
Donne	John Donne, *Pseudomartyr* (1610)
Doran	Madeline Doran, 'What should be in that "Caesar"?: proper names in *Julius Caesar*', in *Shakespeare's Dramatic Language* (Madison, 1976)
Dowden	Edward Dowden, *Shakespeare: A Critical Study of his Mind and Art* (1875)
Drakakis	John Drakakis, '"Fashion it Thus": *Julius Caesar* and the Politics of Theatrical Representation', *SS*, 44 (1992), 65–73
Dryden	John Dryden, *Poetry, Prose and Plays*, selected by Douglas Grant (1964); *An Essay of Dramatic Poesy* (1668), 373–435; *Aureng Zebe* (1676), 497–583
Eedes	Richard Eedes, *Caesar Interfectus*; Epilogue in Bullough, vol. 5, 194–5
EiC	*Essays in Criticism*
ELR	*English Literary Renaissance*
Elyot	Thomas Elyot, *The Book named the Governor* (1531), ed. S.E. Lehmberg (1962)
Evans	Bertrand Evans, *Shakespeare's Tragic Practice* (1979)
Farmer	Richard Farmer, *An Essay on the Learning of Shakespeare* (1767)
Fairfax	Edward Fairfax, *Godfrey of Bulloigne, or the Recovery of Jerusalem* (1600)
Foakes, 'Approach'	R.A. Foakes, 'An approach to *Julius Caesar*', *SQ*, 5 (1954), 260–70

Foakes, *KL* R.A. Foakes, *King Lear*, Arden 3 (1997)

Fowler W. Warde Fowler, *Roman Essays and Interpretations* (Oxford, 1920)

Foxe John Foxe, *Acts and Monuments* (1563), ed. J. Pratt, intr. J. Stoughton, 8 vols (1877)

FQ Edmund Spenser, *The Faerie Queene*, ed. J.C. Smith, 2 vols (Oxford, 1909)

Fuzier Jean Fuzier, 'Rhetoric versus Rhetoric: A Study of Shakespeare's *Julius Caesar*, Act III, Scene 2', *Cahiers Elizabéthans*, 5 (1981), 25–65

Garrick *The Letters of David Garrick*, ed. David M. Little, George M. Kahrl and Phoebe deK. Wilson, vol. 1 (Cambridge, Mass., 1963)

Garnier Robert Garnier, *Cornélie, Tragédie* (Paris, 1573)

Geneva 1560 *The Bible and Holy Scriptures contained in the Old and New Testament ...* (1560)

Geneva 1599 *The Bible, that is, The holy Scriptures contained in the Old and New Testament ...* (1599)

Gielgud, *Stage* John Gielgud, *Stage Directions* (1964)

Gielgud, *Shakespeare* John Gielgud, *Shakespeare, Hit or Miss* (1991)

Golding *The Fifteen Books of P. Ovidius Naso*, trans. Arthur Golding, ed. W.H.D. Rouse (1961)

Grant Michael Grant, *Myths of the Greeks and Romans* (1962)

Granville-Barker Harley Granville-Barker, *Prefaces to Shakespeare*, First Series (1927)

Greene Gayle Greene, ' "The power of speech / To stir men's blood": the language of tragedy in Shakespeare's *Julius Caesar*', *RenD*, II (1980), 67–93

Greg W.W. Greg, *The Shakespeare First Folio* (1955)

Grene Nicholas Grene, *Shakespeare's Tragic Imagination* (1996)

Greville, *Monarchy* Fulke Greville, *Of Monarchy*, ed. G.A. Wilkes (Oxford, 1965)

Greville, *Mustapha* Fulke Greville, *Mustapha* (1596), in *The Poems and Dramas of Fulke Greville*, ed. Geoffrey Bullough (1939)

Grévin Jacques Grévin, *Julius César*, ed. E.S. Ginsberg (Geneva, 1971)

Guntermann Paula Guntermann, 'Die Erstbelege im Wortschatz von Shakespeares *Hamlet*', *SJW* (1978/9), 58–72

Gurr Andrew Gurr, 'You and thou in Shakespeare's Sonnets', *EiC*, 32 (1982), 9–25

Harbage & Schoenbaum Alfred Harbage, rev. S. Schoenbaum, *Annals of English Drama, 975–1700* (1964)

Hart Alfred Hart, 'Vocabularies of Shakespeare's plays' and 'The growth of Shakespeare's vocabulary', *RES*, 19 (1943)

Hayward	John Hayward, *The First Part of the Life and Reign of Henry the Fourth*, ed. John Manning, Camden Society Fourth Series, vol. 42 (Offices of the Royal Historical Society, 1991)
Hazlitt, *Characters*	William Hazlitt, *Characters of Shakespeare's Plays* (1817: 1903)
Hazlitt, *Works*	*The Collected Works of William Hazlitt*, ed. P.P. Howe and A. Glover, 21 vols, (1930)
Henslowe	*Henslowe's Diary*, ed. R.A. Foakes and R.T. Rickert (Cambridge, 1961)
Hinman	Charlton Hinman, *The Printing and Proof-Reading of the First Folio of Shakespeare*, 2 vols (Oxford, 1963)
Homily	*Certain Sermons or Homilies and A Homily Against Disobedience and Wilful Rebellion* (1547), ed. R.B. Bond (Toronto, 1987)
Honigmann	E.A.J. Honigmann, ed., *Othello*, Arden 3 (1997)
Hulme	Hilda M. Hulme, *Explorations in Shakespeare's Language* (1962)
Hunter	Sir Mark Hunter, 'Politics and character in Shakespeare's *Julius Caesar*', in *Essays by Divers Hands, being the Transactions of the Royal Society of Literature*, n.s. 10 (1931), 109–40
Hurstfield	Joel Hurstfield, *Elizabeth I and the Unity of England* (1971)
'I.B.B.'	'I.B.B.', *Observations upon the Lives of Alexander, Caesar, Scipio. Newly Englished* (1602)
Jackson	MacD.P. Jackson, 'The transmission of Shakespeare's text', *The Cambridge Companion to Shakespeare Studies*, ed. Stanley Wells (Cambridge, 1986)
Johnson	*Samuel Johnson on Shakespeare*, ed. H.R. Woudhuysen (1988)
Jones, *Form*	Emrys Jones, *Scenic Form in Shakespeare* (Oxford, 1971)
Jones, *Origins*	Emrys Jones, *The Origins of Shakespeare* (Oxford, 1977)
Jonson, *Alchemist*	Ben Jonson, *The Alchemist* (1610), ed. F.H. Mares (1967)
Jonson, *Every Man Out*	Ben Jonson, *Every Man Out of his Humour* (1599), in *Ben Jonson*, ed. C. Herford and Percy Simpson, vol. 3 (1927), 405–601
Jonson, *Timber*	*Timber, or, Discoveries* (1640), in *Ben Jonson*, ed. Ian Donaldson (Oxford, 1985), 521–94
Jonson, *Staple*	*The Staple of News* (1625), in *Ben Jonson*, ed. C. Herford and Percy and Evelyn Simpson, vol. 6 (1938), 271–382
Jorgens	Jack J. Jorgens, *Shakespeare on Film* (Bloomington, Ind., 1977)
Jowett	John Jowett, 'Ligature shortage and speech-prefix Variation in *Julius Caesar*', *The Library*, Sixth Series, vol. 6 (1985), 244–53

Kahn	Coppélia Kahn, *Roman Shakespeare: Warriors, Wounds, and Women* (1997)
Kemble	*John Philip Kemble Promptbooks*, ed. Charles H. Shattuck, vol. 4 (Charlottesville, Va., 1974)
Kermode	Frank Kermode, '*Julius Caesar*', in the Riverside Shakespeare (Boston, 1974: 1997), 1100–4
King	T.J. King, *Casting Shakespeare's Plays* (Cambridge, 1992)
Kirschbaum	Leo Kirschbaum, 'Shakespeare's stage blood and its critical significance', *PMLA*, 64 (1949), 517-29
KJB	*The Holy Bible, containing the Old Testament, and the New* ... (1611) (The Authorised Version or King James Bible)
Knight	G. Wilson Knight, *The Imperial Theme* (1931)
Kyd, *Cornelia*	Thomas Kyd, *Cornelia (Pompey the Great His Fair Cornelia's Tragedy)*, in *The Works of Thomas Kyd*, ed. F.S. Boas (1901)
Kyd, *Spanish*	Thomas Kyd, *The Spanish Tragedy* (1587), ed. J.R. Mulryne (1970)
Lamb	Mary Ellen Lamb, *Gender and Authorship in the Sidney Circle* (1990)
Laroque	François Laroque, *Shakespeare's Festive World* (Cambridge, 1993)
Lee & Onions	Sidney Lee and C.T. Onions, *Shakespeare's England: An Account of the Life and Manners of his Age*, 2 vols (Oxford, 1917)
Lucan	Lucan, *Pharsalia*, trans. Robert Graves (Harmondsworth, 1956)
McAlindon, *Tragic*	Thomas McAlindon, *Shakespeare's Tragic Cosmos* (1991)
McAlindon, 'Numbering'	Thomas McAlindon, 'The numbering of men and days: symbolic design in *The Tragedy of Julius Caesar*', *SP*, 81 (1984), 373–93
MacCallum	M.W. MacCallum, *Shakespeare's Roman Plays and Their Background* (1910)
Marlowe, *Massacre*	Christopher Marlowe, *The Massacre at Paris* (c.1589), ed. H.J. Oliver (1968)
Marlowe, *Tamburlaine*	Christopher Marlowe, *1 Tamburlaine the Great* (1590) in *The Works of Christopher Marlowe*, ed. C.F. Tucker Brooke (Oxford, 1910), 5–70
Maxwell, 'Brutus'	J.C. Maxwell, 'Brutus' Philosophy', *N&Q*, NS, 19 (1972), 139
Maxwell, 'Roman'	J.C. Maxwell, 'Shakespeare's Roman Plays: Criticism 1900–1956', *SS*, 10 (1957), 1–11
Merchant	W. Moelwyn Merchant, 'Classical costume in Shakespearian productions', *SS*, 10 (1957), 71–6

Meres	Francis Meres, *Palladis tamia: Wit's Treasury* (1598), ed. D.C. Allen (New York, 1938); extracts in E.K. Chambers, *William Shakespeare* (Oxford, 1930), ii, 193–4
Miles	Geoffrey Miles, *Shakespeare and the Constant Romans* (Oxford, 1996)
Miola, *Rome*	Robert S. Miola, *Shakespeare's Rome* (Cambridge, 1983)
Miola, 'Sources'	Robert S. Miola, 'Shakespeare and his sources: observations on the critical history of *Julius Caesar*', *SS*, 40 (1988), 69–76
Miola, 'Tyrannicide'	Robert S. Miola, '*Julius Caesar* and the tyrannicide debate', *RenQ*, 38 (1985), 271–89
Mirror	*The Mirror for Magistrates* (1559–1610), ed. Lily B. Campbell (Cambridge, 1938)
MLN	*Modern Language Notes*
MLR	*Modern Language Review*
Moulton	R.G. Moulton, *Shakespeare as a Dramatic Artist* (1901)
Muir	Kenneth Muir, *The Sources of Shakespeare's Plays* (1972)
Muret	Marc Antoine Muret, *Julius Caesar* (1544), ed. G.A.O. Collischorn (Paris, 1886)
N&Q	*Notes and Queries*
Nashe	Thomas Nashe, *The Unfortunate Traveller* (1564), in *The Works of Thomas Nashe*, ed. R.B. McKerrow, 5 vols (1904–10) 2, 207–328
Nicholl	Charles Nicholl, *The Chemical Theatre* (1980)
Nicholson	Samuel Nicholson, *Acolastus His Afterwit* (1600)
Nicoll	Allardyce Nicoll, 'Passing over the stage', *SS*, 12 (1959), 47–55
North	Sir Thomas North, trans., *The lives of the noble Grecians and Romanes ... by Plutarch* (1579)
OCD	*The Oxford Classical Dictionary*, ed. S. Hornblower and A. Spawforth (Oxford, 1996)
OED	*The Oxford English Dictionary*, second edition, ed. J.A. Simpson and E.S.C. Weiner, 20 vols (Oxford, 1989)
Onions	C.T. Onions, *A Shakespeare Glossary*, enlarged and revised by Robert D. Eagleson (Oxford, 1986)
Orrell	John Orrell, *The Quest for Shakespeare's Globe* (Cambridge, 1983)
Painter	William Painter, *The Palace of Pleasure* (1566)
Palmer, 'Error'	D.J. Palmer, 'Tragic Error in *Julius Caesar*', *SQ*, 21 (1970), 399–401
Palmer, *Characters*	John Palmer, *Political Characters of Shakespeare* (1945)
Parsons	Robert Parsons, *A Conference about the Next Succession to the Crown of Ingland* (1594)

Paster   Gail Kern Paster, '"In the spirit of men there is no blood": blood as trope of gender in *Julius Caesar*', *SQ*, 40 (1989), 248–98

Peacham   Henry Peacham, *The Garden of Eloquence* (1593)

Pelling   Christopher Pelling, 'Caesar', in *Plutarch and his Intellectual World*, ed. Judith Mossman (1997)

Pepys   *The Diary of Samuel Pepys* (1660–9), ed. Robert Latham and William Matthews, vols 2 (1970) and 9 (1976)

Perrin, *Brutus*   Plutarch, 'Brutus', trans. Bernadotte Perrin, *Plutarch's Lives*, vol. 6, *Loeb Classical Library* (1918)

Perrin, *Caesar*   Plutarch, 'Caesar', trans. Bernadotte Perrin, *Plutarch's Lives*, vol. 7, *Loeb Classical Library* (1919)

Perrin, *Cato*   Plutarch, 'Cato the Younger', trans. Bernadotte Perrin, *Plutarch's Lives*, vol. 8, *Loeb Classical Library* (1919)

Pescetti   Orlando Pescetti, *Il Cesare* (1594), trans. Geoffrey Bullough, in Bullough, vol. 5, 174–94

Petrarch   'Julius Celsus' (Francesco Petrarca), *Historia Julii Caesaris*, in *De viris illustribus* (Florence, 1473)

Pettet   E.C. Pettet, 'Hot irons and fever: A note on some of the imagery of *King John*', *EiC*, 12 (1954), 128–44

Plutarch, *Latin*   Plutarchi, *Opus, quod Parallela* (Basel, 1561)

PMLA   *Publications of the Modern Language Association of America*

Pollard   Alfred W. Pollard *et al.*, *Shakespeare's Hand in the Play of* 'Sir Thomas More' (1923)

Pye   Christopher Pye, *The Regal Phantasm: Shakespeare and the Politics of Spectacle* (1990)

Rea   John D. Rea, '*Julius Caesar* 2.110–34', *MLN*, 37 (1932), 374–6.

Rees, 'Caesar'   Joan Rees, '*Julius Caesar* – an earlier play, and an interpretation', *MLR*, 50 (1955), 135–41

Rees, *Greville*   Joan Rees, *Fulke Greville, Lord Brooke, 1554–1628: A Critical Biography* (1971)

RenD   *Renaissance Drama*

RenP   *Renaissance Papers*

RenQ   *Renaissance Quarterly*

RES   *Review of English Studies*

Revenge   Anon., *The Tragedy of Caesar and Pompey, or Caesar's Revenge* (1595): extracts in Bullough, vol. 5, 196–211

Rheims *NT*   *The New Testament of Jesus Christ, translated faithfully into English, out of the authentical Latin ...* (1582), in *The English Hexapla*, ed. Samuel Bagster (1841)

Rieu   E.V. Rieu, trans., Homer, *The Iliad* (Harmondsworth, 1950)

Ringler   W.A. Ringler, 'The number of actors in Shakespeare's early plays', in *The Seventeenth-Century Stage*, ed. G.E. Bentley (Chicago, 1968)

Ripley	John Ripley, *'Julius Caesar' on stage in England and America 1599–1973* (Cambridge, 1980)
Rosalynde	Thomas Lodge, *Rosalynde: Euphues Golden Legacy* (1590), in Bullough, vol. 2, 158-256
Rose	Mark Rose, 'Conjuring Caesar: ceremony, history, and authority in 1599', *ELR*, 19 (1989), 291–304
Rostron	A.A. Rostron, 'John Philip Kemble's *Coriolanus* and *Julius Caesar*', *Theatre Notebook*, 23 (1968), 36–44
RP	Richard Proudfoot, private communication
Russell	D.A. Russell, *Plutarch* (1973)
Schanzer, *Problem*	Ernest Schanzer, *The Problem Plays of Shakespeare* (1963)
Schanzer, 'Platter'	Ernest Schanzer, 'Thomas Platter's observations on the Elizabethan stage', *N&Q*, 201 (1956), 465-7
Schiappalaria, *Osservationi*	Stefano Ambrosio Schiappalaria, *Osservationi politiche, et discorsi pertinenti a' governi di stato ... con la vita di Caio Giulio Cesare* (1600)
Schiappalaria, *Vita*	Stefano Ambrosio Schiappalaria, *La vita di C. Iulio Cesare* (1568)
Scott	William O. Scott, 'The speculative eye: problematic self-knowledge in *Julius Caesar*', *SS*, 40 (1987), 77–89
Shackford	Martha Hale Shackford, *Plutarch in Renaissance England, with Special Reference to Shakespeare* (Wellesley College, 1929)
Sidney, Mary	Mary Sidney, afterwards Herbert, *The Tragedy of Antony* (1590), ed. A. Luce (1897)
Sidney, Philip	Sir Philip Sidney, *An Apology for Poetry* (1595), ed. Geoffrey Shepherd (1975)
Siemon	James R. Siemon, *Shakespearean Iconoclasm* (Berkeley, Cal., 1985)
Sinfield	Alan Sinfield, *Faultlines: Cultural Materialism and the Politics of Dissident Reading* (Oxford, 1992)
SJW	*Shakespeare Jahrbuch (West)*
Skeat	W.W. Skeat, *Shakespeare's Plutarch* (1875)
Slater	Ann Pasternak Slater, *Shakespeare the Director* (Brighton, 1982)
S.McB.	Sean McBride, private communication
Smith, Alan	Alan R. Smith, 'Then burst his mighty heart' *Explicator*, 42 (1984), 9–10
Smith, Irwin	Irwin Smith, 'Their exits and entrances', *SQ*, 18 (1967), 7–16
Smith, Warren	Warren D. Smith, 'The duplicate revelation of Portia's death', *SQ*, 4 (1953), 153-61
Sohmer	Steve Sohmer, *Opening Shakespeare's Globe* (Manchester, forthcoming)

SP	*Studies in Philology*
Speaight	Robert Speaight, 'Shakespeare in Britain', SQ, 19 (1968), 367–75
Spencer	T.J.B. Spencer, 'Shakespeare and the Elizabethan Romans', *SS*, 10 (1957), 27–38
Spevack	Marvin Spevack, *The Harvard Concordance to Shakespeare* (Cambridge, Mass., 1973)
Spurgeon	Caroline Spurgeon, *Shakespeare's Imagery and What It Tells Us* (Cambridge, 1935)
SQ	*Shakespeare Quarterly*
SS	*Shakespeare Survey*
SSt	*Shakespeare Studies*
Stirling	Brents Stirling, 'Brutus and the death of Portia', *SQ*, 10 (1959), 211–17
Strong	Roy Strong, *Portraits of Queen Elizabeth* (1963)
Suetonius, Holland	*Suetonius' Life of the Twelve Caesars*, trans. Philemon Holland (1606)
Suetonius, Rolfe	Suetonius, *The Lives of the Caesars*, trans. J.C. Rolfe, 2 vols, Loeb Classical Library (1913)
Swinburne	A.C. Swinburne, *A Study of Shakespeare* (1879)
Tacitus	Cornelius Tacitus, *The First Book of the Annals of Cornelius Tacitus*, trans. R. Grenewey (1598)
Taylor	Gary Taylor, '*Musophilus, Nosce teipsum*, and *Julius Caesar*', *N&Q*, 229 (1984), 191–5
Temkin	Owsei Temkin, *The Falling Sickness: A History of Epilepsy from the Greeks to the Beginning of Modern Neurology*, 2nd edn (Baltimore, 1971)
Thomas	Sir Keith Thomas, *Religion and the Decline of Magic* (1971)
Thomson	J.A.K. Thomson, *Shakespeare and the Classics* (1952)
Tilley	M.P. Tilley, *A Dictionary of Proverbs in England in the Sixteenth and Seventeenth Centuries* (1950)
TLN	Through line numbering in *The Norton Facsimile: The First Folio of Shakespeare*, prepared by Charlton Hinman (New York, 1968)
True Tragedy	[Shakespeare], *The True Tragedy of Richard, Duke of York* (1595)
Tyndale, *NT*	*The New Testament, diligently corrected and compared with the Greek by William Tyndale* (1534): modern spelling edition, ed. David Daniell (1989)
Tyndale, *Obedience*	William Tyndale, *The Obedience of a Christian Man* (1528)
Ulrici	Herman Ulrici, *Shakespeare's Dramatic Art* (1846)
Ure, *R2*	Peter Ure, ed., *King Richard II*, Arden 2 (1956)
Ure, *JC*	Peter Ure, ed., *Shakespeare, Julius Caesar: A Casebook* (1969)

Valerius	Valerius Maximus, *Facta et dicta memorabilia* (1585)
Velz, '*Orator*'	John W. Velz, '*Orator* and *Imperator* in *Julius Caesar*', *SSt*, 15 (1982), 55–75
Velz, 'Undular'	John W. Velz, 'Undular Structure in *Julius Caesar*', *MLR*, 66 (1971), 21–30
Vickers	Brian Vickers, *The Artistry of Shakespeare's Prose* (1968)
Virgil	Virgil, *Aeneid*, trans. H. Rushton Fairclough, 2 vols, Loeb Classical Library (1919)
Virgil, *Georgics*	Virgil, *Georgics*, trans. H. Rushton Fairclough, Loeb Classical Library (1957)
Vulgate	*Biblia sacra vulgate editionis* (Rome, 1592)
Warnicke	Retha M. Warnicke, *William Lambarde: Elizabethan Antiquary* (1973)
Weever	John Weever, *The Mirror of Martyrs, or The Life and Death of Sir John Oldcastle* (1601)
Weinstock	*Divus Julius* (Oxford, 1971)
Wilders	John Wilders, *Antony and Cleopatra*, Arden 3 (1995)
Williams	George Walton Williams, 'Pompey the Great', *RenP* (1976), 31–6
Williamson	George Williamson, *A Reader's Guide to T. S. Eliot* (1953)
Wilson, Dover	J. Dover Wilson, 'Ben Jonson and *Julius Caesar*', *SS*, 2 (1949), 36–43
Wilson, Richard	Richard Wilson, ' "Is This a Holiday?": Shakespeare's Roman Carnival' *ELH*, 54 (1987), 31–44
Womersley	David Womersley, '*Julius Caesar* and Caesar's *Commentaries*', *N&Q*, 232 (1987), 215–6
Wright, 'Hendiadys'	George T. Wright, 'Hendiadys and *Hamlet*', *PMLA*, 96 (1981), 168–93
Wright, *Metrical*	George T. Wright, *Shakespeare's Metrical Art* (Berkeley, California, 1988)
Zandvoort	R.W. Zandvoort 'Brutus's Forum Speech in *Julius Caesar*', *RES*, 16 (1940), 62–6

INDEX